AA

KEYGUIDE

FLORENCE AND TUSCANY

CONTENTS

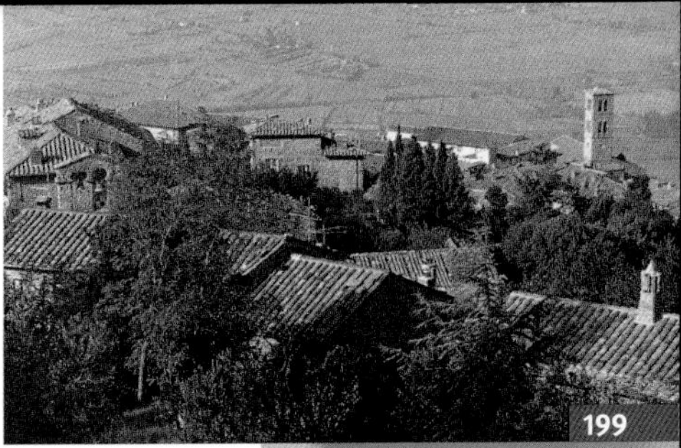
199

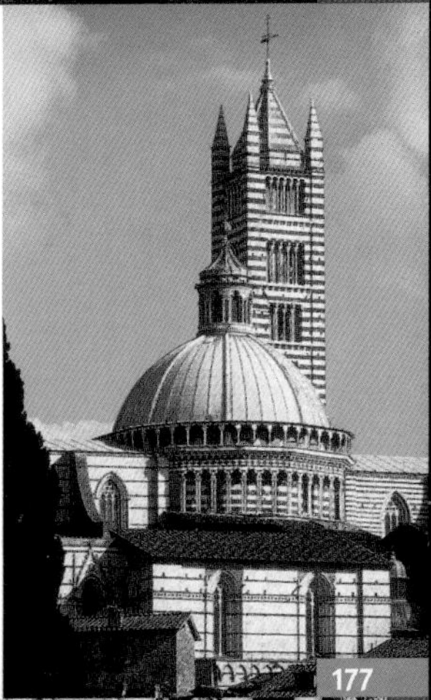
177

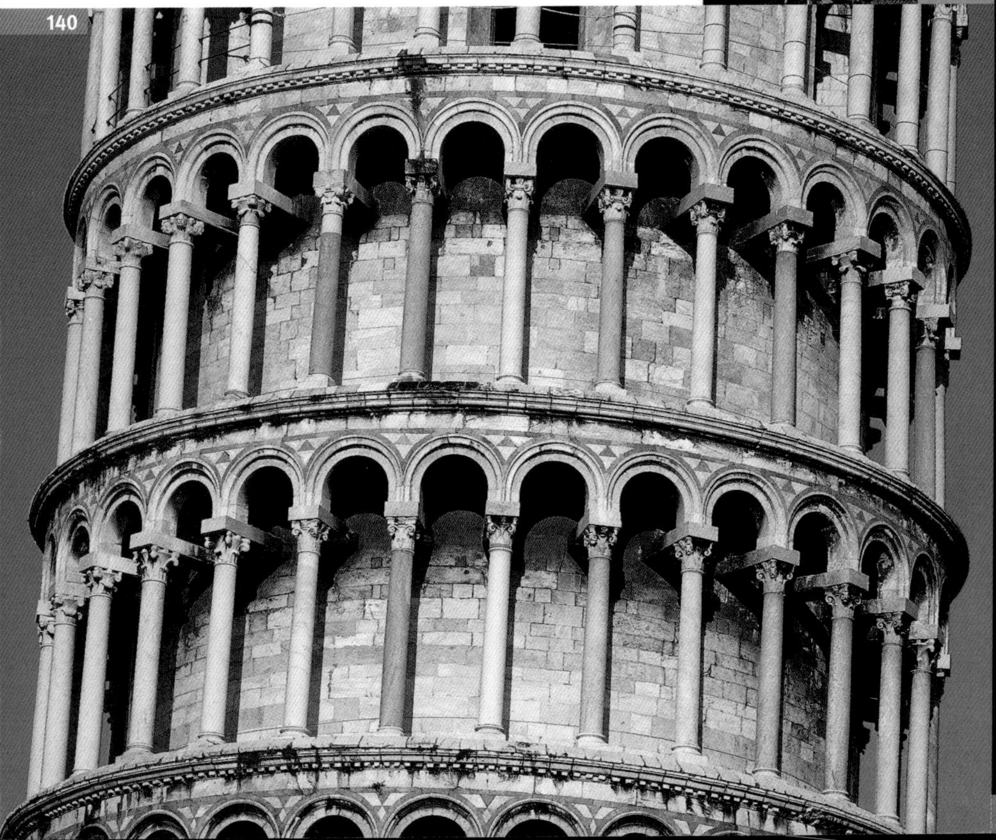
140

UNDERSTANDING | FLORENCE AND TUSCANY

4

UNDERSTANDING FLORENCE AND TUSCANY

Understanding Florence and Tuscany is an introduction to the region, its geography, economy, history and its people, giving a real insight into the area. Living Florence and Tuscany gets under the skin of Tuscany today, while The Story of Florence and Tuscany takes you through the region's past.

Tuscany is probably the most visited region in Italy and its capital, Florence, ranks with Rome and Venice as one of the most popular destinations in the country. But the wealth of art and architecture in the city is only half the story. There is an extraordinary concentration of smaller art towns across Tuscany. Chianti is an area of great natural beauty. The shopping—from designer fashions to handmade paper—is excellent. There is some of the best food and wine in the country. There are mountains and beaches, and many places to go sailing, walking, skiing and diving and to play golf. With this comes a seductively easygoing lifestyle and a sense that, here, there is always plenty of time.

LANDSCAPE

Tuscany is an extraordinarily diverse region. Florence lies to the north on the River Arno; the wide river basin that runs due west and into the sea near Pisa is probably the flattest part of the region. Elsewhere, with the exception of the Val di Chiana, hills and mountains dominate the terrain. Chianti is famous for its characteristic rolling hills dotted with oak woodland, striped with vines and littered with villas, farmhouses and castles. However, there's more to Tuscany than hills and vales: the heavily wooded Casentino; the barren landscapes of the Val d'Orcia and the Crete Senesi; the verdant Mugello, with its alpine feel in parts; Elba, Giglio and Capraia, the principal islands of the Tuscany archipelago; the gentle hills and Etruscan sites of the Maremma. You can swim off the wide, safe beaches of the Riviera di Versilia, dive off the rocky coast of Monte Argentario, ski on the Apennine slopes near Abetone and walk the paths of Monte Amiata, southern Tuscany's highest mountain.

CLIMATE

Florence is in a basin, surrounded on three sides by hills, which gives it an unpredictable climate. It is likely to be among the coldest places in winter and the hottest in summer, and humidity levels, particularly in July and August, can be unbearable. Once out of the city, things improve, but other Tuscan towns such as Siena, Lucca, Pisa and Arezzo also suffer from extreme temperatures. In high summer, head for the hills; even some height above sea level will make all the difference. Areas such as the Casentino and the Alta Versilia will stay cool, at least at night, when the rest of the region is sweltering. The best months to visit are May, June, September and October.

POLITICS

In Italy, elections are held on four different levels: national, regional, provincial and communal or municipal. So, in theory, while Italy might be under the rule of a right-wing government, a particular region could be governed by the left, one of its provinces by the right and the principal town of that province by something in between. Tuscany has a long history of left-wing politics, so while President Silvio Berlusconi's right-wing Forza Italia party has made inroads into various left-wing strongholds, Tuscany on the whole has remained staunchly left or centre-left.

THE ECONOMY

Agriculture provides the backbone of Tuscany's economic existence: Tuscan olive oils and wines are exported throughout the world. However, tourism is playing an increasingly important role. On an industrial level, Prato is important for the production of textiles and Arezzo is famous for its gold jewellery; every year it exports some two billion euros' worth of the stuff. Tuscany is known for leather goods and has many factories making shoes, clothing and accessories. This, however, is changing quickly as designers move to countries where manufacturing costs are much lower.

GETTING THE BEST FROM YOUR STAY

Tuscany offers the visitor great art, fabulous scenery, arguably the best food and wine in the country, remote hilltop towns and villages, good beaches, and a variety of activities, from cooking or language courses to horseback riding and sailing. Given that the road network is good and public transport is excellent, it's possible to fit a lot into your stay. If you want to concentrate on seeing art and are not worried about the weather, the best months to come are November and February, when there will be fewer people about. If you want a mixture of rural relaxation and city culture, May, June and September are good months as it's not too hot for either. Avoid the coastal resorts in July and August—this is when Italian families take their holidays. If you are based in the country and want to spend the day in Florence, use public transport to get there as parking is very difficult. Florence, Siena and other popular towns like San Gimignano become very busy in summer, so make sure you arrive early or late, when the crowds have thinned out.

Try to catch one of the many traditional festivals that take place in Tuscany annually. The biggest are the *Giostra del Saracino* in Arezzo (▷ 227), the Palio in Siena (▷ 187), the *Scoppio del Carro* in Florence (▷ 117) and the *Gioco del Ponte* in Pisa (▷ 157). However, there are many smaller festivals held in towns throughout the summer, and spending a few hours at one of these is a great way to sample country life in Tuscany.

Whatever you do, allow plenty of time and don't expect opening hours to be accurate. You can always go and have lunch while you wait.

Clockwise from opposite *Traditional villa near the village of Camigliano, east of Lucca; the medieval towers of San Gimignano; the Fountain of Neptune in Florence's Piazza della Signoria*

THE PROVINCES OF TUSCANY

The region of Tuscany (Toscana) covers an area of
nearly 23,000sq km (8,880sq miles) and is divided
into 10 provinces. These enjoy a certain amount
of administrative independence, but are ultimately
controlled by the central Italian government.

Provincia di Firenze Florence (Firenze) is the regional
capital and the place that most visitors to Tuscany are
likely to spend time in given its extraordinary artistic
wealth. The province extends north through the green
and little-visited area of the Mugello to the border with
Emilia-Romagna, west a little way along the Arno valley,
south and west to include much of the Chianti area and
east to the wooded slopes of the Vallombrosa.

Provincia di Siena After Florence, many visitors head
south to Siena, capital of possibly the richest province in
Tuscany in terms of things to see. Covering a large area
that stretches from San Gimignano in the northwest
to the borders of Lazio in the southeast, the area has

fascinating towns and villages, gorgeous scenery, some
of the best wine-growing areas in Italy and richly fertile
agricultural land.

Provincia di Arezzo The wealthy town of Arezzo is
known for its production of gold jewellery. It is more
or less in the middle of its surrounding province, which
borders Chianti to the west and Umbria to the east. To
the north are the relatively unknown high, wooded hills
of the Casentino, which borders Emilia-Romagna.

Provincia di Prato Tuscany's newest and smallest
province came into being in 1992 and has prosperous,
industrial Prato at its heart. Although this lively town is
dedicated to the production of cloth, it also has historical
and artistic significance. The province is made up of a
narrow strip running north to south.

Provincia di Pistoia The town of Pistoia has an
abundance of art and refreshingly few visitors. The
province reaches north into the Apennine mountain

range (Florentines flock to Abetone in winter to ski) and includes the two spa towns of Monsummano Terme and Montecatini Terme.

Provincia di Lucca The lovely walled town of Lucca lies between Florence and the sea. The province has dramatic contrasts: to the west it borders the sea where the beaches of the Versilia coast are a popular holiday destination for Italians; inland from here is the wooded Alta Versilia, dotted with tiny villages clinging to the mountains and popular with walkers; north and west of the town of Lucca is the verdant Garfagnana.

Provincia di Massa-Carrara This province is bordered by Liguria in the north and west and by Emilia-Romagna in the northeast. The marble industry dominates life along the coast, which is overshadowed by the dramatic and rugged Alpi Apuane. Michelangelo chose the marble for some of his greatest works from a quarry near Carrara, and the local near-white marble (with its characteristic dark grey vein) is still quarried and exported around the world. Many artists and sculptors live along the coast from Carrara to Pietrasanta. The beautiful Lunigiana, to the northwest, is one of the most remote corners of Tuscany.

Provincia di Pisa Pisa is world-famous because of its iconic Leaning Tower, though there is much more to the town than just this. It sits in the north of its province; the southern part is characterized by rolling hills and some pretty country villages. The magnificent Etruscan town of Volterra lies to the south.

Provincia di Livorno Livorno has the feel of a hard-working port. It's one of the biggest container ports in Europe, but is not without charm and is full of wonderful fish restaurants. Its province is made up of a narrow

coastal strip that runs south, and one of its most attractive features is the Isola d'Elba, off the south coast. Inland, rolling hills form part of the north and there are some interesting archaeological sites in the area.

Provincia di Grosseto Grosseto is the chief town of the Maremma, an area of reclaimed swamp where malaria was endemic until the middle of the 20th century. Today its long beaches and coastline, particularly the rugged Monte Argentario, are popular with glamorous Florentines and Romans. At Alberese a beautiful national park begins and runs south along the coast, delightfully preserved due to severe restrictions on the number of visitors allowed to enter. Inland, the rolling hills are relatively empty in spite of many remarkable towns. To the east is Monte Amiata, the highest mountain in southern Tuscany at 1,738m (5,700ft). To the south is a lonely and remote area of great archaeological importance because of its Etruscan sites. It includes the towns of Pitigliano, Sorano and Sovana.

Clockwise from above Florence's famed Ponte Vecchio, crossing the River Arno; a vineyard in the Chianti region, an area renowned for its wines; Pisa's spectacular Campo dei Miracoli (Field of Miracles)

FLORENCE

Beccofino, Florence (▷ 119) Modern Italian food at its best in contemporary surroundings.

Cappella Brancacci, Florence (▷ 67) The frescoes illustrating the life of St. Peter by Masaccio and Masolino are considered masterpieces that profoundly influenced the course of Florentine Renaissance art.

Cappella dei Magi, Florence (▷ 83) This tiny chapel in the Palazzo Medici-Riccardi is decorated with delightful frescoes by Benozzo Gozzoli.

Caffè Rivoire, Florence (▷ 120) A famous bar that was once a chocolate factory overlooking Piazza della Signoria.

Cibreo, Florence (▷ 121) This is one of Florence's most famous restaurants, serving excellent food and wine.

Enoteca Pinchiorri, Florence (▷ 121) One of Italy's best-known restaurants and one of the few in the country to possess three Michelin stars.

Florence (▷ 60–129) The best city in the world to see Renaissance art and architecture.

Loggiato dei Serviti, Florence (▷ 128) A beautiful hotel in an ex-convent opposite Brunelleschi's famous Ospedale.

Scoti, Florence (▷ 129) Is a simple, inexpensive and friendly hotel with a surprisingly smart location.

Santa Croce, Florence (▷ 97) A Franciscan church, Santa Croce was rebuilt starting in 1294; it contains the tombs of many notable Florentine citizens and much important art. Look out for Giotto's frescoes in the Bardi and Peruzzi chapels and Agnolo Gaddi's painting in the Sanctuary of this vast Franciscan church.

Santa Maria Novella, Florence (▷ 100) This major Gothic church begun by the Dominicans in 1246 has a beautiful symmetrical marble façade by Leon Battista Alberti. It also houses some extraordinary frescoes, among them fresco cycles by Filippino Lippi, Ghirlandaio, Nardo di Cione and Andrea di Buonaiuto.

San Miniato al Monte, Florence (▷ 101) This Romanesque church dominates Florence from its position high on a hill just south of the river.

Tornabuoni Beacci, Florence (▷ 129) Writers have been attracted to this hotel since the 1920s.

Villa San Michele, Fiesole (▷ 129) Exclusive and luxurious hotel in an ex-monastery overlooking Florence.

Vivoli, Florence (▷ 125) This ice cream parlour changes its flavours to suit the seasons.

NORTHERN TUSCANY

Alpi Apuane (▷ 133) The tall, jagged mountains that rise above the Riviera di Versilia provide some dramatic scenery; white scars left by the marble quarries are easily mistaken for snow.

Casentino (▷ 133) Chestnut woods, pine forests, pastoral meadows, isolated monasteries and little-visited towns characterize this peaceful region.

La Darsena, Viareggio (▷ 161) This *trattoria* hidden away among the boatyards serves delicious fish and seafood.

Hotel Relais dell'Orologio, Pisa (▷ 164) This luxury

hotel in a magnificent former manor house also boasts five stars.

Lucca (▷ 136–139) A lovely walled town with rich pickings in its galleries and churches, Lucca has an all-round allure.

Mugello (▷ 144) This lovely, hilly region was popular with the powerful Reniassance family, the Medici, who built weekend retreats here; it's an excellent area for walking.

Osteria dei Cavalieri, Pisa (▷ 160) A restaurant with excellent, imaginative Tuscan food and a good wine list in the old town.

Pisa (▷ 140–143) There is much more to see in Pisa than just its most famous monument, the Leaning Tower.

Duomo, Pisa (▷ 142) One of Italy's most celebrated Romanesque churches and an example of typical Pisan church architecture.

Duomo, Prato (▷ 144) The choir stalls of Prato's striped cathedral are decorated with beautiful frescoes by Filippino Lippi.

Villa Il Poggiale, San Casciano, Val di Pesa (▷ 165) A refined villa in a pretty setting with surprisingly reasonable prices.

SIENA

Siena (▷ 166–191) The Sienese school of painting in the early 14th century produced many masterpieces, all set in a beautiful medieval city.

Duomo, Siena (▷ 176–179) Siena's Gothic Duomo dates from the 13th century and has a fabulous marble pavement.

Grand Hotel Continental, Siena (▷ 190) The city's only five-star hotel is also a cultural highlight.

Museo Civico, Siena (▷ 174) Frescoes by artists of the famous Sienese school of painting: Simone Martini, Sodoma and Ambrogio Lorenzetti are some of the best in Tuscany.

Palazzo Ravizza, Siena (▷ 191) This comfortable and atmospheric hotel in a converted 18th-century palace is set in a lovely garden.

Clockwise from left The hilly Mugello region, lying close to Tuscany's border with Emilia-Romagna, has many scenic villages; Florence is noted for its ice cream

SOUTHERN TUSCANY

Abbazia di Monte Oliveto Maggiore, near Asciano (▷ 195) Frescoes of the life of St. Benedict by Sodoma and Luca Signorelli adorn the walls of the great cloister of this monastery.

Abbazia di Sant'Antimo, near Montalcino (▷ 195) The beautiful Romanesque church of Sant'Antimo, partly built in luminous alabaster from Volterra, has an incomparable, isolated setting.

Arezzo (▷ 197) This wealthy town has several good museums and is home to *The Legend of the True Cross* by Piero della Francesca.

Il Carlino d'Oro, San Regolo, Gaiole in Chianti (▷ 229) Expect to enjoy the essence of a simple country *trattoria*; this is a wonderful place to sample authentic home cooking.

Chianti (▷ 198) The classic image of the Tuscan landscape with vineyards, olive groves, cypresses, crenellated towers and villas adorning rolling hills.

Crete Senesi (▷ 200) A strange lunar landscape of exposed chalk cliffs to the north towards Asciano.

Il Falconiere, Cortona (▷ 230) If you are in search of something special, head to this elegant, Michelin-starred restaurant set in lovely surroundings just north of Cortona.

Gambero Rosso, San Vincenzo (▷ 233) Enjoy some truly excellent food in a delightfully unstuffy atmosphere. at this wonderful Michelin-starred fish restaurant overlooking the sea.

Montalcino (▷ 203) This small walled town is beautifully surrounded by olive groves and vineyards, the latter producing its most famous asset, Brunello wine.

Montepulciano (▷ 205) A handsome town dominating the Val di Chiana in southeast Tuscany.

Monteriggioni (▷ 206) A tiny medieval hill town enclosed by perfectly preserved walls.

Pienza (▷ 207) Built by Pope Pius II and a perfect example of Renaissance town planning.

Pitigliano (▷ 206) Dramatically built on an outcrop in the southern Maremma, Pitigliano has Etruscan origins and is known for its excellent dry white wine.

San Gimignano (▷ 208–210) This town has managed to preserve its medieval atmosphere in spite of huge numbers of visitors. The town's Collegiata, decorated with important fresco cycles by Taddeo di Bartolo, Ghirlandaio and masters from the workshop of Simone Martini, is not to be missed.

Sant'Agostino, San Gimignano (▷ 210) Scenes from the life of St. Augustine by Benozzo Gozzoli and assistants decorate the choir of this 13th-century church.

Val d'Orcia (▷ 214) The remote valley of the River Orcia in the southeastern corner of Tuscany is dominated by Monte Amiata and dotted with tiny fortified hill towns and castles.

Volterra (▷ 213) A rather austere medieval town in a magnificent position, famous for its production of alabaster.

TOP EXPERIENCES

Enjoy a lazy, al fresco lunch involving *bistecca* (steak) and a glass of Chianti at a simple countryside *trattoria.*

Cross the Ponte Vecchio (▷ 95) in Florence at sunset on a golden summer evening.

Watch one of the major festivals such as the *Palio* in Siena (▷ 187) or the *Giostra del Saracino* in Arezzo (▷ 227).

Take in the view from the top of the Campanile in Florence (▷ 93).

Hear Gregorian chants at the Abbazia di Sant'Antimo (▷ 195).

Go for an early morning walk in the magnificent Giardino di Boboli (▷ 69) in Florence.

Pisa's Campo dei Miracoli (▷ 142–143) is a remarkable sight with its Romanesque buildings in gleaming white marble.

Visit the Galleria degli Uffizi (▷ 72–77) in Florence—the greatest collection of Renaissance art in the world.

Il Campo (▷ 172–175) in Siena is arguably the most beautiful square in Tuscany and a great place to sit and watch the world go by.

A climb into Brunelleschi's dome (left) at Florence's Duomo (▷ 90–91) is the best way to appreciate this extraordinary feat of engineering.

Watch a performance of Italian opera at Florence's Teatro del Maggio for a taste of theatrical magic.

Above *Brunelleschi's magnificent dome dominates Florence's skyline*
Below *The Ponte Vecchio, silhouetted at sunset*

LIVING FLORENCE AND TUSCANY

Tuscany's beauty is matched by only a few places on Earth. The region is a natural marvel of ever-changing scenery: golden meadows of sunflowers with cypress trees on the horizon, green rolling hills, dusty grey olive groves and the glistening waters of the Tyrrhenian Sea under an azure sky. Inspiring artists and writers for centuries, no other region in Europe conjures images so evocative nor is spoken of in such terms that it can often seem like a country all of its own. But Tuscany is more than sweeping countryside, as its villages and spectacular hilltop towns also contribute to its distinctive character. Life in rural Tuscany continues to be based on tradition and agriculture, a fact reflected in rural events, often promoting local customs.

THE FAKE LAKE
Following the 1966 flood of the Arno (▷ 39), a plan was drawn up to build a dam that would regulate the flow of the River Sieve, one of its tributaries, and hopefully prevent a similar disaster. So the vast Lago di Bilancino, a few kilometres outside the town of Barberino di Mugello, was created. The lake is just over 31m (100ft) at its deepest point, with a total surface area of 5sq km (1.95sq miles). For many Tuscans it has become a popular alternative to going to the coast. Indeed, this artificial seaside has numerous sandy beaches and a variety of water sports. It's also a must for birdwatchers—the lake forms a large part of the World Wide Fund for Nature's Gabbianello Nature Reserve, which is on the migration route between Europe and Africa.

Clockwise from top A typical Tuscan hill town, medieval Anghiari overlooks a fertile plain; age-old ways continue throughout Tuscany; houses in Anghiari, southeastern Tuscany

IN BLOOM

Tuscany may be famed for its wine-making and olive oil production, but few realize that the cultivation of flowers accounts for around 30 per cent of commercial agricultural production in the region, 15 per cent of national production and 6 per cent of all EU production. Around 4,700 companies are devoted to this blooming industry, most of which are based in and around Pistoia, 'the city of plants in the land of gardens'. Travel between Lucca and Florence and you will see swathes of trees, shrubs and flowers in market gardens. Pistoia represented Italy at the prestigious Floriade 2002 flower show, held in the Netherlands once every 10 years. Plans are underway to establish a Denomination of Protected Flowers for Pistoia. This EU award recognizes the flowers' origins and quality, and the town eventually hopes to secure the title of European Capital of Flower Growing.

ON LOCATION

Film-makers have long been enchanted by Tuscany. But it was the huge success of James Ivory's *A Room with a View* (1985) that catapulted the area to stardom. In the 1990s Tuscany almost became as common a location on the silver screen as Manhattan or Hollywood. One of the latest releases set against this gorgeous backdrop is Audrey Wells' *Under the Tuscan Sun*, adapted from Frances Mayes' bestseller and shot in the hills of Cortona. Tuscany has also produced one of Italy's best-loved comic actors, Roberto Benigni, protagonist of the award-winning *La Vita è Bella (Life is Beautiful)*, made in 1998. As to why the region is so popular with movie-makers, Giorgio Galliani, location scout for almost 100 Tuscan-set films, explains: 'Tuscany has great attributes—if you stick a nail in the ground and stretch a string for a radius of 50km (30 miles), you'll find everything.'

A VILLAGE RESTORED

If pieces of art and even entire villas can be completely restored, then why not a whole village? This is exactly what happened in Borgo Montefienali, a small village in the borough of Gaiole in Chianti. The tiny hamlet sat abandoned and forgotten for more than 45 years, until a palace owned by the Albizi family, a rich and powerful Renaissance dynasty, was discovered. The entire village was given a makeover by Germana Costruizioni, a Tuscan specialist construction company that had already given a new lease of life to several derelict villages in Siena, Castellina in Chianti and Barberino Val d'Elsa. An inauguration ceremony was held for Montefienali's official rebirth. This included the symbolic presentation of keys to the owners of each property.

BURNT SIENA

The Sienese countryside has provided more for painters than just inspiration. The town's buildings and fields, and the region to the south, known as the Crete, are distinctive for their orange and red tones, which are at their best in the autumn, when the fields reveal a warm brown palette, baked by the sun. This earth is the origin of the painting pigment burnt sienna, which is taken from the very soil of the area, *terre di Siena*. A mixture of iron oxide and clay, it was one of the earliest paint pigments and is found in many cave paintings. The Renaissance painters found it the best medium to translate the warmth of the Tuscan landscape onto canvas. These days, you won't find real earth in the paint, but its name and colour will always conjure up images of Tuscany.

Tuscans are among Italy's greatest individualists, proud of their region and its traditions. They consider themselves Tuscans first, Italians second. This strong feeling of regionalism, felt by most Italians, is known as *campanilismo*. The word derives from *campanile* (bell tower), meaning that everything of significance happens within the sound of the bells of your local church. It is loyalty to the region, not country, that is important. Tuscans tend not to follow the trends that are closely followed by the rest of Italy. Consequently, Tuscany's artistic output in the fields of cinema, music and entertainment often reflects an individual attitude. However, this does not mean the region has abandoned what went before, and often events or institutions combine modernity with tradition—the Chianti League, for example. Tuscany continues to respect and draw on its cultural independence, its history, its beauty, and its position as an important focus for art, study, business, fashion and tourism.

TUSCANY'S OTHER CULTURE

When you think of Tuscany and culture, the chances are you think of art and architecture. But the region also boasts some of Europe's finest music festivals, superb choirs and orchestras, Italy's most spectacular pageants, and a plethora of small-town events that celebrate and recall centuries of local culture. In Florence, the key musical event is the *Maggio Musicale*, held annually in April and May, but don't miss the *Scoppio del Carro* on Easter Sunday (▷ 117), or the *Calcio Storico*, a mass game of football in Piazza Santa Croce. Siena celebrates with the twice-yearly *Palio* (▷ 187), and Torre del Lago has an annual festival of Puccini opera. But this is just to scratch the surface: come to Tuscany for culture, but be sure to look beyond the paintings.

Clockwise from top *Members of one of Siena's contrade (neighbourhoods) prepare for the Palio; wines and olive oils produced in Chianti are a great source of regional pride; world-famous Tuscan tenor Andrea Bocelli performing with Laura Pausini in 2007 at the 8th Annual Latin GRAMMY Awards*

CHIANTI'S LEAGUE

The Chianti League is a promotional association designed to celebrate the history, culture and natural beauty of the region. It was set up in 1384 and was originally intended to settle disputes between Florence and Siena. The new association closely resembles its 14th-century counterpart. The league's head, known as the Capitano Generale, presides over its members, each of whom wears a special hand-sewn robe and hat—red for those who live in the Chianti region, yellow for those who come from outside. Upon entering the league, members must partake in a swearing-in ceremony, promising 'to love nature, to give my life religious motivation, to see the world with optimism and love.' Unsurprisingly, one of the League's principal activities involves the promotion and cultivation of the region's world-famous wine.

TUSCAN TENOR

His voice has been called the most beautiful in the world. Tenor Andrea Bocelli was born in Lajatico, rural Tuscany, in 1958. As a young child he played the organ in his local church. Born with congenital glaucoma, he lost his sight as a boy following a cerebral haemorrhage. His blindness—which he is at pains not to discuss—has not held him back, however, and he won his first award (for singing *O Sole Mio* in Tuscany's Viareggio festival) at the age of 12. His first gold record followed a performance in 1994 at San Remo, Italy's foremost festival of popular song, two years after he had been 'discovered' by the Italian rock star Zucchero, with whom he sang *Miserere*, a Europe-wide pop hit. Bocelli's ability to cross musical borders, seducing many different audiences, has been his trademark, and his CDs have sold millions of copies.

TOSCANA PRIDE

Tuscany has created its own manifesto for sexual equality. Toscana Pride is organized by Pride Nazionale GLBT (Gay, Lesbian, Bisexual and Transsexual) and celebrates 'the right to be different, because to be different is every citizen's right.' For two weeks in June a variety of events, including debates, concerts and film screenings, takes place in Florence, Lucca and Pistoia. The 2004 festival saw a deliberate effort to expand the promotion of gay pride away from the major cities and into Tuscany's provinces, where the main focus of the event was Grosseto, one of the region's lesser-known towns. The finale, 'Rainbow Party', featured a rare performance by Patty Pravo, the legendary Italian singer of the 1960s and gay icon.

A STELLA IS BORN

Even the region's actresses have a certain Tuscan attitude towards independence. Martina Stella was born in Florence in 1984, and made her film debut in *L'Ultimo Bacio* (*The Last Kiss*) in 2001, in which she plays a schoolgirl who begins an ill-judged affair with an older man. The film won a handful of David di Donatellas (the Italian equivalent of Oscars) and an audience award at the US Sundance Film Festival 2002. Since then, Stella has shifted between cinema, theatre and television with effortless grace, including an appearance in *Ocean's Twelve* with George Clooney in 2004. 'I come from a family of women,' she says of her determination to succeed. 'All the men have either died, run off or been kicked out.'

Italy has always been synonymous with style, and even though you might think of Milan or Rome first, Tuscany contributes in its own way. Style can be traced back to the Etruscans, who were pioneers in the ceramic arts. By the Renaissance, Florence was making great developments in paper and textiles, creating many designs and techniques that are still used today. It was perhaps inevitable that an Italian fashion revolution should take place in Tuscany: Florence hosted Italy's earliest fashion shows in the 1950s, and innovative designers Salvatore Ferragamo, Guccio Gucci and Emilio Pucci made their fortunes within the city's medieval palaces. The city becomes the fashion world's focus twice a year during Pitti Immagine week, and today's youngest designers and manufacturers continue to take inspiration from the region's rich heritage and knack for originality. Meanwhile, Tuscany's crafts, such as pottery, continue to thrive thanks to their popularity with visitors and the hard work of local artisans.

I FEEL PITTI

On 12 February 1951, Giovanni Battista Giorgini created the modern notion of Italian fashion overnight. During a party at his Florence home, Italian ladies' outfits were presented to select buyers and journalists. An instant success, it was the first fashion show of its kind in Italy, and in 1952 the event moved to the Palazzo Pitti, where over the next 30 years it helped catapult many Italian names to global stardom. Since 1982 the biannual event has taken place at the Fortezza di Basso trade complex, yet retains its Pitti name. While fashion remains at the heart of the event, numerous art and other exhibitions are organized in conjunction with the key fashion shows. In 2006, for example, the main exhibition (Human Game) looked at the role of sport in society. Details of events can be found at www.pittimmagine.com

Clockwise from top *The region has a long ceramics tradition and ceramic works remain popular souvenirs; flamboyant Pucci prints, the epitome of Florentine design; hand-made papers, particularly marbled papers, have been produced in Florence for centuries*

POTS OF STYLE

Though for centuries an important craft in the region, Tuscan-style ceramic works are becoming hard to find. You have to know where to look. Between Borgo San Lorenzo and Ronta in the Mugello valley, Ceramiche Franco Pecchioli is one of the last few places where you can witness the craftsmanship necessary to create authentic Tuscan ceramics. Here, Vieri Chini and his sons, Cosimo and Mattia, produce home furnishings, plates and vases using traditional firing methods and decorated in blues, greens and yellows. Many original Chini pieces are on display in the Villa Pecori Giraldi museum in Borgo San Lorenzo. It was perhaps inevitable that the Chinis should adopt this craft, as they are descendants of Galileo Chini: painter, ceramicist and an exponent of Italy's art nouveau movement in the early 1900s.

THE PAPER MAKERS

The production of marbled and other decorative paper in Tuscany has been a skill since the rule of the Medicis. Now, there are many traditional Florentine paper stores across the region, as well as many market sellers offering decorative notebooks and writing paper. Each claims to be a Florentine original, but one shop continues to leave all others in its wake: the Giannini Giulio & Figlio store in Piazza de' Pitti. The Giannini family has been creating paper products since 1856. Their leather-bound diaries are hand-sewn, their address books are marbled, and their classic Florentine writing paper, delicately decorated and with matching envelopes, continues to outsell the rest. And in this age of email there's still no greater pleasure than receiving a hand-written letter on a sheet of Giannini's writing paper.

ITALIAN STALLION

Where can you find cowhide in Florence? The answer: Roberto Cavalli. Florence's most celebrated contemporary designer, Cavalli first found success in the 1960s when he patented a process for printing on leather. He's now a leading player in fashion circles, and leather continues to dominate his designs for jackets, bags, trousers and shoes, but he believes it shouldn't be considered a precious material. 'Don't be afraid to ruin it or scratch it,' he says. 'Leather is much nicer with a vintage look.' Cavalli's flagship store is on the corner of Via de' Tornabuoni, with the adjacent café incorporating calfskin stools. As the designer's star continues to rise, he has moved into designing eyewear, watches, homeware and other accessories.

TUSCAN TEXTILES

Embroidery has been a Tuscan craft ever since the times of the *barulli* (peddlers), who would journey around the region selling cloths and fabrics from door to door, carried on their shoulders or with the help of a mule. The textiles left to the peasant wives would then be converted into elegant tablecloths, sheets and towels for the local gentry. The owners of the Gallianino shop in the tiny village of Galliano claim to have real *barulli* among their ancestors. They also have the most renowned laceworks in the region and continue to produce the same quality cloths and linens. Today the seamstresses of Galliano still travel throughout the Mugello area to each of the region's weekly markets, giving the people of other local towns the opportunity to take home an original piece of Gallianino embroidery.

A TASTE OF TUSCANY

Italian food holds a special place in the hearts of millions around the world, and many of the dishes originate from Tuscany. Tuscan cuisine is often praised for its rural simplicity and the use of the finest, freshest ingredients. The key, however, to a dish's success lies in its olive oil. With miles of dry olive groves, Tuscany is the leading region in Italy's olive oil production, and the area's perfect growing conditions also mean an abundance of fruit and vegetables. The Tuscans are jokingly called 'bean-eaters' by other Italians, a reference to their indifference to pasta dishes and preference for pulse-based soups and stews. But many Tuscan delicacies, including an enormous range of cheeses and cured meats, are known throughout the country and proudly celebrated around the region. And that's without even mentioning the wine: While a Tuscan meal in itself can be an unforgettable experience, don't miss the chance to wash it down with a bottle of vintage Chianti.

TIPS FOR TRIPE

Historian Leo Coducci spoke of 'the refinement of tripe', or *trippa*, and though tripe may no longer feature heavily in the diets of many, Florentines continue to devour it with gusto. Not only is tripe an important ingredient on the menu of Florence's restaurants, it is also sold by outdoor vendors, satisfying everyone from children in need of an after-school snack to hungry workers on their lunch break. The pale dish is displayed on a bed of cheesecloth. You can buy a single portion, prepared simply with oil, salt, pepper and garlic, although the classic recipe for *trippa alla fiorentina* involves cooking the tripe before adding it to a rich tomato sauce.

Clockwise from top For an unforgettable view, take a seat at a café terrace overlooking Siena's Campo and enjoy a leisurely drink; Brunello wines, produced in Montalcino, are strong, complex wines, commanding high prices; gelaterie sell a range of ice cream, served in cones or tubs of varying sizes

ETRUSCAN SACRIFICE

Chiusi was a thriving town during the time of the Etruscans, as the many Etruscan objects in the town's museums and tomb sites in the surrounding countryside testify. Today the people of Chiusi may not have much in common with their ancestors, but food is an exception, and certain gastronomic traditions are still very much in evidence. Take the recipe and special preparation of *brustico*. *Brustico*, meaning roasted, is an ancient fish dish directly derived from an Etruscan recipe. Small fish, usually rudd, pike or perch, are cooked on a grill (which, for the Etruscans, would have been the sacrificial altar) over a fire of reeds from the nearby lake. After being fully roasted, the darkened fish are scaled, seasoned and drizzled in olive oil, before being washed down with a dry white wine. And in keeping with Etruscan conventions, the fish is always eaten with the fingers.

THE CREAM OF TUSCANY

Many Florentines claim that ice cream was the brainchild of Ruggeri, chef to Catherine de' Medici (1519–89) and the world's first professional ice-cream maker. So Florence is probably the ideal place to learn more about this fine art. Gelati Fantasiosi is an ice cream making course that is held from time to time at Cordon Bleu, a prestigious school of culinary art. During the afternoon lessons, ice-cream expert Palmiro Bruschi demonstrates the preparation of ice creams inspired by the tastes of the region; evening classes teach the delicate marrying of flavours in combination with a whole meal. Students learn from the best, as Bruschi knows his sorbet from his *semi-freddo* (semi-frozen dessert). He owns the famous Ghignoni gelateria in Sansepolcro and is a member of the Italian Ice Cream Academy.

THE BREAD TREE

Over the centuries chestnuts were an irreplaceable source of food for many Tuscans, to such an extent that the chestnut tree was known as 'the bread tree', since the nut's flour was used to prepare bread, pasta and polenta. Today Tuscany is still home to some of Italy's largest chestnut groves. The best chestnuts, including the Amiata from Siena and Grosseto, and the Mugello Marron, are sold and eaten boiled or roasted, while the smaller ones become flour. The flour-making process takes place in a stone building, where on the lower floor a chestnut wood fire is kept slowly burning, over which the chestnuts are dried on a mat upstairs for around 30 days. The chestnuts are then roasted for an additional 10 hours, before being stone-milled and sieved into flour, which is the best product to make *castagnaccio toscano*, a Tuscan chestnut cake.

LOYAL TO THEIR OIL

Not only is olive oil a vital ingredient in Tuscan cooking, it is also appreciated in its purest form. Olive-oil sampling sessions are now almost as common as meetings for wine. Experts can distinguish between brands and their types, such as *extra vergine* (extra virgin) or *delicato* (a finer extra virgin), as easily as a wine connoisseur can separate Brunello from Barolo. Such tastings follow strict procedures. First, the palate must be cleansed with apple. Then the oil is poured into a dark container (so the taster is not influenced by its colour) warmed in the hands and gently swirled to release its full aroma and subtle flavours. Eventually, the delicate qualities of the oil are savoured in small sips. You do not, however, need to be an expert to buy good oil. Tuscan oils are of high quality, particularly those produced in the area around Lucca.

TUSCANY AND TOURISM

More than 10 million visitors descend on Tuscany every year in search of culture and history—especially that of the Renaissance. Florence in particular recognizes the importance of its most celebrated epoch. It now devotes itself to the preservation and promotion of Renaissance masterpieces, often at the expense of the growth of the modern city—for example, an underground metro system was shelved in the 1980s when excavators kept unearthing priceless pieces of art. Although the region has been cunning in exploiting its number-one industry, many Tuscans feel it is ill-equipped to deal with the endless flow of visitors, as the resulting over-crowded cities and traffic-clogged streets testify. Florence has become one of the most expensive cities in Italy, and many Florentines lament the commercialization of their town and its surroundings, fearing it will soon resemble a Renaissance theme park, with Michelangelo's *David* as its mascot.

Clockwise from top *Magnificently illuminated, the Duomo and Palazzo Vecchio dominate Florence's skyline at night; special shows, like the the 2004 exhibition of works by Sandro Botticelli and Filippino Lippi, focus on the city's artistic heritage; cookery courses are increasingly popular among visitors*

THE WEIGHT OF LOVE

Anyone passing over Florence's Ponte Vecchio in recent years will have noticed a mass of padlocks tied to two metal cables projecting from the bridge. This tradition was started by military academy students who left the padlocks of their lockers on the bridge on finishing their course. The rite soon grew popular with young lovers, who fastened a padlock to the cables before tossing the keys into the Arno as a gesture of everlasting love—much like the Etruscans, who threw amulets into the river. This custom was soon adopted by visitors to Florence. That was until it became apparent that the weight of the padlocks was damaging the cables and putting stress on the bridge. Fearing an overload on St. Valentine's Day, on 13 February 2004 the municipal police removed the padlocks, much to the dismay of romantics, as they will have to find another way to pledge their devotion.

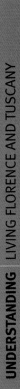

BOTTICELLI'S BLOCKBUSTER

A major exhibition of the work of Filippino Lippi (1457–1504) began in Florence to commemorate the fifth centenary of his death. But it was the far more popular Sandro Botticelli (1445–1510), his friend and teacher, who stole the show. It was Botticelli who appeared on the banners and posters all over the city, and even on the carriages of the intercity trains. Filippino continued to play a supporting role inside the magnificent Palazzo Strozzi, where the artworks were displayed: Just 16 of his paintings, compared to 26 of Botticelli's, were on show. The pulling power of a big-name Renaissance artist was the bankable option and the event was a huge success, as more than 30,000 tickets were sold before it even opened.

CASTAGNO'S CONFESSIONS

Many writers throughout history have recounted the trials and tribulations they faced when visiting Tuscany. Native Dario Castagno decided to reverse this trend by reporting events from the viewpoint of a resident. Castagno is perhaps in a better position than most to comment on the attitude of tourists to Tuscany, having worked as a tour guide for more than 12 years. Entitled *Too Much Tuscan Sun: Confessions Of A Chianti Tour Guide*, the book affectionately pokes fun at the cultural differences between Italians, Americans and the British. On sale throughout Tuscany and in English-language bookshops in Italy's major cities, the book has also been published in the UK and US, and the film rights have been sold.

DAVID'S DUSTING

Michelangelo's statue *David* has had an eventful life. The figure's toe was accidentally broken off with a hammer, it lost an arm when a chair was thrown by rioters, and it has been struck by lightning. It also spent over 350 years exposed to the elements outdoors in the Piazza della Signoria. In 2004 the statue underwent restoration to celebrate 500 years as Western art's most revered male beauty. But the work was hampered by controversy, resulting in the chief restorer storming out after a row over techniques. Her replacement, Cinzia Parnigoni, confessed to being daunted by the responsibility of restoring such a masterpiece. 'Sometimes it was hard to find the inner strength,' she admitted at the unveiling of the newly restored *David*. Yet she confounded critics who felt she wasn't up to the task. 'The doubts and second thoughts weren't so much to do with technique,' Parnigoni explained, 'as with having to measure up to Michelangelo.'

THE BRITISH EXPERIENCE

Tuscany is one of Europe's most popular destinations for people who want to study abroad. But many students are tired of the classroom atmosphere, and wish to learn in a more informal setting. The region is teeming with schools designed especially for visitors, and the British Institute of Florence is the leader in this field. Originally founded in 1917 to improve cultural relations between the UK and Tuscany, 'il British' offers the study of the Italian language and other popular courses and social events. After all, why sit behind a desk when you can cook in a Tuscan kitchen, learn to sing opera, understand fresco painting or create your own masterpiece in a Tuscan meadow? Ironically, as increasing numbers of students come to Tuscany, more and more Italian graduates are seeking their fortune abroad, a trend that could have serious consequences for the country's economy.

In Italy *calcio*, or soccer, is a national obsession, built on local pride and sporting enthusiasm. Nowhere is this more apparent than in Tuscany, where a prevailing sense of regionalism means that support for its teams is particularly intense. Yet the Florentines were for many years the only fans with anything to shout about. Famous for its purple strip, Fiorentina was one of the few Tuscan clubs to have achieved any kind of success. However, in recent years smaller Tuscan teams have started to make an impact, and Tuscany is now represented by four teams in the Serie A (Division One) championship: Fiorentina, Livorno, Empoli and Siena. The region is justifiably proud of this achievement, but when Tuscan sides meet, expect one or two medieval feuds to resurface on the soccer field.

Above left *Two teams battle it out in the Piazza Santa Croce, Florence, during the annual* Calcio Storico
Above right *Fiorentina is currently one of four Tuscan teams playing in Serie A*

THE ROOTS OF THE GAME

As early as the 16th century Florence had developed its own version of *calcio*. Groups of aristocrats and youths chased a ball and each other around the squares of Florence. This medieval scene is recreated every summer in a sand-covered Piazza Santa Croce in *Calcio Storico* (Soccer in Costume). Players are selected as early as Easter, and four teams of 27 players (all in historical dress) take part, each side representing a different area of the city. Before each game a formal procession parades from Santa Maria Novella to Santa Croce, where a flag-throwing display then precedes the main event. But some traditions have been abandoned: the game is now played with a ball rather than the head of a decapitated prisoner.

TOD'S TEAM

In the late 1990s Fiorentina was doing well in European soccer. But in 2001 it was discovered that team president Vittorio Cecchi Gori had been using the club's money for his own business ventures. Fiorentina was banished to Serie C2 (Italy's lowest professional division) and forced to start the 2002 season with the new name of Fiorentia Viola 1926. After gaining promotion to C1, in summer 2003 La Viola was pulled up a further division after a shake-up in the league system. Under the patronage of Tod's shoes mogul Diego Della Valle, Fiorentina won back its original name. In June 2004 Fiorentina regained its place in Serie A. La Viola is the only team in history to go from the first to the fourth division and back in two years. As of 2008, the team continued to flourish in Italy's top division.

THE STORY OF FLORENCE AND TUSCANY

Tuscany was first settled on a large scale by tribes from present-day Emilia-Romagna in the 10th century BC. It was then inhabited by the Etruscans, probably a mixture of indigenous peoples and settlers from Greece and Asia Minor. They established many settlements that exist to this day, notably Fiesole, Arezzo, Cortona and Volterra, where extensive tombs, statues and jewellery bear witness to their passing. The Etruscans were overrun by the Romans, who consolidated the original towns and founded new ones—Florence being the most famous. After the fall of Rome in AD410, the region was subject to a series of invasions from the north, culminating in the arrival of Charlemagne, the leader of the Franks, in AD774. Tuscany then became part of the Carolingian Empire, later the Holy Roman Empire, but was increasingly ruled on behalf of Charlemagne's northern-based emperors by a succession of Lucca-based princes known as the margraves. In time, the margraves became more independent, transferring their allegiance from the distant emperors to the popes in Rome. This allowed the emergence of some of the towns and city states, such as Siena, Pisa and Florence, that would grow rich through trade and banking, and which would dominate Tuscan and Italian history for some 500 years.

THE DEFEAT OF FIESOLE

By 283BC Fiesole was under the control of Rome, but until 63BC it continued to enjoy relative independence. In that year, according to legend, a spirited fugitive and renegade soldier, Catiline, assumed control of the town. Rome dispatched a force led by a soldier named Fiorino to dislodge the upstart. The general decided against a frontal attack on the hilltop town. Instead, he chose to starve the inhabitants into submission from a nearby base on the Arno—present-day Florence. Fiorino's tactics won the day, though Catiline escaped, eventually being defeated near Pistoia in 62BC. Fiorino's fate is less clear. Some say he died in a raid on his camp, others that he never existed.

WHAT'S IN A NAME?

It's one of Europe's most celebrated cities, but nobody knows how Florence (Firenze) came by its name. Some claim it derives from Fiorino, the Roman commander reputedly sent to subdue Fiesole in the 1st century (see The Defeat of Fiesole). Others say that it comes from *fluentia*, either after the River Arno that 'flows' through the city, or the 'confluence' of the Arno and nearby Mugnone river. The origin of the name may lie in the flowers (*fiori*) that would have covered the meadows around the city, in particular the *giaggiolo*, or *Iris florentia*, a purple iris. The flower is still the symbol of the city and of the Virgin Mary, and the cathedral's formal name is Santa Maria del Fiore.

ACIUS AND SENIUS

The She-Wolf was the mythical creature that suckled the twins Romulus and Remus, legendary founders of Rome. But why is this same She-Wolf, along with the suckling twins, depicted so often in the statues and paintings around Siena? The answer is overlapping myth, for the Sienese took the story of Romulus and Remus one stage further. Apparently the brothers could not agree on a name for their settlement, and after one dispute Remus was killed by Romulus, who chose Roma as the name. Remus had two sons, Senius and Acius, who went forth from the city to found a settlement of their own, a place that took the name of the former: Senius, hence Siena.

Clockwise from left The 13th-century campanile of Lucca's Duomo dominates the city centre; the clock tower in Fiesole, northeast of Florence; statues of Romulus and Remus abound in Siena

THE MOVE TO FLORENCE

Tuscany's 10th-century rulers, the margraves, were originally based in Lucca, but in 978 the widow of the Margrave Uberto, Willa, founded the Benedictine Badia Fiorentina in Florence in honour of her husband. Willa's son, the Margrave Ugo, shared her fondness for the city and he transferred the region's capital to Florence in 1001. He also continued the story of the Badia, richly endowing it in the wake of a vision in which he saw 'damned souls all' and was informed that his own soul was similarly damned unless he repented. Repent he did, selling many of his lands and funding the Badia, an institution that would become Florence's focal point for centuries. Its bell tolled the divisions of the city's day and its cells housed one of its first hospitals.

THE PRICE OF A PORT

The story of the Leaning Tower of Pisa reflects the story of the city itself. The tower, like Pisa's Duomo, was started in the early 12th century, many years before construction of the Duomo in Florence began. Such an expensive project was possible thanks to the city's considerable wealth, the result of its port and the maritime trade it allowed. Many of the motifs and architectural ideas on the tower reflect the breadth of this trade and the scope of Pisa's empire, which embraced Corsica, Sardinia and the Balearic Islands. But the fact that the tower started to lean almost from the moment it was begun was a hint of Pisa's fate. The lean was caused by the area's sandy subsoil, created when an area is under or close to the sea. Pisa's port eventually silted up, and the city eventually fell to Florence.

Florence and Tuscany's golden age, a period that laid the foundations of their artistic, cultural and economic supremacy, began in the 13th century. Florence's prosperity was founded primarily on textiles, which in turn encouraged the development of banking and other industries. As trade blossomed, so the city developed a system of guilds, or *arti*, the leading lights of which often rose to positions of administrative power. Wealth and power inevitably lead to conflict, both between individuals and rival banking families, but also between supporters of the two major powers of the day: the papacy and Charlemagne's imperial descendants, known as the Holy Roman emperors. Supporters of the pope were Guelphs and supporters of the emperors were Ghibellines. Like Florence, towns across Tuscany evolved into independent city states, able to flourish in the power vacuum created by the weakness of the papacy and the emperors. As the prosperity of cities such as Pisa, Lucca and Siena increased, so their citizens wished to make conspicuous displays of their new wealth. As a result, both the cities' ruling councils *(comuni)* and rich individuals began to commission ever-more sophisticated works of art.

FLORENCE'S FLORIN
Banking was one of the pillars of the Florentine economy, the business that made the Medici and other families their fortunes. But before banking and trade could flourish, a stable and trustworthy currency was required. In 1252 the Florentines created the gold *fiorino*, or florin, a coin that bore the likeness of St. John the Baptist (the city's patron saint) on one face and the city's name, Florentia, and a fleur-de-lis floral symbol on the other. To prevent the coinage from becoming debased, high standards were applied at the city's mint. By the 15th century, when the coin was accepted across Europe, some two million had been minted.

A WAY WITH WOOL

During the 12th and 13th centuries, groups of Benedictine monks from Lombardy in northern Italy began to move south to Florence. The Umiliati, as they were known, were skilled in the weaving of woollen cloth, and Florence had all that was needed for a thriving textile industry. They settled first on the banks of the River Arno, whose water they used to wash and rinse finished cloth. In time they became a mainstay of the district, and in 1256 founded a church in the area, Ognissanti, which survives to this day. It was the start of an industry that was soon employing 30,000 people, a third of the city's population, and which processed raw wool imported from as far afield as northern England and exported finished cloth to much of Europe and beyond. The monks became so wealthy that they were able to commission Giotto's great *Maestà* altarpiece for their church, now in the Uffizi.

DUBIOUS DUTIES

St. Francis had encouraged peaceful principles in his followers. But this didn't stop 13th-century Franciscans of Florence, who were based in the church of Santa Croce, from taking over the duties of the feared papal Inquisition in 1254. The Dominicans proved equally zealous, making a pun of their name—*domines canes*, or the hounds of the Lord—to underline their dogged determination in matters of doctrine. Two armed friars would roam the city in the company of a lawyer, hunting down heretics. Confessions were often extracted with torture, and those found guilty could be fined or burned at the stake. One third of the fines went to the papacy and Inquisition, one third to the city (the money was used to build the walls) and one third towards the building and upkeep of Santa Croce and Santa Maria Novella, the Dominicans' church in Florence.

Clockwise from left Its historic towers are testimony to San Gimignano's troubled past; Santa Croce, Florence; reliefs at Orsanmichele, Florence, depict the work of the city's trade guilds

A CONFLICT IN BLACK AND WHITE

Factions and conflicts were a way of life in Tuscan cities. All it took in Pistoia to create bloody discord, for example, was an accident. A child, so the story goes, was sent by his parents to apologize for hurting his friend while playing with a sword. The friend's father chopped off the child's hand, saying 'Iron, not words, is the remedy for sword wounds.' The punishment divided Pistoia into rival camps—the Neri and Bianchi (the Black and White), the ancestral names of the families concerned. The same names were eventually taken up by factions of Florence's ruling papal, or Guelph, supporters. Dante, for example, was a White sympathizer, and the power of the rival Black faction one of the reasons he was exiled from Florence in 1302.

A SAINT'S LIFE

Santa Fina, one of San Gimignano's much-loved patron saints, led a strange life, even by the standards of medieval saints. Born in the village in 1238, she was only 10 when she vehemently repented her sins after contracting a serious illness. One of her worst transgressions had been to accept an orange from a boy. She passed the next five years on a wooden board awaiting her death, which had been announced to her by St. Gregory in a vision. At the same time she worked the miracles that would bring her sainthood: She restored a choirboy's sight, healed her nurse's paralyzed hand and caused angels to ring the bells of the cathedral. At her death, violets blossomed from her board and flowers sprang from the walls of San Gimignano's towers.

Life in medieval Tuscany was often turbulent, and never more so than in the 14th century, when the continued prosperity enjoyed by cities and the artistic and cultural awakening of the period were tempered by catastrophes such as the collapse of major Florentine banks like the Peruzzi and Bardi in 1339, and the Black Death in 1348. Civic unrest also continued to be a problem, and it was against this background that the Medici, in the shape of the dynasty's founding father, Giovanni di Bicci de' Medici (1360–1429), first began to make their presence felt. It was also in this period that the process of artistic and other cultural change gathered pace as new artists built on the work of early innovators such as Cimabue and Giotto in Florence, and Duccio and Simone Martini in Siena. Painters, writers and scholars such as Donatello and Piero della Francesca began to make Florence their home. One of the wealthiest cities in the known world, it was a sophisticated and cosmopolitan place in which a freethinking and energetic atmosphere fostered creativity and innovation.

LAW AND ORDER

As Tuscan city states became more sophisticated they made attempts to rule and regulate themselves. Florence's approach, based on a written constitution, was typical. Names of selected guild members were drawn from eight leather bags every two months (the short time span was designed to prevent their power from becoming entrenched). The nine men whose names were drawn became Priori, or Signori, and formed a government called the Signoria. They consulted numerous committees and other elected councils, and had to take heed of permanent officials such as the Podestà, a chief magistrate brought in from outside to guarantee his impartiality. During their period of office, the members of the Signoria were kept virtual prisoners, but were waited on hand and foot, and kept entertained by a professional joke-teller, the Buffone.

Clockwise from top A reproduction of Orcagna's fresco The Triumph of Death *at Pisa, painted in the wake of the Black Death;* Cosimo de' Medici established the Medici as a political and financial dynasty; *detail of one of the bronze panels of the Gates of Paradise at the Baptistery in Florence*

COSIMO DE' MEDICI

Cosimo de' Medici (1389–1464), also known as Cosimo il Vecchio (Cosimo the Elder), was the man whose business sense and political acumen laid the foundations for more than 300 years of Medici dominance in Tuscany. Cosimo's father, Giovanni, had built up a textile and banking business from just two wool workshops, but Cosimo increased the family fortune tenfold. At the same time he was careful to avoid ostentation and overt political interference, knowing that his rivals could destroy him at any time. Yet he also gave to charity and commissioned numerous works of art and buildings. Pope Pius II would describe him as 'master of the country' and 'king in everything but name'. His simple tomb lies at the heart of San Lorenzo church, the Medici's parish chruch.

THE BLACK DEATH

The Black Death arrived in Italy in 1347 or early 1348. In Florence, the plague inspired Giovanni Boccaccio (1313–75), a merchant, man of letters and diplomat, to write the *Decameron*, a masterpiece of medieval European literature. It begins in the Cappella di Filippo Strozzi in the city's church of Santa Maria Novella. Here, one Tuesday after Mass, seven ladies decide to leave the plague-ravaged city for the safety of the countryside to 'hear the birds sing, and see the green hills, and the plains and the fields covered with grain.' Over 10 days they would tell the 100 stories that form the basis of Boccaccio's literary monument to 'the most deadly pestilence, which, either because of the movement of the heavenly bodies or because of our sinful deeds provoked the righteous wrath of God.'

THE BAPTISTERY DOORS

The Renaissance had no distinct beginning. Instead, it was a gradual process of cultural evolution that spanned at least two centuries. Many, however, have identified 1401 as the year that it finally burst into life. This was when a competition was announced in Florence to design the doors for the Baptistery. The judges could not decide between the entries of two young goldsmiths, Filippo Brunelleschi and Lorenzo Ghiberti. Asked to collaborate, the pair fell out: Brunelleschi went off to Rome in a sulk, but would eventually design Florence's great cathedral dome, while Ghiberti remained to work on the project, a task that would take almost 25 years and produce one of the masterpieces of the Florentine Renaissance.

BAPTISMS AND BIRTHRATE

The Annunciation—the announcement of the Incarnation to the Virgin by the angel Gabriel—was long a popular subject for Florentine painters, not least because the Feast of the Annunciation (25 March) marked New Year's Day in the old Florentine calendar. It was also the day on which a mass-baptism of children born each year in Florence took place in the city's Baptistery. When a child was born, a counter was placed in an urn in the Baptistery—black for a boy, white for a girl—and the data recorded. By this means, historians have been able to calculate that the average birthrate in Florence during the 14th century was about 6,000 a year from a city population of 90,000.

Cosimo de' Medici's son, Piero de' Medici (1416–69), enjoyed a brief period in the Florentine limelight, a prelude to the arrival of the most famous of the Medici: Lorenzo de' Medici (1449–92), better known as Lorenzo the Magnificent. Lorenzo's life coincided with the height of the Renaissance, an era during which many of the region's most celebrated artists and sculptors—Leonardo da Vinci, Michelangelo, Sandro Botticelli and others—were creating their best-known work. Lorenzo, like his predecessors, controlled affairs from behind the scenes—few Medici ever held public office. Florence and the rest of the region enjoyed a period of relative peace and prosperity, though Lorenzo did arouse the enmity of rivals. After his death in 1492, however, the fortunes of Florence began to change. Turmoil followed his demise, and a weakened city found itself a pawn in a much larger power struggle between France, the papacy (two popes of the period were from the Medici line) and Holy Roman Emperor Charles V. The sack of Rome in 1527 by Charles V would mark a watershed in Tuscan and Florentine affairs. From then on, the city and the region would largely be ruled by foreign powers.

THE PAZZI CONSPIRACY

The Medici's wealth and power often caused resentment, but never as dramatically as in 1478, when a group of conspirators was brought together in a plot to murder Lorenzo the Magnificent and his brother, Giuliano. Among them were representatives of the pope, angry at having been refused a Medici loan; Franceso Salviati, incensed at having been overlooked as Archbishop of Pisa on Medici prompting; and Francesco de' Pazzi, a member of a rival banking family. In the end Giuliano was killed, his body mauled with 19 stab wounds as he and his brother attended a service at the cathedral. But Lorenzo managed to escape, allowing Medici supporters, city officials and a pro-Medici mob to capture, torture and eventually kill the plot's protagonists.

Clockwise from left The Birth of Venus *by Botticelli hangs in the Uffizi; a portrait of Niccolò Machiavelli, author of* The Prince, *by Santi di Tito; hilltop Pariana, near Carrara, in the foothills of the Alpi Apuane*

MACHIAVELLI

Niccolò Machiavelli (1469–1527) came from impoverished noble stock, but still rose to prominence in the Florentine republic, in which he first served as a diplomat. He visited several Italian and European courts, acquiring a first-hand knowledge of the machinations of princes and other rulers. He had the ear of the city's de facto ruler at a time when the Medici had been replaced. But after 1512, when the Medici returned, he fell from favour, retiring for a while to write books, notably *The Prince*, for which he is best known. These were masterpieces of political analysis, skilfully linking political science with the study of human nature. Machiavelli himself was not 'Machiavellian'—the term was coined later by the French to denigrate all things Italian.

MICHELANGELO'S GENIUS

Michelangelo (1475–1564) was born not in Florence but in the remote village of Caprese, about 96km (60 miles) east of the city. In later life he became convinced that the reason he acquired his skill as a sculptor was his wet nurse, a woman who came from the Carrara region, part of the Alpi Apuane mountains in northwest Tuscany. The area was known for its stone, and the marble for Michelangelo's *David* came from the region. Michelangelo fondly imagined it was the marble dust in his nurse's milk that accounted for his genius as a sculptor. He would also claim to have introduced the art of quarrying to the region, and made pilgrimages to distant parts of the mountains in search of perfect marble.

BOTHERED BOTTICELLI

His delicate paintings might suggest a mild-mannered individual, but Botticelli (1445–1510) was a man of ingenuity when affronted. Life in his studio was interrupted when a weaver moved in next door. The noise and vibrations from the looms forced the painter out of his studio. His pleadings with the weaver—who claimed he could do as he wished in his own home—were to no avail. In response, Botticelli had a boulder winched to the top of his own house, which overlooked the weaver's lower property. He then balanced the stone precariously, so it appeared that any tremor would make it fall. The weaver appealed to Botticelli, who merely said he could do as he pleased in his home. The weaver had no option but to remove his looms.

SAVONAROLA

Reformer Girolamo Savonarola was born in Padua in 1452, moving to Florence, where he achieved high rank in the Dominican order. A strange but charismatic figure, his stirring sermons drew crowds of 10,000, including Michelangelo, who claimed in old age that he could still hear the monk's speeches ringing in his ears. Following Lorenzo de' Medici's death in 1492, as the armies of France advanced on Italy, Savonarola gained effective control of Florence, encouraging its cowed citizens, among other things, to burn their more decadent possessions in a great bonfire in Piazza della Signoria. By 1497, unsettled by plague, poor harvests and war with Pisa, the people turned against him, and he was burned as a heretic in the same square.

After the Sack of Rome in 1527 by the Holy Roman Emperor Charles V, Florence and the Medici lost any real power on the wider European stage. Instead they were minor players in a game dominated by Austria and Spain. When Florence's nominal ruler, Alessandro de' Medici, whom Charles V arranged to marry to his daughter, was murdered in 1537, there was no obvious successor. Charles and his imperial advisors installed Cosimo de' Medici (1519–74), a member of an obscure branch of the family. Despite his ostensible role as a stooge, Cosimo I, the first of Tuscany's self-styled Grand Dukes, managed a long and autocratic rule while being careful not to antagonize his imperial masters. His successors, however, were less able, and a string of ever-more feeble Medici descendants presided over a period of decline, dissipating the family's proud heritage, and with it the last vestiges of Florentine and Tuscan power. The family struggled on for more than 150 years after Cosimo's death, the Medici line finally petering out with its last member, Anna Maria, who died in 1743, thus bringing to an end almost 300 years of continuous Medici power and influence in the region.

THE ORIGINS OF OPERA

Many scholars trace the origins of opera to Florence, and in particular to the *intermedii* of Florentine weddings—displays of dance, singing and static performance. Members of the city's Camarata, a cultural academy, inspired by these entertainments, began to combine their musical elements with portions of Greek drama. In 1597, two of the academy's members, Jacopo Peri and Ottavio Rinucc, produced *Dafne*, a piece generally considered to be the first ever opera. They also created *Euridice*, the first opera to survive in its complete form, performed as part of the celebrations of the marriage of Maria de' Medici to the French king, Henri IV. Such performances continued to be part of Florentine and Tuscan life during the 18th century, paving the way for the region's pre-eminent 19th-century composer, Giacomo Puccini (1858–1924).

Clockwise from left *The Duomo and Leaning Tower on Pisa's Campo dei Miracoli; the Medici family crest on the façade of the church of Ognissanti in Florence; Giambologna's equestrian bronze of Cosimo de' Medici in the Piazza della Signoria in Florence*

THREE TOES SHORT OF PERFECTION

Benvenuto Cellini's great bronze statue of Perseus was nearly ruined before it was started. Cellini (1500–71) was outraged when Cosimo I, the man who commissioned the statue but whom Cellini despised, suggested that the plaster model could never be cast in bronze. Cellini, in a rage, stoked his furnaces so high that the heat gave him a fever, forcing him to bed. When an assistant allowed the bronze to start cooling, the project was at risk as the casting would not be filled properly. Cellini was back in action, throwing every available piece of metal into the furnace. His roof caught fire, but the bronze was cast. Two days later, when the metal cooled, the statue was found to be perfect, except for three missing toes, which were put on later.

STRANGE DEATHS

Grand Duke Francesco I of Tuscany had many problems during his reign, but one in particular. His second marriage, to Bianca Cappello, who had left her Venetian lover to be with him, was going well. Unfortunately, his first wife managed to ban Bianca from Florence, a city whose Catholic citizens took a dim view of second marriages, and who further ostracized the duke's new wife. Bianca became a social outcast, and Francesco was forced to build her an apartment at Poggio a Caiano, one of the Medici's old villas outside Florence (▷ 145). The refuge was not enough to save Bianca, nor Francesco, for both died in 1587. Some claim they succumbed to a virulent illness, but the fact that they died within a few hours of each other suggests they were poisoned.

SIENA'S LAST STAND

After hundreds of years of fighting with Florence, the proud Sienese Republic was brought to its knees—but not before a rousing last stand. Lasting more than a year, the siege of Siena (1554–55) left only 8,000 of the 40,000 residents alive. After the city fell, about 700 families fled south to Montalcino, determined to keep the Republic's flag flying. Here, with the support of the French, they survived the almost constant onslaught of the Medici and Spanish armies for four years. Surrender was made official only when the Spanish and French signed a treaty in 1559. This last stand is still commemorated today at the *Palio* in Siena, when the Montalcino group takes pride of place at the head of the opening procession under a medieval banner proclaiming 'The Republic of Siena in Montalcino'.

A CELEBRATED EXPERIMENT

Pisa-born scientist Galileo Galilei (1564–1642) insisted on the use of experiment to prove or disprove a theory. In one of his most famous, he dropped a cannon ball and a wooden ball from the top of the Leaning Tower in front of his students from Pisa University to disprove Aristotle's assertion that an object falls at a speed proportional to its weight. If this were true, a 10kg (22 lb) ball should fall ten times faster than a 1kg (2.2 lb) ball. The scientist also asked his students to imagine a brick falling from the tower: as it falls, he said, it breaks in two. Will it suddenly slow to half the speed, as Aristotle's theory suggests, or will the two pieces continue falling side by side? Displays connected with the scientist and his experiments can be seen in Florence's Science Museum (▷ 82).

VIVET·DVX·ALEXANDER MED·SECVLA·PER·OMNIA

TOWARDS NATIONHOOD

After the death of Anna Maria de' Medici, Florence and most of Tuscany passed by treaty to the House of Lorraine, whose members were cousins of the Austrian Habsburgs. The first Duke of Lorraine, the future Francis I of Austria, brought stability and reform to the region, ushering in a period of resurgence that was interrupted by the arrival of Napoleon, who defeated Austria in 1799. Napoleon lingered briefly in Italy, including a period of exile on Elba, though his troops remained in the region until his ultimate defeat at Waterloo in 1815. The House of Lorraine, and by implication Austria—which held sway over much of Italy—was then returned to power, remaining in control until removed by the Risorgimento, a series of revolutionary uprisings in Italy during the 1850s. These culminated in the unification of Italy in 1860, after which Florence briefly became the country's capital, as Rome remained occupied by French and papal troops until 1870. Political unrest aside, the 18th and 19th centuries were periods of cultural renewal, particularly in music. It was also the time of the Grand Tour, the trip around Europe, including Italy, made by wealthy English and Americans.

ARISTOCRATIC LARGESSE

Florence's 19th-century aristocracy extended extravagant hospitality, as Thomas Trollope's account of the balls held in the Palazzo Pitti makes clear. 'Guests,' observed the writer in *From What I Remember* (1887), 'used to behave abominably. The English would seize the plates of bonbons and empty the contents bodily into their coat pockets…I have seen huge portions of fish, sauce and all, packed up in newspaper and deposited in a pocket. I have seen fowls and ham share the same fate, without any paper at all. I have seen jelly carefully wrapped in an Italian countess's laced mouchoir…I never saw an American pillaging the supper table; though I may add that American ladies accepted any amount of bonbons from English blockade-runners.'

Clockwise from left *The Venus Italica in the Sala di Venere, in the Palazzo Pitti's Galleria Palatina; cover to the score of Puccini's La Bohème; the Tuscan island of Elba, where Napoleon Bonaparte was exiled*

A DIFFICULT RELATIONSHIP

Lucca-born composer Giacomo Puccini (1858–1924) had an almost lifelong friendship with the conductor Arturo Toscanini. It started with the premiere of *La Bohème* in 1896, which Toscanini was chosen to conduct, despite being just 28. The two continued to work together, but regularly fell out over questions of art and interpretation. On one occasion when they were on bad terms, Puccini sent the conductor a *panettone* cake at Christmas. Then he remembered they were not speaking, and dispatched a telegram: 'Panettone sent by mistake.' Toscanini's reply came back: 'Panettone eaten by mistake.' Yet Toscanini would be Puccini's only real enduring friendship, and it was fitting that the former should conduct the premiere of the composer's last, unfinished, opera, *Forzano*, in 1926. He brought the performance to a close, saying 'the opera finishes here for at this point the Maestro died'.

MODIGLIANI'S LAST LAUGH

Artist Amedeo Modigliani was born in Livorno in 1884, into an intellectual family and grew up speaking French, Italian, English and Hebrew. He studied at art school in the town but left when he was just 16 and spent much of the rest of his life in Paris. He returned to the city towards the end of his life, and announced that he was going to drink himself to death. This he did, dying at the age of just 35. Before doing so he asked the students of his old art school where he might store some of his work. 'Throw it in the canal,' they allegedly replied. In 1984, on the 100th anniversary of his birth, Livorno's council acted on the story and dredged the old canal around the city. They were delighted to find three Modigliani sculptures, but less delighted when three schoolboys appeared on television and showed how they had created the so-called originals with power tools.

SHELLEY'S FUNERAL

English poet Percy Bysshe Shelley (1792–1822) was one of several major poets and many Grand Tourists to visit Tuscany. His sojourn would end in tragedy, however, for he drowned off the Tuscan-Ligurian coast, his body washing ashore near Viareggio. His friends, including writers Edward Trelawny, Leigh Hunt and Lord Byron, conducted a Greek-style funeral on the desolate beach. Trelawny called the ceremony 'beautiful and distressing', describing how the pyre burned yellow with the wine and frankincense poured on the body as libations. In a final twist, Trelawny noticed that among the detritus left as the flames subsided— little more than fragments of jaw and skull—Shelley's heart had remained entire. Trelawny plunged into the embers to 'snatch this relic from the fiery furnace'.

NAPOLEON ON ELBA

Napoleon arrived in exile on Elba, a place he claims he chose for the gentleness of its climate and its inhabitants, on 4 May 1814. On his way to the island he spent the journey musing over plans for his pocket principality, and doodling designs for a new island flag: a red diagonal on a white background—a deliberate echo of the Medici banner—plus the bees of his own imperial emblem. On arrival in the island capital, Portoferraio, he was offended by the stench, and one of his first acts was to give the town drains. This was one of many public works he instigated, partly to occupy and help pay for the 500-strong Napoleonic Guard that had stuck with him. In the end, though, Napoleon was to remain on the island barely 10 months before returning to France.

Italy was a largely reluctant participant of World War I (1914–18), but paid as high a price as other combatant countries—a fact confirmed by the sombre war memorials in many of Tuscany's towns and villages. The region also suffered in the political and economic chaos that followed the war, and in the ensuing period of Fascist rule under Mussolini. Many of the region's hill towns, however, provided some of the most resolute of the *partigiani*, or partisans, who fought Italian fascism and then the Nazis during World War II (1939–45). The region also saw its share of action as the Nazis withdrew, not least in Florence, where all but one of the city's bridges were destroyed. After the war, Tuscany was part of the economic miracle of the 1950s, when Italy, then still largely an agricultural and undeveloped country, was transformed in a few short years into one of the world's leading industrial nations. While the region retained its rural and agricultural traditions, many thousands of farmers or landless peasants abandoned the land for jobs in the service sector, fashion and textiles, or in the small family businesses that have been the motor of economic change in Italy for more than 50 years.

A CHANGING FACE

It is easy when visiting central Florence to be so blinded by the medieval and Renaissance city that you miss the changes that altered its architectural face during the 20th century. The most obvious is the controversial Santa Maria Novella railway station (1935), which owes an obvious debt to the Fascist and other architecture of the 1930s. Similar influences can be seen in the Campo di Marte stadium (1932), now declared a national monument. The station's chief architect, Giovanni Michelucci, also designed the striking Cassa di Risparmio bank building (1957) at Via Bufalini 6. On the River Arno, the graceful Vespucci bridge was built from scratch after the war, while among the art nouveau creations is the lovely house squeezed between old buildings at Borgo Ognissanti 26.

Clockwise from left *Furniture stacked outside Santa Maria dei Fiori in Florence following the devastating 1966 flood; flood waters in Piazza Santa Croce in Florence; Guccio and Rodolfo Gucci in the Florence store during the late 1940s*

GUCCIO GUCCI

Milan may be modern Italy's fashion capital, but Florence can claim one of the biggest designer names of all: Guccio Gucci (1881–1953). Gucci opened a small workshop and his first saddlery store in Florence in 1921, selling leather goods; Gucci's bit-and-stirrup motif dates from these early days, while the distinctive red webbing (introduced in the 1950s) is also taken from its original place on a saddle girth. The success of this store meant Gucci expanded and, as horses gave way to cars, began to sell luggage, bags and other leather goods. In 1938 he opened a shop on Rome's prestigious Via Condotti. In the year of his death in 1953, Gucci opened a store in New York, marking the start of the company's international reputation and association with high-class chic.

THE 1966 FLOOD

The River Arno has flooded throughout its history, but the flood of 1966 that followed 40 days of rain was of a different order. Just before dawn on 4 November, 500,000 tonnes of mud, water and debris crashed through the Arno's breached banks, killing 35 people, destroying hundreds of homes and damaging untold numbers of paintings (including 8,000 in the cellars of the Uffizi), manuscripts, sculptures and other works of art. In some places the water was 6m (20ft) above street level. Helicopters lifted people from rooftops, water and power failed for several days, and bread and milk had to be distributed from the Palazzo Vecchio. Volunteers poured in to the city to help, not least with restoration, which continued for many years.

THE DEATH OF A VILLAGE

Today the Tuscan village of Sant'Anna di Stazzema is almost deserted because of a tragedy that occurred more than 60 years ago. It began when Mussolini was deposed in 1943, and an armistice was signed. The German army then poured into the vacuum left by the Italians in southern and central Italy. A year later, as the Allies pushed up the peninsula, Italian partisans began harrying the retreating Nazi troops. In northern Tuscany the 16th tank division of the SS was clearing villages to deny the partisans support. When villagers in Sant'Anna heard that the SS was approaching, some of the men fled, little thinking that women and children would be harmed. They were wrong. The Nazis killed and then burned 560 people, mainly women, children and the elderly.

A BRIDGE TOO FAR

In 1944, as the American Fifth Army advanced towards Florence from the south, the defending Germans reneged on a promise to demilitarize the city, which would have saved its buildings and artistic heritage from bombing and other attack (Rome had successfully been protected in a similar way a few months earlier). Instead, all the bridges across the River Arno were destroyed on 4 August to hamper the Allied advance. All the bridges save one, that is. Field Marshall Kesselring, commander of the German forces, spared the Ponte Vecchio, almost certainly on the direct orders of Hitler, who was swayed by its historic importance. However, many precious medieval buildings on both banks of the river and the Ponte Santa Trinita were razed to prevent easy access to the surviving bridge.

Since the 1960s Tuscany has shared Italy's economic and social transformation, but also suffered the political upheavals and left- and right-wing terrorism of the 1970s and early 1980s. However, these have done little to derail the resurgence of fashion, design and textiles as major industries, both in and around Florence and farther afield. Nor have they damaged Tuscany's artistic heritage, which has proved a mixed blessing since the advent of mass tourism. While this heritage has attracted millions of visitors to Florence and the rest of the region, with all the economic benefits that accrue, by their sheer numbers these visitors threaten the very works of art they come to admire, placing an enormous strain on Tuscany's already burdened infrastructure.

A TUSCAN TURNAROUND

In the 1950s the tiny hilltown of Montalcino was an impoverished community; a place that was officially the second-poorest *comune* in the province of Siena. It had been making wine for centuries: In the 1660s, the British king, Charles II, had praised 'Mont Alchin' wine. But by 1960 its Brunello wines were only known locally, if at all. This changed in 1966, when it acquired official DOC recognition (Italy's wine classification system). By 1980, it became the first Italian wine to be awarded the rare and elevated DOCG status. The effect on Montalcino was profound, as agricultural and other tourist initiatives paid dividends and all available officially designated land was snapped up and planted with vineyards. Almost one million people a year now visit the village, which has become the second-richest of the province's *comuni*.

UFFIZI BOMBING

Tuscany had been largely free of the terrorism that ravaged Italy in the 1970s and 80s, so the country was stunned when an enormous bomb planted in central Florence exploded in the early hours of the morning on 27 May 1993. The blast, close to the Galleria degli Uffizi, killed five people, including the gallery curator and her family, destroyed three (relatively minor) Renaissance paintings, and damaged some 200 other works of art. The Vasari Corridor was also damaged, along with the Gregoriophilius library. To this day, no one has claimed responsibility or been charged, though there has been no shortage of theories, ranging from Mafia agents to government conspiracy. More than five years later, in December 1998, the damage was finally fully repaired, and new areas of the gallery were opened after a substantial refurbishment.

Above left *View of the Vasari Corridor and the Ponte Vecchio*
Above right *The hilltown of Montalcino*

ON THE MOVE

On the Move gives you detailed advice and information about the various options for travelling to Tuscany before explaining the best ways to get around the region once you are there. Handy tips help you with everything from buying tickets to renting a car.

ARRIVING BY AIR

A large percentage of visitors to Italy arrive by air, the number increasing steadily with the growing popularity of short breaks and the choice of budget airlines for Europeans. Most visitors will land at Pisa, an hour or so from the city. Florence has its own airport and there are plans to extend the runway, but only visitors who can afford regular airline fares fly to Florence directly. Those wanting inexpensive flights go to Pisa or Bologna.

If you are flying from outside Europe you will probably arrive at Rome or Milan. You can catch connecting flights from either airport to Pisa (▷ 43). Delta has direct flights from New York.

Alternatively, you could fly to London Heathrow for a direct flight to Tuscany. Many US visitors coming to Florence and Tuscany fly to Germany and catch a flight to Florence from there.

There are two main airports within the region: Florence and Pisa.

Above *Tuscany's two main airports are in Florence and Pisa*

Florence's airport, **Amerigo Vespucci** (FLR), is 4km (2.5 miles) northwest of the city. You may also hear it called Peretola, which is its old name. It handles mainly domestic flights, with a limited number of daily departures to other European cities. There are two terminal buildings: a smaller one for arrivals with tourist information, car

TRANSFERS FROM AIRPORTS

AIRPORT (CODE)	FLORENCE AMERIGO VESPUCCI (FLR)	PISA GALILEO GALILEI (PSA)
DISTANCE TO CITY	4km (2.5 miles) to Florence	2km (1 mile) to Pisa
TAXI	Price: €18–€20; journey time: 15 min	Price €8; journey time: 10–20 min
TRAINS	n/a	Hourly shuttle. Journey time: 6 min to Pisa Centrale
BUS	SITA 'vola in Bus' buses to Santa Maria Novella (SMN) station	Price: €1.10
	Frequency: every 30 min between 6am and 8.30pm; every hour from 8.30pm to 11.30pm	CPT No. 3 from Pisa airport to Pisa city
	Price: €4.50	Frequency: every 15 min
	Journey time: 20 min	Price: €1
	ATAF bus No. 55	Journey time: 10–15 min
	Frequency: every 30 min between 6am and 8.30pm	www.cpt.pisa.it
	Price: €1.20	
	Journey time: 30 min	
CAR	Journey time: 30 min	Journey time: up to 30 min

rental, banking services and a bar, and a larger one for departures with a café-bar, luggage storage, banking services and some shops.

Pisa Galileo Galilei (PSA) is the region's main entry point, 2km (1 mile) outside Pisa and 91km (56.5 miles) west of Florence. It has good road and train connections to Florence, and handles domestic and European flights. The one spacious terminal has information desks, an adjoining rail station and ticket office, banks, bureau de change, luggage facilities and car rental desks, as well as a bar, a restaurant and a number of shops. There is a building project to help the airport cope with increased visitor numbers.

Two other airports you might fly to are outside Tuscany. Bologna's **Guglielmo Marconi** (BLQ) is 105km (65 miles) northeast of Florence in the Emilia-Romagna region. It handles a large volume of European charter and scheduled flights, as well as budget airline flights. From the airport you have to catch a bus to the main rail station, then it's a rail journey of about an hour to Florence. Alternatively you can rent a car and drive yourself into the region. The airport has banking and exchange services, car rental desks, a bar and a small number of shops.

Rome's **Leonardo Da Vinci airport** (FCO), more commonly known by its colloquial name, Fiumicino, is 32km (20 miles) west of central Rome and about 425km (264 miles) from Florence. If your flight lands here and you don't wish to catch a connecting flight, then you can rent a car to drive to Tuscany. Alternatively you can catch a train to Florence, but you have to get a train into Rome (Termini station) itself first.

The airport has three terminals: A for domestic flights, B for domestic and international, and C for international flights only. A satellite terminal is connected to the main terminal C building by monorail. All three terminals are big, so allow plenty of time for connections. Fiumicino has airport information

desks, a tourist information office, a hotel reservation desk, a lost-luggage office, car rental desks, shops, banks, restaurants and luggage facilities. There are interactive touch-screen information points in both the arrival and departure areas.

CAR RENTAL

The major groups are all represented in the region and have offices at airports, rail stations and in the

bigger cities. You will get a better deal if you shop around before you leave home and book from your own country. Smaller, local companies will often have airport pickup points, but you may be unable to arrange car rental through them in advance from home. If you book with a tour operator, they will be able to arrange car rental in advance.

Before you leave, check your car insurance and see if you will need any additional coverage. You will

USEFUL TELEPHONE NUMBERS AND WEBSITES

AIRPORTS

	TELEPHONE	WEBSITE
General		www.worldairportguide.com
Florence	055 306300 (switchboard)	www.aeroporto.firenze.it
Pisa	050 849111 (switchboard)	www.pisa-airport.com
	050 849300 (flight info)	
Bologna	051 647 9615	www.bologna-airport.it
Rome Fiumicino	06 65951	www.adr.it

AIRLINE CONTACTS

	UK	ITALY	WEBSITE
Alitalia	0870 544 8259	06 2222	www.alitalia.co.uk
British Airways	0870 850 9850	199 712266	www.ba.com
easyJet	0905 821 0905	848 887766	www.easyjet.com
Meridiana	0870 224 3711	892 928	www.meridiana.it
Ryanair	0906 270 5656	899 678910	www.ryanair.com

	US		WEBSITE
Alitalia	800/223-5730		www.alitaliausa.com
American Airlines	800/433-7300		www.aa.com
Continental	800/231-0566		www.continental.com
Delta	800/221-1212		www.delta-air.com
KLM	800/225-2525		www.klm.com
Lufthansa	800/225-2525		www.lufthansa.com
Northwest Airlines	800/399-5838		www.nwa.com
United	800/538-2929		www.ual.com
US Airways	800/622-1015		www.usairways.com

TRANSFERS BETWEEN CITIES

PISA TO FLORENCE

DISTANCE	91km (56.5 miles)
TRAINS	Pisa airport through to Florence Santa Maria Novella
	Frequency: 6 daily direct (extra connections via airport shuttle/Pisa Centrale)
	Price: €5.40
	Journey time: 1 hour 28 min
BUS	Terravision from the airport to Via Alamanni outside Santa Maria Novella station in Florence (tel 050 26080, www.terravision.eu). Services meet incoming flights 8.40am–10.35pm. Price: €8 one way
	Journey time: 1 hour 10 min
CAR	Journey time: 1 hour 15 min

CAR RENTAL COMPANIES

You can book your rental car before you leave home through one of the major international rental groups.

	UK		USA	
Alamo	0870 400 4562	www.alamo.co.uk	800/462-5266	www.alamo.com
Avis	0844 581 0147	www.avis.co.uk	800/331-1212	www.avis.com
Budget	0844 581 9998	www.budget.co.uk	800/527-0700	www.budget.com
Hertz	08708 448844	www.hertz.co.uk	800/654-3131	www.hertz.com
National	0870 400 4581	www.nationalcar.co.uk	800/227-7368	www.nationalcar.com

BUS INFORMATION

Journey time from London:
Florence 28 hours
Ticket price:
Florence £113

Journey time from Berlin:
Florence 18 hours
Ticket price:
€105

Eurolines services:
France: tel 0892 89 90 91
www.eurolines.fr
Italy: tel 899 325264
www.eurolines.it
Germany: tel 069 790 3501;
www.touring.de

need a credit card to act as a deposit when you pick up the car, and it's rare to pay additional charges for car rental with anything else.

You should also check that the car comes with a warning triangle and a reflective jacket, as these must be used in case of an accident or a breakdown.

Drivers of rental cars must be over 21 or 25, depending on the individual rental company, and have a valid driver's licence. If more than one driver is likely to use the car you must specify this when you pick up the car. Any additional drivers may also have to sign the rental agreement.

If you intend to go off public roads, check that the insurance covers this. You will be offered the choice of returning the car filled with fuel; it is less expensive to fill it up yourself just before you return it. Before driving off, be sure to check thoroughly both inside and outside the vehicle for any damage. If you

find any, report it at once and get a company representative to make a note, or you may find that you are liable for it. For more information on driving ▷ 50–52.

ARRIVING BY BUS

You can catch a long-distance bus to Tuscany from most European countries. Buses from the UK are run by National Express Eurolines (tel 0871 781 8181, www.eurolines. co.uk). They operate from London Victoria three or five times a week, depending on the time of year, and go to Florence, Pisa and Siena. However, this may involve changing at Paris.

Visitors from outside the UK can also make use of the Eurolines service, with information on the website above, or check the details given in the panel. There are a limited number of services, operating mostly from Germany.

The majority of long-distance buses arrive at and depart from the

Autostazione SITA, which is across the road from Florence's Santa Maria Novella rail station. From here you can catch a regional service to other Tuscan cities (▷ 53–55).

TIPS

» In Italy, the earlier you can book a bus ticket, the cheaper the fare will be.

ARRIVING BY RAIL

If you arrive by train you will come into either Florence or Pisa. There are direct services from across Europe, including Amsterdam, Basel, Brussels, Frankfurt, Munich and Paris. If you travel from London via Eurostar, you will need to change at either Brussels or Paris. Changing

RAIL INFORMATION

Eurostar
Eurostar House, Waterloo Station, London
SE1 8SE
tel 08705 186 186
www.eurostar.com

Rail Europe
1 Lower Regent Street, London SW1Y 4XT
tel 08705 848 848
www.raileurope.co.uk

Italian State Railways (Trenitalia)
www.trenitalia.com

French Rail Network, SNCF
www.voyages-sncf.com

Interail
www.interrail.net

at Brussels may be a better option as the route via Paris involves a change of train station at Paris, crossing the city from Gare du Nord to Gare de Bercy. Trains then run direct to Florence.

Both Eurostar and other fast European services include:
» 1st- and 2nd-class seating.
» Bar/restaurant cars.
» Snack service on day trains.
» Baby-changing facilities on day trains.
» Air-conditioning.
» Telephone booths.
» Toilets in each carriage, including some that are accessible to wheelchairs.
» Sleepers are available from Paris on direct routes to Florence. Accommodation varies from couchettes in 3-, 4- and 6-berth sleeper compartments to single and double sleepers with private shower and toilets.

RAIL PASSES

» InterRail passes are available in two forms: a Global Pass, allowing travel in 30 countries, or for travel in individual countries. The Global Pass is the most flexible and is available in first- and second-class versions, and for travellers aged between 12 and 25 (Youth) and over-25 (Adult).

Left *Pisa's rail station has a smart exterior*
Right *Rail services to Tuscany arrive at either Pisa or Florence*

It is available for 5 days' travel in 10 days (€249 Adult, €159 Youth); 10 days in 22 days (€359/€239); 22 days' continuous travel (€469/€309); and one month's continuous travel (€599/€399). Half-price passes are available for children aged 4 to 11. Individual country passes also have Adult and Youth passes plus four price levels depending on the country chosen. Within each level there are four options for 3, 4, 6 or 8 days' travel within a month. The cheapest group (Price Level 4) has Adult Passes at £42 (Youth £27) for 3 days' travel, up to £101 (£66) for 8 days.

» Eurail passes are available for North American visitors. They allow several days' consecutive travel, or a certain number of days with a fixed time period in up to 20 countries. There are many combinations to choose from; visit www.eurail.com for more information.

» Before you invest in a pass, bear in mind that train travel in Italy is not expensive. If you're only planning to go on one or two train journeys, it is likely to work out cheaper to buy individual tickets.

ARRIVING BY CAR

Florence is on the A1, Italy's main motorway (expressway)—the Autostrada del Sole. It links Bologna in the north and Arezzo and Rome in the south. The A11 off the A1 at the exit of Firenze–Nord takes you to Prato, Pistoia and Lucca. The best exits to take for the city of Florence are Firenze–Certosa or Firenze–Signa.

From the UK, you can cross the Channel either by car ferry or through the Channel Tunnel. The main routes south run through France, Switzerland and Germany. All cross the Alps; the main passes are the St. Gotthard (free), the Great St. Bernard (www.sitrasb.it; €18.70 for single car journey), Fréjus (www.sitaf.net, €31.90) and the Mont Blanc tunnel (www.tunnelmb. net, €32.30 for single car journey). To reach these from Calais (where the car ferry arrives from England) take the E15 and E17 to Reims, then pick up the roads towards the different passes.

There are toll roads (turnpikes) all along the route. You should allow between 11 and 14 hours' driving time to reach the north Italian border.

You will need the following documents when driving to Italy: valid driver's licence, original vehicle registration document, car insurance certificate (at least third-party insurance is compulsory) and passport.

ARRIVING BY BOAT

Livorno is Tuscany's main port, but it is unlikely that you will arrive in the region by boat, as there are no services from other countries. The port is used mostly for local routes to and from the surrounding islands.

If you do arrive at Livorno then you are probably on a cruise around the Mediterranean and there will be organized tours into the countryside or the major cities.

The best way to see the Tuscan countryside is by car—exploring the narrow roads is one of the highlights of visiting the region. If you are planning to spend most of your time in Florence you will not need a car, as the city is compact and there are good public transport links.

The biggest problem when driving in Tuscany is parking. The centres of the towns and cities are often walled and closed to traffic, or the roads are very narrow; parking is therefore likely to be on the outskirts, where designated parking areas have been created. At busy times of the year there may well be a shortage of spaces.

You can choose to rely on public transport, which is good between the larger towns and major sights, such as Siena and Pisa. In these cases you can get away without driving. However, getting to the smaller towns without a car is less easy, while rail services and bus connections are generally very limited for the national parks, hills and the valleys.

FLORENCE

The Tuscan capital has no metro or subway system, but the historic part of town is largely traffic-free, and can be crossed on foot in around 30 minutes.

There are conventional bus services, but none of the routes is allowed to enter the traffic-free zone. These buses are useful, however, if you're staying on the outskirts of the city, or for getting around to the more outlying sights, such as the Piazzale Michelangelo (▷ 94).

In addition to the normal bus service there are four bus routes that do enter the city's traffic-free zone (▷ 48). These are powered by electricity to keep down the amount of pollution.

Azienda Trasporti Area Fiorentina (ATAF) is responsible for public transportation in Florence. Visit the website at www.ataf.net, both in Italian and English, for details on routes and services.

See pages 47–49 for more information on getting around in Florence.

TUSCANY

Most of the cities and towns in Tuscany are not very large, making them easy enough to walk around, and this is often the best way in which to see them. If you need a map of the town, the local tourist office should be able to supply you with one.

The best way of getting to the most remote parts of the region is by car (▷ 50–52), but you may be lucky enough to find a bus route suitable for where you want to go (▷ 56).

Most roads and routes in Tuscany are scenic, but particular bus journeys worth a mention are Florence to Siena and Montalcino to Montepulciano. The region also has an excellent rail network, with frequent and inexpensive services.

Above *Bicycling is a good way to explore some of the region's smaller towns*
Right *A bus stop in Florence*

GETTING AROUND IN FLORENCE

The best way to see Florence is on foot. A large number of the major sights are in the heart of the city, which is closed to cars. There is no metro system, but buses are useful for getting to the outskirts of town. The electric buses act as unofficial tour buses, as they cut through the traffic-free zone.

USEFUL ROUTES AND MAJOR STOPS

7	Stazione–Duomo–San Marco–Fiesole
10	Stazione–Duomo–San Marco–Settignano
12	Duomo–Porta Romana–San Miniato al Monte
13	Stazione–Piazza Mazzini–Piazzale Michelangelo

BUSES

ATAF (freephone 800 424500 in Italy or 199 104245 when calling from a cell phone, www.ataf.net) has information desks at Piazza San Marco (Mon–Fri 7.15am–7.45pm, Sat 8–12) and Piazza della Stazione (daily 7.15am–7.45pm), which provide timetables and details of routes and sell tickets.

The city's orange buses do not run through the pedestrian-only zone, but can be useful for getting to your hotel after a day's sightseeing or for returning to your car if it's parked on the outskirts. Most lines either originate at or pass the bus station (next to Santa Maria Novella

rail station) or the Piazza del Duomo. Services run from around 6am to midnight, after which the night buses take over (▷ 48).

Routes are not always the same on the return leg, so check the map at the bus stop (*fermata*) to be sure you can get off at the stop of your choice.

TIPS

» You board a bus through the front or rear door, but exit through the middle ones.

TICKETS

» Tickets are sold at *tabacchi* (tobacconists), bars and newsstands displaying ATAF signs and at ATAF offices (see above).
» All tickets must be validated by inserting the ticket into the orange machine behind the driver.
» Tickets can be bought from the driver for an extra €0.80.
» Your ticket becomes valid from the time it is stamped on board the bus. This is because tickets are not bought on the basis of how many trips you want to make, but how long you want to use your ticket for (see Types of Tickets on this page).
» Both the city buses and the electric buses (▷ 48) use the same ticketing system.

TYPES OF TICKETS

» A single ticket costs €1.20.
» The **70 minuti** (70-minute) ticket is valid for 1 hour, from the first time that it is stamped on the bus, and costs €1.20 (€2 on board). You can then use as many different bus routes as you choose within the 70 minutes. You don't need to validate your ticket each time you change buses with this ticket—just the first time you board.
» The **3 ore** (3-hour) ticket works in the same way as the 60-minute

ticket, but for three hours. It costs €1.80.
» The **multiplo** (multiple) gives you four 70-minute tickets, costing €4.50. Although the financial savings aren't great, it is very useful to have the tickets to hand, rather than having to find a shop to buy them in. And because they are only valid once they are stamped on board a bus, you can store them up to use during your visit.
» The **24 ore** (24-hour) ticket works in the same way as the 60-minute ticket, but for 24 hours. It costs €5 and is a good option if you are visiting the outer edges of the city.
» You can also buy tickets for three days costing €12, plus 1- or 3-day Iris tickets for adults, costing €8 and €23 respectively, or for children aged under 15 costing €5 and €12 respectively. These are valid for city buses and trains in the provinces of Florence and Prato (excluding airport Volainbus). The Firenze PassePartour (Adult €22, child under-15 €11) is valid for 24 hours on the Firenze Sightseeing Bus.
» An electronic ticket, the Carta Agile, costs €10 for 12 70-minute tickets and €25 for 21 70-minute tickets.
» All the above passes can be shared as long as a ticket is stamped for each person. For example, four different people can use the tickets that you get with a *multiplo*, but each of the tickets is only valid for the one hour, so if four of you go through the system at once, that's the *multiplo* used up.

TIPS

» Children travel free if they are less than 1 metre (3.28ft) tall. Their height is checked against the box in which you validate your ticket—it's at 1 metre (3.28ft), so below this line your child travels free.

ON THE MOVE   GETTING AROUND

» Smoking is not allowed on buses.
» A limited number of buses are adapted for passengers with disabilities.

ELECTRIC BUSES

Four orange, single-decker, environmentally friendly buses run through the city centre. They are offically known as Bussini Ecologici. Each bus is identified by a letter—A, B, C or D. Bus D runs south of the River Arno to the Palazzo Pitti, which is useful for tired legs.

The map opposite shows these routes around the city; Trenitalia routes are rail connections to other cities; and Vola in Bus is a bus connection to Florence airport (▷ 42).

NIGHT BUSES

Only one bus, No. 70, runs through the night in the city centre (12.30am to 6am). The main stops are: Santa Maria Novella, Duomo, Piazza San Marco, Piazzale Donatello, Piazza Beccaria, Campo di Marte, then back to Santa Maria Novella via Piazza Indipendenza. Fares are the same as on the day buses.

SIGHTSEEING BUSES

If you really want to avoid any leg work, take an open-top bus ride with City Sightseeing (Piazza Stazione 1, tel 055 290451, www.city-sightseeing.it). You buy a ticket on the bus or at an appointed

MAIN STOPS	
The main stops along the routes are:	
Bus A:	Santa Maria Novella–Palazzo Strozzi–Orsanmichele–Piazza della Repubblica
Bus B:	Ognissanti–Santa Trinita–Piazza del Limbo–Uffizi
Bus C:	Piazza di San Marco–Museo Archeologico–SS Annunziata–Sant'Ambrogio–Santa Croce
Bus D:	Santa Maria del Carmine–Santo Spirito–Palazzo Pitti

agent, which is valid for 24 hours from the first time you get on. You are then free to hop on and off any number of times at designated stops. Each bus has a commentary in Italian, English, French, Spanish, German, Portuguese and Japanese.

Line A starts at Santa Maria Novella rail station, and Line B at Porta San Frediano, south of the Arno. Tickets cost €20 for adults, €10 for children (5–15) and €60 for 2 adults and 3 children and can be used on both routes. The buses operate from April to the end of September, and with limited winter service.

DRIVING

It really is not worth driving around Florence. Much of the city is closed to traffic, there is a one-way system and parking is difficult. If you have a rental car, try to book a hotel with parking.

PARKING AREAS

Parcheggio Stazione S. M. Novella
Tel 055 5030 2209, www.firenzeparcheggi.it
Open 24 hours
Built under the square outside Santa Maria Novella. Pay at a cash machine (credit cards are not accepted) before leaving, or at the cash desk if open.
First two hours €2, then every following hour €3; 5-day ticket €140 payable before parking

Parcheggio Oltrarno
Tel 055 223274
Piazza della Calza
Open 24 hours
Entrance is alongside Porta Romana in Piazza della Calza
Each hour €1.50; €15 for 24 hours

TAXIS

Taxis in Florence are white with a yellow design. The start fee is €2.64 (€4.48 Sundays and public holidays). Rates for journeys farther out must be agreed before starting your journey.

There are also a number of surcharges: for journeys between 10pm and 6am (€5.70), travel to and from the airport, travel on a Sunday or public holiday, and for carrying luggage (each piece is €0.62).

Taxi stands are at Piazza della Repubblica, Santa Maria Novella, Piazza della Stazione, Piazza del Duomo, Piazza San Marco, Piazza Santa Croce and Piazza della Santa Trinita.

You can hail taxis in the street—the light indicates they are available. But you may wait a long time before one passes you.

If you call for a taxi, be aware that you will be charged from the moment it sets off, not from when you get in. For radio taxis call 4390, 4798, 4242 or 4499.

Only some taxis are adapted for passengers with disabilities, and they should be booked ahead on one of the telephone numbers above.

Smoking is permitted at the discretion of the driver.

Left *A brightly coloured tour bus does the rounds in Florence*

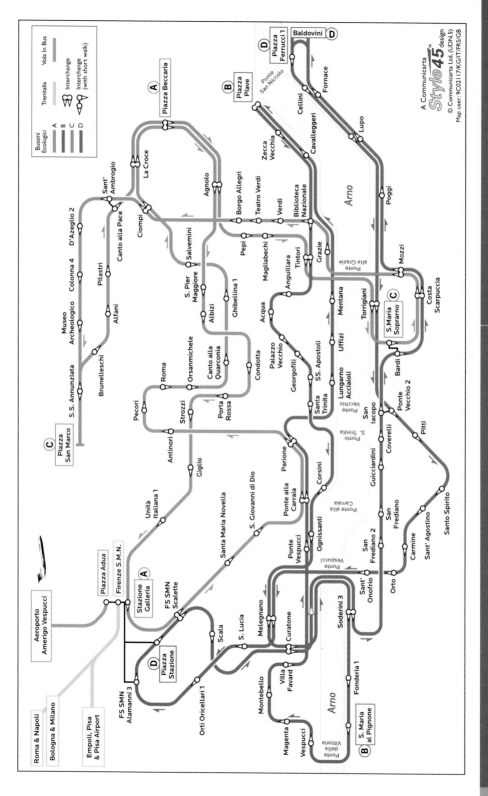

DRIVING

Tuscany's road system ranges from motorways (expressways) and dual carriageways (divided highways) all the way down to narrow, winding country lanes. Driving around the region outside the towns and cities is easy and a pleasure.

A car is ideal if you are concentrating on visiting the smaller towns and cities and rural areas. Tuscan drivers are fairly safe and cautious—Siena has the lowest rate for insurance in Italy—but be prepared for traffic jams in August, when the whole of Italy is on holiday and everyone heads for the roads, particularly on Saturdays and Sundays.

The best bet is to steer clear of cities. One-way systems, narrow streets, lack of parking, traffic congestion and the occasional bit of aggression make city driving stressful.

BRINGING YOUR OWN CAR
Before you leave:
» Well before your departure, check out what you must do to adjust headlights for driving on the right. For many newer cars, this adjustment may have to be made by a dealer for your make of vehicle.
» Remove any device to detect radar speed traps as they are banned in most European countries. Even if not in use, possession of such a device will incur a fine and may result in confiscation of the car.
» Contact your car insurer or broker at least one month before taking your car to Italy.
» Have your car serviced and check the tyres.
» Ensure you have adequate breakdown assistance cover. Contact driving organizations such as the AA in the UK, tel 0800 444500, www.theAA.com.

You will need with you:
» A valid driver's licence (if you have a UK photocard licence, you'll need this as well as the counterpart).
» The original vehicle registration document or certificate.
» A car insurance certificate; at least third-party (liability) insurance is compulsory.
» A warning triangle.
» A distinguishing nationality sticker (but this is unnecessary if you have Euro-plates and are not motoring outside the EU).
» A reflective jacket to wear in emergencies (compulsory).
» A set of replacement headlight bulbs is recommended.
» If you're driving in winter you may need winter tyres or snow chains, depending where you go.

DOCUMENTS
Carry documents with you whenever you are driving. If you are stopped by the police they will want to see them.

The American Automobile Association (AAA) and the Canadian Automobile Association (CAA) advise holders of US and Canadian driver's licences to always carry an International Driving Permit (IDP), together with their national licence.

RULES OF THE ROAD
» Drivers must be at least 18 (or older to drive a rented car) and hold a full driver's licence.
» Drive on the right and give way to traffic from the right. However, at intersections displaying a give way (yield) sign (an inverted triangle with the words *dare precedenza*) give way to traffic approaching from both the left and right.
» Seat belts must be worn in the front of a vehicle and (where available) in the back.
» Children under 4 must have a suitable restraint system and babies under nine months a specially adapted rear-facing child seat (but not in the front seat in cars with airbags). Children aged between 4 and 12 cannot travel in the front of the car without a fitted restraint system.

» It is now compulsory to have dipped headlights on at all times when driving on all roads outside built-up areas. In built-up areas lowered head-lights are only necessary when it's dark.
» There are severe penalties for drinking and driving. The legal level is below 0.05 per cent of alcohol in the bloodstream. You should never drive under the influence of alcohol.
» Italy uses international road signs.

TOLL ROADS AND MOTORWAYS (TURNPIKES AND EXPRESSWAYS)
» As you approach the *autostrada* take the ticket from the automatic box to the left of the car or press the red button to get one. The barrier will lift. Keep your ticket safe, as you will need it to pay when you leave the *autostrada*.
» Cash payment is normally made to the official in the booth; the amount is displayed on a screen outside the pay window. If you are using a pass or paying by credit card, follow the signs into the Viacard booth.
» Slip roads (entrance and exit ramps) on to and off Italian *autostrade* are short. You may have to stop and wait for traffic to pass before you can join.
» Only use the outer lanes for overtaking and be prepared to move to allow faster drivers behind you to pass.

TUSCANY'S ROADS
» The region has three main *autostrade*:
A1 (Rome–Florence–Bologna); A11 (Lucca–Florence); and A12 (Livorno–Genova).
» The SS1 Via Aurelia runs up the coast from Rome and becomes the A12 just south of Livorno. Much work has been done to make this a highway and it will probably become a motorway (expressway).

» The SS2 Via Cassia runs from Rome, passing through Bagno Vignoni, Buonconvento and Siena before going on to Florence. For almost all its length, the road has only two lanes.

» The four-lane Superstrada del Palio was built in the 1960s and links Florence and Siena.

» The newest road, some of which is still being widened, is the much-needed cross-Italy route. In Tuscany it goes through Grosseto, Siena and Arezzo and to Sansepolcro before crossing the Apennines and ending at Faro. For most of its length the road has just two lanes, but the plan is for it to have four.

PROBLEMS

» If your car breaks down outside built-up areas, turn on your hazard warning lights, put on the reflective jacket and place the warning triangle 50m (55 yards) behind the vehicle on ordinary roads, and 100m (110 yards) on motorways. Your rental car should come with both a jacket and triangle.

» If you are driving your own car on non-motorway roads, you can obtain assistance from the Automobile Club d'Italia (ACI) by calling 803 116 or, if using a foreign network mobile, 800 116 800. This is not a free service, so it is a good idea to arrange breakdown coverage with a motoring organization before you leave home. On motorways, you must use the emergency telephones to obtain assistance.

» If your rental car breaks down, call the rental company on the emergency number included with the car's paperwork.

» If you have an accident call the police (113), but do not admit liability. Witnesses should make statements and exchange details.

» If you are stopped by the police, they will want to see your papers. They may give no reason for stopping you, in which case it is likely to be a random spot check. The commonest offence is speeding, for which there is a substantial on-the-spot fine. The police are legally

SPEED LIMITS
Built-up areas: 50kph (31mph)
Outside built-up areas: 70kph (44mph) to 110kph (68mph)
Four-lane highways (*superstrade*) without an emergency lane: 90kph (56mph)
Four-lane highways with an emergency lane: 110kph (68mph)
Motorways/expressways (*autostrade*): 130kph (81mph)
Motorways/expressways (*autostrade*) in bad weather conditions: 110kph (68mph)

obliged to issue fined drivers with a receipt.

SAFETY

In the countryside be aware of animals, slow-moving agricultural vehicles, soft roadsides and unsurfaced roads, which can be hazardous in long spells of drought or heavy rain.

PARKING

Parking is often difficult, as towns and villages were not built to accommodate vehicles.

» Invest in a parking dial; in permitted parking areas these are displayed on your windscreen to indicate when you arrived. Rental cars are normally equipped with one; otherwise they are available at tourist offices.

» Many cities have parking zones: Blue zones (with blue lines) have a maximum stay of 4 hours. Pay the attendant or at the meter. White zones (with white lines) are free and unlimited in some cities, but reserved for residents in others. Yellow zones (with yellow lines) are generally for residents only.

» Traffic-free zones allow cars in to deposit luggage—you may have to obtain a permit first from your hotel.

» A *zona di rimozione* is a tow-away zone.

BUYING FUEL

There are two grades of unleaded fuel (*senza piombo*), 95 and 98 octane, diesel (*gasolio*) and LPG. Leaded petrol (gasoline) is virtually unobtainable; you will have to buy lead-substitute additive.

Motorway (expressway) service areas and petrol (gas) stations in major towns accept credit cards. If you need fuel at night, you will need to find a petrol (gas) station with a 24-hour (*24 ore*) automatic pump. These take €5, €10 and €20 notes. Feed in the money; the fuel stops when the money runs out. These can be temperamental and often reject old notes.

SCOOTERS

Most large towns and holiday resorts have scooter rental outlets—ask at a tourist office for details. To rent a scooter you must be over 21 and hold a full driver's licence. You need to leave your passport and/or a credit card as a deposit. Crash helmets are compulsory.

There are more scooters in Florence than in any other Italian city. Because Florence has less traffic than some other cities, the roads can be less dangerous. But scooters are not for the faint-hearted. If you have never ridden one in a big city, don't start in

HOW TO NAVIGATE A ROUNDABOUT
» When you come to a roundabout (traffic circle), you must give way to traffic approaching from the left.
» If road markings allow you to approach without giving way, proceed, but look left before joining.
» Always look forward before moving onto the roundabout to check traffic is moving.
» To take the first exit, signal right, approach in the right-hand lane, keep right and continue signalling right.
» To take the intermediate exit, select the appropriate lane, signalling as necessary, stay in this lane and signal right after you pass the exit before the one you want.
» To take the last exit or go full circle, sign a left, approach in the left-hand lane, keep left until you need to exit and signal right after you pass the exit before the one you want.

Florence. However, in quieter areas, a scooter is economical and easier to park than a car. Italian scooter drivers weave in and out of the traffic; unless you are experienced, do not be tempted to copy them.

Use the chart below to work out the distance in kilometres (green) and estimated duration in hours and minutes (blue) of a car journey between key towns. The times are based on average driving speeds using the fastest roads.

TRANSLATIONS OF ITALIAN ROAD SIGNS

Accendere Switch on lights	**Incrocio** Crossroads
Accendere i fari Switch on headlights	**Parcheggio** Parking
Banchina non Keep off hard shoulder	**Parcheggio autorizzato** Parking allowed
Caduta massi Falling rocks	**Passaggio a livello** Level crossing
Crocevia Crossroads (intersection)	**Pericolo** Danger
Dare precedenza Give way (yield)	**Rallentare** Reduce speed
Curva pericolosa Dangerous bend	**Senso unico** One way
Discesa pericolosa Dangerous downhill	**Senso vietato** No entry
Divieto di accesso No entry	**Sosta autorizzata** Parking permitted
Divieto di sorpasso No overtaking (passing)	**Svolta** Bend
Divieto di sosta No parking	**Uscita** Exit
Entrata Entrance	**Vietata ingresso veicoli** No entry for vehicles

Distance/duration chart

Upper-right triangle (distances in km / times in hours and minutes):

```
Arezzo                230 215 239 035 059 210 205 139 123 051 059 156 122 159 114 134 043 114 152 158
Barga                     140 021 251 146 302 134 055 311 250 258 122 128 357 137 223 307 233 118 223
Carrara                       122 234 128 227 059 048 253 233 241 050 112 339 121 201 250 216 035 153
Castelnuovo di Garfagnana         258 149 309 143 103 318 257 305 128 133 404 144 232 313 240 124 229
Cortona                               119 206 225 159 109 037 047 216 141 149 134 142 100 109 212 159
Firenze                                   208 118 050 144 118 126 106 032 226 024 058 135 107 103 121
Grosseto                                      152 208 059 139 123 156 225 122 217 144 241 114 208 154
Livorno                                           041 236 221 229 027 105 303 115 126 237 204 041 118
Lucca                                                 216 156 204 028 035 303 044 130 212 139 024 128
Montalcino                                                041 025 235 201 123 153 120 153 050 232 137
Montepulciano                                                 016 215 141 122 133 139 122 106 211 156
Pienza                                                            222 148 112 141 132 130 102 219 149
Pisa                                                                  051 306 100 119 229 155 029 112
Pistoia                                                                   246 026 112 155 121 047 136
Pitigliano                                                                    240 231 228 200 318 247
Prato                                                                             104 147 113 058 128
San Gimignano                                                                         209 043 139 034
Sansepolcro                                                                               144 227 232
Siena                                                                                         154 059
Viareggio                                                                                         133
Volterra
```

Lower-left triangle (distances in km):

```
181
206  61
193  14  49
 30 212 230 223
 78 106 123 115 107
133 217 205 230 140 149
165  85  73  96 194  90 138
150  37  55  48 179  71 183  50
 73 209 226 220  66 114  55 185 174
 54 215 232 226  33 110  91 196 180  37
 61 222 239 233  46 117  77 203 187  23  14
177  65  56  76 206  98 160  23  30 203 209 216
119  78  96  84 148  40 180  91  44 145 151 158  71
141 300 274 312 127 197  70 206 267  80  73  67 226 234
101  89 108 100 130  22 161 102  55 127 133 140  82  22 219
119 153 133 165 110  60 109  83 120  75  98  91  75  86 148  69
 39 220 237 227  69 115 167 201 185 109  86  93 212 152 190 135 156
 65 170 187 180  72  75  76 151 135  41  61  57 162 102 114  85  36 100
175  63  33  74 204  96 184  50  28 201 207 214  31  66 250  81 108 209 162
141 105 142 119 123  83 112  74  70  89 112 104  64 109 162  92  29 175  50 118
```

TRAINS

Italy has one of Europe's cheapest and most efficient rail networks, and if you're planning to cover a lot of ground without a car, trains are the best option. There are a number of good links to Tuscan towns, and Florence's Santa Maria Novella station acts as a hub.

Trenitalia, the state railway system, covers the whole country. Its trains run on time, with clean and comfortable carriages. Trenitalia is also known as Ferrovie dello Stato (FS), which is its older name, and the FS logo can still be seen at smaller stations.

TYPES OF TRAIN

» Eurostar Italia (ES) A super-fast (250kph/155mph) service connecting the main Italian cities (eg Rome to Florence). First-class tickets are available and include newspapers and refreshments. All trains have a restaurant car and trolley service (snack cart). You should book ahead, especially for a weekend journey (book at stations; via Trenitalia agents; by telephone on 892021; or online at www.trenitalia.com).

» Intercity (IC) High-speed trains connecting the main Italian cities and important regional towns. Almost all trains have restaurant/ trolley facilities. Advance

Above Trains at Santa Maria Novella railway station in Florence

reservations are advisable (see above).

» Intercity Plus (IC Plus) These are Intercity trains with new carriages and improved service.

» Espressi (E) Long-distance express trains connecting major cities and towns all over Italy. Espressi services include overnight trains, and seats and sleeping compartments can be reserved in advance (see above).

» Inter-Regionali (IR) Similar to Espressi, they call at larger stations. No seat reservations. Sometimes called Diretti (D).

» Regionali (R) Local trains operating within 100km (62 miles) of their departure station. They stop at every station and can be very slow. There are no seat reservations available and smoking is not permitted.

TICKETING AND FARES

» Italian trains have first- and second-class tickets, which can be purchased online (www.trenitalia. com), at railway stations or through a Trenitalia agent.

» Train fares are calculated by the kilometre. A single second-class fare between Siena and Florence costs €5.90.

» Supplements are charged for the faster services, such as Eurostar and Intercity. You are issued with a separate ticket for the supplement. (A supplement means you are basically paying for a faster service, or in the case of Eurostar, all its extra facilities.)

» There are no discounts for return (round-trip) journeys.

» Children aged 4–12 travel at 50 per cent of the normal fare; children under 4, not occupying a seat, travel free.

» Tickets are valid for up to two months, but must be used within six hours of being validated (see below).

BUYING A TICKET

» Large stations have separate ticket windows for advance booking, and sometimes for first- and second-class travel. Major city stations may also have a travel office for enquiries and advance bookings.

» Ask for either *andata* (one way) or *andata e ritorno* (return/round trip). The price and kilometres are displayed on a board next to the clerk. Specify which train you are taking in case there is a supplement to pay. This can be paid directly to the ticket inspector on the train, but it is cheaper to pay it in advance.

» Payment can be made in cash or by credit card, though credit cards are often not accepted for low-cost tickets.

» Once you have purchased your ticket it must be validated before you board. Do this by inserting your ticket into one of the yellow boxes found in the station and on platforms. If you fail to do this, you are liable to an on-the-spot fine. Your ticket is inspected during your journey.

TIPS

» There are two very helpful information desks at Santa Maria Novella Station in Florence, both open daily 7am–10pm.

RAIL PASSES

» Trenitalia Pass Basic (for Europeans): This is the best discount pass for non-Italians who plan to do a great deal of rail travel. It is valid for 4–10 days' travel within a two-month period and is issued for first- and second-class travel. It can be purchased through Trenitalia in your own country up to six months in advance, or up to two months in advance once you arrive in Italy. You must specify the number of days' travel required when you buy the pass, which also gives discounts on the journey to Italy. Before your pass is used for the first time, it must be validated at any Italian station ticket window or information office. The staff will stamp it and write the first and last day of validity and your passport or ID number on the ticket.

» Other versions of the above are the Trenitalia Pass Youth for 12- to 25-year-olds and the Trenitalia Pass Saver for groups of up to five people.

LOCATIONS OF RAIL STATIONS

CITY (NEAREST STATION)	DISTANCE TO CITY
Arezzo	on edge of old city
Cortona (Camucia)	6km (4 miles)
Lucca	on edge of old city
Montepulciano	10km (6 miles)
San Gimignano (Poggibonsi)	11km (7 miles)
Siena	2km (1.2 miles)
Viareggio	on edge of town; 1km (0.5 mile) to seafront
Volterra (Saline di Volterrra)	9km (6 miles)

» Eurail Pass is available for US and Canadian visitors. It allows 15 days' rail travel in a two-month period for US$588, but there is a complicated fare structure with longer options.

» Eurail Selectpass is valid for train and ferry travel on Eurail group transport for five, six, eight or ten days within two months in three, four or five bordering countries (from $319). It is useful if you are planning to move around a lot. The Eurail Italy Pass is valid for travel for three, four, five, six, seven, eight, nine or ten days within a two-month period. Three days costs €142, seven days costs €215 and 10 days costs €268. Visit www.eurail.com or www.raileurope.com for more details.

INFORMATION

» Visit www.trenitalia.com for online train and timetable information. Alternatively, for phone inquiries tel 892021 (within Italy) or 039 06 6847 5475 (from outside Italy).

» Travel agents displaying the Trenitalia logo have up-to-date timetables, and you can also book tickets there.

» Visit www.raileurope.com for more detailed information on rail passes or www.eurail.com for advice on Eurail Passes.

» Stations display departure and arrival times in the entrance hall. In addition there are timetables for arrivals (*arrivi*) and departures (*partenze*) from the station displayed on boards on every platform.

POINTS TO REMEMBER

» For lost property, call the station at either your departure or arrival point.

» If you have a connection to make, head for the timetable board on the platform where your train has pulled in. Find your connection by looking for the train number, its final destination, or its departure time from the station where you are. The platform will be listed under *binario*.

» All Italian stations, except for very small ones, have a ticket office, newsstand, bar, toilets and luggage facilities.

» Station bars sell food to take out; in larger stations there are also carts selling drinks, water, sandwiches and snacks.

» Luggage trolleys (baggage carts) are few and far between, even at major stations.

» Announcements are clear, but they are made in Italian only, except for airport train announcements at Florence, which are also given in English.

» All trains have on-board toilets.

TRAIN SERVICES IN TUSCANY

Tuscany has an extremely good rail network, and trains can be used to visit most of the large—and many of the smaller—towns and cities across the region. Florence is at the hub of services, with fast main-line connections north to Bologna, south to Arezzo and Rome; and west to Pisa and the coast.

You can reach Siena from Florence on the Pisa line, either directly or with a change at Empoli. Lucca is on a separate line west from Florence, a route that also provides access to Prato and Pistoia. The line south to Rome via Arezzo also provides access to Cortona.

Above *Santa Maria Novella train station*

The chart below shows the duration in hours and minutes of a train journey between these stations in Tuscany. The large numbers are hours, the smaller numbers are minutes. In some cases the journey is quicker if a bus is taken for part of the journey, shown as :

A = bus between Piombino and Campiglia Marittima
B = bus between Cecina and Volterra

	Arezzo	Barga-Gallicano	Buonconvento	Camucia-Cortona	Carrara-Avenza	Empoli	Firenze S.M.N.	Grosseto	Livorno Centrale	Lucca	Montepulciano	Orbetello-Monte Argentario	Piombino	Pisa Centrale	Pistoia	Poggibonsi-S. Gimignano	San Miniato-Fucecchio	Sansepolcro	Siena	Viareggio
Barga-Gallicano	317																			
Buonconvento	258	404																		
Camucia-Cortona	017	344	322																	
Carrara-Avenza	301	148	307	339																
Empoli	122	210	121	155	120															
Firenze S.M.N.	029	212	151	106	156	029														
Grosseto	341	258	054	416	207	211	248													
Livorno Centrale	215	143	222	301	051	050	120	103												
Lucca	213	040	323	248	059	109	113	204	048											
Montepulciano	108	431	150	049	446	216	148	304	315	334										
Orbetello-Monte Argentario	336	353	127	412	256	238	308	018	132	228	326									
Piombino	354	342	A226	425	250	210	244	058	120	236	501	118								
Pisa Centrale	157	119	204	231	033	031	049	118	013	020	306	146	138							
Pistoia	122	135	256	204	142	110	033	302	126	036	237	326	323	058						
Poggibonsi-S. Gimignano	218	255	049	228	231	032	102	146	135	159	139	218	318	116	152					
San Miniato-Fucecchio	141	203	139	214	123	006	037	231	048	104	259	251	230	024	118	049				
Sansepolcro	243	638	550	227	613	432	338	559	534	530	350	631	704	508	448	506	457			
Siena	212	322	026	158	255	053	125	120	201	226	100	155	258	143	213	020	119	527		
Viareggio	229	112	240	256	016	102	133	135	030	016	342	204	227	014	056	150	055	550	211	
Volterra-Saline-Pomarance	400	440	B359	426	214	224	255	142	114	219	521	213	A200	132	354	339	214	736	408	152

BUSES

Italy has no single national long-distance bus company. Buses are operated by several different companies, which mainly run services within their own region, though there are a few that operate more widely.

With the low cost of rail travel, longer journeys are often less expensive by train. For example SENA run buses from Siena to Rome (eight to eleven per day, costing €18) and Milan (three per day, costing €25.50) and Bologna (one to two per day, costing €14.50). However, buses can be much more useful for reaching smaller places.

INTER-TOWN SERVICES

» Buses that run between major towns are known as pullmans or *corrieri*. They link such places as Pisa, Lucca, Siena and Florence.
» It is rare to find a dedicated bus station apart from in Florence and Siena. Services tend to depart from the rail station or the main square.
» If there is a bus station it is likely to have a newsstand, toilets, a bar and lost-property office.
» Inter-town buses are almost always blue.

RURAL BUSES

Rural buses link outlying small towns and villages with the main regional towns or the larger local towns.
» Buses stop at designated places, either at points along the route or in the main piazzas of the villages.
» Services are geared to the local population's needs, so many buses operate to suit working and school hours and are drastically reduced on Saturdays and Sundays and during school holidays.

SAMPLE FARES		
Florence to	Siena	€7.50
	San Gimignano	€6
	Volterra	€6.95
Siena to	San Gimignano	€5.30
	Montepulciano	€5
	Montalcino	€3

BUS COMPANIES IN TUSCANY	
ATAF	Piazza della Stazione, Florence: tel 800 424500, www.ataf.net
SENA	Piazza Gramsci (underneath bus station), Siena: tel 0577 247934, 800 930960 (free phone in Italy) or 0577 283 203, www.sena.it
SITA	Piazza Gramsci (underneath bus station), Siena; for local and regional services: tel 055 834651, 055 478 2250, www.sita-on-line.it
LAZZI	Via Mercadante 2, Florence: tel 055 363041, www.lazzi.it
CAP	Piazza Duomo 18, Prato; for services in northern Tuscany: tel 0574 6081 or 800 570530 (free phone in Italy), www.capautolinee.it
TRA-IN	Piazza Gramsci (underneath bus station), for services in Siena and the Siena province: tel 0577 204111 or 0577 204246 (call centre), www.trainspa.it

CITY-BASED BUSES

» Services that operate specifically around a town or city are called *autobus*.
» Most of the cities have bus services, but these are largely aimed at bringing workers and schoolchildren from the suburbs to the heart of the city, and their schedules are set according to these demands.
» Once you are in the historic part of a town you will find there are few buses. For example, in Siena there is no bus that runs around the Campo. In some towns, such as Montepulciano, there is a shuttle service that runs around inside the town, useful for taking you from the bottom to the top of a steep hill.
» See pages 47–49 for services in Florence.

INFORMATION

» You can get timetables and information from the bus company office or the tourist information office.
» Tickets are available from bus station ticket offices or on board.
» Seat reservations are not generally available.
» Air-conditioning is generally available.
» Smoking is not permitted.

TAXIS

Taxis are available in all towns and cities. Government-regulated vehicles are predominantly white. Always check that the taxi is registered and that the meter is running—avoid taxis without a meter, as they may not be insured.

All charges should be listed on a rate card displayed inside the vehicle. It can be difficult to hail a cab, so it is often better to go to a stand or book over the phone. Supplements are added for telephone bookings, luggage and additional passengers. You can expect to pay higher rates at night, and on Sundays and public holidays. Many city taxis have set rates from airports to cities, so confirm the price before you begin your journey.
» Taxi stands can always be found outside the rail station and in the main city squares.
» For radio taxis call Florence (tel 055 4390, 055 4798, 055 4242, 055

BICYCLE COMPANIES
FLORENCE
Florence by Bike
Tel 055 488992
www.florencebybike.it
A growing company that rents bikes and scooters within the city and has a cycling tour of Chianti. Bicycle rental is €2.70 per hour for use in the city (€14 a day), €3.70 an hour (€20 a day) for a mountain bike; rental also available for three days, five days and a week
Alinari
Via San Zanobi 38r, 50129 Florence
Tel 055 280500
www.alinarirental.com
Scooters and bicycles available for rental—lowest prices range from €2.50 per hour to €12 a day for a city bike
SIENA
D.F. Bike
Via Massetana Romana 54
Tel 0577 271905
www.dfbike.it
Bicycle rental is from €15 per day

4499), Siena (tel 0577 49222), Lucca (tel 0583 495575, 0583 492691, 0583 494989).

» The maximum number of passengers a taxi will take is four.

DOMESTIC FLIGHTS

Domestic flights within Tuscany are non-existent, but you can fly from Pisa or Florence to a number of other cities such as Milan, Rome and Bologna. Tickets for domestic flights are relatively expensive, but advance booking may secure you one of the limited number of inexpensive seats available on each flight. If you fly to Italy with Alitalia (www.alitalia.it) you are eligible for a Visit Italy Pass, which allows you to take three domestic flights for around €125.

DOMESTIC FERRIES

Tuscany has five main islands that you might visit. Elba, Giglio, Giannutri, Pianosa and Montecristo are served by ferries from the mainland. It is essential to book ferries and accommodation in advance for the summer months of July and August. Out-of-season services are drastically reduced, or even non-existent. See the table below for more details.

BICYCLES

Cycling around the Tuscan countryside is a real pleasure and is a good way to see the national parks. In many of the more rural areas, such as the Garfagnana, the Alpi Apuane, Crete Senesi, Monte Amiata and Monti dell'Uccelina,

Above *Moby ferries serve Isola d'Elba. In the summer months it is essential to make ferry reservations in advance*

there are marked trails for mountain bikes. Ask at the nearest tourist office for further information. Safety helmets are not obligatory, but it might be wise to bring your own if you are planning to do a lot of cycling.

There are few city-based bike routes, but you can go more or less anywhere; one good example is along the top of the walls of Lucca. Cycling in Florence is more of a lottery, thanks to the fast-moving traffic and other vehicles using bicycle lanes. However, you can cycle in the traffic-free zone. See panel (left) for more information.

DOMESTIC FERRIES

	ISOLA D'ELBA	ISOLA DEL GIGLIO	ISOLA DEL GIANNUTRI
MAINLAND PORT	Piombino	Porto Santo Stefano	Porto Santo Stefano
ARRIVAL PORT	Portoferraio	Giglio Porto	Giannutri
JOURNEY TIME	1 hour	1 hour	1.5 hours
FERRY COMPANY	**Moby**, Nuova Stazione Marittima, Piombino or Via Ninci 1, Portoferraio, tel 199 303 040 (call centre) or 039 02 7602 8132 (from outside Italy), www.mobylines.it **Toremar**, Nuova Stazione Marittima, Piombino, or Calata Italia 23, Portoferraio, tel 199 123199, www.toremar.it	**Maregiglio**, Giglio Porto, tel 0564 812920, www.maregiglio.it **Toremar**, Porto Santo Stefano, tel 892 123 (call centre) or 039 081 017 1998 (from outside Italy) www.toremar.it	**Maregiglio**, Porto Santo Stefano, tel 0564 812920, www.maregiglio.it
COST (ONE-WAY ONLY)	Cars: €1–€20 Passengers: €6.50	Cars: €31–€36 Passengers: €8–€10	Foot passengers only €8 (service runs Easter to end Oct)

There is a mixed overall picture of facilities in Tuscany for those with disabilities. The major problems are often not with transport, accommodation or public buildings, but with the layout and nature of the cities and towns themselves. Many of the region's medieval walled towns present difficulties for those in a wheelchair, with their cobbled streets and hill-top locations.

Things are progressing, particularly with regard to public transport and access to museums and galleries. It is now the law in Italy that hotels, restaurants and bars must provide facilities for guests with disabilities. However, with some key exceptions, facilities have not yet caught up with those in northern European countries and North America.

FLORENCE
» There are a number of green/grey buses that are adapted for wheelchair use, as is the D electric bus (▷ 48).
» Many of the larger museums have ramps, elevators and specially adapted toilets.
» Santa Maria Novella station is adapted for people with disabilities.

RAIL TRAVEL
There are Centro Assistenza Disabili (Customer Assistance) offices in more than 180 stations across Italy, where you will be given help and advice on your journey, plus help to board and leave trains at stations with these offices. You should call at least 24 hours in advance if you require this particular service. The offices are open 7am to 9pm, with the same number for all stations: 199 303060. This service is available at all big cities if you want to travel outside Tuscany.
» If you have a disability, plan

TUSCAN STATIONS WITH ASSISTANCE DESKS
Arezzo; Campiglia; Empoli; Florence (Santa Maria Novella); Grosseto; Livorno; Lucca; Massa Centro; Montecatini; Piombino; Pisa; Pistoia; Prato; Siena; Viareggio

carefully or consider booking your holiday with a specialist tour operator.
» You should contact your airline in advance of your date of travel. They will let the airports know what assistance you will need.
» The airports in the region are modern, or in the process of being upgraded, so you should find good facilities. They are small enough for visitors not to have to walk long distances between gates.
» Only some Tuscan buses have been adapted for visitors with disabilities; if you are unsure, call one of the numbers on page 56.
» Trains sometimes have wheelchair access, and this is indicated on the timetable by a wheelchair symbol. If you need assistance at the station, contact them 24 hours in advance (3 hours' notice is sufficient from big city to big city).
» Taxis can take wheelchairs folded and stored in the boot (trunk), but Italian taxis are saloon (sedan) cars and getting in and out may be difficult. There are some taxis that are converted for wheelchairs, but you will need to book well ahead. Ask when calling.
» If you are driving and from the UK, you can use your blue Disabled Person's Parking Badge in Italy.
» Major pedestrian crossings in cities have a sound signal for the visually impaired.
» An increasing number of public places and some museums have information in braille.
» Book well in advance and be specific about your requirements when reserving accommodation.
» For a more relaxed Italian holiday, steer clear of the major cities and

use a car to explore rural areas and smaller towns and villages of artistic or architectural interest.
» Contact the local tourist office for more details (▷ 251).

TIPS
» The telephone number 199 303060 can be called from anywhere in the country, and the operator will be able to help or advise you on rail travel.

USEFUL CONTACTS
IN ITALY
Unione Italiana dei Ciechi
(Italian Society for the Blind)
Via Borgognona 38, 00187 Roma
tel 06 699881 or 800 682682, fax 06 678 6815; www.uiciechi.it
Accessible Italy (Regency San Marino srl)
Via C. Manetti 34, 47891 Dogana
Borgomaggiore
Repubblica di San Marino 47031
tel +378 0549 941111, US fax 01139 378 941110; Fax from elsewhere 0039 378 941110; www.accessibleitaly.com
ABROAD
Australia: The Disability Information and Resource Centre Inc, 195 Gilles Street, Adelaide SA 5000 tel (08) 8236 0555; www.dircsa.org.au
Canada: The Easter Seals Society, One Concorde Gate, Suite 700, Toronto ON MC3 3N6, tel 416/421-8377 or 800-668-6252; www.easterseals.org
New Zealand: National Assembly of People with Disabilities, PO Box 27–524, Wellington 6035 tel 04 801 9100; www.dpa.org.nz
UK: RADAR, 12 City Forum, 250 City Road, London EC1V 8AF tel 020 7250 3222; www.radar.org.uk
US: SATH, 347 5th Avenue, Suite 605, New York City, NY 10016 tel 212/447-7284; www.sath.org

REGIONS

This chapter is divided into four regions of Tuscany (▷ 8–9). Places of interest are listed alphabetically in each region.

Florence and Tuscany's Regions 60–238

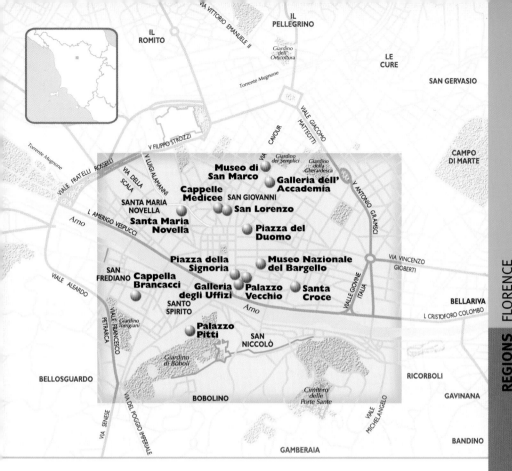

FLORENCE

Florence was the birthplace of the Renaissance and the creative hub for some of the world's greatest artistic talents. The city's churches and museums contain masterpieces and its narrow streets are lined with splendid palaces and elegant shops. The best way to see Florence is to stay for a while, but with some planning, it's feasible to experience the city's glories in a day. Most of the highlights lie within a traffic-free zone on the north bank of the River Arno, an area split by the Via dei Calzaiuoli. This runs south from the Duomo complex to Piazza della Signoria, Florence's main square and home to the Palazzo Vecchio. Just off here is the Galleria degli Uffizi, one of the world's greatest galleries, while south lies the Ponte Vecchio. North of the Duomo is San Lorenzo which stands within easy reach of the Galleria dell'Accademia and the monastery of San Marco. Other major churches and museums are scattered throughout the city. Crossing the river, you'll come to the Oltrarno district; its major draws are the Palazzo Pitti and its galleries, Santa Maria del Carmine and some beguiling artisan shops. The best way to explore is on foot, starting at either the Duomo or Piazza della Signoria, though you may want to hop on a bus to visit the more outlying sights.

   The Romans founded the colony of Florentia in 59BC, which quietly prospered until the fall of Rome in 410. Florence only re-enters the history books during the 13th-century struggle between supporters of the papacy and the Holy Roman Empire. From this, individual city-states emerged, and by the 13th century Florence had a civic leader, the Podestà, and a number of *arti* (guilds) that represented the interests of the merchant classes. From the latter emerged the Medici, a dynastic family that controlled Florence during the Renaissance. By the 16th century the Medici were the Grand Dukes of Tuscany, continuing their patronage of the arts, but overseeing a duchy that was in steady economic decline. In 1737 Medici rule ended and Florence fell into the hands of the Austrian dukes of Lorraine, who, except during the Napoleonic years, ruled Tuscany until 1859. In 1860 Florence became part of united Italy, serving as the capital briefly in 1861. Today it is capital of one of Italy's richest regions.

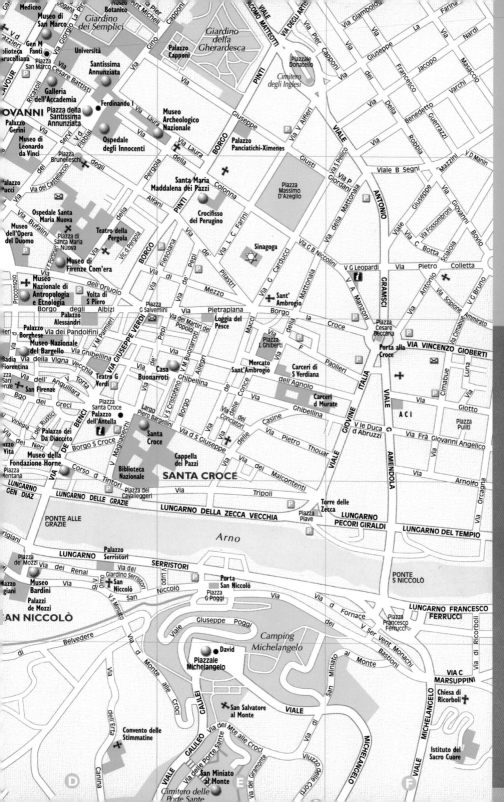

Medicea
Dogana
a Pier
Capponi
Giardino
Botanico
Museo di
San Marco
Giardino
dei Semplici
Giardino
della
Gherardesca
Palazzo
Cadotti Micheli
Gen M
Fanti
Università
Palazzo
Capponi
Piazzale
Donatello
Cimitero
degli Inglesi
Galleria
dell'Accademia
Santissima
Annunziata
Ferdinando I
Museo
Archeologico
Nazionale
Piazza della
Santissima
Annunziata
Museo di
Leonardo
da Vinci
Ospedale
degli Innocenti
Palazzo
Panciatichi-Ximenes
Santa Maria
Maddalena dei Pazzi
Ospedale Santa
Maria Nuova
Crocifisso
del Perugino
Museo
dell'Opera
del Duomo
Piazza di
Santa Maria
Nuova
Teatro della
Pergola
Piazza Massimo
D'Azeglio
Museo di
Firenze Com'era
Sinagoga
Museo
Nazionale di
Antropologia
e Etnologia
Volta di
S Piero
Sant'
Ambrogio
Palazzo
Alessandri
Loggia del
Pesce
Palazzo
Borghese
Museo Nazionale
del Bargello
Casa
Buonarroti
Mercato
Sant'Ambrogio
Carceri di
S Verdiana
Badia
Fiorentina
Teatro G
Verdi
Carceri
d Murate
San Firenze
Piazza
Santa Croce
Palazzo
dell'Antella
Santa
Croce
Museo della
Fondazione Horne
Cappella
dei Pazzi
SANTA CROCE
Biblioteca
Nazionale
Porta alla
Croce
A C I
LUNGARNO
GEN DIAZ
LUNGARNO DELLE GRAZIE
LUNGARNO DELLA ZECCA VECCHIA
Torre delle
Zecca
LUNGARNO
PECORI GIRALDI
LUNGARNO DEL TEMPIO
PONTE ALLE
GRAZIE
Arno
Palazzo
Serristori
Piazza
de Mozzi
Porta
San Niccolò
PONTE
S NICCOLÒ
Museo
Bardini
Giardino
Serristori
San
Niccolò
Palazzi
de Mozzi
LUNGARNO FRANCESCO
FERRUCCI
AN NICCOLÒ
Piazza
Francesco
Ferrucci
David
Camping
Michelangelo
Piazzale
Michelangelo
VIA C
MARSUPPINI
San Salvatore
al Monte
Chiesa di
Ricorboli
Convento delle
Stimmatine
San Miniato
al Monte
Istituto del
Sacro Cuore
Cimitero delle
Porte Sante

D
E
F

63

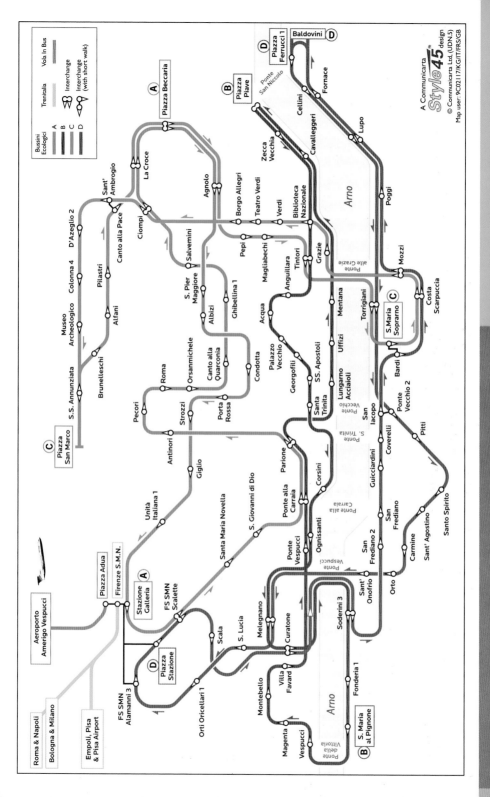

CAPPELLA BRANCACCI

This small chapel, entered via a separate entrance, lies at the end of the right transept of the church of Santa Maria del Carmine and has some of the most significant works of the Florentine Renaissance. Although the church's exterior is dull—a rough stone façade was rebuilt after a fire in 1771—the frescoes survived and, thanks to restoration carried out in the 1980s, are vibrant once again. Advance reservation here is now compulsory for much of the year, so call ahead to book tickets.

THE FRESCOES

Rich merchant Felice Brancacci commissioned the frescoes in 1424. Masolino and his apprentice Masaccio began the work a year later. Both died before the cycle could be completed and, since the patron Brancacci was exiled by Cosimo de' Medici after 1436, the frescoes were untouched for 50 years. They were eventually finished by Filippino Lippi (1457–1504), who copied the style of his two predecessors.

The chapel (which can only accommodate 30 people at one time) is covered from top to bottom with paintings. The entire cycle, apart from two paintings, depicts scenes from St. Peter's life. In particular, look for Masaccio's dramatic *Expulsion of Adam and Eve* and *Tribute Money*, probably the most famous of the images and the first monumental Renaissance fresco painting. In contrast to the two-dimensional portrayals characteristic of Masaccio's predecessors, the depiction of Adam and Eve in their anguish is particularly moving and forms a striking contrast to Masolino's depiction of the same event. Other highlights are *St. Peter Healing the Sick* and *Distribution of Alms*.

INFORMATION

www.museoragazzi.it

✚ 62 A3 ✉ Piazza del Carmine, 50124 ☎ 055 238 2195 🕐 Mon, Wed–Sat, 10–5, Sun 1–5; last entrance 4.30 ♿ Adult €4, under 18 €1.50 🚇 D ❓ Combined ticket with Palazzo Vecchio available: Adult €8, under 18 €3

Opposite *The Cappella Brancacci lies within the church of Santa Maria del Carmine*

Below *This chapel is embellished by a fresco cycle that marks a watershed in the development of painting and is among the earliest true Renaissance works*

CAPPELLE MEDICEE

The chapels are at the eastern end of the church of San Lorenzo (▷ 99) and consist of the crypt, the Cappella dei Principi (Chapel of Princes) and the Sagrestia Nuova (New Sacristy). Most members of the Medici family are buried within the chapels, the minor ones interred in the vaulted crypt where there are numerous tombstones. Glass cases display gold and silver objects from the church treasury, including a 16th-century pearl-encrusted mitre.

CAPPELLA DEI PRINCIPI

Stone steps lead from the crypt to this chapel, the Grand Dukes' (▷ 34) octagonal mausoleum. It was begun in 1604 and is entirely lined with marble and gems. It is a magnificent example of pietre dure craftsmanship (a technique of inlaying stones) at which the Florentines of the time were particularly skilled. The massive sarcophagi set high around the walls contain the remains of the most illustrious of the Medici: (from left to right) Fernando II, Cosimo II, Fernando I, Cosimo I, Francesco I and Cosimo III. The huge, gilded bronze statues (1626–42) above two of the tombs are by Pietro and Ferdinando Tacca.

SAGRESTIA NUOVA

The Sagrestia Nuova is totally different in style from its predecessor. The grey pietra serena (stone taken from the hills of Fiesole, ▷ 69) against white marble and the classical lines are a sober contrast to the extravagance of the Cappella dei Principi. Work is thought to have been begun by Giuliano da Sangallo in 1491, and was continued (though never completed) by Michelangelo between 1520 and 1533. Inspired by Brunelleschi's Old Sacristy (access through the main church), it was used as a funeral chapel for the Medici family. Here you will find two superb examples of tombs and statues by Michelangelo. The tomb of Lorenzo, Duke of Urbino and grandson of Lorenzo de' Medici, is on the left of the entrance and is decorated with the reclining figures of *Dawn and Dusk*. The corresponding statues on the tomb opposite, that of Giuliano, Duke of Nemours, represent *Day and Night* and are considered among Michelangelo's finest. The beautiful statue of the Madonna and Child (1521) is also by Michelangelo, along with the two carved candelabra on the altar.

INFORMATION

www.firenzemusei.it

✚ 62 C2 ✉ Piazza Madonna degli Aldobrandini 6, 50120 ☎ 055 238 8602 🕐 Daily 8.15–5.50. Closed 2nd and 4th Sun and 1st, 3rd and 5th Mon of each month ✋ Adult €6, under 18 free 🚌 A, 1, 17 🎧 Audiotours in English and Italian for €5 📖 A wide selection is available. the official book is €8, and an inexpensive leaflet €1.55 🏛 Sells the usual books, guides, postcards, calendars, posters and gift items ❓ Advance booking (€3) not required but advisable in high season (tel 055 294883)

Above *The Medici family's monumental private chapels are remarkable for their scale—visible proof of the dynasty's tremendous wealth*

Opposite *The 14th-century Carthusian monastery at Certosa di Galluzzo*

CASA BUONARROTI

www.casabuonarroti.it

The Casa Buonarroti, once a Renaissance townhouse, is now the Michelangelo museum, providing an insight into the life of one of the world's most famous artists. Michelangelo Buonarroti (1475–1564) bought the house in 1508. He left the property and several works of art to his nephew Leonardo, who left it to his son, also named Michelangelo. This Michelangelo was an art collector, and in 1612 he turned part of the house into a gallery dedicated to his great-uncle. The museum is not packed with works, but you can see several portraits of the great artist, and the marble bas-relief of *The Madonna of the Steps*, his earliest-known work.

✚ 63 E3 ✉ Via Ghibellina 70, 50122 ☎ 055 241752 🕐 Wed–Mon 9.30–2, ticket office closes 30 min earlier ✋ Adult €6.50 🚌 A, 14 ♿

CERTOSA DI GALLUZZO

This great Carthusian monastery was once occupied by 18 monks, who lived silent lives in self-contained apartments. They tended gardens around the Chiostro Grande, a cloister decorated with tondi by brothers Andrea (1435–1525) and Giovanni (c1469–1529) della Robbia. The visit includes the Palazzo degli Studi, which holds the great *Scenes from the Passion* frescoes, executed by Pontormo while he sheltered there during the 1522 plague. Insensitively restored in the 1970s, they are ghosts of what they were, though nothing can detract from the power of the composition.

✚ 278 G5 ✉ Certosa di Galluzzo, Via Buca di Certose, 50124 ☎ 055 204 9226 🕐 Apr–end Oct Tue–Sun 9–12, 3–6; Nov–end Mar 9–12, 3–5 ✋ Free 🎫 Guided tours only

FIESOLE

www.comune.fiesole.fi.it

Perched on a hillside 7km (4 miles) northeast of Florence, Fiesole was originally an Etruscan settlement, which grew in importance under the Romans. Evidence of both periods can be seen in the Area Archeologica east of the main square, Piazza Mino da Fiesole. It has a well-preserved Roman amphitheatre, Roman baths, a Roman temple and some sixth-century BC Etruscan ruins. From the piazza you can climb Via San Francesco for sweeping views of Florence below. The Museo Bandini (currently closed for restoration) has ivories, ceramics and paintings on display, while the church of San Domenico, dating from the 15th century, has a delicate Madonna with Saints and Angels by Fra Angelico.

✚ 278 G4 🚹 Via Portigiani 3, 50014 Fiesole, ☎ 055 598720 🕐 Mar–end Oct Mon–Sat 9–6, Sun 10–1, 2–6. Closed 5pm Nov–end Feb

GIARDINO DI BOBOLI

This green space in the middle of Florence, a cool oasis on a hot summer's day, is the perfect fresh-air antidote to the many indoor sights in the city. Even at the height of summer the warren of small lanes and pathways provides a welcome refuge with elaborate fountains, grottoes, elegant buildings, formal gardens, lichen-covered statues and secluded glades.

The gardens are laid out on a hillside behind the Palazzo Pitti (▷ 84–85) and stretch from the palace up to Forte di Belvedere (▷ 105). They were designed by Niccolò Tribolo (1500–50) for Cosimo I de' Medici and were opened to the public in 1766. Near the main courtyard of the Palazzo Pitti is the magnificent Grotta Grande. In each of the four corners are copies of Michelangelo's unfinished *Slaves*; the originals are in the Galleria dell'Accademia (▷ 70–71). Walk up the terraces to the Neptune fountain (1571), where you can either take a detour to the elegant pavilion Kaffeehaus, for wonderful views and refreshments, or continue up to the top of the garden to the large statue, *Abundance*.

Off the beaten track, follow the magnificent Viottolone, a wide, steep path lined by cypress trees and statues leading to the lower part of the garden. At the bottom is the magical Isolotto, an island surrounded by an oval moat, adorned with statues, lemon trees and the Oceanus fountain. You can reach the Museo delle Porcellane (the Porcelain Museum, ▷ 85) from the top of the gardens. Before you leave, be sure to see the Bacchus fountain.

✚ 62 B5 ✉ Palazzo Pitti, Piazza de' Pitti, 50125 ☎ 055 265 1838 🕐 Jun–end Aug daily 8.15–7.30; Apr, May, Sep 8.15–6.30; Mar, Oct 8.15–5.30; Nov–end Feb 8.15–4.30, ticket office closes 1 hour earlier. Closed 1st and last Mon of each month ✋ Adult €7, under 18 free. Combined ticket available with Museo degli Argenti, Museo delle Porcellane, Museo del Costume in the Pitti Palace, valid for 3 days, for €4 🚌 D, 11, 36, 37 💻 ♿

INFORMATION

www.sbas.firenze.it/accademia

✚ 63 D1 ✉ Via Ricasoli 60, 50122
☎ 055 238 8609 🕐 Tue–Sun 8.15–6.50
(hours often extended in summer), ticket
office closes 45 min earlier 🖐 Adult
€6.50 (mid-Jul to end Aug €10), under 18
free 🚌 1, 6, 7, 11, 17 🎧 Audiotours
in English, French, Spanish, German,
Japanese, Italian, €5 for a single, €7 for
a double. For organized guided tours,
☎ 055 294883 📖 Shorter book for
€9.50, and another for €14 with more
photos 📖 A selection of art books,
posters, postcards, gifts and stationery
❓ Advance booking (€3) not required but
advisable in high season (tel 055 294883)

INTRODUCTION

The Accademia, second only to the Galleria degli Uffizi (▷ 73–77) in visitor numbers, contains many rooms full of glorious Renaissance and other paintings, but it is Michelangelo's *David* that is the main attraction, drawing a constant stream of people. In summer, you'll have to wait for hours if you haven't booked ahead; advance booking, whatever the time of year, will save you much time and frustration (▷ 75).

Florence's first school of drawing, the Accademia was founded in the 1560s, moving to its current home in 1764, when its role expanded to cover the visual arts generally. Named the Accademia di Belle Arti, it obtained its own gallery in 1784, quickly building up a teaching collection of art, used to aid students working on all aspects of painting, drawing and sculpture. It was augmented with numerous paintings during the 19th century and became home of the *David* in 1873, when the statue was moved indoors from the Piazza della Signoria. A replica now stands in the square.

The entrance to the gallery is by way of the large Sala del Colosso, from where you pass through to the gallery containing the *David*, protected (since an attack in 1991) by glass in a specially built alcove. But don't become so preoccupied with the *David* that you miss the Accademia's other highlights, not least several other works by Michelangelo (the four *Slaves* and a statue of St. Matthew, which you'll see in the corridor leading to the *David*), and a large collection of 13th- to 16th-century Florentine paintings. The latter include works by Pontormo and Botticelli.

WHAT TO SEE

DAVID

Liberated, if only temporarily, from the shackles of the Medici rulers and the fanatical religious reformer Girolamo Savonarola (▷ 33), the city fathers

Above *The gallery is home to Michelangelo's* David, *one of the world's best-known sculptural pieces, and to other works by this Renaissance artistic giant*

decided to commemorate this rebirth of civil liberty with a large public statue. In 1501 the group that looked after the Duomo, the Opera del Duomo, chose the subject of David the Giant-Killer as a suitable theme to invoke Florence's success against more powerful forces, and commissioned Michelangelo, then only 26, to carve the piece. The block of marble available was huge (more than 4m/13ft), misshapen, cracked and thin; it had already defeated sculptors including Jacopo Sansovino and Leonardo da Vinci. Where they failed, Michelangelo succeeded, producing an amazing display of virtuosity, and turning the stone's defects into strengths. The statue shows the young David in meditative pose as he prepares for his fight with Goliath, aware that the salvation of his people depends upon him.

Bear in mind that the statue wasn't intended to be seen in the confined interior space it now occupies, but as a public sculpture to be viewed from below in a large open piazza. In this context, the huge head and over-large hands fall into proportion. It took 40 men four days to move the finished work into the Piazza della Signoria (▷ 87), where it became a symbol of republican liberty.

THE SLAVES

The four *Slaves*—unfinished marble pieces in which the figures appear trapped in the stone—were carved between 1519 and 1536, and originally intended for the tomb of Pope Julius II (1443–1513) in St. Peter's, Rome. Michelangelo held the theory that sculpting was a process of liberating the subject from the stone and started work by cutting the figure in deep relief into the block. This process was often carried out by his assistants, Michelangelo then stepping in to 'set free' the three-dimensional figure. These works are a perfect example of the process, and may also have been intended to act as an illustration of the 'imprisonment' of the arts following Julius' death. Julius' tomb was never assembled in its intended form, so the *Slaves* remained in Florence. There were originally six figures; two are now in the Musée du Louvre, in Paris. The four in the Accademia were moved there in 1909 from the Giardino di Boboli (▷ 69), where they had been placed by the Medici in 1564.

MORE TO SEE

You will find the figure of St. Matthew by Michelangelo in the same corridor as the *Slaves*. It was intended to be the first of a set of all twelve apostles, although this is the only one ever started. The *Cassone Adimari*, a painted panel from a marriage chest, shows a lively and much-reproduced wedding scene of the mid-15th century taking place in front of the city's baptistery. *Madonna of the Sea* is an early work by Botticelli (also known as *Madonna and Child with the Young St. John and Two Angels*). *Venus and Cupid* is an early work by Pontormo, probably painted using a Michelangelo cartoon.

Below David *is a sculptural tour de force and confirmed Michelangelo as a leading sculptor of the time*
Below left Tobias with the Archangels Michael, Raphael and Gabriel *by Domenico di Michelino*

GALLERIA DEGLI UFFIZI

INTRODUCTION

Whatever else you do in Florence and Tuscany, set aside plenty of time to see the Galleria degli Uffizi, the world's finest gallery of Renaissance art. While you could skim through the highlights in an hour or so, this is a sight to which you could easily devote two or more visits.

This, more than almost any other sight in Italy, is one where you should strive to reserve tickets in advance. Only 660 people are allowed into the gallery at any time, so pre-book your visit by telephone or online, for which there is a small fee (▷ 75). You will be allocated an entrance time and booking number. Collect your tickets at Entrance 2 in the west ground-floor arcade. The alternative is to wait in line, but this could mean standing for hours in summer. If you arrive in the city without having made a booking, ask your hotel concierge if he or she can help with a last-minute reservation.

The Palazzo degli Uffizi, which houses the gallery, was originally intended to be government offices (*uffizi*) of the Grand Duchy of Tuscany and was built between 1560 and 1574 by Giorgio Vasari, under the orders of Cosimo I de' Medici. His son, Francesco I (1541–87), had the upper floor converted to house his art collections, which were available for public inspection from 1591, making the Uffizi one of the oldest museums in Europe. Succeeding Medici dukes added to the collections, which were bequeathed to Florence by the last member of the family, Anna Maria Lodovica, in 1737, on the condition that the works never leave the city.

Not only are these collections enormous, but so too is the palace in which they are housed, a building that essentially consists of two long wings, with most of the exhibits ranged in 45 rooms on their upper floors. So don't attempt to see the entire collection in one day, but use your first visit to concentrate on Rooms 1 through 18 in the East Corridor, which present major Florentine, Tuscan Gothic and Renaissance works, all arranged in chronological order. This is where you'll find most of the familiar paintings and famous names—Botticelli, Giotto, Duccio, Leonardo da Vinci and many more—and most of your fellow visitors. Return to tackle 16th-century and later Italian and other major European artists in the remainder of the East Corridor and the rooms along the West Corridor. Many visitors to the Uffizi are surprised to find that it contains

INFORMATION

www.firenzemusei.it

✚ 62 C3 ✉ Piazzale degli Uffizi, 50123 ☎ 055 238 8651 🕐 Tue–Sun 8.15–6.50 (hours usually extended in summer); ticket office closes 45 min earlier; booking in advance Mon–Fri 8.30–6.30, Sat 8.30–12.30 ☎ 055 294883 or online at www.firenzemusei.it (€4 booking fee) 🖐 Adult €6.50 (10 Jun–2 Nov €10), under 18 free, free to all in Cultural Week (24–30 May) 🚌 B, 23 🎧 Audiotours in English, French, Spanish, German, Japanese, Italian from €6.50 📖 Official guidebook from €4.50 ☕ Good, if expensive, café serving drinks and snacks at the end of the West Corridor. It has a superb terrace overlooking Piazza della Signoria 🏛 A good book and gift shop, selling art books and guidebooks, posters, prints, and the usual gift items

Opposite *A detail of the Madonna from Madonna with Child and Two Angels by Filippo Lippi (c1455)*
Below *The U-shaped Palazzo degli Uffizi was originally designed as government offices*

THE DEVELOPMENT PLAN

The Uffizi's management has long been aware of its shortage of display areas and visitor facilities. A huge redevelopment plan has been launched, which will eventually almost double the museum's space, as well as provide much-needed visitor infrastructure in the shape of better access, more cloakrooms and refreshment facilities. Works in storage will emerge, and the aim is to open up on a regular basis the Corridoio Vasariano (▷ 95), which links the Uffizi with the Palazzo Pitti. Work will continue throughout the first decade of the century; while it's in progress the museum will remain open as usual, although some galleries will close on a rotating basis.

masterpieces by non-Italian painters, notably Rembrandt, Goya, Rubens and Van Dyck.

Don't overlook the occasional works of sculpture, survivors from the 19th century, when much of the formerly extensive sculpture and archeological collections were transferred elsewhere, making the Uffizi essentially a painting gallery. And don't assume that what you are seeing in the 45 rooms is the gallery's entire collection: most is in storage. The Uffizi continues to acquire paintings and drawings but, with space at a premium, a huge development project is under way to increase the museum's space and visitor infrastructure.

WHAT TO SEE

THE DUKE AND DUCHESS OF URBINO

This double portrait was painted in 1465 by Piero della Francesca, two years after the death of the Duchess, Battista Sforza. It shows the sitters in profile; the Duke, Federigo da Montefeltro, lost his right eye in battle and was always portrayed from the left. Piero painted few portraits and it is worth comparing this with his religious works in Arezzo (▷ 197) and Sansepolcro (▷ 211). The town behind Battista is Gubbio, the place of her death in childbirth.

ADORATION OF THE MAGI

This altarpiece, epitomizing the intricacy and richness of International Gothic, was commissioned in 1423 by Palla di Strozzi for the family chapel in Santa Trinita (▷ 101). It was painted by Gentile da Fabriano, and Strozzi's culture, learning and wealth are reflected in the richness of detail and lavish use of gold in the Magi procession. The panels above the altar, showing the Nativity, the Rest on the Flight into Egypt and the Presentation, move stylistically towards the Renaissance, as can be seen by the realistically blue sky.

Above right Piero della Francesca's 15th-century diptych of the Duke and Duchess of Urbino
Opposite Primavera *by Botticelli, dating from 1477*

MADONNA RUCELLAI

Painted by Duccio di Buoninsegna for the Rucellai Chapel in Santa Maria Novella (▷ 100) in 1285, this watershed painting came to the Uffizi in 1937. Though heavily influenced by the work of Cimabue (born c1240), it breaks new ground stylistically with the introduction of delicate Gothic overtones and brilliant colours, features that were to become the hallmark of Sienese painting. These are strongly evident in the rendition of the throne, with its Gothic pointed shapes, and the supporting angels all gazing devoutly at the Virgin, a totally new concept—formerly, they would have been background figures. The roundels in the lower section contain images of saints revered by the Dominicans, the commissioners of the work.

PRIMAVERA

Probably dating from around 1477, this instantly familiar painting by Sandro Botticelli (1445–1510) is associated with the nuptials of Lorenzo di Pierfrancesco de' Medici, cousin of Lorenzo the Magnificent: It was placed outside the wedding chamber. The symbolism of this picture celebrates fecundity and new life through the freshness of spring. The identities of the figures reflect the Renaissance interest in the classical world; on the right Zephyrus, the wind god, pursues the nymph Cloris, who is transformed into Flora, the pregnant goddess of spring. The central figure is Venus, goddess of love, flanked by the Three Graces with Cupid above and Mercury fending off stormy winter clouds. Art historians have argued for years over the exact meaning of the painting, but the picture probably celebrates the triumph of Venus, typified by the burgeoning of spring after winter.

THE BIRTH OF VENUS

This is another of Botticelli's instantly recognizable pictures and the last of his mythological works. It was painted about 1484 for the villa of Pierfrancesco de' Medici, which also housed the *Primavera*. Its theme is often interpreted as the myth of Venus' birth, which taught that the goddess was born from the sea after it had been impregnated by the castration of Uranus, an allegory for the creation of beauty. Zephyrus, god of the west wind, accompanied by the nymph Cloris, blows the goddess ashore to be clothed by Hora, daughter of Aurora, goddess of dawn. The liberties taken with anatomy—note the unnatural length of Venus' neck and shoulders and the awkward left arm—serve to add to the beauty of the central figure, creating a dreamlike picture of grace and harmony.

TIPS

» Advance booking is highly recommended; waiting times for entrance, even in the quieter winter months, can be up to 3 hours. All state-run museums belong to the Firenze Musei association (www.firenzemusei.it) and set aside a daily number of tickets that can be booked in advance by phone or online (tel 055 294 883; Mon–Fri 8.30–6.30, Sat 8.30–12.30). You can also book online for the Uffizi and other Florentine and Italian museums at a commercial site, www.weekendafirenze.com. There is a booking fee of around €8.

» Plan what you want to see before you start and remember that backtracking is difficult.

» Be patient—the highlights are often blocked by large groups, making them virtually invisible.

» There are frequently long waits for the toilets; go before you come or after you leave.

» The audioguides will help you get more out of your visit.

Clockwise from left *Although primarily a painting gallery, the Uffizi displays some works of sculpture;* Madonna of the Goldfinch *(1505) by Raphael; the Uffizi and Corridoio Vasariano seen from the River Arno*

ANNUNCIATION

Previous depictions of the Archangel Gabriel announcing the news of her pregnancy to the Virgin Mary were almost all interior scenes, set against a vertical background. This early Leonardo da Vinci departs from the convention, showing the Virgin and angel against a lovingly detailed background of both architecture and landscape, where soft light falls on the distant mountains and water, and every detail is depicted with the greatest precision. It was probably painted about 1475, when Leonardo was still a pupil of Andrea del Verrocchio.

THE TRIBUNA

The octagonal room 18, known as the Tribuna, once held some of the greatest of the Medici treasures. It is still home to important classical sculptures, notably the *Medici Venus*, a first-century BC Greek copy of the Aphrodite of Cnidos. The walls are hung with some of the Uffizi's most compelling portraits, depictions of the ruling Medici and their children by Agnolo Bronzino. Ice-cold and perfect, they epitomize the power and wealth of the family at its zenith. High on one wall you can also see Rosso Fiorentino's *Musical Cherub*.

THE HOLY FAMILY

Michelangelo created this painting, also known as the *Doni Tondo*, between 1504 and 1505 for the marriage of Agnolo Doni and Maddalena Strozzi. It's his only completed easel painting, and a precursor to the Sistine Chapel frescoes at the Vatican Museums in Rome. The composition is perfectly aligned with the shape of the picture, an eye-satisfying series of circular forms.

THE RAPHAEL PAINTINGS

Several important works hang in room 26, including the luminous *Madonna del Cardellino*, a self-portrait and the portrait group *Leo X with Giulio de' Medici*, a wonderfully sinister group of clerics, painted shortly before Raphael's death.

THE VENUS OF URBINO

This sensual, earthy nude was painted c1538 by Tiziano Vecellio, better known as Titian (c1488–1576). This is no idealized female beauty, but a warm-blooded, provocative woman who serves as an allegory for the delights of married love. It's a superbly composed piece, the relaxed figure gazing out with a mischievous expression, while the domestic touches of the servants in the background and the little dog lend the whole scene a feeling of temporal reality.

MADONNA DAL COLLO LUNGO

The Uffizi is rich in Mannerist paintings and none better illustrates the genre than the *Madonna of the Long Neck*, a sinuous and eccentric composition, full of elongated forms and brittle refinement. Painted for a church in Parma by Francesco Parmigianino (1504–40), it's actually unfinished, which may explain discrepancies such as the extraordinary row of shadows caused by a single column and the odd, three-legged scroll.

GALLERY GUIDE

SECOND FLOOR

Rooms 2–6: Giotto, 14th- and 15th-century Florentine, Sienese and International Gothic
Rooms 7–9: Early Renaissance
Rooms 10–14: Botticelli
Room 15: Leonardo da Vinci
Room 18: Bronzino portraits (Tribuna)
Rooms 16–24: Perugino, Signorelli, Giorgione, Correggio, Bellini, Mantegna, Dürer
Rooms 25–26: Michelangelo, Raphael and Andrea del Sarto
Rooms 27–29: Raphael, Mannerism and Venetian painting
Room 30: Emilian painting
Room 31: Veronese
Room 32: Tintoretto
Rooms 33–45: 16th- to 18th-century—Rubens, Caravaggio, Rembrandt, Goya, Velázquez, Canaletto, Tiepolo

FIRST FLOOR

The New Galleries: ongoing museum expansion with galleries devoted to displaying artists and their schools and followers, and temporary exhibitions
Gabinetto dei Disegni: temporary small exhibitions of works from the prints and drawings department

MUSEO ARCHEOLOGICO NAZIONALE

www.comune.firenze.it

The Museo Archeologico Nazionale has an excellent collection of art and ancient objects, including one of the most important Etruscan and Egyptian collections in Italy. One of the museum's highlights is the restored bronze *Idolino*, which is exhibited in a room on the ground floor. The torso of this statue of a young man, probably once used as a lampstand, is thought to date from the first century BC. The Etruscan collection includes the famous bronze *Chimera*, part lion, part goat and part snake, dating from the late fifth to the early fourth century BC. Here also is the monumental *Arringatore*, or *Orator*, dating from the Hellenistic period (fourth to first century BC), and a statue of Minerva.

The Egyptian collection includes mummies, statuettes, sarcophagi and vases, along with a 14th-century BC Hittite chariot made of bone and wood. On the second floor is a collection of vases dating from the sixth and fifth centuries BC. Outstanding among these is the François Vase. Made in Athens around 570BC, this huge, highly decorative piece is one of the earliest examples of its kind.

➕ 63 E1 ✉ Piazza Santissima Annunziata 9/B, 50122 ☎ 055 235750 🕐 Mon 2–7, Tue, Thu 8.30–7, Wed, Fri–Sun 8.30–2 🖐 Adult €4, under 18 free 🚌 21, 22

MUSEO BARDINI

Art collector and antiques dealer Stefano Bardini (1836–1922) built the Palazzo Bardini in 1883 to house his vast and eclectic art collection. The huge variety of art on show includes paintings, medieval and Renaissance sculpture, furniture, ceramics, arms and armour and musical instruments. In addition, Bardini was particularly fond of reclaiming doorways, staircases and ceilings from demolished buildings, and many of these architectural bits and pieces have been incorporated into the palazzo. On his death, he bequeathed the house and its entire contents to the city.

➕ 63 D4 ✉ Piazza de' Mozzi 1, 50125 ☎ 055 234 2427 🕐 Closed for restoration

MUSEO DELLA CASA FIORENTINA ANTICA

www.sbas.firenze.it

This stately 14th-century palace, also known as the Museo del Palazzo Davanzati, was once the residence of the wealthy Davizzi family. It was converted into a museum, giving a rare and vivid insight into the life of city merchants, artists and noblemen during the Middle Ages. The exterior is typical of a house of its period, with three floors rising above arches. The interior, as well as the furnishings, tapestries, ceramics, paintings and domestic objects, are all typical of a Florentine house built between the 15th and 17th centuries.

On view to the public is the spacious entrance hall, temporarily housing furniture and other objects, two upper floors with beautifully furnished bedrooms, and a kitchen with cooking utensils, looms, a spinning machine and other fascinating pieces that illustrate daily life in a Florentine home.

➕ 62 C3 ✉ Via Porta Rossa 13, 50122 ☎ 055 238 8610 🕐 Daily 8.15–1.50. Closed 2nd and 4th Sun and 1st, 3rd and 5th Mon of the month 🖐 Free

Below left *Sculpted busts on display at the Museo Bardini*
Below *A painted sarcophagus at the Museo Archeologico Nazionale*

MUSEO DI FIRENZE COM'ERA

www.comune.firenze.it

The Museum of Florence As It Was gives you a glimpse of what the city looked like at the various stages of its development through maps, plans, engravings and paintings, beautifully illustrating how many of the city's old landmarks have survived intact. A large model at the beginning of the museum shows how Florence might have appeared in the Roman era. The Pianta della Catena map is an outstanding exhibit. A copy of the 1490 original fills a wall in the first room and shows the city at the height of the Renaissance. The bridges are all marked, and most of the churches are there, as are many of the streets and piazzas. The series of lunette paintings (1599) of Medici villas is by the Flemish painter Giusto Utens. Other illustrations show Florence as it was before the 19th-century demolition of the medieval buildings and streets around the Mercato Vecchio, the area now filled by the Piazza della Repubblica (▷ 94).

➕ 63 D2 ✉ Via dell'Oriuolo 24, 50122 ☎ 055 261 6545 🕐 Apr–end May, Oct Mon, Tue 9–2, Sat 9–7; Jun–end Sep Mon, Tue 9–2, Sat 9–2; Nov–end Mar Mon–Wed 9–2, Sun 9–7 💷 Adult €2.70, under 17 €1 🚌 14, 23

MUSEO DELLA FONDAZIONE HORNE

English art historian and collector Herbert Percy Horne (1864–1916) lived in Florence from 1904 and is best known for a pioneering biography of Botticelli, a work that helped bring to the painter to the prominence that he enjoys today. Horne bought the Renaissance Palazzo Corsi, built in 1489, to house his collection of paintings, furniture and sculpture. He carefully restored the building and, on his death, left the palazzo and its contents to the people of Italy.

The collection is arranged on three floors of the building, which has an attractive courtyard with elaborate capitals and a decorated frieze. In one of the rooms off the courtyard is a portrait of Horne along with a copy of his book on Botticelli. Another room contains an excellent collection of drawings including works by Raphael, Bernini, Giulio Romano, Guido Reni and Rubens. Other important pieces in the museum include an age-darkened *Deposition* by Benozzo Gozzoli (c1421–97) and a *Holy Family* by Domenico Beccafumi (1486–1551) in an elaborate gilt frame.

A beautiful depiction of the young St. Stephen by Giotto (c1267–1337), one of his most important paintings, is the highlight of the collection. There is a striking array of Renaissance furniture, including some splendidly inlaid chests, and several of the rooms have fine fireplaces. Also on display is a good collection of household objects.

➕ 63 D3 ✉ Via de' Benci 6, 50122 ☎ 055 244661 🕐 Mon–Sat 9–1; ticket office closes 30 min earlier 💷 Adult €5, child (6–16) €3, under 6 free 🚌 B, C, 23

MUSEO NAZIONALE DI ANTROPOLOGIA E ETNOLOGIA

The anthropological museum, founded in 1869, was the first of its kind in Europe and is the most important anthropological and ethnological museum in Italy. The museum occupies the magnificent Palazzo Nonfinito, begun in 1593 by Buontalenti, but not finished, hence the name nonfinito. It is one of the finest on a street of exceptionally fine Renaissance palaces.

The 35 rooms are filled with old-fashioned showcases displaying a huge variety of items: Peruvian mummies collected in 1883, objects from Oceania probably gathered by the explorer Captain James Cook on his last voyage in 1776–79, shrunken heads from Ecuador, articles made by the Ainu people from Japan, items from places as far apart as Sumatra and Eritrea, as well as musical instruments from around the world.

The museum's rare collection of material from the extraordinarily rich Kafiri culture of northern Pakistan is among its highlights.

➕ 63 D2 ✉ Via del Proconsolo 12, 50122 ☎ 055 239 6449 🕐 Mon, Tue, Thu, Fri and Sun 9–1, Sat 9–5; ticket office closes 30 min earlier 💷 Adult €4, child (6–25) €2, under 6 free 🚌 A, 14

Above left *The Pianta della Catena map at the Museo di Firenze Com'era*
Below *Wooden sculptures at the Museo Nazionale di Antropologia e Etnologia*

INFORMATION

www.sbas.firenze.it

➕ 63 D3 ✉ Via del Proconsolo 4,
50122 ☎ 055 238 8606 🕐 Daily
8.15–6. Closed 2nd and 4th Mon of the
month; ticket office closes 40 min earlier
♿ Adult €4, under 18 free 🚌 A, 14
📖 Small bookshop selling art books,
museum guides, posters and gifts
❓ Advance booking (€3) not required but
advisable in high season (tel 055 294883)

MUSEO NAZIONALE DEL BARGELLO

The forbidding, crenellated Palazzo del Bargello, home to the Bargello
Museum, was built in 1255 as the Palazzo del Popolo, the seat of the city's
government. In the 16th century the police headquarters were here, along with
a prison, which was in use until 1858. The museum was first opened to the
public in 1865.

GROUND FLOOR

Begin in the Gothic courtyard with its statues and sculptures. Until 1786,
executions were carried out here, and condemned prisoners spent their last
night in the chapel on the first floor. Off the courtyard, the hall contains the
gallery's most celebrated sculptures by Michelangelo and his contemporaries.
Michelangelo's works include an early *Drunken Bacchus* (c1497)—a humorous
portrayal of the god of wine—and the marble tondo of the Madonna and Child
with the infant St. John, known as the *Pitti Tondo* (c1503). Important works by
Benvenuto Cellini (1500–71) include *Narcissus*, carved from a block of Greek
marble, and *Apollo and Hyacinth*. There is also a life-size preliminary bronze
cast of his famous *Perseus* (▷ 87).

FIRST FLOOR

The loggia has bronze birds by Giambologna (1529–1608), while the Gothic
Salone del Consiglio Generale has works by Donatello (1386–1466) and his
contemporaries. Donatello's *Marzocco Lion*, the symbol of Florence, is the
focus of the room, although his *St. George* and the sexually ambivalent
bronze *David* are far more important artistically. On the walls hang two of the
trial bronze panels made by Lorenzo Ghiberti and Filippo Brunelleschi for the
Baptistery doors (▷ 92), a marble relief of the *Madonna and Child with Angels*
by Agostino di Duccio (1418–81) and a number of attractive glazed terracotta
Madonnas by Luca della Robbia (1400–82).

DECORATIVE ARTS

There are several rooms dedicated to European and Middle Eastern decorative
art, including carpets and clocks. The Renaissance bronzes on display here form
the most important collection of its kind in Italy.

Below The Annunciation *in glazed
terracotta by Andrea della Robbia*

MUSEO DI SAN MARCO

The convent of San Marco, home to the museum, is next to the church of the same name. The original convent on the site was of the Silvestrine order, but it was given to the Dominicans by Cosimo de' Medici, who commissioned the expansion of the existing buildings. Fra Angelico (*c*1387–1455), also known as Beato Angelico, lived here from 1436 to 1447, during which time he painted these ethereal images, full of endlessly fascinating detail. The museum was founded in 1869, and in 1921 most of Fra Angelico's panel paintings were transferred here from other museums in Florence.

THE CLOISTERS AND THE PILGRIMS' HOSPICE

A visit starts in Michelozzo's peaceful cloister of Sant'Antonio. In the middle is an old cedar of Lebanon and at each corner is a small lunette fresco by Fra Angelico. The Pilgrims' Hospice is off this cloister, a long room full of beautiful paintings, glowing in bright jewel shades and gold leaf. At one end of the room is the superb *Deposition from the Cross* (*c*1435–40), and at the other the *Linaiouli Tabernacle* (1433) with its saints and enthroned Madonna; the border consists of musical angels, often reproduced on Christmas cards. This room also contains the great *Last Judgement* altarpiece (1431) and a series of reliquary tabernacles in gold frames showing 35 tiny scenes from the life of Christ.

There are paintings here by Fra Bartolomeo, Giovanni Sogliani and Lorenzo Lippi, among others. Before climbing the stairs to the monks' quarters, visit two more frescoes: Fra Angelico's large *Crucifixion and Saints* (1441–42) in the Chapter House and Domenico Ghirlandaio's *Last Supper* in the small refectory.

THE MONKS' CELLS

At the top of the stairs to the dormitory is one of Fra Angelico's most famous frescoes, the *Annunciation* (1442). Each of the 44 tiny cells where the monks lived has a shuttered window and a small fresco by Fra Angelico or one of his assistants. Those by the master himself are in cells one to nine—look for the beautiful angel in cell three and the nativity scene in cell five. Famous inhabitants of the cells include Girolamo Savonarola (▷ 33), the rebel priest, who was prior in 1491, and the painter Fra Bartolomeo, who was a friar.

INFORMATION

www.sbas.firenze.it

✚ 63 D1 ✉ Piazza San Marco 1, 50121 ☎ 055 238 8608 ⊙ Mon–Thu 8.15–1, Fri 8.15–6, Sat–Sun 8.15–7. Closed 1st, 3rd and 5th Sun and 2nd and 4th Mon of each month; ticket office closes 30 min earlier ♿ Adult €4, under 18 free 🚌 1, 6, 7 🏠 Small shop selling guidebooks to this and other museums, some art books, good reproductions of paintings, postcards, bookmarks and gift items

TIP

» Only 120 people are allowed up to the dormitories at one time, so book your visit in advance (tel 055 294883, www.firenzemusei.it), arrive early in the morning, or be prepared to wait.

Above *The fresco depicting the Adoration of the Magi is one of the many beautiful paintings to adorn the walls of San Marco*

MUSEO SALVATORE FERRAGAMO

www.salvatoreferragamo.com

This unusual museum is heaven for footwear fetishists. Salvatore Ferragamo's life story is a classic tale of rags to riches. Born near Naples in 1898 and one of 14 children, he emigrated to the US at the age of 16 and soon began designing shoes to be worn by actors in movies. In 1927 he moved back to Italy and opened his workshop in the Palazzo Spini Ferone in Florence, which is still the company's business headquarters as well as the museum. Ferragamo shod some of the world's most famous feet, and shoes made for such glamorous names as Judy Garland, Lana Turner, Lauren Bacall, Audrey Hepburn, Marilyn Monroe and Eva Perón are on display.

While all the shoes are quite exquisite, some are totally fantastical, decorated with intricate beadwork, rhinestones and ostrich feathers or stacked on enormously high platform soles in bands of suede. Each pair of shoes is accompanied by an anecdote about the owner from Ferragamo himself, which is a great way of supplying an intimate glimpse into the tastes of celebrities from the past. Look out in particular for Marilyn Monroe's red stilettos, made from satin and covered entirely in red Swarovski crystals, and the sandals made from 18-carat gold chain created for the wife of an Australian tycoon.

🕂 62 C3 ✉ Piazza di Santa Trinita 5r, 50120 ☎ 055 336 0456 🕓 Mon–Fri 9–1, 2–6. Closed Tue Aug 🖐 Adult €5 🚌 A 🏛

MUSEO DI STORIA DELLA SCIENZA

www.imss.fi.it

This absorbing museum explores the history of physics, chemistry, astronomy and medicine through scientific and mathematical instruments, many of them beautifully decorated. As you look at the exhibits, the contribution made by Florence and Tuscany to the history of science becomes apparent.

Room IV is dedicated to Galileo Galilei (1564–1642), who was born in Pisa and died in Florence, having spent years in the service of the Medici family. One of his many achievements was the perfection of the telescope, and here you can see the instrument through which he observed Jupiter's four moons. The museum also charts the progressive improvement of the telescope from Galileo's first examples, made in 1610.

Room XII is dedicated to the development of the mechanical clock, with beautiful examples of pocket watches. Room XVIII has some gruesome 18th-century anatomical waxworks and terracotta models that demonstrate possible complications of childbirth, along with sets of surgical instruments dating from that time, including one for amputation.

🕂 62 C3 ✉ Piazza dei Giudici 1, 50121 ☎ 055 265311 🕓 Jun–end Sep Mon, Wed–Fri 9.30–5, Tue 9.30–1; Oct–end May Mon, Wed–Sat 9.30–5, Tue 9.30–1, 🖐 Adult €4, child (7–14) €2, under 7 free 🚌 B, 23

OGNISSANTI

The principal reason to visit this church to the west of the city is to see Domenico Ghirlandaio's (c1448–94) celebrated *Cenacolo*, which is actually in the convent next door.

But the church, which dates from the 12th century, has a few riches of its own. The elaborate exterior in travertine, a light-coloured stone, positively glows; there is an attractive lunette of the *Coronation of the Virgin* above the door. Inside, in addition to a beautiful high altar inlaid with marble and mother-of-pearl, there are a few paintings and a couple of tombs of note, including that of Botticelli, whose tombstone lies in the south transept, and of the explorer Amerigo Vespucci (1451–1512), whose family lived on Borgo Ognissanti; their family tombstone is in the floor to the left of the altar. It is said that Amerigo gave his name to the Americas. Look for Ghirlandaio's early frescoes above the second altar on the south side; Botticelli's fine *St. Augustine in his Study* (1480); and a fresco depicting St. Jerome (1480) by Ghirlandaio.

Ghirlandaio's *Cenacolo (Last Supper)* is in the vaulted convent refectory to the left of the church. The theme was a popular one, particularly for a painting in a room in which people gathered to eat, and similar works are found in several monasteries around Florence. Ghirlandaio himself painted four such scenes in the city, of which this one, dating from 1480, is the best and is said to have inspired Leonardo da Vinci's *Last Supper*. The scene is set against the background of a garden with charming details such as birds, flowers and fruit trees. *The Annunciation* by the same artist dates from 1369.

🕂 62 B2 ✉ Borgo Ognissanti 42, 50123 ☎ 055 238 8720 🕓 Church: Daily 7.30–12.30, 4–7.30; Convent and Cloister: Mon, Tue, Sat 9–12 🖐 Free 🚌 B, 12

Left *The name Salvatore Ferragamo has become a byword for glamorous shoes*

ORSANMICHELE

Orsanmichele was built as a grain market in 1337, and the original building had a granary on the upper floor. When the market was moved in 1380, the ground floor became a church. The city's guilds commissioned some of the best artists of the day to make statues of patron saints to sit in the canopied niches, and so created a permanent outdoor exhibition of 15th-century Florentine sculpture. These statues are being removed one by one for restoration and copies are being put in their places; some of the original statues are still here, including Lorenzo Ghiberti's bronzes of St. Matthew (1419–22) and St. Stephen (1427–28). Inside, frescoes of patron saints decorate the walls, but the church's focal point is the Gothic tabernacle, a large decorative work commissioned by the survivors of the Black Death in 1349. Classical music concerts are often held in the church. Look for flyers or contact the tourist office for details.

✚ 62 C3 ✉ Via Arte della Lana, 50123 ☎ 055 284944 ⏰ Tue–Sun 10–5 👆 Free

OSPEDALE DEGLI INNOCENTI

The Ospedale degli Innocenti opened as a foundling hospital in 1445. It was the first of its kind in Europe and remained open as an orphanage until 2000. It was home to the first school of obstetrics in Italy, and groundbreaking research into nutrition and vaccination was carried out here. The building, an important architectural landmark because of its beautiful portico by

Filippo Brunelleschi (1377–1446), is an early Renaissance masterpiece.

A portico with nine arches borders Piazza della Santissima Annunziata (▷ 94) and is adorned with blue-and-white tondi (glazed terracotta medallions) of babies in swaddling clothes by Andrea della Robbia (1435–1525). At the other end of the portico is the window-wheel where babies were left anonymously by their mothers. Brunelleschi also designed the two cloisters. The Chiostro degli Uomini, reserved for men, is rather sober, whereas the Chiostro delle Donne, for women, is beautiful—a slim oblong, with a loggia above. From the Chiostro degli Uomini, stairs lead up to the Galleria dell'Ospedale degli Innocenti, where some fine paintings are hung, including Ghirlandaio's vivid Adoration of the Magi (1488). At one end of the room is a collection of identification tags left by mothers in the hope that one day they might see their children again.

✚ 63 D1 ✉ Piazza della Santissima Annunziata 12, 50122 ☎ 055 203 7308 ⏰ Mon–Sat 8.30–7, Sun 8.30–2; ticket office closes 30 min earlier than museum 👆 Adult €4, child (6–18) €2 🚌 C, 6

PALAZZO MEDICI-RICCARDI

The massive Palazzo Medici-Riccardi was built by Michelozzo some time after 1444 as a town mansion for Cosimo il Vecchio, and was the residence of the Medici until 1540. The Riccardi family bought the palace in 1659 and enlarged it. It is now the headquarters of the

provincial government. The Medici-Riccardi's surprise, after the slightly rugged and stately exterior, is one of the most pleasant little spaces in Florence, the Cappella dei Magi. Renovation work is going on here, but the palace is still open.

The main, columned courtyard is suitably noble, and the adjacent gardens are filled with lemon trees in huge terracotta pots. The principal staircase off the courtyard leads to the chapel, which is covered by Benozzo Gozzoli's restored frescoes of the Procession of the Magi to Bethlehem (1459–63). The glorious colours have tremendous immediacy and you can almost feel the textures of the rich fabrics. Gozzoli dotted the scene with members of the Medici family and other well-known people of the day; the beautifully dressed young ruler on a horse on the right-hand wall is believed to be an idealized portrait of Lorenzo il Magnifico (▷ 32). The gallery is a large and elaborate baroque room decorated with mirrors, plasterwork and ceiling frescoes by Luca Giordano (1683). Look for the Madonna and Child by Filippo Lippi in the adjoining room.

✚ 62 C2 ✉ Via Cavour 3, 50129 ☎ 055 276 0340 ⏰ Thu–Tue 9–6.30 👆 Adult €4, child (6–12) €2.50, under 6 free 🚌 1, 7, 17 🏛

Above left A decorative fleur-de-lis adorning the exterior of Orsanmichele
Below Four statues of saints in a niche on the façade of Orsanmichele

PALAZZO PITTI

INFORMATION

www.firenzemusei.it

✚ 62 B4 ✉ Piazza de' Pitti, 50125
☎ 055 238 8614 ⊘ Palatina and
Appartamenti: Tue–Sun 8.15–6.50.
Argenti, Costume and Porcellane:
Jun–end Aug daily 8.15–7.30; Apr, May,
Sep, Oct 8.15–6.30; Jan, Feb, Nov, Dec
8.15–4.30; Mar 8.15–5.30. Closed 1st
and last Mon of the month; ticket office
closes 30 min earlier. Arte Moderna:
Daily 8.15–1.50. Closed 2nd and 4th Sun,
and 1st, 3rd and 5th Mon of the month.
Carrozze: By appointment (tel 055 238
8611) ♿ Argenti, Costume, Porcellane,
Giardino di Boboli: Adult €7, under 18
free. Palatina and Appartamenti: Adult
€8.50 (more during special exhibitions),
under 18 free. Ticket to all Palazzo Pitti
museums: Adult €11.50 (except during
special exhibitions), under 18 free
🎧 Audiotours of the Palatina in several
languages, €3.50 📖 A range available
☕ Good but pricey café on the main
courtyard 🛍 Small shop in the Palatina;
shop in main courtyard selling books
and gifts

Above A Concert by Paganini, *painted
by Annibale Gatti (1827–1909) in the
Galleria d'Arte Moderna*

INTRODUCTION

Most cities would be content with one superlative gallery of Renaissance
art, but Florence has two, the Uffizi and the Galleria Palatina, one of several
museums and galleries contained in the vast Palazzo Pitti. In any other city,
the Pitti's paintings would be a major attraction, but are often overlooked
by visitors. The art here is the equal of much in the Uffizi, and the painters
represented—notably Raphael, Titian, Filippo Lippi and Caravaggio—are just as
pre-eminent.

With eight museums and galleries in all, the Pitti's collections are vast. It
makes sense to concentrate on the Galleria Palatina, a suite of 26 rooms, their
walls almost entirely covered with paintings. The works are displayed much
as they were in the 17th century, covering the walls from floor to ceiling in no
discernible chronological order. Allow 2–3 hours to appreciate the paintings
fully before moving on to another gallery that takes your fancy. Be prepared for
crowds, and also for sections or collections to be closed; you can book ahead
to avoid disappointment (tel 055 294883). There is much to see, but make
sure you leave time to relax afterwards in the Giardino di Boboli behind the
palace (▷ 69). Combined tickets can be bought to various combinations of the
museums in the Pitti complex, as well as the gardens (▷ Information).

The Palazzo Pitti was begun in 1457, supposedly to a design by Filippo
Brunelleschi. It was originally the residence of the banker Luca Pitti, a rival of
the Medici, and his descendants, but in 1549 the family funds dried up and it
was purchased by Cosimo I's wife, the Grand Duchess Eleonora. It became
the residence of the Grand Dukes of Tuscany and was occupied by ruling
families until 1919, when it was presented to the state by Vittorio Emanuele
III. Under the Medici it was repeatedly enlarged, notably in the 16th century,
when Ammanati lengthened the façade and built the courtyard; the side wings
were added in the 18th and 19th centuries. The Medici began amassing the
collections in the 17th century. The main galleries opened to the public in 1833
and the Galleria d'Arte Moderna, Florence's modern art museum, joined the
gallery complex in 1924.

WHAT TO SEE

APPARTAMENTI REALI

The royal apartments have been expertly and sensitively restored to their 19th-century condition. From the 17th century they were the residence by turn of the Medici, the dukes of Lorraine and members of the house of Savoy, including Italy's first monarch, King Umberto I. They are hard to beat in terms of extravagance, with their gilding and stuccowork, rich damask hangings, vast chandeliers, enormous gilt mirrors, period furnishings, paintings and sculptures.

THE COURTYARD

The main entrance to the palace leads you through to a grand courtyard (1560–70), an excellent example of Florentine Mannerist architecture by Bartolomeo Ammanati (1511–92), best known for the Ponte Santa Trinita (▷ 95). It was used as a stage for lavish spectacles between the 16th and 18th centuries, and is still the venue for concerts and ballet in the summer.

GALLERIA PALATINA

Madonna and Child (Sala di Promoteo)

Painted in 1452 and known as the *Pitti Tondo*, Filippo Lippi's famous work perfectly combines exquisite painting and intense spirituality. The eye is drawn to the pure face of the Virgin, who forms the central point, and the Christ Child lying on her knee; around her are scenes from the life of her mother, St. Anne.

Madonna della Seggiola (Sala di Saturno)

Raphael painted this tondo in Rome in 1514, and it has been in the Pitti since the 18th century. Although heavily influenced by Venetian painting, evident in its use of light and shade, the painting follows a strictly Florentine form, its circular shape emphasizing the tender curves of the Virgin and Child. According to legend, the round panel used for the painting came from the end of a wine barrel. For centuries the work was one of Italy's most popular—in the 19th century copyists has a five-year waiting list.

Pietro Aretino (Sala di Promoteo)

Portraiture gained importance during the High Renaissance as the Church lost its control over subject matter, and new money brought self-made men to prominence. Titian painted this portrait of the satirical poet Pietro Aretino in 1545, after Aretino had moved from Mantua to Venice, Titian's native city. The same room contains other prized paintings by Titian including *Mary Magdalen* (c1531), plus Rosso Fiorentino's vast *Madonna and Child with Saints* (1522), which once stood in the church of Santo Spirito.

Sleeping Cupid (Sala dell'Educazione di Giove)

This plump little sleeping Cupid is full of allegorical references to passion and lost love. Caravaggio painted it when he was in Malta in 1608. By this time he had already lived in Rome, where he had studied and grasped the fine details of human anatomy, and was beginning to concentrate on the development of chiaroscuro, the contrast of light and dark, a technique he expertly employed in his later work.

MUSEO DEGLI ARGENTI

In a series of sumptuous state rooms, this museum concentrates on luxury items amassed by the Medici dukes. Exhibits include antique vases, stunningly worked figurines and a vast number of inlaid pieces. One of the museum's highlights is a set of *pietre dure* vases once owned by Lorenzo il Magnifico. They include Roman, Byzantine and Venetian pieces, though Lorenzo, in an act of minor vandalism, had each one inscribed with his monogram. He believed that such artefacts were better investments than paintings and sculptures.

GALLERY GUIDE

Galleria Palatina: The main collection, strong on 16th-century works; in wing of main palace.

Galleria d'Arte Moderna: Works spanning the mid-18th to mid-20th centuries; in main building on the floor above the Palatina.

Museo degli Argenti: Objects, gold and jewellery from the Medici collections; accessed from the main courtyard.

Museo del Costume: Rotating exhibitions of clothing from the 18th to mid-20th centuries; in Palazzina Meridiana in the south wing.

Museo delle Porcellane: French, Italian, German and Viennese porcelain and ceramics; in a pavilion at the top of the Giardino di Boboli.

Appartamenti Reali: Lavishly decorated state apartments following on from the Palatina.

Collezione Contini Bonacossi: A picture collection on long-term loan; next to the Museo del Costume in the Palazzina Meridiana.

Museo delle Carrozze: Carriage collection—closed at present.

Below *Within the Palazzo Pitti there are eight museums and galleries*

INFORMATION

www.comune.fi.it
www.museoragazzi.it

🔲 62 C3 ✉ Piazza della Signoria,
50123 ☎ 055 276 8465; 055 276 8224
to book an activity (see Tip) 🕐 Fri–Wed
9–7, Thu 9–2, ticket office closes 60 min
earlier 🎫 Adult €6, under 18 €2 🚌 A,
B 🎧 Audioguides in Italian and English
€4.30 📖 Different formats for €11 and
€4.65 📚 A good bookshop selling books
for children, art books, posters, postcards
and gift items

TIP

» A number of activities now make a
visit to the palazzo more entertaining. For
example, you can go on a guided tour led
by costumed actors, or take the children
to a themed games room.

Above *The vaulted arcades surrounding
the Palazzo Vecchio's courtyard are the
work of Michelozzo and date from 1453*

PALAZZO VECCHIO

This is the grand embodiment of Florentine civic purpose dating from the
14th century, with both elaborately decorated public rooms and intimate private
apartments. Florence's town hall stands on the site of the medieval Palazzo dei
Priori, which was demolished and rebuilt at the beginning of the 1300s. The
Palazzo Vecchio was built as the seat of the government, and the bell in the
tower summoned the citizens to the piazza below for public meetings in times
of trouble. The Palazzo Vecchio is still home to the City of Florence council
offices.

THE COURTYARD

The courtyard, reconstructed by architect Michelozzo in 1453, is beyond
the main entrance. It was elaborately decorated by Giorgio Vasari in 1565 to
celebrate the marriage of the son of Grand Duke Cosimo I to Joanna of Austria.

FIRST FLOOR

The largest room is the Salone dei Cinquecento, a meeting room for the
500-member Consiglio Maggiore (Grand Council). Vasari painted the frescoes
here to celebrate Cosimo I's triumphs over Pisa and Siena. The most notable
sculpture is Michelangelo's *Victory*. Next door, in the tiny, windowless Studiolo
di Francesco I there are allegorical paintings by Vasari and assistants from
his workshop. It was here that the melancholic son of Cosimo I pursued his
interest in alchemy. On the same floor, Vasari and his assistants decorated
the Quartiere di Leone X with ornate illustrations depicting the history of the
Medici family.

SECOND FLOOR

Access to the apartments of Cosimo I's wife, Eleonora di Toledo, is via a
balcony across the end of the Salone dei Cinquecento. This gives you a close-
up view of the ceiling. The chapel is decorated with frescoes of various saints.
The Sala dei Gigli owes its name to the lily (*giglio*) motif, a symbol of the city;
here you can see Donatello's bronze statue, *Judith and Holofernes* (1455). The
writer Niccolò Machiavelli (▷ 33) used the Cancellaria next door as an office
from 1498 to 1512, when he was a government secretary.

PIAZZA DELLA SIGNORIA

Florence's most noble and famous piazza is a vast, open-air, traffic-free sculpture gallery with elegant cafés and restaurants. This wide, open square next to the Galleria degli Uffizi (▷ 73–77), marks the heart of the *centro storico* (old town). The Piazza della Signoria has been the political focus of Florence since the Middle Ages. Surrounded by tall buildings, notably the grand, austere Palazzo Vecchio (see opposite), this is where the ruling city elders called open-air public assemblies in times of crisis. The crowd was often provoked by speeches from the *arringhiera* (oration terrace), a raised platform, and the gatherings frequently degenerated into violence. The area in front of the Palazzo Vecchio was named Piazza del Popolo in 1307.

THE SCULPTURES

The enormous Loggia dei Lanzi (also known as the Loggia della Signoria) was designed to be used by dignitaries for formal meetings and ceremonies. It was completed in 1382 and has been used as an open-air sculpture museum since the late 18th century.

The front is dominated by Benvenuto Cellini's Mannerist bronze *Perseus* (1545). Considered his greatest work, it shows Perseus triumphantly holding aloft the severed head of Medusa. Near it is Giambologna's (1529–1608) last work, the *Rape of the Sabine Women*, completed in 1583. Donatello's *Judith and Holofernes* was the first of the statues to be placed in the piazza, but what you see is a copy—the original is in the Palazzo Vecchio.

In front of the main entrance to the Palazzo Vecchio stands a copy of Michelangelo's *David* (the original is in the Accademia, ▷ 70–71). The other large statue nearby is Baccio Bandinelli's *Hercules and Cacus* (1534), described by his rival Cellini as an 'old sack full of melons'. At the corner of the Palazzo Vecchio is Bartolomeo Ammanati's massive fountain (1575), with the undignified figure of Neptune. The watery theme is said to reflect Cosimo I's naval ambitions. The large equestrian bronze, Giambologna's monument to Cosimo I (1595), shows detailed scenes of the Grand Duke's coronation and his victory over the Sienese.

The plaque in the pavement in front of the fountain marks the spot where Girolamo Savonarola was burned at the stake as a heretic and traitor on 23 May 1498 (▷ 33). A ceremony to mark his death is held in the square annually on this day.

INFORMATION

✚ 62 C3 ☒ Piazza della Signoria, 50122 🚾 Free 🚌 A, B

TIPS

» An elegant (if expensive) table at the Café Rivoire is a good place to people-watch. Otherwise, perch on a stone bench under the Loggia dei Lanzi.

» Free open-air concerts are held here in summer.

Below Cellini's bronze Perseus dominates the Loggia dei Lanzi in the piazza

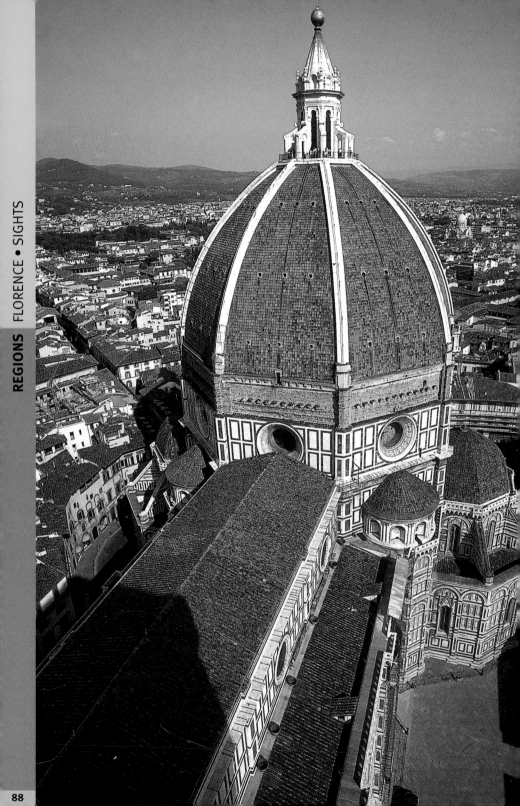

PIAZZA DEL DUOMO

REGIONS FLORENCE • SIGHTS

INTRODUCTION

The sublime Piazza del Duomo forms the religious heart of Florence, a counterpart to Piazza della Signoria to the south, which—with the Palazzo Vecchio at its heart—has long been the focus of civic power in the city. As its name suggests, the focal point of the Piazza is the Duomo (cathedral), one of the largest churches in Europe. Set slightly apart from its church is the Campanile (bell tower), the work of Giotto and other leading artists, architects and sculptors. In front of the Duomo is the distinctive octagonal Battistero (baptistery), occupying a part of the square known as Piazza San Giovanni, after St John the Baptist, to whom building is dedicated.

For much of its long history, the cathedral has been supervised and repaired by a body known as the Opera del Duomo, which had its headquarters behind the cathedral, in a building now given over to the relatively unvisited Museo dell'Opera del Duomo. Many of the finest works of art given to or commissioned by the cathedral authorities, or those removed from the church or Campanile for safe-keeping, are now found in the museum. These include some of the most important of all Florentine works of art, including a sculpture of the *Pietà* by Michelangelo and the original panels created by Lorenzo Ghiberti (1378–1455) for the baptistery doors (the present panels are copies).

The Duomo is constantly busy with visitors, especially visitors who want to climb the great dome, designed by Filippo Brunelleschi (1377–1446) and one of the miracles of Renaissance engineering (the entrance to the dome is by the Porta dei Canonici on the cathedral's south side of the Duomo). Fewer people climb the Campanile, but in many ways the view from the bell tower is better,

INFORMATION
DUOMO
www.duomofirenze.it

✚ 62 C2 ✉ Piazza del Duomo, 50122 ☎ 055 230 2885 🕐 Mon–Wed, Fri 10–5, Thu 10–3.30, Sat 10–4.45 (1st Sat of month 10–3.30), Sun 1.30–4.45 🚌 Free 🚏 1, 7, 17 🎧 Free guided tours in English, French, German, Spanish, Italian, Mon–Sat 10–12.30, 3–5, Sun 3–5; audioguide in English, French, Spanish, Italian for €1 📖 Guidebooks cover the whole complex, in Italian, English, French, German and Spanish, for €10 🛍 Bookshop sells guidebooks, art books, gifts and posters

Opposite *The dome of the Duomo is one of the iconic images of Florence*
Above *The magnificent fresco of the Last Judgement decorates the inside the dome*

89

CUPOLA

✚ 62 C2 ✉ Piazza del Duomo, 50122
☎ 055 230 2885 🕐 Mon–Fri 8.30–7,
Sat 8.30–5.40, last entry 40 min before
closing 💷 Adult €6

BATTISTERO

✚ 62 C2 ✉ Piazza del Duomo,
50122 ☎ 055 230 2885 🕐 Mon–Sat
12–7, Sun and 1st Sat of month 8.30–2
💷 Adult €3, under 6 free 🎧 Audioguide
€2

MUSEO DELL'OPERA DEL DUOMO

✚ 63 D2 ✉ Piazza del Duomo 9, 50122
☎ 055 230 2885 🕐 Mon–Sat 9–7.30,
Sun 9–1.40 💷 Adult €6, under 6 free
🎧 Audioguide €5 🛒 Sells art books,
postcards, gifts and posters

CAMPANILE

✚ 62 C2 ✉ Piazza del Duomo, 50122
☎ 055 230 2885 🕐 Daily 8.30–7.30
💷 Adult €6, under 6 free

Below *The Campanile is 85m (278ft) high*
Opposite *A detail from one of the panels
of Luca della Robbia's* cantoria, *now
on display in the Museo dell'Opera del
Duomo*

if only because it includes the cathedral dome itself, as well as a wonderful
bird's-eye view of the baptistery below.

Although Florentines long believed it was a Roman building, the baptistery
probably dates from the 6th or 7th century. It was originally Florence's
cathedral, replacing the old church of San Lorenzo, which was also, at one
time, the city cathedral. The baptistery's role was later ceded to the cathedral
of Santa Reparata, the patron saint whose remains, and the remains of whose
church, lie beneath the present Duomo.

In the 13th century the city fathers decided to build a new cathedral, largely
to flaunt the city's political power and growing wealth and size. In 1294 the
project was entrusted to Arnolfo di Cambio, and work continued throughout
the 14th century, with various architects realizing Arnolfo's plan. The Duomo's
Campanile was finished by 1359 and by 1418 the nave and tribunes were
complete. The building awaited the massive dome planned for the crossing,
because nobody had yet worked out how it would be built. Brunelleschi
offered his services, refusing to explain his solution. The building committee
finally gave him the job, insisting that he work with his rival Lorenzo Ghiberti,
whose work on the baptistery doors had secured his reputation. In 1436 the
first freestanding dome since Roman times was completed, and the cathedral
consecrated. The lantern was finished in the 1460s. Only part of the gallery
remains unfinished (you can see the obvious bare brick and stone), abandoned
after Michelangelo reputedly compared its proposed appearance to a 'cage for
crickets'. The rest of the dome, however, left the great man awestruck. Looking
at it when he came to plan the dome of St Peter's he said: '*Come te non
voglio, meglio di te non posso*'—'*Similar to you I will not build, better than you
I cannot build*'.

WHAT TO SEE

THE DUOMO'S EXTERIOR

The Duomo of Santa Maria del Fiore, to give it its full name, is huge—there is
room inside for 20,000 people. Walk all the way around its green- and white-
striped marble exterior to appreciate the vast proportions. The marble came
from all over Tuscany: white from Carrara, red from the Maremma and green
from Prato. Several doors punctuate the walls, the most elaborate being the
Porta della Mandorla with its relief of the Assumption sculpted by Nanni di
Banco in 1420. Also look out for the late 14th-century Porta dei Canonici and
the unfinished gallery round the base of the dome. Work on this ceased after
Michelangelo disparagingly described it as a 'cricket's cage'. The ornate Gothic-
style façade dates from the 19th century; the original was destroyed in the late
1500s.

THE DUOMO'S INTERIOR

Compared with the outside, the interior of the cathedral is remarkably austere.
Over the years many of the finest artworks have been moved to the Museo
dell'Opera del Duomo (▷ 91–92), leaving the Duomo relatively bare. But you
are better able to appreciate the soaring space beneath the Gothic arches,
the patterned marble flooring, the scale of the dome itself and the superb
mid-15th-century stained-glass windows, which are among Italy's finest. There
are two equestrian memorials in fresco dedicated to two of Florence's most
famous *condottieri* (mercenary soldiers): Niccolò da Tolentino (1456) by Andrea
del Castagno, and a far sharper-edged portrait (1436) of Englishman Sir John
Hawkwood, by Paolo Uccello. Terracotta reliefs by Luca della Robbia (1400–82)
decorate both north and south sacristy doors, and a superb bronze reliquary
urn by Lorenzo Ghiberti stands in the central apse.

Steps to the crypt of Santa Reparata lead down from the south aisle. The
church was excavated in the 1960s and dates from anywhere between the
sixth and 12th centuries. This space has archaeological finds dating from

Roman times and including palaeo-Christian and Romanesque elements, as well as mosaics and early frescoes. It's a confusing and complicated maze, so it might be better, and certainly more inspiring, to take in the tomb of Filippo Brunelleschi (1377–1446), architect of the cathedral's remarkable dome. You'll find this behind a grille to the left of the bottom of the steps.

INSIDE THE DOME

Climbing the rather claustrophobic 463 steps of the dome (*cupola*) is a must; not only will you be rewarded with some of Florence's best views from the top but you'll also get an insight into the construction of Brunelleschi's great plan. He beat Ghiberti in a competition to win the commission—a reversal of the Baptistery doors competition (▷ 92). First stopping point is the gallery that runs round the interior of the dome, with vertiginous views to the street beneath and close-ups of the stained-glass roundels. From here up, you're climbing between the inner and outer shells of the dome itself, all slanting space, arches and brickwork, a fine example of the sophistication of Renaissance building techniques and the genius of the architect.

MUSEO DELL'OPERA DEL DUOMO

The Museo dell'Opera del Duomo contains the sculptures and paintings from the Duomo complex, too precious to be left to the mercy of modern pollution. The building, behind the east end of the Duomo, is also home to the workshops that are responsible for the maintenance of the cathedral and its works of art. Ghiberti's Gates of Paradise (▷ 92) steal the show, but the collection as a whole provides a splendid overview of the best of Florentine sculpture, with works by many of the city's leading sculptors.

TIP

» You will not be allowed into the Duomo wearing skimpy shorts or a sleeveless top.

Luca della Robbia

Don't miss the *cantoria* by this artist, a superb contrast to that by Ghiberti. The frame of this choir loft is inscribed with the words from Psalm 33, 'Praise the Lord with harp, sing unto him with psaltery and the instrument of ten strings', and the sculpted solemn young musicians follow this command perfectly.

Donatello

The collection contains several works by Donatello (1386–1466), the greatest of Michelangelo's predecessors. He was involved with sculpting the 16 statues that once stood in the niches of the Campanile, and created the powerful figure of the prophet Habbakuk. It is so realistic he is said to have seized it, crying 'Speak, speak!' He was also responsible for the wood carving of the gaunt and bedraggled Mary Magdalene, while his lighter side emerges in the choir gallery (*cantoria*) from the Duomo, where he carved capering infants and cherubs.

Arnolfo di Cambio

This artist (active mid-13th century) sculpted figures for the earlier façade of the Duomo, demolished in 1587. These, which include a Madonna, are displayed in the first rooms. One of these is of Santa Reparata, who is one of Florence's patron saints and gave her name to the first church on the site of the Duomo.

Michelangelo

The sculptor was 80 when he created his *Pietà*, said to be his last work. He intended it for his own tomb, but never finished it; the figure of Nicodemus is traditionally believed to be a self-portrait.

GHIBERTI'S BAPTISTERY DOORS

Having finished the north doors of the baptistery in 1424 (see below), Ghiberti set to work on the doors for the east side, a work of such beauty that Michelangelo named them the Gates of Paradise. Completed in 1452, they are made up of 10 relief panels of biblical subjects, exquisitely carved in low relief and highlighted in gold to give wonderful perspective and pictorial effects. Their artistic importance is in their use of perspective, extending the scenes far into the background, which was a totally new concept at the time that became typical of work produced during the Renaissance. The composition is far more naturalistic than in the earlier baptistery doors, with figures grouped so as to intensify the drama of each scene. The subjects are taken from the first books of the Bible, and each panel contains several scenes from each selected story, while the border panels show Old Testament figures, busts, vegetation and flowers, inhabited by insects, frogs and lizards.

Below *Michelangelo's* Pietà, *one of the works on display in the Museo dell'Opera del Duomo*

The panels read left to right, top to bottom, starting with Adam and Eve and the story of their creation, temptation and expulsion from Eden. Next is a panel devoted to the murder of Abel by Cain; this is followed by the story of Noah and his ark—look out for the quirkily observed animals, which include an elephant. This is followed by the tale of Abraham and Isaac, then Jacob and Esau, and, finally, Joseph and his brothers, three panels that tell complex stories and are rich in detail. The next panel is essentially a single scene, showing Moses on Mount Sinai receiving the tablets of the Ten Commandments from God, while the frightened people gather below. This contrasts with Joshua's story, the next relief, which shows the crossing through the dried-up River Jordan and the walls of Jericho tumbling down. The final two scenes are devoted to the story of David and Goliath and the visit by the Queen of Sheba and her retinue to King Solomon. Look on the frame of the left-hand door for Ghiberti's self-portrait—the rather smug-looking, bald-headed man. The doors, restored after they were damaged by the 1966 floods (▷ 39), are now on display at the Museo dell'Opera del Duomo—those on the Battistero are replicas.

THE BATTISTERO

The octagonal baptistery, entirely encased in green and white marble, is one of Florence's oldest buildings, probably dating from around the sixth to seventh century, and remodelled in the 11th century. It is most famous for its three sets of bronze doors, the south set dating from the 1330s by Andrea Pisano, and the north and east by Lorenzo Ghiberti. Ghiberti, aged 20, won the commission for the north doors in a competition and worked on them from 1403 to 1424, embarking on his finest achievement, the east set (see above), immediately afterwards. The panels in the doors here are reproductions; the originals are kept away from pollution in the Museo dell'Opera del Duomo.

The interior of the dome glitters with Florence's only mosaic cycle, the earliest dating from 1225. Look above the entrance door and follow the history of the world from the Creation to John the Baptist, before taking in the main image of Christ and the Last Judgement, together with the Apostles and the Virgin.

THE CAMPANILE

Giotto designed the campanile in 1334, but died before it was completed. Both Andrea Pisano, who took over after Giotto's death in 1337, and Francesco Talenti altered the original design considerably, strengthening the walls and adding large windows. The building is covered with bands of green, white and pink marble and is decorated with copies of sculptures and reliefs showing prophets and scenes from the Old Testament; the originals are in the Museo dell'Opera del Duomo. There are 414 steps to the top of the bell tower, which commands 360-degree views of Florence and the surrounding hills. The empty octagon marks the original site of the city's font, in which every child born the previous year was once baptized on New Year's Day.

Above Christ Enthroned *is the focal point of the Battistero's golden mosaic cupola by Jacopo da Torrita*

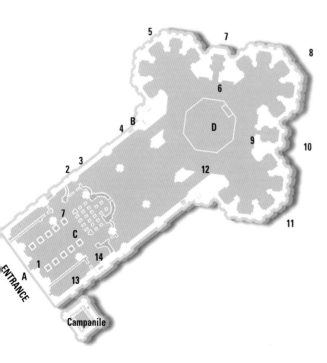

KEY

A Portale Maggiore with relief Maria in Gloria by A. Passaglia
B Porta dell Mandoria
C Crypt, with remains of old cathedral
D Chancel and High Altar
1. L'Assunta window by Ghiberti Incoronazione di Maria
2. Equestrian portrait of Niccolò da Tolentino, by A. del Castagno
3. Equestrian statue of Giovanni Acuto (John Hawkwood) painted by P. Uccello
4. 14th-century window, and below, Dante and the Divine Comedy by D. di Michelino
5. Marble altar (Buggiano)
6. In the door, lunette, Risurrezione, by Luca della Robbia
7. Sagrestia Nuova o della Messe
8. Above the altar, two angels (Luca della Robbia), below the altar reliquary of St. Zenobius by Ghiberti
9. Lunette, Risurrezione, terracotta by della Robbia
10. Sagrestia Vecchia o dei Canonici
11. Altar by Michelozzo
12. Entrance to the dome
13. Bust of Brunelleschi, by A. Cavalcanti
14. Stairs to the Crypt

PIAZZA DELLA REPUBBLICA

This is not Florence's prettiest square, but it is traffic-free, one of the few open spaces at the heart of the city, and bustling with activity. It stands on the site of the Roman forum which, by the Middle Ages, was occupied by a market square and the Jewish ghetto. The Mercato Vecchio (old market), as it was known, was pulled down in the late 19th century in a wave of urban renewal; this is generally considered to have been a grave error of judgement on the part of the city authorities of that time. Lined with important-looking buildings, which nowadays largely house the headquarters of banks and insurance company, Piazza della Repubblica is also a place where you will find lively outdoor cafés, street vendors and street performers. Dominating the western side of the square is a vast triumphal arch and opposite this is the luxurious Savoy hotel (▷ 129). On the corner of Via Roma is the lovely belle-époque Caffè Gilli, a great place for a rather expensive cappuccino.

✚ 62 C2 ⊠ Piazza della Repubblica, 50123 🕅 Free 🚌 A, 22

PIAZZA DELLA SANTISSIMA ANNUNZIATA

This space, arguably the loveliest piazza in Florence, remains much as it was when built. Designed by Filippo Brunelleschi (1377–1446), it is surrounded on three sides by graceful porticoes. The church of Santissima Annunziata (▷ 95) has elegant, neoclassical arches. To the right of the church is the Ospedale degli Innocenti (▷ 83), its portico adorned with Andrea della Robbia's blue and white tondi of swaddled babies. The later portico of Antonio da Sangallo and Baccio d'Agnolo (1516–25) is to the left, mirroring the Ospedale across the square, on which they based their design. In the middle of the piazza is a large equestrian statue of Grand Duke Ferdinand I by Giambologna, the artist's final work. The south side of the piazza is open, which means there are fine views of the cathedral dome (▷ 89–90). The wide steps under the left and right porticoes are a good vantage point, and they are often full of people chatting, eating or simply taking a break.

✚ 63 D1 ⊠ Piazza della Santissima Annunziata, 50122 🕅 Free 🚌 C, 6

PIAZZALE MICHELANGELO

It is worth making the climb, or taking a bus, to Piazzale Michelangelo, on a hillside south of the Arno, for the unrivalled views over Florence. The best approach on foot is to walk to the Forte di Belvedere on Costa di San Giorgio from behind the church of Santa Felicita. From the Forte take Via di Belvedere to Porta San Miniato and then climb the steps on the left to Viale Galileo Galilei, a short distance south of the Piazzale. There's a huge replica of Michelangelo's *David* (▷ 70–71) in the middle of the square, and terraces well placed for the panoramic views, which on a clear day extend beyond the city to the surrounding hills. The sunsets are glorious and on Sunday afternoons the piazza is packed. Piazzale Michelangelo is halfway along the broad, leafy road that winds through this part of the city, where traffic can be heavy.

✚ 63 E5 ⊠ Piazzale Michelangelo, 50125 🕅 Free 🚌 12, 13

Above *From Piazzale Michelangelo there are panoramic views of the city—on clear days these extend to the surrounding hills*

PONTE SANTA TRINITA

www.firenzeturismo.it

The original Santa Trinita bridge was destroyed by bombs in 1944 during World War II, along with all the other bridges in Florence except the Ponte Vecchio (▷ below). It was carefully reconstructed using stone from the original quarries, and what you see today is a faithful replica of Bartolomeo Ammanati's (1511–92) bridge of 1567. With three wide, graceful arches, it links the elegant Via de' Tornabuoni on the north bank of the Arno to the Oltrarno on the south side of the river. At each of its four corners stands one of the original *Four Seasons* statues, which fell into the river during the bombing, but were salvaged and reassembled; the last piece, the head of Spring, was only fished out of the river in 1961.

Ponte Santa Trinita is also where you get the best view of the Ponte Vecchio.

✚ 62 B3 ✉ Piazza di Santa Trinita, 50123 ✋ Free 🚌 A, B

PONTE VECCHIO

The medieval bridge over the Arno, with its line of overhanging shops, is one of the immediately recognizable emblems of Florence.

If you can ignore the crowds and the many modern stores selling gold and jewellery, the Ponte Vecchio gives you a taste of what medieval Florence was like—as well as a good view of the River Arno, its palaces and the next bridge along the river, the Ponte Santa Trinita (▷ above).

The present bridge was built in 1345, a reconstruction of an earlier structure (until 1218 the only crossing over the river) washed away by a flood. At the end of the 16th century Grand Duke Ferdinand replaced the evil-smelling hog-butchers' shops that lined the bridge with gold- and silversmiths, and the trade has prevailed here ever since. The bridge has survived two major traumas in recent history: In 1944, while all the other bridges in Florence were destroyed by bombing, the Ponte Vecchio was

preserved on Hitler's orders; and in 1966 the waters of the Arno rose to such a level that a fortune in gold was washed away in the floods (▷ 39).

Small shops and houses painted in mellow shades of yellow line the bridge on both sides, supported on brackets that overhang the river. With their wooden shutters, wrought-ironwork and awnings, they have retained their medieval appearance.

The sun sets directly downriver from the bridge, and the golden tones of the structure itself are magical on a good evening.

Clearly visible running over the top of the eastern shops is the Corridoio Vasariano, a passageway designed by Giorgio Vasari in 1565 as a secret route for Cosimo I. It joins the Galleria degli Uffizi (▷ 73–77) and the Palazzo Pitti (▷ 84–85).

✚ 62 C3 ✉ Ponte Vecchio, 50123 ✋ Free 🚌 B, D

SANTISSIMA ANNUNZIATA

In the mid-15th century this grand building was one of the most important churches in Florence. It was founded in 1250 to protect a picture of the Virgin (said to have been painted by a monk with help from an angel), and expanded between 1444 and 1481 by Michelozzo. He also designed the Chiostrino dei Voti in front of the church, a glass-roofed atrium

decorated with frescoes by Andrea del Sarto (1486–1531) and some of his contemporaries.

The church stands on the north side of Piazza della Santissima Annunziata, its façade made up of a graceful portico that leads into the Chiostrino dei Voti. On the right are frescoes by Rosso Fiorentino of the Assumption and to the left is Jacopo Pontormo's *Visitation*. The dim interior is lavishly decorated with marble and gold leaf. The tabernacle commissioned by the Medici family in the 15th century contains the painting of the Virgin mentioned above. The large apse behind the main altar is entered by way of a triumphal arch, clearly influenced by Roman architecture.

Notable works of art in the main body of the church include, in the left aisle, an *Assumption* by Perugino (c1450–1523) and *The Holy Trinity with St. Jerome* by Andrea del Castagno (c1421– 57). The splendid organ in the nave, built between 1509 and 1521, is the oldest in the city and the second-oldest in Italy.

The Chiostro dei Morti (Cloister of the Dead) is to the left of the church and houses Andrea del Sarto's *Madonna del Sacco*, one of his most famous works.

✚ 63 D1 ✉ Piazza della Santissima Annunziata, 50122 ☎ 055 266181 🕒 Daily 7.30–12.30, 4–6.30 ✋ Free

Below *Ponte Santa Trinita, a faithful replica of the original 16th-century bridge*

SANTA CROCE

In the heart of one of Florence's most attractive areas, Santa Croce was begun in 1294 and completed in the 1450s. The original plain front was replaced in the 19th century with an elaborate neo-Gothic façade. The interior is vast, with a wide nave and superb stained-glass windows by Agnolo Gaddi (c1300–66). Some of the frescoes are in a disappointing condition, but there are some exceptional works.

THE LEFT (NORTH) AISLE

Lorenzo Ghiberti (1378–1455) is buried under the tomb-slab with the eagle on it. There is also a monument to Galileo (1564–1642), the great scientist, who spent his last years in Florence (▷ 35).

THE EAST END

The polygonal sanctuary in the east end is covered with vivid frescoes by Gaddi. On either side are small chapels, each dedicated to an eminent Florentine family of the day, with frescoes by Giotto (c1267–1337). The Bardi di Libertà Chapel has frescoes by Bernardo Daddi, a contemporary of Giotto, and an altarpiece by Giovanni della Robbia (c1469–1529). The Bardi di Vernio Chapel has frescoes (c1340) by Maso di Banco, while Donatello's wooden crucifix hangs in the Bardi Chapel in the north transept. The frescoes in the Castellani Chapel are by Gaddi, whose father was responsible for the beautiful paintings in the Baroncelli Chapel. Next to the Baroncelli Chapel a passage leads to the Medici Chapel by Filippo Brunelleschi.

THE RIGHT (SOUTH) AISLE

In the right aisle are the tombs of Michelangelo the poet Dante and the political writer Niccolò Machiavelli (▷ 33).

CAPPELLA DEI PAZZI, THE CLOISTERS AND MUSEUM

You can access the Cappella dei Pazzi from the right aisle and through the 14th-century cloister. Brunelleschi was still working on this tranquil masterpiece when he died in 1446. Inside, the grey stone, simply carved in classical lines, is set against a white background. At the base of the elegant dome, 12 terracotta roundels by della Robbia depict the Apostles. There are more fine works of art in the Museo dell'Opera di Santa Croce, the entrance to which is off the cloister.

INFORMATION

www.firenzeturismo.it

➕ 63 D3 ✉ Piazza Santa Croce, 50122 ☎ 055 244619 ⏱ Church, Cappella, Museum: Mon–Sat 9.30–5.30 (also Mar–end Oct Sun 1.30–5.30) 💶 Adult €5 (also covers cappella and museum), child (11–18) €2.50, under 11 free 🚌 B, C 🚶 Free tours in English, French, German, Spanish, Italian Mon–Sat 10–12.30, 3–5, Sun 3–5 (tours given by volunteers, so times and availability of languages may vary). Audioguides at fixed points: English, French, Spanish, Italian €1 📖 Official book €8 🏬 One shop sells gifts, books, posters and postcards; another sells leather goods, which you can watch the artisans making

Opposite *Santa Croce, the largest Franciscan church in Italy, incorporates one of Brunelleschi's most important works, the Cappella dei Pazzi*
Below *Many illustrious Italians are buried at Santa Croce*

Above *The frescoed trompe l'oeil ceiling at Santa Maria Maddalena dei Pazzi is superb*

SANT'APOLLONIA

Andrea del Castagno's *Last Supper*, or *Cenacolo* (1447), is housed in the refectory of the former convent of Sant'Apollonia and is one of the finest paintings of that subject in Florence. Few visitors make time to see it, so you may well have the place to yourself. The painting shows Christ's table in the unusual surroundings of a marble loggia. The predominant dark greens, browns, blues and reds are sombre while the faces of the disciples are vivid. Above the *Cenacolo* is a faded fresco of the Crucifixion also by Castagno, and on the opposite wall of the long room is the *sinopia*, the rough outline on plaster that the artist followed. The lunette frescoes are also by Castagno.

✚ 62 C1 ✉ Via XXVII Aprile 1, 50129 ☎ 055 238 8607 ◷ Daily 8.15–1.50. Closed 1st, 3rd, 5th Sun and 2nd, 4th Mon of each month; ticket office closes 30 min earlier ♿ Free 🚍 1, 6, 7

SANTA FELICITA

Santa Felicita, off the busy Via de' Guicciardini, often gets overlooked by visitors hurrying between the Ponte Vecchio and the Pitti Palace. The church itself is not outstanding, its chief allure lying in the harmonious use of the local grey stone *pietra serena*, but it has a long history. It is thought to be one of the city's oldest churches, founded by Syrian Greek merchants in the second century. Since then it's been rebuilt several times, notably in 1565 by Vasari, who added a portico to accommodate his *corridoio*, the covered passage linking the Uffizi (▷ 73–77) and the Palazzo Pitti (▷ 84–85); you can see a window into the passageway high in the church's interior. The present façade dates from 1736.

To the right of the main door is the Cappella Capponi, containing Jacopo Pontormo's extraordinary painting of the Deposition (1528). The chapel itself was designed in the 1420s by Brunelleschi, and frescoed a century later by Pontormo and his adopted son, Bronzino. The right wall has an *Annunciation*; under the cupola are four tondi of the Evangelists, but it is the *Deposition* that draws the eye. The composition makes this one of the greatest of all Mannerist works. Scale means nothing here—note the Virgin and her attendants—and all the usual elements of this subject are lacking: Where are the cross, the soldiers, the mourners? The virulent tones (their acidic quality is caused by low light levels) light up the chapel with pinks, blues, lime-green, oranges and reds and form a luminous contrast to the monotonous grey elsewhere in the building. Make sure you have a €1 coin for the light box that illuminates the painting.

✚ 62 C4 ✉ Piazza Santa Felicita 50125 ☎ 055 213018 ◷ Mon–Sat 9.30–12.30, 3–6, Sun 9–1 ♿ Free 🚍 D

SANTA MARIA MADDALENA DEI PAZZI

The convent of Santa Maria Maddalena dei Pazzi was named after a Carmelite nun, famed for her religious devotion of covering herself in boiling wax; she lived from 1566 to 1607 and was canonized in 1669. The entrance to the church is through a large, rather sober cloister, but the church itself is built to grand dimensions, with a lavishly frescoed trompe l'oeil ceiling and a series of chapels under beautifully carved arches. The main chapel surrounding the altar was built in extravagant marble in 1675 in homage to Santa Maddalena herself. However, the main reason for visiting the church lies in the chapter house, entered by passing through the crypt under the church. Here you'll find Perugino's superb fresco of the *Crucifixion and Saints*, painted between 1493 and 1496, considered one of his masterpieces. The picture's strength lies as much in its peaceful rural background as in the Crucifixion itself—a continuous panorama across the wall of a beautiful spring landscape around Lake Trasimeno in Umbria.

✚ 63 E2 ✉ Borgo Pinti 58, 50121 ☎ 055 247 8420 ◷ Daily 9–12, 5–9 ♿ Church: free; Perugino: donation 🚍 C, 6

SAN MARTINO DEL VESCOVO

The tiny oratory of San Martino del Vescovo, right in the heart of medieval Florence, is a rewarding stop-off. A church founded on the site in the 10th century was the poet Dante's parish church. It was rebuilt in 1479 and became the headquarters of the Compagnia dei Buonomini di San Martino, a charitable institution. Inside, a series of lunette frescoes by the workshop of Domenico Ghirlandaio decorates the upper walls. These illustrate scenes from the life of St. Martin and acts of charity, and show Florentines going about their daily business. There are also two lovely paintings of the Madonna on the walls, one Byzantine and the other attributed to a close follower of Perugino. Near the latter is a small, blocked window marked with a plaque; from here bread was distributed during the Black Death in 1348.

✚ 62 C3 ✉ Piazza San Martino, 50122 ☎ 055 281259 ◷ Mon–Sat 10–12, 3–5 ♿ Donation 🚍 A

SAN LORENZO

The Medici family church is a superb example of archetypal Renaissance architecture. The basilica that originally stood on the site of San Lorenzo was consecrated in AD393 and is thought to have been the oldest church in Florence. The Medici commissioned Filippo Brunelleschi to rebuild it in 1425, enlisting Michelangelo for certain projects. There are few important works of art, but the church is a wonder in itself and houses the Cappelle Medicee, the family mausoleum (▷ 68).

THE CHURCH

The interior is mainly grey shades of *pietra serena* stone columns, with a grey-white marble floor designed by Brunelleschi. The overall effect is elegant, as the wooden ceiling, painted white and gold, creates a feeling of light. The aisles are lined with chapels, and paintings to look out for include Rosso Fiorentino's *Marriage of the Virgin* (1523) in the second chapel on the right and the fresco of the Martyrdom of St. Lawrence by Bronzino along the left aisle. The most important works within the church are Donatello's massive rectangular pulpits in the nave, which were his last work.

SAGRESTIA VECCHIA

The left transept leads you to the Sagrestia Vecchia (Old Sacristy) by Brunelleschi, a partner to the Sagrestia Nuova (New Sacristy) in the Cappelle Medicee. The vault with terracotta tondi is by Donatello, who also made the bronze doors. The small dome above the altar is decorated with frescoes of the zodiac in midnight-blue and gold. The tomb in the middle of the room is of Giovanni and Piccarda, founders of the Medici wealth. You can wander out of the main door on the left into the graceful two-tiered cloisters that frame the garden.

BIBLIOTECA LAURENZIANA

The Biblioteca Laurenziana is on the first floor and is entered via a hall dominated by an extraordinary freestanding staircase, built to a design by Michelangelo. The long reading room is full of closely packed desks and has a beautiful carved wooden ceiling. None of the library's collection of great manuscripts is on permanent display. A selection is brought out twice a year for periods of roughly three months.

INFORMATION

✚ 62 C2 ✉ Piazza San Lorenzo, 50123
☎ 055 216634 ⓘ Church and cloister: Mon–Sat 10–5.30 (also Mar–end Oct Sun 1.30–5.30) 💶 Adult €3, under 6 free 🚌 1, 6, 17, A 🔖 Free tours Mon–Sat 10–12.30, 3–5, Sun 3–5 in English, French, German, Spanish, Italian (tours given by volunteers, so times and availability of languages may vary). Audioguides at fixed points in English, French, Spanish, Italian €1 📗 Official guide €8 📚 Small bookshop selling guides

Below *The cloisters of San Lorenzo, the Medici family church and a superb example of Renaissance architecture*

INFORMATION

www.smn.it

⊕ 62 B2 ✉ Piazza Santa Maria Novella, 50123 ☎ Church: 055 215918. Museum: 055 282187 🕐 Church: Mon–Thu, Sat 9–5, Fri, Sun 1–5. Museum: Mon–Thu, Sat 9–5. Public holidays 9–2 ✋ Church: Adult €2.50, under 18 free. Museum: Adult €2.70, child (12–20) €2.70, under 12 €1.90 🚌 A, 12 and all buses to Santa Maria Novella rail station 🎫 Free tours Mon–Sat 10–12.30, 3–5, Sun 3–5 in English, French, German, Spanish, Italian (tours given by volunteers, so times and availability of languages may vary) 📖 Official guidebook €8 🏬 Small bookshop in the church sells posters, postcards and some guidebooks

SANTA MARIA NOVELLA

Santa Maria Novella is one of the great Florentine churches, full of superb artworks and with the advantage of being relatively uncrowded. The Gothic church with its adjoining museum is immediately striking thanks to the remarkable black-and-white marble exterior. Inside it has outstanding stained glass and important frescoes, while the museum includes cloisters decorated by Paolo Uccello.

THE INTERIOR

The church is entered through the old cemetery, via the side door. Its lofty interior, with stone vaulting decorated with stripes, is calm and uncluttered. One of the first things you notice is Giotto's crucifix (c1300) hanging dramatically in the middle of the nave. Opposite the door is the church's most famous fresco, Masaccio's *Trinità* (c1425), remarkable for its use of perspective; it depicts the Virgin and St. John with the painting's sponsors above a skeleton. The sanctuary has frescoes (1485–90) by Domenico Ghirlandaio of the lives of the Virgin Mary, John the Baptist and the Dominican saints. Next to it is the Filippo Strozzi Chapel, with frescoes by Filippino Lippi of scenes from the lives of St. Philip and St. John. Before leaving, be sure to stop for a few moments to admire the enchanting little nativity scene by Botticelli above the main door of the church.

MUSEO DI SANTA MARIA NOVELLA

There are yet more important frescoes in the Museo within the convent of the church. Here the first cloister, known as the Chiostro Verde, takes its name from the greenish hues that characterize the great but fading frescoes by Paolo Uccello. His scenes from the book of Genesis cover the walls straight in front of the entrance. At the far end of the cloister is the entrance to the Cappellone degli Spagnoli (Spanish Chapel), so-called because the Spanish members of Eleonora di Toledo's court used it in the 16th century. It was once the headquarters of the Inquisition. The vault and walls are covered in vivid frescoes (1365–67) by a relatively unknown artist called Andrea di Buonaiuto, who chose as his subject matter the Dominican cosmology.

Other rooms in the museum contain fresco fragments, holy vestments and 16th- and 17th-century reliquaries. The Chiostro Grande is occupied by a military school and is not open to the public.

Above *A detail of St. Thomas Aquinas on one of the stained-glass windows at Santa Maria Novella*

Opposite *The mosaic on the exterior of San Miniato al Monte*

SAN MINIATO AL MONTE

The church of San Miniato al Monte, on a hill to the south of the city, is one of the finest Romanesque churches in Tuscany. Apart from being a beautiful church in itself, it has wonderful views across the Arno, the old town and neighbouring Fiesole (▷ 69), perched on a hillside 7km (4 miles) away. A visit requires an uphill walk from town or a bus ride, but is well worth the effort.

Built in 1013, the exterior can be seen from all over the city. White-and-green geometrical marble designs surround a glittering 13th-century mosaic of Christ between the Virgin and St. Minias. Little has changed inside the church since the 11th century. In the middle of the nave, the marble floor is made up of intarsia (a kind of inlay) panels decorated with animals and constellations of the zodiac. The Cappella del Crocifisso has a freestanding tabernacle carved by Michelozzo (1396–1472) and terra-cotta pieces by Luca della Robbia (1400–82).

🕇 63 E5 ✉ Via Monte alle Croci, 50125 ☎ 055 234 2731 🕐 Apr–end Oct daily 8–7; Nov–end Mar daily 8–12, 3–6 🖐 Free 🚌 12, 13

SANTO SPIRITO

www.firenzeturismo.it

The beautiful Santo Spirito was the last church designed by Filippo Brunelleschi. He began designing it in 1444 and the work was finally finished in 1481. Its most notable feature is the simple 18th-century façade, now an emblem for the Oltrarno district of Florence, and the huge structure dominates the attractive Piazza Santo Spirito. In spite of its grandeur, it is still a parish church and its broad steps are a convenient outdoor sitting room for the local residents. Inside, grey *pietra serena* stone dominates, with massive columns, arches and vaults creating a harmonious space, and the walls are lined with 38 chapels. This is a great place to escape the crowds. The *Cenacolo* (refectory), next door to the church,

has an assortment of carvings and a Crucifixion fresco by Orcagna (c1308–68).

🕇 62 B4 ✉ Piazza Santo Spirito 29, 50125 ☎ 055 210030 (Church); 055 287043 (Cenacolo) 🕐 Church: Thu–Tue 9.30–12.30, 4–6. Cenacolo: Apr–end Oct Sat 9–5; Nov–end Mar Sat 10.30–1.30 🖐 Church: Free. Cenacolo: Adult €2.20, under 20 €1.60 🚌 D

SANTA TRINITA

Although it is right in the heart of town, this church is often ignored by those on the popular visitor route. But it's worth a short visit for the stunning painting and frescoes in the Sassetti chapel. Inside, the mid-13th-century church is a dark, rather mystical place with pools of light picking out the choicer works of art from the gloom. The interior is square with a series of chapels running down each side. The Sassetti chapel is on the right of the altar and is decorated with exquisite frescoes of the life of St. Francis (1483) by Ghirlandaio. He also painted the superb altarpiece of the Adoration of the Shepherds (1485). On the left of the altar is the tomb of Benozzo Federighi with a finely carved marble effigy (1454–57) by Luca della Robbia. Along the left aisle, the fourth chapel has an Annunciation (1475) by Neri di Bicci and, next to this, there is an altarpiece, the *Coronation of the Virgin* (1430) by Bicci di Lorenzo. Outside the church, in the square, notice the Colonna della Giustizia (Column of Justice), which Pope Pius IV removed from Rome's Terme di Caracalla and presented to Cosimo I in 1565. Two years later, Cosimo ordered the building of the adjacent bridge, Ponte della Trinita, which was destoyed by the Nazis in 1944 but rebuilt to the original design with the original towers.

🕇 62 B3 ✉ Piazza di Santa Trinita, 50125 ☎ 055 216912 🕐 Daily 8–12, 4–6, 🖐 Free 🖐 Free tours Mon–Sat 10–12.30, 3–5, Sun 3–5 in English, French, German, Spanish, Italian (tours given by volunteers, so times and availability of languages may vary) 🚌 A, B

LA SPECOLA

www.msn.unifi.it

Known as La Specola because of the observatory (*specola* meaning looking glass or lens) founded in the same building by Grand Duke Pietro Leopoldo, the Palazzo Torrigiani was built in 1775 as a zoological museum. It now houses the Department of Natural Sciences of the University of Florence, but the museum (on the third floor) still functions and the zoological collection here is the largest in Italy. Old-fashioned wood and glass cases are filled with every creature imaginable that walks, crawls, flies, swims or slithers: insects, butterflies, crustaceans, reptiles, birds and mammals, both small and large. But it is the collection of anatomical wax models that are the real attraction, although anyone of a squeamish disposition should take a deep breath before embarking on this section. The models in wax are unique and extraordinary. Made between 1775 and 1814 by Clemente Susini, they graphically illustrate every bone, muscle, ligament and blood vessel in the human body, both in close-up section and through lifesized models with their skin peeled off or their internal organs exposed.

On the first floor of the palazzo is the Tribuna di Galileo, built in 1841 in honour of the great scientist Galileo and elaborately decorated in marble and mosaic.

🕇 62 B4 ✉ Via Romana 17, 50125 ☎ 055 228 8251 🕐 Mon, Tue, Thu, Fri, Sun 9–1, Sat 9–5; ticket office closes 30 min earlier 🖐 Adult €6, child (6–14) €3, under 6 free 🚌 D, 11, 36, 37 🏛

THE HEART OF FLORENCE

This walk starts and ends with two of Florence's great churches and is a good way to get a general feel for the city. Weaving in and out of the main visitor route, it takes in some of the lesser-known churches, palaces and small museums of the city's historic heart.

THE WALK

Distance: 2km (1.2 miles)
Allow: 1.5 hours
Start at: Duomo
End at: Piazza Santa Maria Novella

★ Begin at Piazza del Duomo (▷ 88–93), Florence's religious heart and one of the city's three main squares.

❶ The Piazza is home to Florence's Duomo, one of Italy's most familiar landmarks, while the Battistero holds a significant place in Florence's spiritual history. The views from the top of Giotto's campanile are spectacular. On the corner with Via de' Calzaiuoli is the 14th-century Loggia del Bigallo, built for the Misericordia, a charitable institution that cared for plague victims in the 13th and 14th centuries. The finely carved porch served as a drop-off point for unwanted babies.

On the southwest side of the square is Via de' Calzaiuoli (street of the shoemakers), built on the site of a Roman road. Follow this pedestrian-only, shop-lined street—the medieval city's main thoroughfare—to Piazza della Signoria, passing the unusual church of Orsanmichele (▷ 83) on your right along the way. Piazza della Signoria (▷ 87) is the second of the city's three large squares and has been its political and civic focus since medieval times. Leave the square on Via Vaccherccia, which emerges near the top of Via Por Santa Maria, once lined with medieval palaces that were destroyed by German bombing in 1944. A right turn brings you out to the Mercato Nuovo.

❷ The Mercato Nuovo is also known as Il Porcellino (the Little Pig), after the famous bronze statue of a boar, a copy (1612) by Pietro Tacca of the marble classical original. Its snout is worn shiny by the daily caresses of thousands of visitors. There has been a market on this site since the early 11th century. The elegant loggia was built by Cosimo I in 1547; it now shelters stands selling gifts and leather goods.

Pass the market, turn left and walk down Via Porta Rossa. On the left is the Palazzo Davanzati or the Museo della Casa Fiorentina Antica (▷ 78), complete with top-floor loggia. At the end of the street is Piazza di Santa Trinita (▷ 101).

❸ The Piazza and its church are artistically rich. In the middle of the square is the tall Column of Justice, a monolith brought from the Baths of Caracalla in Rome and given to Cosimo I in 1560 by Pope Pius IV. On the left stands the fine Palazzo Bartolini-Salimbeni, built between 1520 and 1523 by Baccio d'Agnolo, and beyond this the splendid Palazzo Spini-Feroni, one of the best-preserved private medieval palaces in Florence, now housing Ferragamo's flagship store and close to its shoe museum (▷ 82, 110).

Take the left exit down Borgo Santi Apostoli, which leads to a tiny sunken square.

❹ Piazza del Limbo is so-called because it stands on the site of a cemetery for unbaptized babies, which were believed to spend eternity in limbo. The church of Santi Apostoli is also here. This is one of the oldest churches in the city, founded in the 11th century, with a carved tomb by Benedetto da Rovezzano (1474–1554) inside. He also designed the entrance door.

Return to Piazza di Santa Trinita and take Via del Parione to the right of the church of Santa Trinita, then turn right down Via Parioncino. You will emerge onto Via del Purgatorio. Walk to your left to the intersection with Via della Vigna Nuova. With your back still to Via del Purgatorio, the Palazzo Rucellai will be in front of you.

❺ Palazzo Rucellai's exterior was designed by Leon Battista Alberti and built by Bernardo Rossellino between 1446 and 1451. The lovely Loggia dei Rucellai, now home to a fashion store, is on your right.

Turn left here onto Via della Vigna Nuova. Cross over Via della Vigna Nuova, turn right up Via dei Palchetti (at the corner of the Palazzo Rucellai), then right again onto Via dei Federighi. This leads onto Piazza San Pancrazio.

❻ Piazza San Pancrazio is home to the deconsecrated church of San Pancrazio, now the Museo Marino Marini, dedicated to the work of the Florentine sculptor Marino Marini (1901–80). Just around the corner from here, on the right at Via della Spada 18, is the tiny Cappella di San Sepolcro. Built in 1467 for the Rucellai family, this chapel has a superbly carved marble inlay model of the Church of the Holy Sepulchre in Jerusalem.

From the Cappella di San Sepolcro, walk back a little way along Via della Spada and turn left down Via del Moro, which is full of antiques shops. At Piazza Goldoni turn right and continue along Borgo Ognissanti. No. 60r is one of Florence's more unusual buildings, a well-preserved example of art deco architecture.

❼ The wide Piazza d'Ognissanti is just a few doors down, site of the church and adjacent convent that give the square its name. When facing the church, the 15th-century Palazzo Lenzi—now the French Consulate—is on the left-hand side. Across the river you can see San Frediano in Cestello, one of the many churches in Florence with a façade left unfinished.

Backtrack a little and turn left up Via della Porcellana, lined with workshops, then turn right down Via della Scala. At the top is the huge Piazza Santa Maria Novella.

❽ The superb Gothic church of Santa Maria Novella (▷ 100) stands at the north end of the square.

WHEN TO GO
Morning is the best time to explore Florence. During the afternoon, and on Mondays, many of the smaller churches are closed.

WHERE TO EAT
CAFFÈ RIVOIRE
▷ 120.

CANTINETTA DEI VERAZZANO
Off Via de' Calzaiuoli, this restaurant serves coffee and cakes along with excellent wines and snacks.
✉ Via dei Tavolini 18–20r ☎ 055 268590
🕐 Mon–Sat 8am–9pm

PLACES TO VISIT
MUSEO DELLA CASA FIORENTINA ANTICA
▷ 78.

SANTI APOSTOLI
✉ Piazza del Limbo 🕐 Mon–Sat 10–12, 4–6, Sun 4–6

MUSEO MARINO MARINI
✉ Piazza San Pancrazio 🕐 Wed–Sat, Mon 10–5. Closed Aug 👤 €4

CAPPELLA DI SAN SEPOLCRO
✉ Via della Spada 18 🕐 Mon–Sat 10–12 (hours vary)

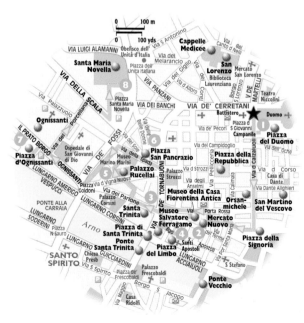

Opposite *Santa Maria Novella*

THE OLTRARNO

The Oltrarno is the part of Florence to the south of the river. The walk begins amid the bustle of the city, yet only a short distance to the west is a tranquil district where you can catch glimpses of everyday local life. Soon city turns to countryside, and you will find yourself in a landscape of mellow villas, olive groves and cypress trees.

THE WALK

Distance: 5km (3 miles)
Allow: 3 hours
Start/end at: Ponte Vecchio

★ Set off from the south side of the Ponte Vecchio (▷ 95). With your back to the bridge, turn right and walk parallel to the river down Borgo San Jacopo.

❶ The buildings on Borgo San Jacopo include several medieval tower houses such as Torre dei Belfredelli on the left at No. 9, and the Torre dei Barbadori opposite. Farther on, the 11th-century church of San Jacopo Soprarno has a graceful, three-arched portico, and often hosts concerts.

Just after a little marble fountain on the left, the street ends in Piazza de' Frescobaldi. To the left is Via Maggio, lined with elegant palaces and expensive antiques shops. Cross this road and turn left onto the narrow Via del Presto di San Martino.

This emerges alongside the church of Santo Spirito (▷ 101).

❷ Santo Spirito is on the tranquil, tree-lined piazza of the same name. This is the heart of a lively and vibrant district of artisans' workshops, narrow streets and medieval houses. A small morning market is held here each Monday to Saturday, as well as a flea market on the second Sunday of each month.

With your back to the church, leave the square by the bottom (southern) corner, passing the 16th-century Palazzo Guadagni on the corner, and turn left into Via Mazzetta. This leads to Piazza San Felice.

❸ Piazza San Felice has a tall marble column dating from 1572, and a 14th-century church. On the first floor of No. 8, on the left towards Via Maggio, is the Casa Guidi, where the poets Robert and Elizabeth Barrett Browning lived between 1847 and 1861.

Cross the square and walk into Piazza de' Pitti, passing Palazzo Pitti (▷ 84–85) on the right. It was in the row of houses opposite the palace, at No. 22, that Dostoyevsky wrote the novel *The Idiot* (1868). Walk straight on along Via de' Guicciardini and turn right into Piazza Santa Felicità.

❹ Santa Felicità (▷ 98) is one of the oldest churches in Florence. Its dome was lopped off in the mid-16th century to make way for the Corridoio Vasariano, which links the Pitti and Uffizi palaces. Inside is Pontormo's (1494–1557) painting of the Deposition.

Behind the church, Costa di San Giorgio leads out of the piazza climbing steeply uphill, with some wonderful views of the city. Towards the top on the right (No. 19) is a house where the scientist Galileo Galilei once lived (▷ 35). At the top of the hill, the street passes under the old city gate, Porta San

Giorgio. The entrance to the Forte di Belvedere is on the right.

❺ Bernardo Buontalenti (1536–1608) designed the huge, star-shaped Forte di Belvedere in 1590 as part of the city's defences. The ramparts, partially grassed, are popular as a park with locals and visitors alike, and provide magnificent views over the city and surrounding countryside.

After the gate, turn left along Via Belvedere, which follows the 13th-century defensive walls. From here the road heads down to the small gateway of Porta San Miniato. Turn right and head up Via Monte alle Croci. Enoteca Fuori Porta, one of the city's best-known wine bars, is on the right. A little farther up, take the steep Via di San Salvatore al Monte on the left, which crosses the busy Viale Galileo. Cross the road and continue on up the last few steps to the sober Franciscan church of San Salvatore al Monte. From here, Via delle Porte Sante to the right leads to San Miniato al Monte.

Opposite *The Ponte Vecchio*

❻ The church of San Miniato al Monte (▷ 101) has a dazzling marble exterior and a terrace with panoramic views. Benedictine monks still live in the adjoining monastery.

With your back to the church, cross over Via delle Porte Sante and onto Viale Galileo. Turn right and continue downhill until you reach Piazzale Michelangelo.

❼ There are endless photographic possibilities at Piazzale Michelangelo (▷ 94), with Florence and the hills beyond as a backdrop.

From here, the No. 12 bus (the bus stop is on Viale Michelangelo) will take you down to Ponte alle Grazie. It is then a short walk back to the Ponte Vecchio along the river. Or take the path from the Piazzale down to the 14th-century Porta San Niccolò. Turn left onto Via di San Niccolò and follow this to Piazza de' Mozzi, where the 13th-century Palazzo dei Mozzi and the Museo Bardini (▷ 78) face each other. From here, Via de' Bardi leads to the Ponte Vecchio.

WHEN TO GO
This is a long walk with several steep climbs, so avoid the midday sun and take a hat and plenty of water. The views over the city at dusk are stunning, and if you happen to reach San Miniato by 4.30pm in winter or an hour later in summer, you can hear the monks singing Gregorian chants at evening Mass.

WHERE TO EAT
There are bars and cafés on Piazza Santo Spirito, near Piazzale Michelangelo and on Via di San Niccolò.

ENOTECA FUORI PORTA
✉ Via Monte alle Croce 10r ☎ 055 234 2483 🕒 Mon–Sat 12.30pm–12.30am

PLACES TO VISIT
CASA GUIDI
✉ Piazza San Felice 8 ☎ 055 354457 🕒 Apr–end Nov Mon, Wed, Fri 3–6 ✋ Donation

SAN SALVATORE AL MONTE
✉ Via San Salvatore al Monte 🕒 Daily 7–7 ✋ Free

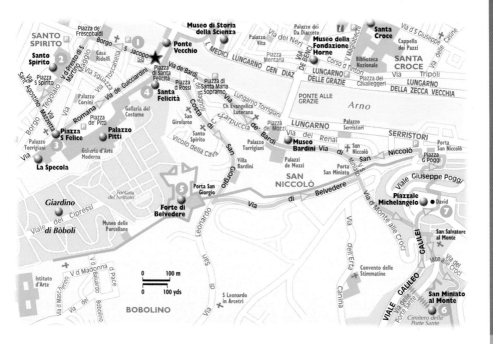

Above *Florentine shops tempt shoppers with their fine fashions*

SHOPPING

ABACUS
www.abacusfirenze.it
The sign on the door says that this bookbindery aspires to 'sturdiness and beauty'. The hand-stitched spines and exquisitely lined covers make the volumes exceptional gifts. Prices are surprisingly low.
✉ Via de' Ginori 28/30r, 50123 ☎ 055 219719 ⊙ Tue–Sat 9.30–1.30, 3.30–7.30, Mon 3.30–7.30. Closed last 2 weeks in Aug 🚌 1, 6, 7, 10

ALICE'S MASKS STUDIO
www.alicemasks.com
Papier-mâché masks in all shapes and sizes are here: animals— mythical and real—as well as more theatrical and surreal characters. They are all hand-painted and finished, making great gifts or wall hangings.
✉ Via Faenza 72r, 50123 ☎ 055 287370 ⊙ Mon–Sat 9–1, 3.30–7.30 (hours vary) 🚌 4, 12, 25, 31, 32, 33

ALINARI
www.alinari.it
Alinari has a superb photographic archive, some of the first photos taken in Italy. You can order any print for a very reasonable price. Beautiful coffee-table books and the kind of

postcards you want to keep rather than send are also for sale.
✉ Largo Alinari 15, 50122 ☎ 055 23951 ⊙ Mon–Fri 9–1, 2–6 🚌 6, 36, 37

ANGELA CAPUTI
www.angelacaputi.com
Angela Caputi is the place to look for bright, bold and highly original costume jewellery. Clothing and accessories to go with the pendant or earrings you have just bought are also stocked.
✉ Borgo Santi Apostoli 44–46r, 50123 ☎ 055 292 993 ⊙ Mon–Sat 10–1, 3.30–7.30. Closed 2 weeks in Aug 🚌 B

ANTICO SETIFICIO FIORENTINO
www.anticosetificiofiorentino.com
This 'old Florentine silk factory' makes fine fabrics for some of Italy's top designers. Much of the fabric is produced by traditional methods, and their finest cloth is woven on 18th-century looms.
✉ Via Lorenzo Bartolino 4, 50124 ☎ 055 213861 ⊙ Mon–Fri 9–1, 2–5 🚌 D

ANTONIO FRILLI GALLERY
www.frilligallery.com
If you've always wanted figures from famous paintings, such as Rubens' *The Three Graces*, to stand whispering and giggling in your garden, you can find them here. Of course these high-quality hand-made and hand-finished sculptures aren't

the real thing, but they come pretty close. Frilli also carries Ionic and Corinthian columns.
✉ Via dei Fossi 26r, 50123 ☎ 055 210212 ⊙ Mon–Sat 9.30–12.30, 3–7. Closed Jul, Aug Sat pm 🚌 A, 36, 37

BABETTE VON DOHNANYI
www.bd-jewellery.com
Highly unusual glass spheres, strung together with finely spun gold and silver, are sold in the maker's shop close to the Giardino di Boboli. Her alternative styles are growing in popularity. Credit cards are not accepted.
✉ Viale Francesco Petrarca 116 int, 50124 ☎ 055 223697 ⊙ Mon–Fri 10.30–1, 3–7 or by appointment 🚌 12, 13

BALLOON
www.balloon.it
This Italian chain sells funky casual clothing made from natural fabrics such as silk and cotton that looks good on all generations.
✉ Via del Proconsolo 69r, 50122 ☎ 055 212460 ⊙ Summer Mon–Fri 10–7.30, Sat 10–1; winter Tue–Sat 10–7.30, Mon 3.30–7.30. Closed 2 weeks in Aug 🚌 A, 14, 23

BARTOLOZZI & MAIOLI
This antiques shop gives a great insight into the Florentine love of ostentatious adornment. It's like wandering around a theatrical prop

department preparing for a new production as craftsmen tap away in the background. You'll find some first-rate pieces in here, but be prepared to spend a lot.

✉ Via Maggio 13r, 50125 ☎ 055 239 8633 🕐 Mon–Sat 9–1, 3–7. Closed Aug 🚌 D, 11, 36, 37

IL BISONTE
www.ilbisonte.net

This brand (everything is stamped with the trademark bison) is at the cutting edge of leather bags and accessories. You can buy mobile phone covers, wallets, belts and travel bags, all made out of leather that takes on a beautiful patina of its own after use.

✉ Via del Parione 31r, 50123 ☎ 055 215722 🕐 Mon–Sat 9.30–7.30 🚌 A, B, 6, 11, 36, 37

BORGO
www.borgovino.com

This well-stocked wine shop focuses on smaller local winemakers. The knowledgeable staff can help you choose. Chiantis from €4.20, up to €210 for a Super Tuscan. Also *biscotti*, pasta and olive oil.

✉ Borgo San Lorenzo 20r, 50123 ☎ 055 215103 🕐 Mon–Sat 10–7.30 🚌 1, 6, 7, 10, 11, 14

LA BOTTEGHINA DEL CERAMISTA
The lively patterns hand-painted on these jugs, bowls and dishes will brighten up any table. Look for the patterned jugs with matching cups, perfect for serving red wine.

✉ Via Guelfa 5r, 50129 ☎ 055 287367 🕐 Closed Jul, Aug Sat pm 🚌 1, 6, 7, 10, 11, 17

LA CASA DELLA STAMPA
Vivianna is the lithographer who hand-tints many of these beautiful prints. There is a huge selection of Florentine scenes, from the Medici era to the early 19th century, alongside rich studies of butterflies and plants. All are printed on thick paper and can be framed.

✉ Sdrucciolo de Pitti 11r, 50125 ☎ 055 223258 🕐 Mon–Sat 10–1, 3.30–6 🚌 D, 11, 36, 37

CASCINE
It's worth an early start to experience the hustle and bustle of this market, in Florence's biggest park, by the Ponte della Vittoria. There are meats, fruit and vegetables, bric-a-brac, clothes and shoes. Credit cards are not accepted.

✉ Parco delle Cascine, Viale Abramo Lincoln, 50144 🕐 Tue 8–1 🚌 B, 1, 9, 12, 13

CELLERINI
www.cellerini.com

Drop in to view some of the wonderfully simple yet cleverly designed bags and purses here. Cellerini bags are very popular among fashion buffs and will elicit envious glances once you get back home.

✉ Via del Sole 37r, 50123 ☎ 055 282533 🕐 Mon–Fri 9–1, 3–7, Sat 9–1 🚌 A, 6, 11, 36, 37

COIN
www.coin.it

This chain is one of the greatest things about Italy. The fashion department always delivers, with versions of the latest trends that are both affordable and of good quality. Good beauty department too, plus everything for the home.

✉ Via dei Calzaiuoli 56r, 50123 ☎ 055 280531 🕐 Apr–end Dec Mon–Sat 10–8, Sun 10.30–7.30; Jan–end Mar Mon–Sat 10–7.30, Sun 11–8 🚌 A

DOLCI E DOLCEZZE
Purveyor of light fluffy cakes, doughnuts and savoury pastries, this bakery is internationally renowned and deservedly so. If you are only in Florence for a day, make sure you come here for your cake stop. Credit cards are not accepted.

✉ Piazza Beccaria 8r, 50121 ☎ 055 234 5458 🕐 Tue–Sun 8–8 🚌 A, 6, 31, 32

DUCCI
www.duccishop.com

A massive selection of tinted lithographs, engravings and prints, both framed and unframed. Also some unusual items that make

excellent gifts, as well as furniture and wooden carvings of shoes and clothing.

✉ Lungarno Corsini 24r, 50123 ☎ 055 214550 🕐 Tue–Sat 9.30–1, 3.30–7. Closed Nov–Apr Mon am, May–Oct Sat pm 🚌 A, B, 6, 11, 36, 37

ECHO
You will not have heard of any of the labels in this shop, but you'll almost certainly be bowled over by the clever designs and the reasonable prices. There's a younger, funkier Echo next door.

✉ Via dell'Oriuolo 37r, 50122 ☎ 055 238 1149 🕐 Tue–Sat 10–1.30, 2–7.30; Mon 3.30–7.30 (also Oct–Christmas Sun 11–7) 🚌 14, 23

EDISON
www.libreriaedison.it

Selling guides and books in English, maps, CDs, magazines and newspapers, Edison is a must for media junkies. The internet café is a great place to watch the world news on huge screens.

✉ Piazza della Repubblica 27r, 50123 ☎ 055 213110 🕐 Mon–Sat 9am–midnight, Sun 10am–midnight 🚌 A, 6

EMILIO CAVALLINI
www.emiliocavallini.com

Come the cooler weather, there's nothing like a whole wardrobe of bright, patterned and textured hosiery to keep your legs warm. Emilio Cavallini is where you can come to get it.

✉ Via della Vigna Nuova 24, 50123 ☎ 055 238 2789 🕐 Tue–Sat 10–7, Mon 3–7 🚌 A, B, 6, 11, 36, 37

ENOTECA MURGIA
www.vinodelizia.com

If you need help choosing an olive oil, the staff at this friendly store will take you through all the different types available, and you can taste and try before you buy. They also have a good selection of local wines and Italian liqueurs.

✉ Via dei Bianchi 45r, 50123 ☎ 055 215686 🕐 Jul–end Aug Mon–Sat 9.30–1.30, 3–8; Sep–end Jun Mon–Sat 9.30–1.30, 3–8, Sun 10–7 🚌 A, 1, 14, 17, 22, 23

FELTRINELLI
www.feltrinelli.it
Feltrinelli is part of a nationwide chain of bookstores, clearly laid out and with a sprinkling of English- and other foreign-language titles dotted around its well-organized shelves. You'll find an even bigger selection of English titles (plus maps, newspapers and magazines) at the sister store, Feltrinelli Internazionale at Via Cavour 20r (tel 055 219524; Mon–Sat 9–7.30), west of the Duomo.
✉ Via de' Cerretani 30r ☎ 055 238 2652 🕐 Mon–Sat 9–8, Sun 10–1, 3–8 🚌 1, 6, 17

FRATELLI PICCINI
www.fratellipiccini.com
Make sure you take in Piccini's if you are jewellery shopping on the Ponte Vecchio. Their gold charms make delightful gifts.
✉ Ponte Vecchio 23, 50123 ☎ 055 294768 🕐 Apr–end Oct Mon–Sat 10–7; Nov–end Mar Tue–Sat 10–1, 3.30–7.30 🚌 B, D

GIOVANNI BACCANI
Florence has many shops and galleries selling prints and paintings, but none, perhaps, as tempting as this beautiful old store, little changed since it was founded in the 1930s. It offers a superb selection of prints of the city and other subjects in all price ranges, framed and unframed. It also has a small selection of other craft items, such as beautiful handmade lamps.
✉ Via della Vigna Nuova 75r ☎ 055 214467 🕐 Tue–Sat 9–1, 3.30–7.30, Mon 3.30–7.30 🚌 A, B

GIOVANNI TURCHI
A huge selection of period pieces just a stone's throw from the Palazzo Pitti. The store has been in the same family for years, and has items from the local area, Venice and the Veneto. Pieces are less expensive than they would be back home, even including the cost of shipping.
✉ Via Maggio 50–52r, 50125 ☎ 055 217341 🕐 Mon–Sat 9.30–1, 4–7.30 🚌 D, 11, 36, 37

GIULIO GIANNINI E FIGLIO
www.giuliogiannini.it
At what may be Florence's oldest papermakers, you can buy gorgeous muted marbled paper, either by the sheet or the box. Also, covered boxes and books for your desk.
✉ Piazza de' Pitti 37r, 50125 ☎ 055 212621 🕐 Mon–Sat 10–7.30, Sun 10.30–6.30 🚌 D, 36, 37

GUALTIERI GANDOLFI
If you are looking for antique jewellery, this little shop just off Borgo Santi Apostoli has some amazing pieces. Look out for gemstones, glass beads and jet, as well as pieces unique to this region.
✉ Piazza del Limbo 8r, 50123 ☎ 055 283318 🕐 Mon–Sat 9.30–1, 3–7.30 🚌 B

GUCCI
www.gucci.com
The famous Gucci label was founded in Florence at this address in 1921, when Guccio Gucci first opened a small leather workshop and saddlery store (▷ 39). The impressive store now on the site still acts as a prestigious showroom for the revitalized company's clothes, shoes and accessories.
✉ Via de' Tornabuoni 73r ☎ 055 264011 🕐 Mon–Sat 10–7, Sun 2–7 🚌 A, 6, 11, 22, 36, 37

HEMINGWAY
A chocolate heaven that caters to chocolate lovers of all descriptions. This is where the region's master chocolate makers come to drink coffee and liqueurs, and to talk—and eat—chocolate.
✉ Piazza Piattellina 9r, 50124 ☎ 055 284781 🕐 Tue–Sat 4.30pm–11.30pm, Sun 11.30am–8pm 🚌 D, 6

INTIMISSIMI
www.intimissimi.it
The simple cotton and silk lingerie and sleepwear here is hard to beat for quality and price. The helpful staff will happily dismantle the shop to ensure you see the entire range.
✉ Via dei Calzaiuoli 99r, 50123 ☎ 055 230 2609 🕐 Daily 9.30–8 🚌 1, 6, 7, 10, 11, 14, 17, 23

LORETTA CAPONI
Loretta Caponi has cornered the market in Florentine lace and luxury embroidered linens. A lot of work goes into these pieces so be prepared to pay. There are exquisite clothes for young children and some beautiful lingerie.
✉ Piazza Antinori 4r, 50123 ☎ 055 213668 🕐 Tue–Sat 9–1, 3.30–7.30, Mon 3.30–7.30 🚌 A, 6, 11, 22, 23, 36, 37

MADOVA
www.madova.com
Madova have been making fine-quality leather gloves in every hue for nearly a century; they come in silk, fur, wool or cashmere lining and are reasonably priced.
✉ Via Guicciardini 1r, 50125 ☎ 055 239 6526 🕐 Mon–Sat 9.30–7 🚌 D, 36, 37

MAX & CO
The clothes at this subsidiary of MaxMara are usually variations of classics, but with a contemporary twist. Great for the sort of clothing you might wear at work.
✉ Via dei Calzaiuoli 89r, 50123 ☎ 055 288656 🕐 Mon–Sat 9–7.30, Sun 11–7 🚌 A

MERCATO CENTRALE
The outside stands are the place to buy leather—make sure it's made in Italy and always be prepared to bargain—as well as clothes and gifts. Inside is the real Mercato Centrale, a cavernous space full of mouthwatering Florentine delicacies. Feast your eyes on the fruit and vegetable stalls as well as the salumeria (delicatessen) counters brimming with meats and cheeses. There are also stands where you can get lunch. Credit cards are not accepted.
✉ Piazza del Mercato Centrale, San Lorenzo, 50123 🕐 Summer Mon–Sat 8.30–7; winter 8.30–2 🚌 4, 12, 25, 31, 32, 33

MERCATO DEI LIBERI ARTIGIANI
This market of free traders (liberi artigiani) sells clothes and jewellery. There are some superb bargains for those with the patience to search,

otherwise there's not that much. Credit cards are not accepted.

✉ Loggia del Grano, Via de Neri, 50122 ⏱ Thu 8–7 🚌 B, 23

MERCATO NUOVO (PORCELLINO)
Full of inexpensive reproductions of Florentine classics—great for gifts. The Italian leather bags and shoes are often a good buy. Look for the bronze boar, its snout polished to a shine by the attentions of visitors. Credit cards are not accepted.

✉ Loggia Mercato Nuovo, Via Porta Rossa, 50123 ⏱ Daily 9–7 🚌 A, 6, 11, 36, 37

MERCATO DELLE PULCI
This flea market is probably Florence's best, with all manner of household goods, antiques and vintage clothing, including second-hand designer clothes and plenty of shoes. Credit cards are not accepted.

✉ Piazza dei Ciompi, 50121 ⏱ Mon–Sat 8–7 🚌 A, 14

MERCATO DI SANT'AMBROGIO
If you are staying in the Santa Croce area, this is your local produce market, off Via de' Macci, but by the time you get there the real business will have been done by the early-risers. Bargain hunters prepared to haggle should check out the cheap clothing stalls. Credit cards are not accepted.

✉ Piazza Lorenzo Ghiberti, 50121 ⏱ Mon–Sat 7–2 🚌 A, C

MOLERIA LOCCHI
www.locchi.com
This shop is reminiscent of a museum, with the most extraordinary examples of glass you will see outside Venice—with prices to match—created using traditional methods.

✉ Via Domenico Burchiello 10, 50124 ☎ 055 229 8371 ⏱ Mon–Fri 8.30–1, 3–6 🚌 12, 13

MONACI DI LANURIO
Next door to the Ognissanti church, this lovely little shop sells organic food grown and produced by monks and fair-trade suppliers. Their *biscotti*, fruit juices, marmalade and tomato sauces all make good gifts.

✉ Borgo Ognissanti 44, 50123 ☎ 055 284727 ⏱ Mon–Fri 10–1, 4–7 🚌 A, B

MOSCARDI
Moscardi's wonderful frames hardly need a picture in them. There are also exquisite mirrors of varying sizes, some of which have been treated to give an antique look.

✉ Lungarno Corsini 36r, 50123 ☎ 055 214414 ⏱ Daily 9–1, 3.30–7.30. Closed Sat pm in summer, Mon am in winter. 🚌 B, 11, 36, 37

ORE DUE
www.oredue.it
This store close to the Uffizi produces jewellery using the same techniques as the original Florentine goldsmiths. Very traditional styles are set in 18-carat gold. Prices are not over the top considering the quality of the materials and craftsmanship.

✉ Via Lambertesca 12r, 50122 ☎ 055 292143 ⏱ Tue–Sat 9.30–7, Mon 3.30–7 🚌 B

ORNAMENTA
This little shop sells small amber rings and silver earrings. Great for those who want an inexpensive reminder of their trip. Credit cards are not accepted.

✉ Via Proconsolo 68, 50122 ☎ 055 292879 ⏱ Daily 9.30–8 🚌 A

Below *Women's fashion at Sisley (▷ 111)*

PAM
www.pamfirenze.it
Rather out of the way, but stocks a wide and impressive selection of bed linen, tablecloths and bath sets, made from damask, Irish linen, silk and perçale. Some are beautifully hand embroidered and everything is immaculately hand finished.

✉ Via Bartolommeo Scala 2r, 50126 ☎ 055 681 3375 ⏱ Mon–Fri 8.30–1, 3–7.30 🚌 3, 8, 23, 31, 31

PAPERBACK EXCHANGE
www.papex.it
Art and history books, both new and secondhand, are sold here. Trade in any books you've already read and take your pick from the out-of-print ones, including some in English.

✉ Via delle Oche 4r, 50122 ☎ 055 293460 ⏱ Sep–end Jun Mon–Fri 9–7.30, Sat 10–1, 3.30–7.30; Jul, Aug Mon–Fri 9–7.30, Sat 10–1. Closed 2 weeks in Aug 🚌 A, 14, 23

PARENTI
www.parentifirenze.it
Even people who say they don't like jewellery end up ooing and aahing at Parenti's eclectic mix of styles and shapes, ranging from art nouveau to 1970s glitz. And the fair prices mean you can indulge yourself.

✉ Via de' Tornabuoni 93r, 50123 ☎ 055 214438 ⏱ Tue–Sat 9.30–1, 3.30–7.30, Mon 3.30–7.30. Closed Aug 🚌 A, 6, 11, 22, 36, 37

Above There is a number of jewellery shops on the Ponte Vecchio

PASSAMANERIA TOSCANA
www.ptfsrl.com

A great place to pick up all those little Florentine decorative touches and flourishes. They have tassels, tiebacks, fringes, coats of arms and trims, as well as brocade cushions, damask runners and wall hangings. Check out their mosquito nets.
✉ Piazza San Lorenzo 12r, 50100 ☎ 055 214670 🕐 Daily 9.30–7.30 🚌 D

PASTICCERIA MARINO
If you are heading south of the river, pull in here for a pastry stop. There is a delicious selection of custard-, chocolate- and marmalade-filled *sfogliatelle*—pastry pockets, rounds and tubes. They also produce a memorable rum baba (a rich sponge cake soaked in rum syrup). Credit cards are not accepted.
✉ Piazza Nazario Sauro 19r, 50124 ☎ 055 212657 🕐 Daily 6am–8pm 🚌 6, 11, 36, 37

PEGNA
www.pegna.it

Florentines have flocked to this wonderful food shop, a city institution, in the pedestrian zone just south of the Duomo, since 1860. It sells tea, coffee and olive oil, plus wine, cheese and various other gastronomic treats from Italy and around the world.
✉ Via dello Studio 26r ☎ 055 282701/2 🕐 Mon–Tue, Thu–Sat 9–1, 3.30–7.30, Wed 9–1 (also in summer open Wed pm, closed Sat pm) 🚌 1, 7 and other services to Piazza del Duomo

PIANEGONDA
www.pianegondaitalia.com

This silversmith uses twinkling amethysts, topaz and moonstones alongside bold, sometimes theatrical styles. The pieces are ultramodern but don't lack feminine charm, and prices are reasonable.
✉ Via dei Calzaiuoli 96r, 50123 ☎ 055 214941 🕐 Mon–Sat 10–7, Sun 2–7 🚌 A

PINEIDER
www.pineider.it

Used by Napoleon Bonaparte, Lord Byron and Marlene Dietrich, Pineider's beautifully crafted tinted papers and inks have been prized since the late 18th century. Also exquisite leather-bound notebooks and desk accessories.
✉ Piazza della Signoria 13r, 50122 ☎ 055 284655 🕐 Mon–Sat 10–7, Sun 10–2, 3–7. Closed 2 weeks in Aug 🚌 23

PRINCIPE
www.principedifirenze.com

Mature customers are the target at this decidedly old-fashioned store. But any generation will appreciate the classic Italian home and kitchen ware.
✉ Via del Sole 2, 50123 ☎ 055 292764 🕐 Tue–Sat 9.30–7.30, Mon 10.30–7.30 (also Sep–end Jun last Sun of each month) 11–7.30 🚌 A, 6, 11, 36, 37

PUCCI
www.emiliopucci.com

Exuberant and hugely distinctive prints prevail here. Separates, silk shirts, dresses, shoes, scarves and accessories are all superb, but very pricey. Pucci style devotees can even buy or order a chair or carpet. The couture collection can be seen at Palazzo Pucci, Via de' Pucci 6.
✉ Via de' Tornabuoni 20–22r, 50123 ☎ 055 294028 🕐 Mon–Sat 10–7, last Sun of month 2–7 🚌 A, 6, 11, 22, 36, 37

QUELLE TRE
www.quelletre.it

While some of the clothes border on the bohemian, the wealth of shades, textures and shapes makes this shop a superb find for individual dressers and those looking to enliven a sober wardrobe.
✉ Via de' Pucci 43r, 50123 ☎ 055 293284 🕐 Tue–Sat 11–1.30, 2–7, Mon 3.30–7.30 🚌 1, 6, 7, 10, 11, 14, 17, 23

LA RINASCENTE
www.rinascente.it

This classy department store drips designer labels, which extend to the bedding department as well as men's and women's fashion. The cosmetics and perfume counter stocks exclusive Italian brands unavailable back home.
✉ Piazza della Repubblica 1, 50123 ☎ 055 219113 🕐 Mon–Sat 10–9, Sun 10.30–8 🚌 A, 6

ROMANO
www.romanofirenze.com

Romano sells a huge variety of shoes, boots and sandals for both men and women and catering to all ages: You'll see trendy young Florentines trying on kitten heels next to matrons looking at shoes seemingly from a bygone age.
✉ Via degli Speziali 10r, 50123 ☎ 055 216535 🕐 Tue–Sat 10.30–7.30, Mon 3.30–7.30 (also Sep–end Apr Sun 11–7.30) 🚌 A

SALVATORE FERRAGAMO
www.ferragamo.it

Perhaps the leading brand in Italian shoes and bags, Ferragamo is expensive. But the styles are timeless and made to last, so you should think of a Ferragamo as an investment. To find out about the legend behind the shoes, visit the Museo Salvatore Ferragamo (▷ 82).
✉ Via de' Tornabuoni 16r, 50123 ☎ 055 292123 🕐 Mon–Sat 10–7.30, Sun 2–7 🚌 B, 6, 11, 36, 37

SANTO SPIRITO
Right across from the church of the same name, this store is worth a visit for some of the most beautiful antique Florentine frames you're likely to find, restored on the premises. New frames are also made. Credit cards are not accepted.
✉ Piazza Santo Spirito 17r, 50125 ☎ 055 239 8139 🕐 Mon–Fri 8.30–12.30, 3–7, Sat 8.30–12.30 🚌 D, 11, 36, 37

SANTO SPIRITO

There are stands daily at Santo Spirito, selling bedding, shoes, clothing and haberdashery, but the Sunday markets are particularly worth visiting. On the second Sunday of the month there's an ethnic flea market, while the third Sunday is devoted to organic foods, clothing and herbal remedies. Credit cards are not accepted.

✉ Piazza Santo Spirito, 50125 🕐 2nd and 3rd Sun of the month 8–6 🚌 D, 11, 36, 37

SCRIPTORIUM

www.scriptoriumfirenze.com

Those who reject ballpoints and palmtops can step back in time at Scriptorium. Leather-bound notebooks, thick quality papers and a huge variety of quills, inks and waxes are sold to clients with an eye for tradition and quality.

✉ Via dei Servi 5/7r, 50122 ☎ 055 211804 🕐 Mon–Sat 10–2, 3.30–7.30 🚌 7, 10, 14, 23

SCUOLA DI CUOLO DI SANTA CROCE

www.leatherschool.it

Come to this workshop, at the back of the Santa Croce church, to learn how to spot quality and craftsmanship in leather working. If you make a purchase at the on-site shop, they'll personalize the goods for you with a stamp.

✉ Piazza Santa Croce 16, 50122 ☎ 055 244533 🕐 Apr–end Oct Mon–Sat 9–6, Sun 10.30–4.30 🚌 B, C, 23

SISLEY

www.sisley.it

Italian Sisley has a wider selection of stock than their counterparts outside Italy, and tend to be less expensive. The Benetton subsidiary has a wide range of separates and accessories, as well as a number of the season's unmissable buys.

✉ Via de' Cerretani 53r, 50123 ☎ 055 210683 🕐 Mon–Sat 9–8, Sun 11–8 🚌 A

STANDA

Standa sells all the sorts of things you need on holiday—shorts, beach towels, picnic baskets—all under one roof and at low prices.

✉ Via Pietrapiana 42/44r, 50122 ☎ 055 234 7856 🕐 Mon–Sat 8–9, Sun 9–9 🚌 A, 14

UMBERTO LEATHER

www.umbertoleather.com

Close to the glove shop Madova is Umberto Leather. Excellent for robust but classic satchels and briefcases that last a lifetime.

✉ Via Guicciardini 114r, 50125 ☎ 055 293091 🕐 Mon–Sat 9–7 🚌 D, 36, 37

VALLI

Valli's shop window showcases fabrics designed by Valentino, Armani and others. It has a very luxurious array of gleaming and plush fabrics, most of which you can't find back home.

✉ Via degli Strozzi 4r, 50123 ☎ 055 282485 🕐 Tue–Sat 9.30–7 (Jul, Aug closed 1–3.30), Mon 3–7 🚌 A, 6, 11, 22, 36, 37

VALMAR

www.valmar-florence.com

This store is like a big sewing box, with ribbons, trims and buttons tumbling out of trays and baskets. It takes time to work your way through everything, but you're sure to find some unique bits and bobs for great finishing touches. You can even take in your own fabric and they will create something for you.

✉ Via Porta Rossa 53r, 50123 ☎ 055 284493 🕐 Mon–Sat 9–7.30 🚌 A, 6, 11, 36, 37

ENTERTAINMENT AND NIGHTLIFE

AMICI DELLA MUSICA

www.amicimusica.fi.it

The prestigious Teatro della Pergola (▷ 115) hosts regular classical concerts by the Amici della Musica organization. Leading musicians from around the world appear in the grandiose Sala Grande and the more intimate Saloncino della Pergola during the concert season (Oct–end Mar).

✉ Via Pier Capponi 41, 50121 ☎ 055 607440 or 055 608420 ✋ €15–€20 🚌 C, 14, 23

ASTOR CAFFÈ

The sleek contemporary glass-and-chrome appearance of this bar in the shadow of the Duomo may be at odds with its historic surroundings, but it makes a perfect place for a coffee or light lunch by day (there are often art exhibitions), while in the evenings there's occasional live music downstairs by the bar and you can eat dinner or sip cocktails upstairs.

✉ Piazza del Duomo 20r ☎ 055 284305 🕐 Daily 10am–2am 🚌 All services to Piazza del Duomo

AUDITORIUM FLOG

www.flog.it

This is Florence's best alternative music venue. As well as Italian indie acts like 99 Posse, the Flog attracts some well-known international artists and many tribute bands. Every night there is something different: from rock 'n' roll to ska and reggae to electronic trance.

✉ Via Michele Mercati 24b, 50139 ☎ 055 487145 🕐 Tue–Sun 9.30pm–2am ✋ €5–€25 🚌 4, 8, 14

BASILICA DI SAN LORENZO

www.filarmonicarossini.it

It may have changed quite a few times since its consecration in AD393, but the church of San Lorenzo remains one of the most evocative places in the city to hear classical music. The celebrated home-grown orchestra, the Filarmonica di Firenze Gioacchino Rossini, regularly plays here.

✉ Piazza San Lorenzo 9, 50123 ☎ 055 216634 ✋ Free 🚌 1, 6, 7, 10, 11, 17

BATTISTERO DI SAN GIOVANNI

www.operaduomo.firenze.it

Florence's Baptistery makes a wonderful setting for classical concerts. Look out especially for events organized by the O flos colende orchestra. The Musicus Concentus organization occasionally puts on more innovative concerts.

✉ Piazza San Giovanni, 50123 ☎ 055 230 2885 ✋ Free 🚌 1, 6, 11, 14, 17, 23

BLOB CLUB

www.theblobclub.com

Grab a sofa upstairs to get the best view of the live music action below. If you prefer hot and sweaty jumping, then join the throng on the floor swaying and nodding to the mainly rock cover bands.

✉ Via Vinegia 21r, 50122 ☎ 055 211209 🕐 Daily 6pm–2am ✋ Annual membership €10, taken out on door 🚌 23

CAFFÈ CONCERTO PASZKOWSKI

In the summer, the seating outside this bar is swamped with locals. Where once this was the meeting place of the 19th-century intelligentsia, it's now the domain of the well-groomed Florentine.

✉ Piazza della Repubblica 31–35r, 50123 ☎ 055 210236 🕐 Tue–Sun 7am–1am 🚌 A, 6, 22

CAFFÈ MEGARA

Vistors and locals alike make good use of this central café-bar at lunch (noon–3pm). By night, it's a good spot to sit inside (or outside in summer) with a drink.

✉ Via della Spada 15–17r ☎ 055 211837 🕐 Daily 8am–2am

CAFFÈ NOTTE

There are plenty of board games to occupy you in this Oltrarno café-bar. The jovial staff are happy to recommend one of their fine grappas, or create a lethal cocktail before your increasingly bleary eyes. Credit cards are not accepted.

✉ Via delle Caldaie 28r, 50125 ☎ 055 223067 🕐 Mon–Sat 8am–2am. Closed Aug 🚌 D, 11, 36, 37

CAFFÈ LA TORRE

www.caffelatorre.it

After a few apéritifs and some free nibbles, try some of this trendy, art-filled café's cocktails while soaking up the eclectic live music. Expect anything from smooth samba to drum and bass two-step between 7.30 and midnight. The Sunday brunch menu is well worth sampling.

✉ Lungarno Cellini 65r, 50125 ☎ 055 680643 🕐 Daily 11am–3am ✋ Free 🚌 12, 13, 23

CARACOL

www.cafecaracol.com

Tequila is one of the specialties of this South American-style bar. Happy hour is popular here, but there's not much in the way of seating, so treat this as a good place to start the evening before moving on, rather than a place to unwind after a day of sightseeing.

✉ Via dei Ginori 10r ☎ 055 211427 🕐 Tue–Thu, Sun 6pm–1.30am, Fri–Sat 6pm–2.30am 🚌 1, 6, 11, 17 to Via Cavour

CARUSO JAZZ CAFÉ

www.carusojazzcafe.com

Accomplished and often well-known Italian and international jazz musicians perform at this large, brick-vaulted bar and club not far from the Duomo, usually on Thursday and Friday nights.

✉ Via Lambertesca 14–16r ☎ 055 281940 🕐 Mon–Sat 10am–3.30, 6–12 ✋ Usually free, but admission for some events 🚌 A, B

CENTRAL PARK

This is a house-music complex, complete with garden, eight bars, four dance floors, restaurant and a VIP terrace. Italian house dominates but there's also plenty of room for lounge and smooth piano-bar music.

✉ Via del Fosso Macinate, 2, 50144 ☎ 055 353505 🕐 Summer Tue–Sat 11pm–4am; winter Fri–Sat 11pm–4am ✋ €17, free for visitors (show your passport) and students 🚌 1, 9, 12, 80

CHIESA DI SANTA MARIA

If you would like to sample Florentine organ music, then this is the place to visit. A wonderfully evocative setting in which to hear music similar to that heard by Dante here in the 13th century.

✉ Via del Corso, 50122 ☎ 333 307 4339 ✋ From €5 🚌 A, 14

CINEHALL ODEON

www.cinehall.it

To avoid the frustrating (if comic) experience of seeing an English-speaking film dubbed into Italian, head to the Cinehall Odeon. Films are regularly shown here with their original soundtrack intact.

English-language films are usually shown on Mondays, Wednesdays and Thursdays Reduced prices on Wednesday and in the afternoons.

✉ Piazza degli Strozzi 2, 50123 ☎ 055 295051/295337 ✋ €5–€7.50 🚌 A, 6, 11, 22, 36, 37

CINEMA FULGOR

www.staseraalcinema.it/cinemafulgor

This wonderful art deco cinema is between Ognissanti and the banks of the Arno. It's a great place to watch the likes of Robert De Niro (usually dubbed) amid the 1930s cinema surroundings.

✉ Via Maso Finiguerra 24r, 50123 ☎ 055 238 1881 ✋ €5–€7 🚌 A, 11, 36, 37

CLUB MONTECARLA

Exotic leopard-skin patterned upholstery, chintz and belle-époque furnishings give this unique club a sophisticated kitsch vibe. Drink mojitos and other cocktails, amid bright cushions and peculiar artworks. Drinks are a little pricey but the friendly atmosphere wins you over. Credit cards are not accepted.

✉ Via de' Bardi 2, 50125 ☎ 055 234 0259 🕐 Sun–Thu 9.30pm–5am, Fri, Sat 9pm–5am ✋ Members only, membership available for €5 on door 🚌 C, D

CRISCO

This is one of Florence's leading gay clubs, near the Duomo in Santa Croce. This is a city famed for its cross-dressing, so expect the most glamorous transvestites you've ever seen. Credit cards are not accepted.

✉ Via Sant'Egidio 43r, 50122 ☎ 055 248 0580 🕐 Sun–Mon, Wed–Thu 10.30pm–3am, Fri–Sat 10.30pm–6am ✋ Varies 🚌 A, 14, 23

DOLCE VITA

One of the trendy places where young Florentines go, in the Oltrarno district. A great place for a refreshing *aperitivo* or a cocktail and to mingle with the pre-club beautiful people.

✉ Piazza del Carmine 5, 50124 ☎ 055 284595 🕐 Summer Mon–Sat 5pm–2am, Sun 6pm–2am; winter Tue–Sat 5pm–2am, Sun 6pm–2am 🚌 D, 6

Above *Classical concerts take place at Palazzo Pitti and the Giardino di Boboli*

ESTATE FIESOLANA

www.estatefiesolana.it
Sunset concerts and operatic productions are held at the Teatro Romano in the Fiesole hills above Florence, a cool, tranquil venue during the heat of summer.

✉ Piazza del Mercato 5, Fiesole, 50014 Firenze ☎ 055 597 8303/800 41 42 43 🕐 Jun–end Sep 👍 From €20 🚌 7

FIDDLER'S ELBOW

The original Florentine Irish pub, popular with students and visitors. Gulp the best Guinness in town and catch up on the soccer action on the widescreen TVs.

✉ Piazza Santa Maria Novella 7a, 50123 ☎ 055 215056 🕐 Fri–Sat noon–2am, Sun–Thu noon–1am 🚌 A, 1, 14, 17, 36, 37

FULL-UP

Clubs in Florence come and go, but Full-Up, like Yab (▷ 115) and Meccano (▷ 114), seems to go on for ever. It owes its popularity in part to the convenient location, near Santa Croce, but also to its friendly staff, good music and various themed nights.

✉ Via della Vigna Vecchia 23r ☎ 055 293006 🕐 Tue–Sat 11pm–4am. Closed Jun–Sep 👍 Free 🚌 B, C

GIARDINO DI BOBOLI

During the summer months, the wonderful Palazzo Pitti courtyard and the Giardino di Boboli, once occupied by the Medici and the alleged setting for Boccaccio's

Decameron, becomes the backdrop for ballet and classical concerts.

✉ Piazza de' Pitti, 50121 ☎ 055 211158 👍 Prices vary 🚌 D, 11, 36, 37

GIRASOL

www.girasol.it
You can hear live Latin music most nights in this colourful bar, and benefit from the occasional free tango and samba lessons from local dance schools. Exotic, if rather expensive drinks, add to the Latin character. There's also a pizzeria for topping up energy levels.

✉ Via del Romito 1 ☎ 055 474948 🕐 Tue–Sun 7 or 8pm–2am 🚌 14

JARAGUA

www.jaragua.it
Italy's first exclusively Latino music club is a lot of fun. The spicy South American food also makes it popular. If you don't know how to dance salsa or merengue, there are lessons available as well as many willing tutors on the dance floor. Credit cards are not accepted.

✉ Via Erta Canina 12r, 50125 ☎ 055 234 3600 🕐 Daily 9.30pm–3am 👍 Free 🚌 C, D

JAZZ CLUB

www.jazzclubfirenze.com
If you like live jazz and a relaxed vibe, head for this central Florence club. Shows start at 10.15pm. Credit cards are not accepted.

✉ Via Nuova de' Caccini 3, 50121 ☎ 055 247 9700 🕐 Fri–Wed 9pm–2am, Thu 7pm–2am. Closed Jun–end Sep 👍 Annual membership €7.50, taken out on door 🚌 C, 14, 23

KIKUYA

www.kikuyapub.it
Drink pints of beer while soaking up the English pub atmosphere in this ever-popular central haunt. Kikuya shows widescreen soccer and serves decent sandwiches. Happy hour is 7–10pm, except on Saturday. The cocktails are particularly generous. Also hosts occasional live music. Credit cards are not accepted.

✉ Via de' Benci 43r, 50122 ☎ 055 234 4879 🕐 Daily 6pm–2am 🚌 B, C, 23

LOONEES

www.loonees.it
The understated entrance hints at hidden depths, which the friendly basement bar delivers. The bands mainly play American and British classic covers that the international crowd laps up. Credit cards are not accepted.

✉ Via Porta Rossa 15, 50123 🕐 Tue–Sun 10pm–3am. Closed Aug 👍 Free 🚌 A, 6, 11, 36, 37

MARACANA

www.maracana.it
Six levels, a carnival stage and a party crowd make this vibrant club popular with lovers of all things Brazilian. It's the place to watch carnival dancers, to samba and sip caipirinhas (the classic Brazilian cocktail of ice, lime, sugar and Caçasa). The bar staff juggle bottles while some of the crowd attempt dance-floor acrobatics.

✉ Via Faenza 4r, 50123 ☎ 055 210298 🕐 Tue–Sun 8.30pm–4am 👍 €10–€20 🚌 31, 32

MAYDAY

Locals swarm around this bar. Live guitar-based acts take the stage from around midnight into the early hours. Credit cards are not accepted.
✉ Via Dante Alighieri 16r, 50122 ☎ 055 238 1290 🕙 Mon–Sat 8pm–2am 💷 Free 🚌 A, 14, 23

MECCANO

www.meccanofirenze.com
Meccano offers a predictable but fun selection of house and other dance music, and is currently one of the city's more popular clubs.
✉ Via degli Olmi 1, 50144 ☎ 055 331371 🕙 Wed–Sat 9pm–4am 💷 €15 🚌 1, 9, 12, 13, 16, 26, 27, 80

MEZZANOTTE E DINTORNI

Come here for an early evening drink or one of the house's divine cocktails. The friendly staff will also serve you substantial tasty meat and vegetable dishes to fill the stomach for the night ahead.
✉ Via Kassel 9, 50126 ☎ 055 653 1651 🕙 Mon–Sat 7am–2am (also Sep–end Jun Sun 6pm–1am) 🚌 3, 8, 23

MULTISALA VARIETY

www.staseraalcinema.it/cinemavariety
There are five screens in this modern multiplex. The Variety has the latest sound system in the large Sala Sole. There is a discount ticket on Wednesday and on weekday afternoons.
✉ Via del Madonnone 84r, 50100 ☎ 055 677902 💷 €5–€7 🚌 14, 34

MUSICUS CONCENTUS

www.musicusconcentus.com
Musicus Concentus pushes the boundaries of contemporary jazz with its innovative concerts. Expect everything and anything from classical and world music to the latest electronic wizardry.
✉ Sala Vanni, Piazza del Carmine 19, 50124 ☎ 055 287347 🕙 See wesbite for details 💷 €15 🚌 D

OFFICINA MOVE BAR

A good choice for some snacks and late-night alcohol-fuelled fun if you plan to be in the Porta a Prato quarter. Subtle lighting and intimate seating arrangements set the scene for a flirtatious adventure. Credit cards are not accepted.
✉ Via Il Prato 58r, 50123 ☎ 055 210399 🕙 Daily 3pm–3am 🚌 1, 2, 9, 17, 27, 29 30, 35

PALASPORT FIRENZE

www.boxoffice.it
This medium-sized venue near Campo Marte hosts some of Italy's most celebrated rock/pop acts. Check in advance for well-known British and American bands who may be swinging into the Palasport.
✉ Viale Pasquale Paoli 1, 50137 ☎ 055 661497/8 🕙 See wesbite for details 💷 €20–€65 🚌 3, 10

PINOCCHIO LIVE JAZZ

www.pinocchiojazz.it
Jazz fans will love this place where some of Italy's top artists can be

heard. Members nod approvingly in this smoky venue while the musicians play their instruments into the night.
✉ Viale Giannotti 13, 50126 ☎ 055 683388 🕙 Nov to mid-Apr Sat 10pm–3am 💷 €9 for membership fee, plus €8 entrance fee 🚌 31, 32

PORFIRIO RUBIROSA

This elegant café-bar is popular with young Florentines and business people. Sit back, sip one of their tempting cocktails and watch the locals at play.
✉ Viale degli Strozzi, 18r, 50123 ☎ 055 490965 🕙 Mon–Sat 7pm–2am 🚌 A, 6, 22

REX CAFÉ

www.rexcafe.it
This popular bar has a spellbinding interior of retro lighting and paint-splashed walls, as well as some eye-catching, constantly changing art exhibits. The global house music complements the array of drinks from around the world, which include mojitos (mint, lime juice, rum and soda) and Green Days (kiwi fruit, vodka and soda). Credit cards are not accepted.
✉ Via Fiesolana 25r, 50122 ☎ 055 248 0331 🕙 Daily 6.30pm–3am. Closed mid-May to mid-Sep 🚌 A, C, 14, 23

SANTO STEFANO

www.orcafi.it
The Orchestra da Camera Fiorentina stage many of their seasonal concerts at Orsanmichele or this church by the Ponte Vecchio. As might be expected from a chamber orchestra, concerts frequently feature works by Vivaldi, Haydn, Bach and Mozart.
✉ Piazza Santo Stefano, 50122 ☎ 055 783374/055 210804 💷 €15–€20 🚌 B

SASCHALL

www.saschall.it
Florence's leading music venue hosts big-name rock/pop acts and well-known musicals. Expect to see international artists like Tori Amos

Left *Jazz music is a popular choice at the city's bars and clubs*

as well as Italian stars. Check the website for the latest events. ✉ Lungarno Aldo Moro 3, 50136 ☎ 055 650 4112 ◉ Performances usually start 9pm 💶 €5–€45 🚍 3, 14, 31, 32, 34

SCUOLA MUSICA DI FIESOLE
www.scuolamusica.fiesole.fi.it
Fiesole's music school is one of Italy's most celebrated, and its resident orchestra, the Orchestra Giovanile Italiana, is the country's leading youth ensemble. The school's annual open day, the Festa della Musica, is held at the end of June, with concerts and workshops. The Concerti per gli Amici concert cycle takes place between September (or October) and June in the school's 200-seat auditorium. ✉ Villa La Torracia, Via delle Fontinelle 24, San Domenico, Fiesole ☎ 055 597851 💶 Ticket prices vary 🚍 7

SHOT CAFÉ
A great place to start a night out near the Duomo. Not surprisingly, this bar has a wide range of shots to knock back. Visitors and party animals get here early, as there are cheap drinks between 5 and 8pm. Credit cards are not accepted. ✉ Via dei Pucci 5a, 50123 ☎ 055 282093 ◉ Daily 7am–2am 🚍 8, 12, 14, 33

SLOWLY CAFÉ
This relaxing contemporary bar is full of vibrant decorative touches. The easy-listening and chilled music sounds complement the subdued lighting and all-round welcoming vibe. There's a wide selection of cocktails at the bar and very good fish dishes served in the dining area. ✉ Via Porta Rossa 63r, 50123 ☎ 055 264 5354 ◉ Mon–Sat 12–3pm, 7pm–2am 🚍 6, 11, 36 37

TEATRO COMUNALE
www.maggiofiorentino.com
Il Teatro Comunale is Florence's major venue for all things orchestral, balletic and operatic. The winter concert season is January through March; opera and ballet season is September through March. Expect popular operatic and ballet repertoire

and a wide range of concert works by seminal composers from Bach to Wagner. ✉ Corso Italia 16, 50123 ☎ 055 27791; 055 213535 (ticket office); 199 112 112 call centre (Italy); +39 0424 600 458 (abroad) 💶 €22–€150 🚍 A, B

TEATRO GOLDONI
www.maggiofiorentino.com
This famous old theatre, with seating for 1,500, hosts opera and ballet, as well as various classical concerts. ✉ Via Santa Maria 12, 50125 ☎ 055 233 5518 💶 €30–€50 🚍 11, 36, 37

TEATRO VERDI
www.orchestradellatoscana.it
www.teatroverdifirenze.it
This is the home of the Orchestra della Toscana, which covers a broad repertoire of classical music, from baroque to contemporary. The theatre also hosts many other concerts by musicians of international repute, most notably during the *Maggio Musicale Fiorentino* (▷ 117). ✉ Via Ghibellina 99, 50122 ☎ 055 212320 💶 €10–€15 🚍 A, 14, 23

TEATRO DELLA LIMONAIA
www.teatrodellalimonaia.it
Fresh, edgy, contemporary productions are the mainstay of the Limonaia. Alongside quality theatrical collaborations with the likes of the National Theatre in London, the venue also holds various classical concerts amid the lush park surroundings. ✉ Via Gramsci 426, Sesto Fiorentino, 50019 ☎ 055 440852 💶 €10–€15 🚍 2, 28a

TEATRO LE LAUDI
Alongside classic literary plays and classical concerts, this theatre also stages family-friendly productions like *Le Avventure di Pinocchio* (The Adventures of Pinocchio) and *Cappuccetto Rosso* (Little Red Riding Hood). ✉ Via Leonardo da Vinci 2r, 50132 ☎ 055 572831 💶 €8–€15 🚍 10, 11, 13, 17, 20, 33

TEATRO DELLA PERGOLA
www.pergola.firenze.it
Well-known theatre productions are regularly held in the sumptuous main hall and the elegant Saloncino, its second hall. As well as staging Italian classics by the likes of D'Annunzio and De Filippo, English-, Irish- and French-language playwrights, including Oscar Wilde, Steven Berkoff, Victor Hugo and Georges Feydeau, are also showcased. ✉ Via della Pergola 12/32, 50121 ☎ 055 226 4316 💶 €15–€20 🚍 C, 14, 23

TEATRO PUCCINI
www.teatropuccini.it
If you wish to improve your knowledge of the Italian language and culture, this is ideal. The Puccini has a full schedule of theatrical productions, which have included the satirical monologues of Paolo Hendel and the classic comedies. 💶 €12–€23 🚍 30, 35

TENAX
www.tenax.org
This is Florence's premier house-music club, attracting big international names like Dimitri from Paris, Thievery Corporation, Grace Jones and the UK's Groove Armada. As a superclub, it has amazing lighting and sound technology, as well as some very curious art installations. Also hosts various live music acts. ✉ Via Pratese 46, 50127 ☎ 055 308160 ◉ Thu–Sat 11pm–4am (plus concerts) 💶 €20–€25 🚍 5, 29, 30, 56

YAB
www.yab.it
Theatrical surroundings and renowned DJs make this one of Florence's most fashionable clubs. House music dominates, with hard house on Fridays and happy house on Saturdays. Monday's Smoove Night sees hip-hop tunes and electric acrobatics on the dance floor. Credit cards are not accepted. ✉ Via Sassetti 5, 50122 ☎ 055 215160 ◉ Mon–Tue, Thu–Sat 11pm–4am. Closed Jun–end Sep 💶 €15 🚍 A, 1, 6, 14

SPORTS AND ACTIVITIES
AZIMUT GROUP
www.azimut.fi.it

For outdoor adventure in the Tuscan hills or farther afield, the Azimut group is a good port of call to arrange mountain walking or climbing. They also run alpine skiing and mountain biking trips. Credit cards are not accepted.

✉ La Casa del Popolo 25 aprile, Via Bronzino 117, 50142 ☎ 055 700460 🕐 Telephone calls only Mon–Fri 4–10pm 🖐 Membership: Adult €13, child €6 🚌 6, 26, 27, 80

BALLOONING IN TUSCANY
www.ballooningintuscany.com

This small (English-speaking) company organizes personalized balloon trips for groups of four with champagne breakfast. It's an hour's drive south of Florence but the views are worth it.

✉ Podere La Fratta, 53020 Montisi ☎ 0577 845211 🕐 Contact for details 🖐 €200 (minimum 4 adults) 🚌 A1 towards Siena, Montisi exit

BASKET FIRENZE
www.firenzebasket.net

I Biancorossi (The White and Reds) of Basket Firenze play their home games here, competing in the second flight of the Italian men's league. Credit cards are not accepted.

✉ Palazzetto S. Marcellino, Via Chiantigiana, 50126 ☎ 055 436 0301 🕐 Sun 6.30pm 🖐 Free 🚌 31, 32

CANOTTIERI COMUNALI FIRENZE
www.canottiericomunalifirenze.it

Try your hand at canoeing, boating and rowing at this club on the River Arno. As well as kayaking sessions, there are a number of other courses available. There's also the chance to try dragon boating, Polynesian canoeing or canoe polo.

✉ Lungarno Ferrucci 4, 50126 ☎ 055 681 2151/681 2649 🕐 Mon–Sat 8.30am–9pm, Sun 8.30–1; ring the information number for the latest details about upcoming courses and other activities 🖐 Joining fee €100 🚌 8, 31, 32

LE CASINE
www.softvision.it

The Ippodromo delle Mulina is the place to go and see horse racing in Florence. If you feel like placing a bet on the *galoppo* (flat racing) or *trotto* (chariot racing) many *tabbachi* (tobacconists) have easy-to-use betting facilities.

✉ Ippodromo delle Mulina, Viale dell' Aeronautica/Viale del Pegaso 1, 50144 ☎ 055 436 9280 🕐 Race season is Jun, Jul, Nov–end Mar 🖐 Free 🚌 17c

CENTRO SPORTIVO DLF
Le Cascine's sports complex, in the largest park in Florence, has nine tennis courts. These can be booked up to three days ahead.

✉ Via Paisiello 131, 51144 ☎ 055 363052 🕐 Daily 8am–11pm 🖐 Outdoor court €9.50; indoor €15.50

CLUB MONTELUPO
www.golfmontelupo.it

This par 36, 9-hole course lies below the Chianti Montalbano hills on the banks of the Arno. Enjoy the wonderful scenery and the excellent facilities, which include a pro shop, practice area and putting greens. Coaching is available: one half-hour lesson costs €22 or six lessons cost €90.

✉ Via Le Piagge 4, 50056 Fibbiana, Montelupo Fiorentino ☎ 0571 541004 🕐 Daily 9am–dusk 🖐 €35 for 9 holes 🚌 Take the Firenze-Pisa-Livorno expressway and leave at Montelupo Fiorentino or Empoli Est exit. Look for directions to Fibbiana

FIORENTINA
www.fiorentina.it

Watch the reborn Viola (the team's kit is violet) at the 47,000-capacity Stadio Comunale Artemio Franchi (named in remembrance of the ex-Fiorentina director). Soccer is the sport in Italy, so expect fervent support from locals for the club, which is once again riding high in Serie A. Credit cards are not accepted.

✉ Viale Manfredo Fanti 14, 50137 ☎ 055 262 5537 🕐 Alternate Sun, Sep–end May 🖐 €5 🚌 3, 10, 11, 17, 20, 34

ICE SKATING IN THE CITY
In December and January each year, a temporary ice rink is constructed in Piazza Santa Croce or the Fortezza da Basso. As you glide around you can admire the magnificent palaces or the imposing fortress.

✉ Piazza Santa Croce, 50122/ Fortezza da Basso, 50129 🕐 Dec, Jan 🖐 €5 🚌 C, 12, 14, 23, 28, 33, 80

PALLAVOLO FIRENZE
Women's volleyball *(pallavolo)* can be seen at Palazzetto dello Sport in Campo di Marte. Italy has some top-rank players and the game has an enthusiastic following, so check ticket availability in advance. Credit cards are not accepted.

✉ Palestra Paolo Valenti, Via Taddeo Alberotti 26, 50139 ☎ 055 896 9042 🕐 Alternate Sun, Oct–end May 🖐 Free 🚌 8, 14, 28

HEALTH AND BEAUTY
CELSUS
For a total overhaul, book a day at Celsus. They will buff, massage and smooth you towards perfection. Their lash-tinting and brow-shaping is particularly recommended.

✉ Viale Gramsci 27r, 50125 ☎ 055 234 2733 🕐 Mon–Fri 9–6 🖐 Body treatments from €50; eyelash tints from €20 🚌 C, D

COIFFEUR RENATO
www.renatocoiffeur.com

This is one of Florence's smartest hairdressers and the perfect place to come for a treat. The interior of the salon is a stylish mix of old and contemporary and the experienced staff are charming and professional.

✉ Via San Gallo 199r, 50129 ☎ 055 483548 🕐 Tue–Sat 9–6 🖐 €20 for a blow-dry 🚌 1, 7, 8, 13, 25, 33

GENNY
Where better to be pampered than the beautiful Palazzo Pucci. You can enjoy shiatsu massage, hydromassage, hydrotherapy, reflexology and a variety of beauty treatments for face, body and nails.

✉ Via de' Pucci 4, 50122 ☎ 055 214823 🕐 Mon–Fri 9–7, Sat 9–1 🖐 Back massage €40 🚌 4, 23

KLAB WELLNESS CENTRE
www.klab.it
Even if you don't feel like a session
on an exercise bike, you can enjoy a
hydro- massage before slipping into
the Turkish bath. A Scottish shower,
targeted jets of alternating hot and
cold water (effective in the battle
against cellulite) is also available.
✉ Via Giambattista Lulli 62a, 50144
☎ 055 718 4300 ⓘ Mon–Fri 9am–
10.30pm, Sat 10–6, Sun 10–2 ✋ Hydro
massage from €25 🚌 22, 23, 33

OFFICINA PROFUMO
www.smnovella.it
This pharmacy, established by
Dominican friars in the 1220s, was
opened to the public in 1612. The
formulae of some of its better-
known preparations, such as the
Pasta di Mandorle (almond hand-
cream) and perfumes, date back to
the days of Catherine de' Medici.
You can also buy from its wide range
of luxury cosmetics.
✉ Via della Scala 16, 50123 ☎ 055
216276 ⓘ Mon–Sat 9.30–7.30, Sun
10.30–6.30 ✋ Almond hand-cream from
€20 🚌 A, 6, 11, 36, 37

FOR CHILDREN
GIARDINO DI BOBOLI
▷ 69.

GIARDINO DEI SEMPLICI
www.unifi.it/giardino/
Laid out between 1545 and
1546 this is the third-oldest
botanical garden in the world. The
greenhouses are home to tropical
flowers and plants, ferns, palms,
orchids and citrus trees. It's a great
place to let the kids loose in.
✉ Via Micheli 3, 50121 ☎ 055 275 402
ⓘ Mon–Tue, Thu–Fri, Sat 9–5, Sun 9–1
✋ Adult €4, child (6–14) €2, under 6 free
🚌 1, 7, 25

MUSEO DEI RAGAZZI
www.museoragazzi.it
Florence's interactive children's
museum runs activities in English
on weekends. The main themes are
Renaissance life, with workshops
explaining how the palazzo was built;
a chance to play with lenses and test

FESTIVALS AND EVENTS

MARCH/APRIL
SCOPPIO DEL CARRO
Florence's *Scoppio del Carro*
(Explosion of the Cart) dates
back to the 11th century, when
a carousel of fireworks was lit to
spread the good news of Easter.
A ceremonial cart stuffed with
incendiaries is wheeled into Piazza
del Duomo, and a wire is run to
the statue of the Virgin on top of
the Duomo and into the cathedral.
At about 11pm the wire is lit and
a mechanical dove slides down to
the cart, causing an explosion that
ignites the fireworks.
ⓘ Easter Sunday

MAY/JUNE
MAGGIO MUSICALE
FIORENTINO
www.maggiofiorentino.it
This is Florence's major music
festival, held at indoor and outdoor
venues across the city. Founded
in 1933, it's Italy's longest-running
music festival with a good mix of
opera, ballet and classical music.
✉ Teatro Comunale, Corso Italia 16,
50123 ☎ 055 213535 or 199 112112
🚌 A, B, 1, 9, 13

out Galileo's ideas; and 'Clothing
and the Body', in which an actress
dresses for a 16th- century day while
discussing clothing and changing
attitudes to the body.
✉ Piazza della Signoria, 50123 ☎ 055
276 8558/8224 ⓘ Mon–Wed, Sat 9–5,
Thu 9–2, Sun 9–7 ✋ Adult €6, under 18 €2
🚌 A, B 🔵 Guided tours only. ❓ Visits
must be booked ahead

MUSEO STIBBERT
www.museotibbert.it
This is an interactive exhibition
of historic weaponry and military
costume. You can try on Ottoman
sultans' and Medici captains'
uniforms, weaponry and regalia.
✉ Via Stibbert 26, Via Vittorio Emanuele II,
50134 ☎ 055 475520 ⓘ Mon–Wed 10–2,

GIOCO DI CALCIO
www.calciostorico.it
A no-holds-barred version of
soccer that is played between
the four city quarters, originally
used to keep the city militia in
fighting shape and to meld the
various factions into a united force.
The final day is celebrated with a
costumed procession and a flotilla
of candlelit boats with fireworks on
the River Arno.
✉ Ufficio Valorizzazione Tradizioni
Popolari Fiorentine, Piazzetta di Parte
Guelfa 1r, 50123 ☎ 055 261 6050/1/6
ⓘ Sundays in Jun ✋ €10–€25 🚌 C, 23

OCTOBER
MUSICA DEI POPOLI
www.flog.it/mus_pope.htm
In October each year, artists from
around the globe descend on
Florence for this international folk
music festival. Italy's finest world
music event has been running for
more than 25 years and attracts
many to its main venue, the
Auditorium Flog (▷ 111).
✉ Via M. Mercati 24/B, 50134 ☎ 055
462 8714 🚌 4, 8, 14

Fri–Sun 10–5 ✋ Adult €6, child (6–12) €3,
under 6 free 🚌 4 🔵 Guided tours only,
lasting 1 hour, departing every half hour

MUSEO DI STORIA DELLA
SCIENZA
▷ 82.

MUSEO ZOOLOGICO
(LA SPECOLA)
▷ 101.

PARCO DELLE CASCINE
Children will love the wide-open
spaces, fountains, monuments,
riding, swimming pool and
playgrounds. Bring a picnic, and
check out the amphitheatre.
✉ Piazza Vittorio Veneto, 50144 ⓘ 24
hours 🚌 1, 17, 17c, 19, 26, 800

Above *Enjoy informal dining at one of the city's pizzerie*

PRICES AND SYMBOLS

The restaurants are listed alphabetically (excluding La, Il, Le and I). The prices given are the average for a two-course lunch (L) and a three-course dinner (D) for one person, without drinks. The wine price is for a bottle of house wine.

For a key to the symbols, ▷ 2.

13 GOBBI

This friendly restaurant is a great place to bring kids. Alongside an unusual assortment of foods there are more standard choices for those who prefer plain food. There are also fabulous desserts, such as *cioccolata con pere* (pears in chocolate sauce) and good Tuscan wine. When the weather is fine, reserve a table in the small courtyard to eat alfresco.

✉ Via del Porcellana 9r, 50123 Firenze ☎ 055 284015 ◷ Daily 12.30–2.30, 7.30–10.30 ♨ L €22, D €36, Wine €16 🚌 B, C, 6, 11, 36, 37

ACQUERELLO

Sardinian restaurants are rare in Florence, but this is one of the best. There are lots of fish and seafood dishes, including marinated anchovies, pasta with mussels, grilled lobster and cooked prawns. Otherwise, try the *petto di pollo alla Vernaccia* (chicken breasts in a white wine sauce). Sardinian wines such as Vermentino or Cannonau are available, along with Sardinian beer.

✉ Via Ghibellina 156r, 50122 Firenze ☎ 055 234 1330 ◷ Daily 7pm–2am. Closed Aug ♨ D €22, Wine €10 🚌 A, 14

ALLE MURATE

An elegant, sophisticated restaurant, known for serving popular Tuscan dishes with an imaginative twist. Choose dishes beautifully prepared from a variety of fish and meat, including duck and turbot, or try home-made pasta such as Puglian *orecchiette* (little ear-shaped pasta) with a meat sauce and *scamorza* cheese (rather like mozzarella). There's a selection of more than 300 wines. The soft lighting and

candles make for an intimate dining experience.

✉ Via Ghibellina 52r, 50122 Firenze ☎ 055 240618 ◷ Tue–Sun 7.30pm–11pm ♨ D €65, Wine €20 🚌 A, 14

L'ANTICO RISTORO DI CAMBI

www.anticoristorodicambi.it
Popular with the local lunchtime crowd, this eatery is in the Oltrarno district south of the river, near the Ponte Vespucci. The food is generally light with an emphasis on fresh produce. Try one of the excellent salads or a platter heaped with such delicacies as buffalo mozzarella, basil, cured meats and pecorino (sheep's milk) cheese.

✉ Via Sant'Onofrio 1r, 50124 Firenze ☎ 055 217134 ◷ Mon–Sat 12.30–2.30, 7.30–10.30 ♨ L €17, D €36, Wine €12 🚌 D, 6

ASTOR CAFFÈ

For something different try this modern, American-style café-bar near the Duomo, a superb place to eat lunch or to grab a snack. Mediterranean cuisine dominates—

try the excellent fish dishes and innovative salads, which make a change from the traditional *insalate* (salads) that are usually served in the city. In the evening DJs and sometimes bands perform in the back room (▷ 111).

✉ Piazza del Duomo 20r, 50123 Firenze ☎ 055 284305 🕐 Daily 11am–2am. Closed 2 weeks in Aug 🖐 L €22, Wine €15 (food only served at lunchtime) 🚌 A, 1, 6, 7, 10, 11, 14, 17, 23

BALDOVINO
www.baldovino.com
This bustling, friendly *trattoria* is run by a Scotsman, whose famous friends from the world of entertainment often drop in when they're in town. Children are always welcome, and most enjoy the great pizzas from the wood-burning oven. The menu includes plenty of soups, beef dishes, various grilled meats and inventive pasta dishes. The wine list includes many Tuscan classics.

✉ Via San Giuseppe 22r, 50122 Firenze ☎ 055 241773 🕐 Mar–end Oct daily 11.30–2.30, 7–11.30; Nov–end Feb Tue–Sun 12–2.30, 7–12 🖐 L €19, D €30, Wine €15 🚌 C, 14

BAR GELATERIA ERMINI
In a popular shopping area, this *gelateria* is a good place to take a break and cool down. Ask for one of the cones as the portions are more generous than those served in the *coppette* (small cups). You can't go wrong with a *palla* (scoop) of *bacio* ice cream, which contains pieces of nuts and chocolate. Credit cards are not accepted.

✉ Via Gioberti 125, 50121 Firenze ☎ 055 244464 🕐 Mon–Tue, Thu–Sat 8am–midnight, Sun 8–8 🖐 Ice cream cone from €1.60 🚌 6, 8, 12, 31, 32, 33, 80

BAR PERSEO
The fresh fruit varieties are the best of all the mountains of delicious ice cream on view at Bar Perseo. They also serve drinks, filled *panini* and ciabattas. Vegetarians will enjoy the croissants with a filling of *carciofi* (artichoke). Your snack will cost you a lot more, however, if you sit at one

of the tables on the street. Credit cards are not accepted.

✉ Piazza della Signoria 16r, 50122 Firenze ☎ 055 239 8316 🕐 Daily 7am–midnight. Closed 3 weeks in Nov 🖐 Cappuccino from €3; ice cream cone from €3; filled *panini* from €3 🚌 A, B

BECCOFINO
www.beccofino.com
This popular restaurant and *enoteca* (wine bar) attracts an international crowd, who enjoy such delights as *gnocchi al nero di seppia* (small dumplings in squid ink) and *faraona alle olive* (roast guinea fowl with black olives). For a lighter meal, try a salad, pasta or risotto dish from the alternative menu. The 500-strong wine list has a superb range of Tuscan and Piedmontese wines.

✉ Piazza degli Scarlatti 1r, 50125 Firenze ☎ 055 290076 🕐 Mon–Sat 7pm–11pm; wine bar remains open later 🖐 L €28, D €52, Wine €15 🚌 6, 11, 36, 37

BELLE DONNE
This tiny, informal restaurant is densely packed with convivial shared tables, decorated with masses of fruit, vegetables and flowers. Choose your Tuscan dish from the blackboard—salads and vegetables are the highlights.

✉ Via delle Belle Donne 16r, 50100 Firenze ☎ 055 238 2609 🕐 Daily 12–3, 7–11 🖐 L €11, D €22, Wine €12 🚌 6, 9, 11

BIBENDUM
This fine restaurant at the five-star Hotel Helvetia & Bristol (▷ 127) attracts international stars and Florentine nobility. In the restaurant and Winter Garden cocktail bar the gilding, chandeliers and draperies give an exclusive, old-world charm. There isn't anything too innovative on the menu, but it offers expertly prepared, traditional Tuscan cuisine and well-known Italian dishes.

✉ Hotel Helvetia & Bristol, Via dei Pescioni 2, 50123 Firenze ☎ 055 287814 🕐 Daily 12.30–3, 7–10.30 🖐 L €40, D €69, Wine €20 🚌 A, 6, 11, 22, 36, 37

BORGO ANTICO
Enjoy some Neapolitan pizza in a

setting reminiscent of Naples itself. There are plenty of meat dishes for the main course, and a fine northern/southern Italian fusion in the risotto with smoked cheese and courgettes (zucchini). Reserve a table—especially if you want to eat outside.

✉ Piazza Santo Spirito 6r, 50125 Firenze ☎ 055 210437 🕐 Daily 12.45–2.30, 7.30–midnight 🖐 L €12, D €33, Wine €13 🚌 D, 11, 36, 37

BORGO SAN JACOPO
www.lungarnohotels.com
Borgo San Jacopo is the restaurant of the Lungarno hotel (▷ 128), and consists of a long, elegant room with large windows at one end that offer superb views over the Arno. If you make a reservation, and are lucky, you may be able to secure one of a handful of tables on the tiny terrace, which offer even better views of the Ponte Vecchio. Despite the stylish setting, the atmosphere is informal, and the food sophisticated without being over-elaborate. Head chef Beatrice Segoni, one of several women chefs making their mark in the city, put the restaurant on the map.

✉ Borgo San Jacopo 14, 50125 Firenze ☎ 055 281661 🕐 Mon, Wed–Sun 7.30–10.30. Closed Tue and Aug 🖐 D €45, Wine €20 🚌 D, 11, 36, 37

Below *For inventive Italian cuisine head to Borgo Antico*

CAFFÈ AMERINI

This is a good spot to take a break during the day, but avoid early afternoon when it's particularly busy. Try one of the excellent snacks, which include filled *panini*, *piadine* (flat bread) and a variety of savoury pastries packed with tasty fillings. Those with a sweeter tooth will be tempted by the array of cakes.

✉ Via della Vigna Nuova 63r, 50123 Firenze ☎ 055 284941 ◷ Mon–Sat 8–8 ✋ Filled *panini* €5 🚌 A, 6

CAFFÈ ITALIANO

www.caffeitaliano.it

It's a pleasure to linger in the high-vaulted rooms of the Palazzo da Cintoia, which are full of wonderful antiques. Classic Tuscan fare includes *cinghiale* (wild boar) and an excellent choice of pasta dishes and chunky soups. The wine list includes plenty of Chiantis and Super Tuscans.

✉ Via Isole delle Stinche 11–13r ☎ 055 289368 ◷ Tue–Sun 12.30–3, 7.30–12 ✋ L €28, D €50, Wine €15 🚌 A

CAFFÈ MEGARA

This is a great place to grab a *merenda* (snack break) while reading one of the newspapers provided. In the heart of the clothes shopping district, the Megara also shows catwalk videos. The adventurous menu includes exotic meats, such as kangaroo and ostrich, prepared *carpaccio* style (very thinly sliced and raw), as well as vegetarian dishes.

✉ Via della Spada 11–17, 50123 Firenze ☎ 055 211837 ◷ Daily 8am–2am ✋ Pasta dishes for around €7.50, Wine €8 🚌 A, 6, 11, 22, 36, 37

CAFFÈ RICCHI

www.caffericchi.it

The Oltrarno's beautiful people make up the bulk of the crowd here. You can eat alfresco in the leafy Piazza Santo Spirito, or inside in the contemporary dining rooms. The menu is crammed with traditional Tuscan dishes made from fresh fish and seafood, such as pasta with oysters and spaghetti with small

clams. Caffè Ricchi also serves meat dishes, plus a good selection of salads.

✉ Piazza Santo Spirito 8–9r, 50125 Firenze ☎ 055 215864 ◷ Bar: summer Mon–Sat 7am–1.30am; winter Mon–Sat 7am–10pm in winter). Restaurant: Mon–Sat 12.30–2.45, 7.30–11. Closed 2 weeks of Aug and Feb ✋ D €39, Wine €15 🚌 D, 11, 36, 37

CAMMILLO

A well-established *trattoria* that attracts an international crowd and a host of Italian celebrities enticed by the excellent home-made pasta, various *baccalà* (salted cod) dishes and expertly cooked meats. Wine lovers have a great choice of Tuscan and Piedmontese wines.

✉ Borgo San Jacopo 57r, 50125 Firenze ☎ 055 212427 ◷ Thu–Tue 12–2.30, 7.30–10.30. Closed Aug, 2 weeks over Christmas ✋ L €25, D €44, Wine €9.50 🚌 D, 11, 36, 37

CAFFÈ RIVOIRE

www.rivoire.it

A Florentine institution, opened in the 1870s, that is a must if you are a first-time visitor or chocolate lover—the Rivoire produces arguably the best chocolate in town. Try one of their exquisite ice creams or the famous Rivoire hot chocolate at one of the tables in the Piazza della Signoria or Loggia dei Lanzi. But remember, you pay for the privilege of sitting down to enjoy your treat.

✉ Piazza della Signoria 5r, 50122 Firenze ☎ 055 214412/211302 ◷ Tue–Sun 8am–midnight. Closed 2 weeks in Jan ✋ Sit down: cappuccino from €5, ice cream from €6 🚌 A, B

IL CANTASTORIE

Paintings of old Florence adorn the walls here. The friendly staff are happy to help you choose from the excellent soups and grilled meats. Although the type of food served here is often called *cucina povera* (poor person's food), it is rich in taste and texture. There is a limited choice of Chianti and other Tuscan wines.

✉ Via della Condotta 7–9r, 50122 Firenze ☎ 055 239 6804 ◷ Daily 12–2.30, 7–11 ✋ L €14, D €28, Wine €12 🚌 A, 23

CANTINA BARBAGIANNI

www.cantinabarbagianni.it

The decorations here include contemporary artworks, and there is an equally inventive menu. Among the highlights are a green pepper risotto with strawberries and mint, duck with blueberries and some unusual salad combinations.

✉ Via Sant'Egidio 13, 50122 Firenze ☎ 055 248 0508 ◷ Mon–Fri 12.30–2.30, 7–11.30, Sat–Sun 7pm–11.30pm. Closed part of Jul ✋ D €33, Wine €12 🚌 14, 23

CANTINETTA ANTINORI

www.antinori.it

This elegant *cantinetta* is famed for its wines. *Bruschetta* (garlic toast), pork, truffles, salted fish, hearty soups and pâté dominate in winter, and lighter pasta dishes, salads and fresh fish in the warmer months.

✉ Via de' Tornabuoni 3, 50123 Firenze ☎ 055 292234 ◷ Mon–Fri 12.30–2.30, 7–10.30. Closed Aug ✋ L €25, D €47, Wine €12 🚌 A, 6, 11, 22, 36, 37

CAPOCACCIA

www.capocaccia.com

This stylish café-bar is one of the places to be seen in Florence. It's famous for its *panini* and American-influenced brunch menu. Eat out in style in the frescoed *salone* or in the bar area overlooking the Arno. There are more than 200 wines available.

✉ Lungarno Corsini 12–14r, 50123 Firenze ☎ 055 210751 ◷ Daily noon–2am, Mon noon–4pm ✋ Filled panini €5–€12, smoked salmon and salad €6 🚌 B

CARABÈ

www.gelatocarabe.com

A Sicilian *gelateria*, Carabè sells ice cream that harks back to the recipes that arrived in southern Italy from the Arabic world. Varieties include pistachio, fig and apricot. Try, too, the refreshing *granite* (crushed ice with fruits and sometimes cream) and *sorbetti* (sorbets). Credit cards are not accepted.

✉ Via Ricasoli 60r, 50121 Firenze ☎ 055 289476 ◷ Jan, Feb daily 12–7.30pm; Mar, Apr daily 10am–9pm; May–end Oct daily 9am–1am; Nov, Dec 10am–8pm ✋ Cone €1.80–€5.50 🚌 1, 6, 11, 14, 17, 22

CIBREO

www.cibreo.com

Fabio Picchi's renowned restaurant is one of Florence's gastronomic shrines, and as such is expensive. Starters include couscous with yoghurt and *insalatina di trippa* (tripe salad). The fish and meat dishes are both innovative and delicious, while for vegetarians there are dishes piled with porcini mushrooms. There are also great Tuscan wines to choose from. Ask about the latest performances at the adjoining Teatro del Sale-Cibreocittà.

✉ Via de' Macci 122r, 50122 Firenze
☎ 055 234 1100 ⏲ Tue–Sat 12.30–2.30, 7.30–11.15. Closed Aug, 1st week in Jan
🖐 L €44, D €78, Wine €16 🚍 A, C

COCO LEZZONE

Coco is a fashionable restaurant with an interesting mix of functionalism and gourmet cuisine. The dining room has communal tables, so you must be prepared to share your space. The cuisine is Tuscan, with particularly good meat dishes. The service is quick, and at busy times you may be asked to move on to make way for new customers. Credit cards are not accepted.

✉ Via del Parioncino 26r, off Lungarno Corsini, 50123 Firenze ☎ 055 287178
⏲ Mon, Wed–Sat 12–2.30, 7–10.30, Tue 12–2.30. Closed Aug 🖐 L €20, D €40, Wine €15 🚍 11, 31, 32, 36, 37

COQUINARIUS

www.coquinarius.com

One of central Florence's better wine bars, full of dark wood and with stylish posters on the walls, Coquinarius is a great place to sample different cheeses, cold cuts, smoked fish, *carpaccio* meats (raw, thinly cut and dressed with lemon and oil) and *stuzzichini* (Italian bar snacks). There are also soups and salads to choose from, plus a large selection of wines, a range of teas and some wickedly rich hot chocolate concoctions.

✉ Via delle Oche 15r, 50122 Firenze
☎ 055 230 2153 ⏲ Mon–Sat 9am–11pm, Sun 9am–4pm. Closed Aug 🖐 L €11, D €25, Wine €10 🚍 A, 14, 23

DA BENVENUTO

A popular restaurant serving good-quality Tuscan food. The walls are adorned with an eclectic collection of artworks, and the clientele is an equally intriguing array of local characters. As for the menu, pasta with a meaty sauce represents good value, or ask about the season's beef and pork dishes, which are served with herbs and accompanied by side dishes of potatoes and crunchy vegetables.

✉ Via della Mosca 16r, 50122 Firenze
☎ 055 214833 ⏲ Mon–Sat 12–2.30, 7–10.30 🖐 L €14, D €25, Wine €7
🚍 B, 23

DON CHISCIOTTE

www.ristorantedonchisciotte.it

A truly wonderful culinary experience awaits you at this popular eatery, serving mostly fish and some meat dishes. Try the warm seafood salad on Tuscan bread or the aubergine (eggplant) mousse stuffed with bread and tomatoes. The wine list includes top-quality Tuscan wines as well as some great choices from overseas.

✉ Via Cosimo Ridolfi 4r, 50129 Firenze
☎ 055 475430 ⏲ Tue–Sat 1–2.30, 8–10.30, Mon 8pm–10pm. Closed Aug
🖐 L €25, D €55, Wine €10 🚍 7, 10, 20, 25, 31, 32, 33

ENOTECA PINCHIORRI

www.enotecapinchiorri.com

This French-influenced establishment is one of Italy's best. The rose-scented courtyard and elegant dining areas are ideal settings to complement the exquisite nouvelle cuisine and wonderful wine list. Try one of the imaginative dishes of liver or pigeon, and finish with a sumptuous dessert. The service is impeccable but the prices are high, and you will need to reserve a table.

✉ Via Ghibellina 87, 50122 Firenze ☎ 055 242777 ⏲ Thu–Sat 12.30–2, 7.30–10, Tue and Wed 7.30pm–10pm. Closed Aug and Christmas 🖐 L €130, D €250, Wine €30 🚍 A, 14

FRANCESCANO

The quality of the food at the Francescano distinguishes it from other restaurants in this part of town. Regulars enjoy the Tuscan dishes created from fresh ingredients. Begin with the cheese and cold meat platter and assorted vegetable starters. If you haven't tried the hearty Tuscan *ribollita* (soup made with beans and black cabbage), this is a good place to enjoy a bowl.

✉ Largo Bargellini 16r, 50122 Firenze ☎ 055 241605 🕐 Wed–Mon 12–3, 7–11. Closed Aug 🍴 L €17, D €28, Wine €10 🚌 C, 14

FUOR D'ACQUA

As its name implies (it means out of water), this restaurant is famed for its fish creations, such as the marine salads with balsamic vinegar dressing or the beautifully prepared *calamari* (squid). White wines dominate the wine list, but there are also some decent reds.

✉ Via Pisana 37r, 50124 Firenze ☎ 055 222299 🕐 Mon–Sat 8–11. Closed Aug 🍴 D €61, Wine €15 🚌 D, 6

LE GIUBBE ROSSE

www.giubberosse.it

This celebrated café was once the haunt of the Florentine avant garde; the red-jacketed waiters and stylish interior hint at this illustrious cultural past. Bring a book, order one of the pasta dishes or a *panino*, and observe the scene on the elegant piazza. For just a taste of history, order a drink at the bar and linger there. It also has a restaurant.

✉ Piazza della Repubblica 13r, 50123 Firenze ☎ 055 212280 🕐 Daily 8am–2am; restaurant 12–3.30, 6.30–11 🍴 Pasta dishes from €4, D €28, Wine €12 🚌 A, 6, 22

GROM

www.grom.it

Florence's newest *gelateria* has caused a stir, its wonderful ice cream threatening to take the crown from the long-established Vivoli (▷ 125) and Perchè No! (▷ 123). There is even now a branch in New York. Although tucked away in a side street of the pedestrian-only zone, it is just a short walk from the main Via de' Calzaiuoli, and almost always has a small crowd of people outside waiting to be served or enjoying their purchase. The Crema di Grom, made from organic eggs, biscuits and Valrhona Ecuadorian chocolate, is already a classic.

✉ Via del Campanile, on the corner of Via delle Oche, 50122 Firenze ☎ 055 216158 🕐 Summer daily 10am–midnight; winter daily 10am–11pm 🍴 Cups and cones from €1.50

GUSCIO

Both fish- and meat-eaters are very well served at this popular *trattoria*. Various beef and goose dishes are served daily. Ask the waiter to suggest a suitable vintage from the superb wine list. Among the tempting desserts is ice cream topped with a warm chocolate sauce.

✉ Via dell'Orto 49a, 50124 Firenze ☎ 055 224421 🕐 Tue–Sat 7.30pm–11pm. Closed Sat, Sun Jul and Aug 🍴 D €30, Wine €10 🚌 D

INCANTO

The restaurant of the Grand Hotel (▷ 127) has a lavish interior yet contemporary feel. The menu changes with the seasons and is always very well balanced. Look out for crustacean treats, like the wonderfully piquant marinated prawns, and the various meat sauces, but save some space for one of the fabulous desserts. Wine buffs will not be disappointed by the list of more than 300 labels.

✉ Piazza Ognissanti 1, 50123 Firenze ☎ 055 27161 🕐 Daily 12.30–3, 7–11 🍴 L €23, D €78, Wine €30 🚌 A, B

IL LATINI

www.illatini.com

This rustic *osteria* serving hearty Tuscan classics attracts a loyal crowd to the long communal tables. Highlights include a traditional *zuppa di farro* (a meat, grain and vegetable soup) and wild boar stewed in honey, dried fruit and pinenut sauce. Save room for the heavenly tiramisu. The Latini family produce some fine wines and their own olive oil.

✉ Via de' Palchetti 6r, 50123 Firenze ☎ 055 210916 🕐 Tue–Sun 12.30–2.30, 7.30–10.30 🍴 L €15, D €30, Wine €10 🚌 A, 6

LA LOGGIA

www.villasanmichele.com

Its evocative former monastery setting and some of the finest cuisine in the area are what attract diners to this Fiesole restaurant in the hotel Villa San Michele (▷ 129). You can eat in the covered courtyard or the vaulted open-air section, which has stunning views of Florence below. Expect plenty of fresh produce and home-made pasta: The mushroom tagliatelle and scampi dishes are delights. Later in the evening a pianist plays in the cocktail area at the far end of the terrace. Reservations are essential.

✉ Via Doccia 4, Fiesole 50014 ☎ 055 567 8200 🕐 Daily 1–2.30, 7–9.30. Closed mid-Nov to mid-Mar 🍴 L €55, D €100, Wine €30 🚌 7 🚗 A1 from Florence (or Via Giuseppe Mantellini—the road to Fiesole); turn right at the sign at the bottom of the hill

OLIVIERO

www.ristorante-oliviero.it

Excellent service and superb Tuscan food are the main characteristics of Francesco Altomare's eatery. Meat-lovers have a lot to choose from, including guinea fowl and rabbit. Delicious soups, wonderfully fresh vegetables and some innovative pasta creations make up the rest. The dessert list includes *zuppa inglese* (trifle). Rare wines and spirits are available.

✉ Via delle Terme 51r, 50123 Firenze ☎ 055 287643 🕐 Mon–Sat 7.30pm–midnight. Closed Aug 🍴 D €50, Wine €17 🚌 A, B, 6, 11, 36, 37

ORUM

Enjoy an *aperitivo* in the Westin Excelsior Hotel's lavish bar before dining in style in a grand salon, with views of the River Arno. The finest seasonal ingredients are used in a fusion of international haute cuisine and traditional Mediterranean and Tuscan influences. Alternative menus exploring specific cuisines are regularly available. There is an excellent wine list.

✉ Piazza Ognissanti 3, 50123 Firenze ☎ 055 264201 🕐 Daily 12–2.30, 7.30–11 ✋ L €33, D €66, Wine €20 🚌 A, B, 6, 11, 36, 37

OSTERIA ANTICA MESCITA SAN NICCOLÒ

The San Niccolò serves a superb range of *antipasti* in its rustic wooden interior. These are followed by traditional dishes such as tripe and tongue. Vegetarians can choose from the heaped salads and the couscous with vegetables.

✉ Via San Niccolò 60r, 50125 Firenze ☎ 055 234 2836 🕐 Mon–Sat 12–3, 7–1am ✋ L €14, D €20, Wine €6.50 🚌 C, D, 23

OSTERIA DEI BENCI

This long-established *osteria* a few minutes from Santa Croce was one of the first in Florence to set the trend for simple, bright and inexpensive bistro-type restaurants. A good, reliable choice in a busy area, it has a single attractive dining room decorated in bold, warm colours, crowned by an attractive medieval brick vault. The staff is young and relaxed, though service is brisk at busy times. The menu changes according to the season, but sticks to simple Tuscan staples such as *bistecca* and *ribollita*, along with more adventurous pastas and some excellent desserts.

✉ Via de' Benci 13r, 50122 Firenze ☎ 055 234 4923 🕐 Mon–Sat 12.30–2.45, 7.30–10.45. Closed Sun and a period in Aug ✋ L €17, D €22, Wine €12 ✋ B, C, 23

OSTERIA DEL CINGHIALE BIANCO

www.cinghialebianco.it

The cooking at the White Boar restaurant is traditional Tuscan, and there is boar on the menu. There are also chicken, rabbit and veal dishes.

✉ Borgo San Jacopo 43r, 50125 Firenze ☎ 055 215706 🕐 Mon–Tue, Thu–Fri 6.30–11, Sat, Sun 12–2.30, 6.30–11 ✋ L €22, D €39, Wine €16 🚌 3, 13, 32

OSTERIA SANTO SPIRITO

This trendy eatery excels in creating adventurous, mountainous salads. There is also a superb choice of cheeses and a decent wine list.

✉ Piazza Santo Spirito 16r, 50125 Firenze ☎ 055 238 2383 🕐 Daily 12.30–2.30, 7.30–11.30 ✋ L €11, D €34, Wine €12 🚌 D, 11, 36, 37

PALLOTTINO

www.trattoriapallottino.com

This traditional *trattoria* has small dining rooms, wooden tables and candles. It is near Santa Croce and is known for its tasty cheese and salami platters. Also excellent pasta dishes with both creamy and tomato-based sauces.

✉ Via Isola delle Stinche 1r, 50122 Firenze ☎ 055 289573 🕐 Tue–Sun 12.30–2.30, 7.30–10.30. Closed 2 weeks in Aug ✋ L €17, D €22, Wine €8 🚌 B, 13, 23

PAOLI

Here Tuscan and other Italian dishes are served in a beautifully frescoed dining room reminiscent of a medieval tavern. Most are served with fresh vegetables; try the sole or pasta with kidneys. Paoli is centrally placed between the Duomo and Piazza della Signoria, making reservations essential.

✉ Via dei Tavolini 12r, 50122 Firenze ☎ 055 216215 🕐 Wed–Mon 12–2.30, 7–10.30. Closed most of Aug ✋ L €29, D €46, Wine €16 🚌 A, 1, 6, 7, 11, 14

PERCHÈ NO!

This *gelateria* has the bonus of tables where you can enjoy your ice cream. There are always new varieties to try, but for a taste of the Mediterranean you can't beat the Malaga, with rich wine grapes. Ask for *due palline* (two scoops) of *meringa gelata* (meringue ice cream) and wait for the server to ask for confirmation and reply *'Perchè no!'* (meaning Oh, why not!). Credit cards are not accepted.

✉ Via dei Tavolini 19r, 50122 Firenze ☎ 055 239 8969 🕐 Mar–end Oct Wed–Mon 11am–12.30am, Tue 11am–7.30pm; Nov–end Feb Wed–Mon 12–7.30pm ✋ Ice cream cone from €2 🚌 6, 17, 23

PITTI GOLA E CANTINA

Sample the Pitti's excellent selection of wines, and feast on the fabulous meat and cheese platters and grilled vegetables. Wine bottles and other paraphernalia fill the wooden interior, and the young staff prepare the simple but wholesome fare in front of your eyes. Choose a table outside overlooking the Palazzo Pitti or grab a stool by the bar.

✉ Piazza de' Pitti 16, 50125 Firenze ☎ 055 212704 🕐 Tue–Sun 11.30–11.30 ✋ Cheese and meat platter from €22, Wine from €4 per glass 🚌 D, 11, 36, 37

RELAIS LE JARDIN

www.regency-hotel.com

The dark wood and carpeted interiors and lush, well-kept gardens make the Hotel Regency's restaurant a welcoming place. The immaculately prepared and presented haute cuisine menu is constantly evolving, as traditional

Below *Indulge yourself with an ice cream from one of the city's* gelaterie

Above *Pasta with a tempting black truffle sauce*

Italian dishes are given a modern twist. Book early to reserve a candlelit table.
✉ Hotel Regency, Piazza D'Azeglio 5, 50121 Firenze ☎ 055 245247 ◷ Daily 12.30–3.30, 7.30–11.30 ✋ L €28, D €100, Wine €25 🚌 C, 6, 31, 32

RISTORANTE ENOTECA PANE E VINO
www.ristorantepaneevino.it
This inviting restaurant is a popular evening choice. Seasonal Tuscan dishes predominate, so the menu changes frequently. However, expect such delights as pumpkin in a buttery sage sauce, fish-filled ravioli, pasta with a wild boar sauce and guinea-fowl breast. There is an excellent wine list.

✉ Piazza di Cestello 3r, 50125 Firenze ☎ 055 247 6956 ◷ Mon–Sat 7pm–11pm. Closed Aug ✋ D €33, Wine €13 🚌 C, 23

RISTORANTE PERSEUS
Ristorante Perseus in Fiesole is one of the best places to sample the famous Florentine steak accompanied by tasty salads, Tuscan cannellini beans and cooked vegetables. For dessert, try the *pannacotta* or a slab of cheesecake. There's a good wine list and a lovely terrace facing the Teatro Romano.
✉ Piazza Mino da Fiesole 9, 50014 Firenze ☎ 055 59143 ◷ Daily 12.30–3, 7.30–11.30 ✋ L €17, D €30, Wine €13 🚌 7

SABATINI
www.ristorantesabatini.it
This elegant restaurant is a Florentine institution. The cuisine

mixes solid Tuscan dishes with international influences. They serve a great Florentine steak, while seafood enthusiasts can try the risotto with scampi. Excellent wine list and professional service.
✉ Via dei Panzani 9a, 50123 Firenze ☎ 055 282802 ◷ Tue–Sun 12.30–2.30, 7.30–10.30 ✋ L €32, D €65, Wine €25 🚌 A, 1, 4, 7, 10, 11, 22, 23, 36, 37

IL SANTO BEVITORE
www.ilsantobevitore.com
A wine bar that has great food and is good value, serving platters of salami, *prosciutto* and various cheeses. Main courses include pumpkin risotto, a soup of the day and pasta with a sardine sauce.
✉ Via di Santo Spirito 64–66r, 50125 Firenze ☎ 055 211264 ◷ Mon–Sat 12.30–2.30, 7.30–11.30 ✋ L €17, D €25, Wine €8 🚌 11, 36, 37

TARGA BISTROT

www.targabistrot.net

The finest international cuisine is served here amid sleek surroundings. The menu includes pasta with swordfish and a scampi risotto. There are plenty of cheeses, a detailed wine list and some delectable *dolci*. Reservations need to be made well in advance.

✉ Lungarno Cristoforo Colombo 7, 50136 Firenze ☎ 055 677377 🕓 Mon–Sat 12.30–2.30, 7.30–11. Closed 1–20 Jan, 1–20 Aug 🖐 L €30, D €50, Wine €14 🚍 31, 32

TAVERNA DEL BRONZINO

Taverna del Bronzino serves a wealth of Tuscan culinary delights alongside more international dishes. Fish and meat dishes change frequently according to the seasons. If it's on the menu, try the expertly prepared sea bass.

✉ Via delle Ruote 25r, 50129 Firenze ☎ 055 495220 🕓 Mon–Sat 12–2.30, 7.30–11.30. Closed Aug 🖐 L €22, D €55, Wine €16 🚍 7, 10, 20, 25, 31, 32, 33

TRATTORIA ANGIOLINO

Angiolino has been a fixture of the Oltrarno district for many years, a simple restaurant that, while undergoing the odd decorative makeover, has remained at heart a *trattoria* of the old school. It has a pretty interior, distinguished by its old brick-vaulted main dining room, and serves a variety of traditional dishes that rarely stray far from the Tuscan mainstream.

✉ Via Santo Spirito 36r, 50125 Firenze ☎ 055 239 8976 🕓 Daily 12.30–2.15, 7.30–10.30 🖐 L €20, D €27, €Wine 13 🚍 D

TRATTORIA ANTELLESI

Antellesi serves excellent Tuscan food at affordable prices. Starters include pâté with *crostini* (toasted crusty bread), as well as an inventive salad with nuts, fruits and pecorino cheese. Equally enticing are the stuffed lamb, beef stew, veal escalope and Florentine steak. Vegetarians will love the artichoke risotto.

✉ Via Faenza 9r, 50123 Firenze ☎ 055 216990 🕓 Daily 12–2.45, 7–10.45 🖐 L €14, D €28, Wine €10 🚍 4, 7, 10, 12, 13, 25, 31, 32, 33

TRATTORIA ANTICHI CANCELLI

Hearty Tuscan food is the mainstay of this *trattoria*. Feast on hearty soups and toast topped with sweet tomatoes and extra-virgin olive oil. The menu changes according to the season, and there's always a substantial meat or fish dish. Vegetarians have a variety of side dishes along with the classic spaghetti with tomato and basil to choose from. The house wine is very reasonable.

✉ Via Faenza 73r, 50123 Firenze ☎ 055 218927 🕓 Daily 12–2.30, 7–10.30 🖐 L €11, D €22, Wine €8 🚍 4, 7, 10, 12, 13, 25, 31, 32, 33

TRATTORIA DEI QUATTRO LEONI

www.4leoni.com

The Four Lions is a welcoming, informal place spread across two high-ceilinged, brick-arched rooms. You can sit outside in spring and summer. The food is generally straightforward Florentine cuisine with a few inventive twists. Good fish options on Friday. Booking is recommended.

✉ Via del Vellutini 1r, 50125 Firenze ☎ 055 218562 🕓 Thu–Tue 12–3, 7–11, Wed 7–11 🖐 L €22, D €34, Wine €10 🚍 6, 11

TRATTORIA PONTE VECCHIO

www.trattoriapontevecchio.com

A stone's throw from the Ponte Vecchio and its crowds, this *trattoria* is inevitably popular with visitors and you cannot fault the Tuscan cuisine. A house special is pasta with mushrooms.

✉ Lungarno Archibusieri 8r, 50125 Firenze ☎ 055 292289 🕓 Daily 12–3.30, 7–10 🖐 L €17, D €48, Wine €15 🚍 D

TRE SOLDI

Tre Soldi is a welcoming and unpretentious *trattoria*. The food is great value with some highly inventive dishes, including a warm vegetable salad with junipers and dumplings with a pumpkin sauce. The wine menu is mostly Tuscan reds.

✉ Via d'Annunzio 4r, 50137 Firenze ☎ 055 679366 🕓 May–end Sep Mon–Fri 12–3, 8–10, Sat–Sun 8pm–10pm; Oct–end Apr Sun–Thu 12–3, 8–10, Fri 12–3. Closed Aug 🖐 L €17, D €28, Wine €8 🚍 3, 6, 20, 34

VIVOLI

www.vivoli.it

The Vivoli family have been making ice cream since the 1930s, and this is Florence's most famous *gelateria*. If you don't mind the wait, the rewards are truly delicious. There are lots of varieties to choose from and all are served in *coppette* (cups of different sizes): Vivoli is strictly a no-cone zone. Credit cards are not accepted.

✉ Via Isole delle Stinche 7, 50122 Firenze ☎ 055 292334 🕓 Tue–Sat 7.30am–1am, Sun 9.30am–1am 🖐 Ice cream cup from €1.60 🚍 A, 14, 23

ZÀ-ZÀ

www.trattoriazaza.it

An old-fashioned, inexpensive *trattoria*, which is very popular with visitors to the city. The Tuscan food is excellent, and the fixed-price menus are great value. The stone-walled interior is especially appealing in the summer heat; arrive early or reserve a table.

✉ Piazza del Mercato Centrale 26r, 50123 Firenze ☎ 055 215411 🕓 Daily 11–11 🖐 L €14, D €39, Wine €9.50 🚍 1, 6, 7, 10, 12, 25

ZIBIBBO

www.trattoriazibibbo.it

Zibibbo has a deservedly good reputation. It specializes in fish dishes, but don't ignore the tasty vegetable side dishes and typically Tuscan creations like tagliatelle with duck *ragù*. There's a superb choice of fish, and plenty of Tuscan wines. There is a good selection of desserts.

✉ Via di Terzollina 3r, 50129 Firenze ☎ 055 433383 🕓 Mon–Fri 12.30–3, 7–11, Sat 7–11. Closed Aug 🖐 L €28, D €44, Wine €14 🚍 14c

Above *The Ponte Vecchio*

PRICES AND SYMBOLS

The prices are the lowest and highest for a double room for one night including breakfast, unless otherwise stated. All the hotels listed accept credit cards unless otherwise stated. Note that rates can vary widely throughout the year.

For a key to the symbols, ▷ 2.

ALBERGO FIRENZE

www.hotelfirenze-fi.it
Between the Duomo and the Piazza della Signoria, this is an inexpensive place to stay if you are not seeking luxury but want to be right at the heart of the city. Almost all rooms have a private bathroom.

✉ Via del Corso-Piazza dei Donati 4, 50122 Firenze ☎ 055 214203 ♨ €80–€109 ❶ 60 🚌 23

ALESSANDRA

www.hotelalessandra.com
This two-star hotel is in a small street parallel to the Arno and its location is its main selling point. The rooms are spacious, clean and neat, but not all have a private bathroom or air conditioning.

✉ Borgo S.S. Apostoli 17, 50129 Firenze ☎ 055 283438 ♨ €110–€185 ❶ 27 🚌 6, 11, 36, 37

BALCONY

www.hotelbalcony.com
A welcoming and dependable no-frills hotel close to Piazza Santa Maria Novella, within walking distance of almost everything in Florence. The rooms are basic but clean and all have a private bathroom (bath or shower), telephone, TV and minibar. There is a communal area with a TV and library, as well as a terrace with fine views of the Duomo.

✉ Via dei Banchi 3r, 50123 Firenze ☎ 055 283133 ♨ €65–€120 ❶ 15 🚌 A, 6, 11, 14, 17

BELLETTINI

www.hotelbellettini.com
Close to the church of San Lorenzo and the Duomo, this hotel dates from the 15th century, making it one of the oldest in Florence. The interior has some attractive Tuscan touches and the rooms come in a variety of sizes, making the hotel perfect for families. The facilities include optional private bathroom, TV, telephone, safe and internet access. Breakfast includes the owner's home baking and should not be missed.

✉ Via de' Conti 7, 50123 Firenze ☎ 055 213561 ♨ €105–€140 ❶ 28, 5 suites 🚌 1, 6, 7, 10, 11, 14, 17, 23

BRUNELLESCHI

www.hotelbrunelleschi.it
In a peaceful spot behind Via dei Calzaiuoli, this excellent hotel is in a medieval tower. There are amazing views of the Duomo from the roof terrace and some of the rooms. Guest rooms are cool and calm in white and cream with red accents. The hotel has a restaurant, a bar, laundry and internet services, and a private museum displaying objects found during the tower's conversion.

✉ Piazza Sant'Elisabetta 3, 50122 Firenze ☎ 055 27370 ♨ €211–€380 ❶ 96 🚌 1, 6, 7, 11, 14

CASCI

www.hotelcasci.com
The Casci, near the Duomo, is especially good for families. Triple-glazed windows cut down on noise in the rooms at the front of the building. Rooms are simple and clean; many have a balcony and all have private bathrooms, telephone, cable TV and minibar.

✉ Via Cavour 13, 50129 Firenze ☎ 055 211686 ♨ €80–€150 ❶ 25 🚌 1, 6, 7, 10, 11, 17, 31, 32

CHIAZZA

www.chiazzahotel.com
The Chiazza, in the Santa Croce area, close to the Duomo, is a

stylish, relaxing budget option. Rooms are modern and immaculate and the breakfast room functions as a small bar in the evening.

✉ Borgo Pinti 5, 50121 Firenze ☎ 055 248 0363 🖐 €60–€85 🛈 14 🔄 🚌 14, 23

DE ROSE PALACE HOTEL
www.hotelderose.it
This hotel is well named, as its pink and peach shades create a rosy glow throughout to the west of the city, it is still within walking distance of Florence's attractions. The rooms are comfortably furnished and have private bathrooms, telephone, TV and hairdryer.

✉ Via Solferino 5, 50123 Firenze ☎ 055 239 6818 🖐 €135–€220 🛈 18 🔄 🚌 B, D

EXCELSIOR
www.westin.com
The Excelsior is characterized by old-fashioned opulence. Walking into the magnificent reception area you get a sense of its splendour. The marble-laden rooms have frescoes, antiques and artworks; many have views of the Arno and the city. The Orum restaurant (▷ 122) and the Bar Donatello make it far too easy never to step outside. Residents have the use of a nearby gym.

✉ Piazza Ognissanti 3, 50123 Firenze ☎ 055 27151 🖐 €275–€824, excluding breakfast 🛈 161 🔄 🚌 B, C, 9

GALILEO
www.galileohotel.it
Bright and cheerful, Galileo is ideal for those who want to make the most of every minute they are in Florence. The rooms are clean with good amenities, including private bathroom, telephone and TV. Welcoming public rooms and helpful staff complete the picture.

✉ Via Nazionale 22a, 50123 Firenze ☎ 055 496661 🖐 €90–€230 🛈 31 🔄 🚌 4, 12, 25, 31, 32, 33

GALLERY HOTEL ART
www.lungarnohotels.com/gallery/
This is Florence's finest hotel for sleek modernity and stylish comfort. With designer furniture, quality

detailing, subtle lighting and state-of-the-art technology the rooms are relaxing. The penthouse has linen sheets and cashmere blankets. The small Fusion Bar Shozan serves light meals and drinks, and has views over the Ponte Vecchio.

✉ Vicolo dell'Oro 5, 50123 Firenze ☎ 055 27263 🖐 €460 🛈 69 🔄 🚌 B

GIGLIO
www.hotelgiglio.fi.it
The Giglio is a small family-run hotel between the Duomo and Piazza San Marco. The family also owns the Osteria del Cinghiale Bianco (▷ 123), which guarantees you a reservation as a hotel guest. The guest rooms are small but relaxing and have private bathroom, telephone and internet access, safe and minibar.

✉ Via Cavour 85, 50129 Firenze ☎ 055 486621 🖐 €85–€770 🛈 19 🔄 🚌 1, 6, 7, 10, 11, 17

GRAND HOTEL
www.starwood.com/grandflorence
The Grand may be smaller than its sister hotel, the Excelsior, but it is more romantic. The luxurious rooms have fabulous bathrooms and sumptuous bed linen. You are also treated to great Tuscan cooking at the hotel's Incanto restaurant (▷ 122).

✉ Piazza Ognissanti 1, 50123 Firenze ☎ 055 27161 🖐 €285–€845 🛈 107 🔄 U 🚌 B, C, 9

HELVETIA & BRISTOL
www.royaldemeure.com
Once a port of call for English ladies on the Grand Tour, the Helvetia & Bristol is still redolent of 19th-century refinement. Each guest room is different, with rich hues creating a warm environment. Amenities such as private bathroom, TV and telephone are carefully blended into the prevailing period style. You can dine in the enchanting Winter Garden or in the Bibendum restaurant (▷ 119).

✉ Via dei Pescioni 2, 50123 Firenze ☎ 055 26651 🖐 €340–€620, excluding breakfast 🛈 67 🔄 🚌 A, B, 6, 11, 22, 36, 37

HERMITAGE
www.hermitagehotel.com
The emphasis here is on a warm and friendly welcome, something that draws visitors back time and again. The hotel is right next to the River Arno with the light, airy roof terrace overlooking the Ponte Vecchio. The rooms have TV and a safe and the hotel has a baby-sitting service, parking (at an extra cost), restaurant, bar and an email service.

✉ Vicolo Marzio 1, 50122 Firenze ☎ 055 287216 🖐 €170–€245 🛈 28 🔄 🚌 B

HOTEL CIMABUE
www.hotelcimabue.it
A small family-owned hotel that claims to be the best-value two-star hotel in Florence. Every bedroom is individually furnished and five have painted ceilings. There is a charming bar-cum-breakfast room. Nearby parking can be arranged for €15–€20 per day.

✉ Via B. Lupi 7, 50129 Firenze ☎ 055 475601 🖐 €79–€155 🛈 16 🔄 🚌 1, 6, 17

HOTEL ORTO DE'MEDICI
www.ortodeimedici.it
This elegant townhouse was converted to a hotel in the 1950s and the original painted ceilings, wallpapers and parquet floors give the feeling of being a guest in a private house. A veranda leads to a large terrace where drinks and breakfast are served.

✉ Via San Gallo 30, 50129 Firenze ☎ 055 483427 🖐 €108–€260 🛈 31 🔄 🚌 1, 7, 10, 17, 25

HOTEL RITZ
www.florenceitaly.net
The Ritz is on the north bank of the Arno, and many of the rooms have good views. Bright hues prevail, and the many reproductions of Old Masters give the illusion you are staying in the Uffizi. It is comfortably furnished, has attractive bedrooms, and the bonus of free email services.

✉ Lungarno della Zecca Vecchia 24, 50123 Firenze ☎ 055 234 0650 🖐 €90–€180 🛈 30 🔄 🚌 14, 23

JOHANNA I
www.johanna.it
The owners of this hotel and its sister hotels, Johanna II, Johlea I, Antica Johlea and Antica Firenze, employ knowledgeable and enthusiastic staff. The rooms are small but attractively furnished and there is a communal room with fridge. Amenities include private bathroom, coffee-making facilities, TV and telephone.
✉ Via Bonifacio Lupi 14, 50129 Firenze ☎ 055 481896 ✋ €95 Johanna I, €85 Johanna II, €95 Johlea I, €125 Antica Firenze, €140 Antica Johlea 🚪 11 🚌 8, 11, 12, 20,

LIANA
www.hotelliana.it
The Liana has all the elegance and atmosphere of a 19th-century residence. The rooms, which vary in size and quality, retain a period feel. The excellent amenities include telephone, private bathroom, minibar, safe and TV.
✉ Via Vittorio Alfieri 18, 50121 Firenze ☎ 055 245303 ✋ €90–€170 🚪 24 ♿ 🚌 6, 8, 13, 31, 32, 33, 80

LOGGIATO DEI SERVITI
www.loggiatodeiservitihotel.it
You can relax under vaulted ceilings, amid dark-wood antiques and rich fabrics in the former monastery of the Serviti. The refurbished guest rooms are enlivened by bright curtains and throws. Many look onto the Brunelleschi-designed arcades of the Piazza della Santissima Annunziata (▷ 94). The breakfast room and bar have views of the Accademia gardens.
✉ Piazza della Santissima Annunziata 3, 50122 Firenze ☎ 055 289592 ✋ €105–€205 🚪 38 ♿ 🚌 C, 6, 31, 32

LUNGARNO
www.lungarnohotels.com
The Lungarno gives you the choice of being more independent by staying in one of its apartments. The richly decorated interiors are reminiscent of a country house. Tall windows frame Florentine vistas and a tranquil central courtyard. Standard rooms have excellent facilities, and each apartment is equipped with kitchen, cable TV, a workstation with high-speed internet access and an espresso machine.
✉ Borgo San Jacopo 14, 50125 Firenze ☎ 055 27261 ✋ €290–€630 🚪 73 rooms, 4 apartments in adjoining building ♿ 🚌 D, 11, 36, 37

MALASPINA
www.malaspinahotel.it
The elegant Malaspina was built in the 14th century, which is borne out by its grand exterior. The rooms, soundproofed and scrupulously clean, are quite modern but retain traditional touches. They have TV, minibar, safe and telephone.
✉ Piazza Indipendenza 24, 50129 Firenze ☎ 055 489869 🕐 Closed 5–25 Aug ✋ €100–€230 🚪 31 ♿ 🚌 7, 10, 20, 25, 31, 32, 33

MARIO'S
www.hotelmarios.com
This family-run hotel is great value for money. Its small size and diligently maintained rooms, together with attentive service, give you the feeling of staying in a private house. The public spaces are adorned with antiques and interesting old photographs. There is also a bar-lounge area. A small apartment is available.
✉ Via Faenza 89, 50123 Firenze ☎ 055 216801 ✋ €85–€195 🚪 16 ♿ 🚌 4, 7, 10, 12, 13, 25, 31, 32, 33

MONNA LISA
www.monnalisa.it
This 15th-century palace is a wonderful mix of old and contemporary. A magnificent staircase leads to the upstairs rooms. Many have elaborate ceilings, Florentine wall hangings and dark antique furniture with modern velvet covers and cushions. Facilities include private bathroom, hairdryer, TV, telephone, minibar and safe. The flower-filled garden is a perfect spot for a glass of wine.
✉ Borgo Pinti 27, 50121 Firenze ☎ 055 247 9751 ✋ €226–€380 🚪 45 ♿ 🚌 14, 23

PALAZZO GALLETTI
www.palazzogalletti.it
The Palazzo Galletti, occupying a single floor of a converted palace, offers a less expensive alternative to the Relais Santa Croce (▷ below) and Palazzo Magnani Feroni (below). Although on a relatively busy road (in the Santa Croce district), seven of the spacious rooms face onto a peaceful courtyard. The best rooms are the two vast and completely frescoed suites.
✉ Via Sant'Egidio ☎ 055 390 5750 ✋ €110–€260 🚪 9 🚌 14, 23

PALAZZO MAGNANI FERONI
www.florencepalace.it
This is a grand place to stay on the south side of the River Arno. It has an inner courtyard, vaulted ceilings and a lavish use of marble. The owners are very hospitable and will make all manner of arrangements for you: They can even arrange for a shoemaker or a tailor to visit you in the privacy of your own room. Facilities include TV, telephone, minibar and safe.
✉ Borgo San Frediano 5, 50124 Firenze ☎ 055 239 9544 ✋ €230–€750 🚪 12 ♿ 🚌 D, 11, 36, 37

PLAZA HOTEL LUCCHESI
www.plazalucchesi.it
A riverside hotel, in the Santa Croce area, that has more understated sophistication than you will find at some of the city's other establishments. Rooms are light and relaxing, decorated in subdued shades. Private bathroom, TV, minibar, telephone and safe included. Some rooms are smaller and have showers, not baths.
✉ Lungarno della Zecca Vecchia 38, 50122 Firenze ☎ 055 26236 ✋ €185–€485 🚪 97 ♿ 🚌 B, C, 12, 13

RELAIS SANTA CROCE
www.relaissantacroce.com
Within a stone's throw of Santa Croce church, this sumptuous hotel is one of a growing number of luxury hotels in Florence to be housed in magnificent former palaces, complete with the frescoes

and other fine period details of the original structure. For a real treat, take the Da Verrazzano Royal Suite or Suite 201, which has magnificent views over the city.

✉ Via Ghibellina 87, 50122 Firenze ☎ 055 234 2230 ✋ €350–€800 ⓘ 18 🔇 🚍 B, C

RIVOLI
www.hotelrivoli.it
The Rivoli is a beautifully renovated Franciscan monastery. The public spaces have cross vaults, arches and pillars. Rooms are simple, with large marble bathrooms; some have a balcony or terrace. Amenities include 24-hour room service, laundry service, TV, radio and telephone.

✉ Via della Scala 33, 50126 Firenze ☎ 055 282853 ✋ €230–€350 ⓘ 80 🔇 🏊 Outdoor heated hot tub 🚍 A, 11, 36, 37

SAVOY
www.roccofortehotel.it
In a 19th-century building, this is one of Florence's top boutique hotels. It has parquet flooring and natural fabric carpets throughout; sleek furniture, cool photography and sculpture give the rooms a designer edge. The private bathrooms have deep bathtubs and are adorned with marble and mosaics. There is a bar and a restaurant, L'Incontro.

✉ Piazza della Repubblica 7, 50123 Firenze ☎ 055 27351 ✋ €539–€902, excluding breakfast ⓘ 107 🔇 🍴 🚍 A, 6, 22

SCOTI
www.hotelscoti.com
Scoti is in a 15th-century building opposite the Palazzo Strozzi in a bustling shopping street. It is a great place to stay—excellent value with period character, and a good central base from which to explore the city. The bedrooms are simple and light. There are no private bathrooms but the shared ones are very clean. The lounge area has 18th-century frescoes of landscapes.

✉ Via de' Tornabuoni 7, 50123 Firenze ☎ 055 292128 ✋ €75–€120 ⓘ 11 🔇 🚍 A, 6, 11, 22, 36, 37

SOGGIORNO ANTICA TORRE
www.anticatorre.com
Part of this hotel is based around an 11th-century tower, the original ceilings complemented by handsome parquet floors. The rooms are beautifully furnished. Each has a private bathroom (with shower or bath), minibar, TV and telephone.

✉ Piazza della Signoria 3, 50122 Firenze ☎ 055 216402 ✋ €90–€180 (suite €150–€200), excluding breakfast ⓘ 6 🔇 🚍 A, B

TORNABUONI BEACCI
www.tornabuonihotels.com
This handsome hotel is great for shopping and sightseeing but its position on a busy road means that it can be noisy. Since the late 1920s it has attracted writers, academics and aeshetes. The large, leafy roof garden and antiques-filled library-cum-lounge are quite retreats from the nearby shopping frenzy. Enjoy an *aperitivo* on the roof, watching the sun set. The design of the guest rooms is simple and uncluttered and each is equipped with private bathroom, telephone, hairdryer, satellite TV, minibar and safe.

✉ Via de' Tornabuoni 3, 20123 Firenze ☎ 055 212645 ✋ €120–€280 ⓘ 40 🔇 🚍 A, 6, 11, 22, 36, 37

TORRE GUELFA BORGO
www.hoteltorreguelfa.com
This 13th-century tower is home to one of Florence's best hotels. The rooms have ornate high ceilings, giving them an airy feel. Some have balconies and canopied beds, and include telephone, private bathroom and TV. The rooftop terrace is a great attraction.

✉ Borgo Santi Apostoli 8, 50123 Firenze ☎ 055 239 6338 ✋ €150–€210 (suites €150–€200) ⓘ 20 🔇 🚍 B, D, 11, 37

VILLA FIESOLE
www.villafiesole.it
The 19th-century Villa Fiesole gives visitors a taste of luxury just a short bus ride from Florence. It has a splendid greenhouse, which contains the breakfast room, a

lounge area and several bedrooms. The guest rooms have every modern comfort as well as private bathroom, TV and telephone.

✉ Via Beato Angelico 35, 50014 Fiesole ☎ 055 597252 ✋ €120–€240 ⓘ 32 🔇 🏊 Outdoor 🚍 7 🚗 Take A1 from Florence (or Via Giuseppe Mantellini—the road to Fiesole), then follow the signs as you enter Fiesole

VILLA LA MASSA
www.villalamassa.com
The Medici family once owned this villa. Rooms are furnished with heavy brocade and Florentine antiques, and have huge marbled bathrooms and views over the grounds. Tuscan cuisine is served at the Verocchio restaurant. Tennis, golf and horseback riding are available, and there is a free bus service to and from the Ponte Vecchio in Florence.

✉ Via della Massa 24, Bagno a Ripoli, 50012 Firenze ☎ 055 62611 🕐 Closed Nov–end Feb ✋ €410–€490 ⓘ 37 🔇 🏊 Outdoor 🚍 48 🚗 Take A1 from Florence and exit Firenze Sud before following signs for Bagno a Ripoli and Candeli

VILLA SAN MICHELE
www.villasanmichele.com
This former monastery, with a façade attributed to Michelangelo, is in the Fiesole hills and surrounded by trees. The bedrooms have every comfort and amenity, while the suites have huge marble-filled bathrooms, DVD, stereo, concierge service and a TV that emerges from a cabinet at the touch of a button. The Cenacolo and Loggia restaurants serve excellent regional cooking in the vaulted-ceilinged cloisters with the backdrop of a Last Supper fresco. The panoramic views of Florence from the terrace bar make this one of the most magical hotel settings in the world.

✉ Via Doccia 4, 50014 Fiesole ☎ 055 567 8200 🕐 Mar–end Oct ✋ €946–€1,890 ⓘ 45 🔇 🏊 Outdoor 🍴 🚍 7 🚗 On A1 from Firenze (or Via Giuseppe Mantellini—the road to Fiesole); turn right at the sign at the bottom of the hill

NORTHERN TUSCANY

Northern Tuscany contains some of the region's loveliest towns and most striking countryside, and yet it remains less visited and less well known than the area to the south, where cities such as Siena and the classic landscapes of Chianti have been celebrated for centuries. There are exceptions, of course, notably Pisa, whose famous Leaning Tower, part of the city's magnificent medieval cathedral complex, is one of Italy's most familiar images, but on the whole this is an area where a little exploration is required. The region's biggest revelation is Lucca, one of Tuscany's loveliest and most rewarding towns, set within imposing walls, and with its Roman, medieval and Renaissance heart almost perfectly preserved. Urbane and unspoiled, the town is full of beautiful Romanesque churches, sleepy squares and atmospheric streets, as well as excellent restaurants, cafés and some food shops. There is enough of interest in Lucca to warrant a stay in its own right, but it also makes a good base for day trips into the surrounding countryside or into Florence. Other towns and villages may lack Lucca's allure, but they don't lack for interest. Carrara, for example, is a fascinating place, at the heart of Europe's most important marble-mining region. Beyond their modern suburbs, Pistoia and Prato have glorious historic centres all but ignored by visitors eager to see nearby Florence. At Montecatini Terme you can bathe in natural hot springs and in Viareggio you can lie on the beach, for northern Tuscany has a long coastline dotted with small, unpretentious resorts much loved by Italian families.

As ever in Tuscany, the region's landscapes are every bit as memorable as its towns. Here, the most spectacular scenery is found in the Alpi Apuane, high, jagged mountains flanking the coast; a landscape that is a world away from the soft, pastoral countryside of southern Tuscany. On the mountains' eastern flanks is the Garfagnana, a lovely, sweeping valley, and to their north the Lunigiana, one of Tuscany's wildest and least-visited corners. East of Florence lies the Casentino, a secret enclave of wooded hills, hidden villages and ancient monasteries, much of which is protected as a national park.

REGIONS | NORTHERN TUSCANY • SIGHTS

ALPI APUANE

www.parks.it
www.parcoapuane.it

The Alpi Apuane mountains, a protected regional park, cut a dramatic swathe for 40km (25 miles) down the Versilian Coast. These are no gently rolling hills, but mountains with knife-like ridges and precipitous slopes. Because of their height and position, the Alpi have different habitats, making them a superb destination for nature-lovers. The flora is particularly special, as the mountains are one of Italy's richest botanical areas. Bird life is also prolific, with more than 300 species within the park's boundaries. There's a network of trails that penetrate deep into the mountains; the best walking area is inland from the marble-quarrying towns of Massa and Carrara. There's a park information office at Seravezza where you can reserve a place on guided walks.

✚ 276 C3 ℹ Park Information Office, Via Corrado del Greco 11, Seravezza 55047 ☎ 0584 75821 🕐 Mon, Wed, Fri, Sat 9.30–12.30, Tue, Thu 9.30–12.30, 3.30–5.30

BARGA

www.barganews.com

Barga is off the beaten track, yet easily accessible, making it an ideal trip into the country if you are staying in Lucca (▷ 136–139) or Pisa (▷ 140–143). You can stroll through the winding streets, shop for local goods such as chestnut flour and pecorino cheese, or stop at one of the town's cafés for a leisurely drink. The long-established Caffè Capretz (▷ 148) is not to be missed.

Barga sits on a hill above the Serchio Valley with fine views of the Alpi Apuane. It has kept much of its medieval appearance and layout, with remnants of the old walls and narrow, steep streets stretching down from the Romanesque cathedral. The Duomo dates mainly from the 13th century; it has a lovely

Opposite *Barga's Duomo*
Right *The countryside around Sita in the Casentino*

exterior and campanile and, inside, a wooden statue of St. Christopher. The climb to the cathedral is fairly steep but worth the effort for the views alone. The town has strong links with Scotland, as many of its residents emigrated to Glasgow. As a result many people speak English.

✚ 277 D3 ℹ Via di Mezzo 45, 55051 Barga ☎ 0583 724743 (freephone in Italy 800 028497) 🕐 Mon–Fri 8–2, Sat–Sun 10–12, 2.30–5 🚉 Barga Gallicano, long uphill walk

CARRARA

Carrara is tucked beneath the Alpi Apuane and the coast, almost on the border between Tuscany and Liguria. Busy and bustling, it feels like an industrial town, which is due to marble. The stone has been quarried from the Alpi Apuane for thousands of years. You can drive the short distance from town to see the quarries, but the best trip is to the village of Colonnata, 8km (5 miles) from Carrara. The drive takes you up a winding road past quarries to the tiny village, the main square of which is paved with marble. On the way there are plenty of places to stop and buy newly quarried marble.

✚ 276 B3 ℹ Via XX Settembre 46, 54037 ☎ 0585 844136/844403 🕐 Apr, May Mon–Sat 9–5; Jun–end Aug Mon–Sat 9–1, 4–7; Sep–end Mar Mon–Sat 9–1, 3–5

CASENTINO

www.parks.it

The wild, richly wooded country north of Arezzo is a rural area known as the Casentino. Its main towns are Bibbiena, focus of Tuscany's tobacco industry, and Poppi, site of the area's

main landmark, the 13th-century castle of Conti Guidi. Much of the Casentino lies within the Parco Nazionale delle Foreste Casentinesi, which combines preservation of the wildlife and the environment with protection of the area's historic villages, especially La Verna and Camaldoli. It was at La Verna, in 1224, that St. Francis of Assisi is said to have received the stigmata, and this mountaintop monastery is a major pilgrimage place, with many relics of the saint. There's another monastery at Camaldoli, in wooded surroundings popular with weekend hikers.

✚ 279 J4 ℹ Parco Nazionale delle Foreste Casentinesi, Via Guido Brocchi 7, 52015 Arezzo ☎ 0575 50301 🕐 Tue–Sun 9–1 🚉 Arezzo

CASTELFIORENTINO

The main reason for paying a visit to Castelfiorentino is to see the church of Santa Verdiana (ask at the tourist office). This is arguably the finest early 18th-century church in Tuscany, with striking architecture and frescoes. If you are historically minded, you will want to see the underground cell where Verdiana (1178–1242), the town's patron saint, lived for the last 34 years of her life; according to legend, she walled herself in along with two snakes. For art-lovers there are two fresco cycles by Benozzo Gozzoli (c1421–97) at the Biblioteca Comunale, depicting the life of the Virgin Mary.

✚ 281 F6 ℹ Via Redolfi, 50051 Castelfiorentino, ☎ 0571 629049 🕐 Daily 9–12/1, 3–5/6 🚉 Castelfiorentino

Above Porto Mediceo, the 16th-century quarter of Livorno, is one of the few areas of the historic port city to have survived bombing during World War II

COLLODI

www.pinocchio.it

The name Collodi is the nom de plume used by Carlo Lorenzini, creator of Pinocchio, Italy's most famous children's character. This unremarkable village, birthplace of Lorenzini's mother, has been the site of the Parco di Pinocchio (▷ 152) since the 1950s. The mazes, tableaux and statues are all related to the book, and presume a good knowledge of the text. Most children will enjoy the park and the excellent toyshop. Adults may prefer to wander through the gardens of the Villa Garzoni next door, laid out in the 18th century around a magnificent villa to a masterly baroque design, with topiary, geometric planting, parterres, cascades and fountains.

🕂 277 E4 ℹ️ Parco di Pinocchio, Via San Gennaro 3, Collodi, 51017 Pescia ☎ 0572 429342 🕐 Daily 9am–dusk 🎟️ Adult €10, child (3–14) €7 🚉 Pescia

GARFAGNANA

▷ 135.

LIVORNO

www.costadeglietruschi.it

Livorno is Tuscany's third-largest city, a booming port and one of the Mediterranean's biggest container docks. It's also a major ferry port, with departures to Corsica, Sardinia and Sicily, as well as the Tuscan islands of Gorgona and Capraia. Heavily bombed in World War II, its rebuilt commercial area is unattractive, so head for the area around the Piazza Grande, the heart of what's left of the old city. This area, the Porto Mediceo, is enclosed by canals and was laid out in 1557. On the piazza is the Duomo, and just a few minutes' walk away is the Fortezza Vecchia (old fortress) overlooking the harbour. Inland from here is the Fortezza Nuova (new fortress). The Museo Civico has nothing on Livorno's most famous son, the 20th-century artist Amedeo Modigliani. Instead, spend your time enjoying the city's excellent seafood.

🕂 280 C6 ℹ️ Piazza Cavour 6, 57100 Livorno ☎ 0586 204611 🕐 Tue, Thu 9–1, 3.30–6.30 Mon, Wed, Fri 9–1 🚉 Livorno

LUCCA

▷ 136–139.

LUNIGIANA

www.lunigiana.net

There are dramatic landscapes and isolated and remote villages in the Lunigiana, Tuscany's northernmost tip. The two main towns of this area around the Magra valley are Aulla, to the south, and Pontrémoli to the north. Between the two is a succession of tiny villages, often high in the hills, many with castles built to extract tolls from anyone passing through. Aulla suffered huge damage in World War II, so you should perhaps head for some of the surrounding villages sitting among the dense woods of sweet chestnut trees, which once provided the area's staple food. Pontrémoli has a baroque cathedral and a museum (Museo del Comune) with a group of extraordinary prehistoric stylized statues dating from 3000–1000BC.

🕂 276 A1 ℹ️ Piazza della Repubblica, 54027 Pontrémoli, Massa Carrara ☎ 0187 831180/833278 (for winter enquiries) 🕐 Jun–end Sep daily 9–12, 2–6 🚉 Pontrémoli

MONTECATINI TERME

Tuscany's finest spa town lies in the district of the Valdinievole (Valley of Mists) in northern Tuscany. A funicular railway is a scenic link to Montecatini Alto, the old upper town, which has fine views over the valley. The town is dominated by the Parco delle Terme, which has most of the spas. The thermal springs and their healing powers were well known to the Romans, and in the 14th century gentlemen came here to indulge in water therapy. In the 18th century the magnificent Leopoldine and Tuttuccio baths were built, to be followed in the early 20th century by the art nouveau Terme Excelsior (▷ 154).

🕂 277 E4 ℹ️ Viale Verdi 66–68, 51016 Montecatini Terme, ☎ 0572 772244 🕐 Nov–Easter Mon–Sat 9–12.30, 3–6; Easter–end Oct Mon–Sat 9–12.30, 3–6, Sun 9–12 🚉 Montecatini

GARFAGNANA

North of Lucca, the Serchio Valley runs south down the east of the Alpi Apuane (▷ 133), an attractive and largely undiscovered area that's dotted with little towns and laced with excellent walking trails. Even without a car, you can reach towns such as Barga, but with your own vehicle you can drive the numerous tiny roads that run up from the valley floor right into the mountains and through to the next valley system to the east. The area is perfect for wildlife-lovers and hikers, since much of it is protected as the regional nature reserve Parco Regionale delle Alpi Apuane. Good bases for exploring the area include the Orecchiella, the most rugged stretch with marked walking trails, Bagni di Lucca and Barga.

THE TOWNS

Only 25km (15 miles) north of Lucca, Bagni di Lucca is a low-key spa town, whose heyday was in the 19th century, when it was among Europe's most popular spas, patronized by English poets Byron, Shelley and Browning. It's still a pleasant place, and has a good range of accommodation. Another good bet for a few days is the town of Barga (▷ 133), some 45km (28 miles) up the Serchio Valley, at the start of the most scenic stretch. Peaceful Barga's main sight is its Duomo, dating mainly from the 13th century.

From Barga, it's a 20-minute drive west to the Grotta del Vento underground cave system (▷ 152). Farther north is the valley's main town, Castelnuovo di Garfagnana, a fair-sized market town that's a good base for both hikers and drivers exploring the mountains and villages.

THE ORECCHIELLA

The Orecchiella, wild country with magnificent views over wooded mountains, is easily reached from Barga. The mountains are rounded, with alpine meadows above the treeline—great hiking country that is still traditionally farmed. If you plan to take to the hills and walk, Corfino makes a good base; the park and visitors' office is 7km (4 miles) from there. Northeast from Castelnuovo is the ancient pilgrimage area of San Pellegrino in Alpe (▷ 149), at 1,524m (5,000ft), where you can get insights into the traditional peasant way of life at the Museo Etnografico Provinciale (▷ 148).

INFORMATION

www.garfagnanavacanze.it

⊕ 277 D2 ⚹ Centro Visite, Parco Regionale delle Alpi Apuane, Piazza delle Erbe 1, 55032 Castelnuovo di Garfagnana ☎ 0583 644242 🕒 Jun–end Sep daily 9–1, 3–7; Oct–end May 9–1, 3.30–5.30 🚉 Castelnuovo di Garfagnana

Below *The spa town of Bagni di Lucca is set among pretty woodlands*

INFORMATION

www.comune.lucca.it
www.luccapro.sns.it

✚ 277 D4 ⓘ Piazzale Verdi, 55100
Lucca ☎ 0583 583150 ⏰ Apr–end Oct
daily 9–7; Nov–end Mar 9–5 🚌 Lucca

Above *Piazza Anfiteatro, Lucca's principal piazza, retains the elliptical shape of the Roman amphitheatre that once occupied the site*

INTRODUCTION

Lucca is a delightful town: peaceful, charming and urbane, and third after Florence and Siena in terms of art, culture and all-round allure. With its intricate grid of streets, a legacy of the Roman colony on the site, the town remains sleepily and perfectly preserved within a ring of tree-lined walls. There is enough of interest in Lucca to keep you occupied for at least two days and it also makes a good base for day trips into the Garfagnana region to the north (▷ 135). Yet it's small enough, and accessible enough, to see as a day trip from Florence either by road or rail.

There has been a settlement in Lucca since around 1000BC. The city became a Roman colony in 180BC and grew in importance from then on. In Lombard times, around the sixth century, it was the capital of the embryonic Tuscany, and by the 11th century banking and silk were starting to prove the mainstay of its economy, helped by its 12th-century recognition as a free Comune. In 1314 the city came briefly under Pisan control, but regained its independence, and defeated Pisa and Pistoia under the leadership of Castruccio Castracani. In the mid-16th century Lucca remained an independent republic and new defensive city walls—those you see today—were erected to replace the earlier Roman and medieval ones. The city remained a republic until the French occupation, when Napoleon Bonaparte presented it to his sister Elisa. After the fall of Napoleon it became a Bourbon duchy and remained independent of the Tuscan Grand Duchy until 1847. Lucca today is one of Tuscany's richest cities, its artistic heritage and high standard of living attracting an increasing number of visitors.

It doesn't matter too much where you start you exploration, although if you arrive by car you will almost certainly have to leave your vehicle in one of the parking areas outside or just inside the walls. Most of Lucca's central streets are pedestrian-only (though bicycles are allowed), but nowhere is far to walk, with all the main sights a few minutes away from the central squares of Piazza Napoleone and Piazza San Michele. Be sure to see the Duomo and its Museo della Cattedrale, before crossing the square to inspect Santi Giovanni e Reparata. Also essential is the church of San Michele in Foro, with its glorious façade, and the best example of the Pisan-Romanesque style churches you find dotted across the city. Via Fillungo (Long Thread Street) is an expensive shopping street that leads north to the Piazza Anfiteatro and San Frediano, another outstanding church. Only the two main museums, housed in the Villa Guinigi and Palazzo Mansi, are slightly peripheral. They lie inside the walls to the west and east of the heart of town. Finally, be sure to allow time to walk or cycle at least part of the way around the walls for an overview of this lovely city —bicycles are easily rented at several points around town.

WHAT TO SEE

DUOMO DI SAN MARTINO

Lucca's stunning Romanesque cathedral, with its asymmetrical façade, has 11th- to 13th-century reliefs on and around the three principal doors. Nicola Pisano, the 13th-century Pisan sculptor, first made his mark here; his panels, *Annunciation*, *Nativity* and *Adoration of the Magi*, are around the left-hand door. The interior is best known for the work of Matteo Civitali, a 15th-century sculptor whose masterpiece occupies the middle of the church. This is the Tempietto, an octagonal structure that holds the *Volto Santo* (Holy Face), a cedarwood crucifix much venerated in the city and said to be an exact likeness of Christ. According to legend it was carved by Nicodemus, a witness of the Crucifixion. Look for the tomb of Ilaria del Carretto, the second wife of a local merchant, tenderly carved between 1407 and 1410 by the Sienese master Jacopo della Quercia. You'll find it in the sacristy, where there's also a *Madonna Enthroned with Saints* by Ghirlandaio.

✚ 139 C3 ✉ Piazza San Martino ☎ 0583 490530 ⏰ Duomo: mid-Mar to end Oct Mon–Fri 9.30–5.45, Sat 9.30–6.45, Sun 9.30–10.45, 12–6; Nov to mid-Mar Mon–Fri 9.30–4.45, Sat 9.30–6.45, Sun 11.20–11.50, 1–4.45. Sacristy: Apr–end Oct Mon–Fri 9.30–5.45, Sat 9.30–6.45, Sun 9.30–10.45, 12–6; Nov–end Feb Mon–Fri 9.30–4.45, Sat 9.30–6.45, Sun 11.20–11.50, 1–4.45 ♿ Duomo: free. Sacristy: Adult €2, child (6–14) €1.50. Combined ticket with Museo della Cattedrale and Santi Giovanni e Reparata: Adult €6, child (6–14) €4

SAN MICHELE IN FORO

The Piazza San Michele, the site of the old Roman forum, has given its name to the church of San Michele in Foro, dating from 1070. The exterior was completed about the middle of the 12th century, a dazzling masterpiece that is an intricate medley of tiny loggias, lavish carvings and decorated columns, all different, the whole topped by the triumphant figure of an archangel. The 12th-century campanile is the tallest in Lucca.

✚ 139 B2 ✉ Piazza San Michele ☎ 0583 48459 ⏰ Apr–end Oct daily 7.40–12, 3–6; Nov–end Mar 9–12, 3–5 ♿ Free

SAN FREDIANO

San Frediano is the third of Lucca's splendid churches, after the cathedral and San Michele. It was built between 1112 and 1147 on the site of a sixth-century basilica and is fronted by a glittering 13th-century mosaic depicting the Ascension. The interior is crammed with sculptures, the best being the Fonte Lustrale, a 12th-century baptismal font finely carved by three different craftsmen, and the Cappella Trenta altarpiece by Jacopo della Quercia. Also of interest are the intricate 12th-century cosmati paving in the presbytery, and the Cappella di Sant'Agostino, frescoed in the early 1500s by a little-known artist, Amico Aspertini.

✚ 139 B1 ✉ Piazza San Frediano ☎ 0583 493627 ⏰ Mon–Sat 8.30–12, 3–5.30, Sun 9–11.30, 3–5.30 ♿ Free

TIPS

» Lucca is easily explored on foot. As the station is only 10 minutes' walk from the old town and parking is not easy, it is better to come by train rather than car.

» Emulate the locals and get around by bicycle; these can be rented from the tourist office or numerous places around town (look for the word *noleggio*—rental).

» At some point in your visit to Lucca you should walk or bicycle along the wide, tree-lined promenade that runs along the top of the ramparts.

Below The glittering mosaic depicting the Ascension on its façade distinguishes San Frediano church from others in Lucca

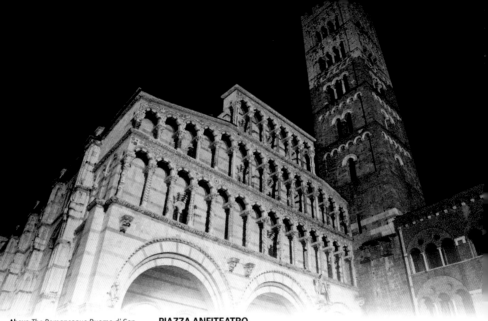

Above *The Romanesque Duomo di San Martino at night*

PIAZZA ANFITEATRO

This extraordinary piazza, dotted with cafés and bright with flower-sellers' displays, draws more visitors than any of Lucca's churches and it's a great place to take a break. Its shape is that of the Roman amphitheatre that was once here, and you can still see traces of arches and columns incorporated in the old buildings that surround the piazza. Stone from here was carted away for building in the 12th century, after which the space was occupied by medieval slum buildings; these were cleared in 1830.

🗺 139 C2

MUSEO NAZIONALE DI VILLA GUINIGI

Lucca's main museum occupies the Villa Guinigi, built for the Guinigi family in the 15th century, and where the exhibits are sensitively displayed. The big and varied collection includes furniture and the applied arts, archaeological finds, sculpture and painting. The sculpture and archaeology are displayed on the ground floor, while the floor above is devoted to paintings. These represent most major Tuscan schools, ranging from early Lucchese and Sienese works to huge 16th-century panels.

🗺 139 D2 ✉ Via della Quarquonia ☎ 0583 496033 🕐 Tue–Sat 8.30–7.30, Sun 8.30–1.30. Ticket office closes 60 min earlier ✋ Adult €4, under 18 €2; combined ticket available with Museo Nazionale di Palazzo Mansi for €6.50 🏛

MUSEO NAZIONALE DI PALAZZO MANSI

The 17th-century palace in which this museum is set is as great a draw as the artworks themselves. You'll pass through a series of ornate rococo rooms, exuberantly frescoed and hung with tapestries, before reaching the rooms with the Pinacoteca Nazionale, the picture collection. Outstanding are portraits by the Mannerists Bronzino (1503–72) and Jacopo Pontormo (1494–1557), sinuous compositions that contrast with the warm and opulent style of those by the Venetian Tintoretto (1518–94). To learn about the source of Lucca's wealth, spend time in the section that traces the development of the silk and damask industries.

🗺 139 A2 ✉ Via Galli Tassi 43 ☎ 0583 55570 🕐 Tue–Sat 8.30–7.30, Sun 8.30–1.30 ✋ Adult €4, under 18 €2; combined ticket available with Museo Nazionale di Villa Guinigi for €6.50

THE WALLS

You can access the walls at any of the bastions and then cycle or walk down the broad tree-lined promenade that runs along the top. The walls were built between 1520 and 1650 and are 12m (40ft) high and 30m (100ft) wide at the base with a moat that is 35m (115ft) wide. They form a complete circle round the town 4.2km (2.6 miles) long.

TORRE GUINIGI

Once the home of a leading Lucchese family, this battlemented tower house is topped by a living holm oak, whose roots have grown into the room below the roof. You can climb the 44m (144ft) tower for the best views over the city.
✛ 139 C2 ✉ Via Sant'Andrea ☎ 336 203221 🕐 Jul to mid-Sep daily 9am–11pm; mid-Sep to end daily Oct 9–7; Nov–end Feb daily 9.30–5; Mar 9–6.30, Apr–end Jun daily 9.30–6.30
🖐 Adult €5, child (6–12) €4

MUSEO DELLA CATTEDRALE

This museum has objects from the cathedral, including illustrated manuscripts, reliquaries, church furnishings and sculpture.
✛ 139 C3 ✉ Piazza Antelminelli ☎ 0583 490530 🕐 Apr–end Oct daily 10–6; Nov–end Mar Mon–Fri 10–2, Sat, Sun and public holidays 10–5 🖐 Adult €4, child (6–14) €2.50. Combined ticket with Duomo Sacristy and Santi Giovanni e Reparata: Adult €6, child (6–14) €4

SANTI GIOVANNI E REPARATA

Dating from the eighth century, this was Lucca's first cathedral. Excavations have uncovered Roman mosaics, Roman columns and a fourth-century pavement.
✛ 139 B3 ✉ Piazza Antelminelli ☎ 0583 490530 🕐 Apr–end Oct daily 10–6; Nov–end Mar Sat, Sun 10–5 🖐 Adult €2.50, child (6–14) €1.50. Combined ticket with Duomo Sacristy and Museo della Cattedrale: Adult €6, child (6–14) €4

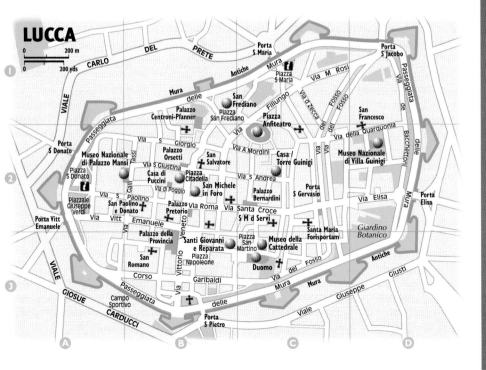

PISA

INTRODUCTION

First stop on a tour of the city has to be the Campo dei Miracoli (Field of Miracles), the green space graced by the Leaning Tower (Torre Pendente), the Duomo and the Battistero. Around it are the Camposanto (cemetery) and two museums relevant to the site (if time's short you may want to leave these off your list). From the Campo, Via Carducci and Borgo Stretto, lined with graceful, mainly Renaissance palaces, lead through the most evocative part of the old city to the river. On the way, you could take a detour west to the Piazza dei Cavalieri, one of Pisa's most attractive squares. The streets around here are lively during the morning market. Cross the river to take in the little church of Santa Maria della Spina. Alternatively, head east along the Lungarno to the Museo Nazionale. Thereafter, you may be surprised to find that much of Pisa is modern in appearance, the result of bombing in the World War II, when Allied forces attempted to destroy the city's major rail installations. It's worth considering a night's stay in Pisa if you're flying in late or out early from the region's main airport; otherwise, it is a good day-trip destination, an hour by train from Florence or just 20 minutes from Lucca, a better overall base.

The Allies' preoccupation with Pisa was hardly surprising, for its strategic position—and, formerly, its port—have always made it important. A naval base under the Romans, Pisa reached its peak in the 11th and 12th centuries, when this maritime city-state was one of the Mediterranean's greatest powers. It defeated the Saracens and expelled them from Corsica, Sardinia and the Balearic Islands, bringing Pisa to the attention of its powerful neighbour, Genoa. The Genoese victory of 1284 marked the start of decline, with Pisa's commercial empire collapsing and the harbour silting up. In 1406 the city was taken over by Florence, and the Medici embarked on major rebuilding, while turning Pisa into a focus for science and learning. The university they founded numbered Galileo among its teachers. Despite this the city gradually sank into obscurity and provinciality, its palaces providing inexpensive accommodation in the 19th century for British exiles like the poet Byron and the Shelleys. Despite the bombing of World War II, the second half of the 20th century saw it re-emerge from the shadows as a provincial capital with growing light industry, a thriving university and as the entry point for the thousands of visitors flying into Tuscany via its airport.

INFORMATION

www.opapisa.it

➕ 280 D5 ✉ Piazza del Duomo 1, 56126 Pisa ☎ 050 560464 ⏰ Jun–end Sep daily 9–7; Oct–end May daily 9.30–5.30/6.30 🚉 Pisa Centrale

Opposite *Detail of the Leaning Tower's exquisite galleries*
Above *The Fontana dei Putti, Duomo and the Leaning Tower*

TIPS

» A variety of combined tickets for some or all of the cathedral, baptistery, Museo and Camposanto (but not the Leaning Tower) can be bought at the ticket office of the Leaning Tower or the Museo; two monuments or museums from €5–€8.50.

» Tickets for the Leaning Tower can be purchased in advance at the ticket office or on website www.opapisa.it.

» There are excellent bus and train connections to the city, so leave the car behind.

WHAT TO SEE

THE LEANING TOWER OF PISA

The Leaning Tower is a fine example of Pisan architecture, but for most visitors its main attraction is the very fact that it leans. You may be surprised to know it always has. Work on the bell tower started in 1173, and by the time three of the eight floors were in place there was a distinct tilt. Despite strenuous efforts, the inclination increased throughout the construction process, and by the time the tower was completed in 1350 the angle was permanent. Unstable ground beneath exacerbated the slant so that by the late 20th century the tower was 4.5m (15ft) off the perpendicular and at a critical angle. In 1990 the tower was shut and 10 steel bands were wrapped around its base to prevent collapse. A 900-tonne lead ingot counterbalance was inserted and the underlying ground drilled to remove water and silt. This operation brought the tower back to its 1838 position, where it should remain for the foreseeable future. You can climb the 294 steps to the top, 54m (177ft) up, from where Galileo is said to have conducted his experiments on the force of gravity (▷ 35).

✉ Piazza del Duomo, 56126 Pisa ☎ 050 560547 🕒 Apr–end Sep daily 8.30–8.30; Nov–end Feb daily 9.30–5; Mar, Oct daily 9–7; mid-Jun to mid-Aug also visits daily 8.30–11pm 💰 Adult €15 (€17 online) 🎫 By tour only, with timed tickets, lasting 40 minutes ❓ No children under 8 allowed

DUOMO

www.duomo.pisa.it

A supreme example of Pisan-Romanesque architecture, the Duomo is among Italy's greatest buildings, the subtlety of its grey-and-white marble the perfect foil for the intricacy of its four-tiered façade. Building started in 1064 and finished in the middle of the 12th century. Spend time admiring the exterior columns and loggias of the front before entering through the Porta di San Ranieri with Bonanno Pisano's bronze doors, cast in 1180. Inside, the five aisles, sheathed in black-and-white marble, provide harmonious surroundings for Giovanni Pisano's marble pulpit, carved between 1302 and 1311, and the apse mosaic (1302) by Cimabue. After a fire in 1595 the pulpit—then considered horribly out of date—was put into storage and was only rediscovered in 1926. It is a wonderful work, the whole surface carved with virtually freestanding figures in a series of tableaux that tell the story of Christ's life.

The huge incense lamp (1587) was for many years thought to have inspired Galileo's theory of the movement of the pendulum.

✉ Piazza del Duomo, 56126 Pisa ☎ 050 560547 🕒 Apr–end Sep daily 8–8; Mar, Oct Mon–Sat 10–6, Sun 1–6; Nov–end Feb Mon–Sat 10–12.45, 3–4.45, Sun 3–4.45 💰 Adult €2 (Mar–end Oct), under 10 free; free to all Nov–end Feb

Below *Pisa's Duomo set the style for buildings across Tuscany*

Below right *The Duomo's intricately carved marble pulpit is the work of Giovanni Pisano*

BATTISTERO

The third structure on the Campo dei Miracoli is the baptistery, built between 1152 and 1350. It's a circular building, its three levels of arcades crowned with an elegant eight-sided dome, whose exterior niches once held statues—now in the Museo dell'Opera del Duomo. Inside the dome is bare and the arcades plain. The pulpit was carved in 1260 by Nicola Pisano, father of Giovanni.

✉ Piazza del Duomo, 56126 Pisa ☎ 050 560547 ⏰ Apr–end Sep daily 9–7; Mar, Oct daily 9–6.30; Nov–end Feb daily 10–4.30 💶 Adult €5, under 10 free

Above *The city's flag is known as the Pisan Cross*

CAMPOSANTO

The north side of the Campo dei Miracoli is edged by a wall of white marble, part of what used to be the cemetery for Pisa's most eminent citizens. The Camposanto (literally the Holy Field), said to have been built around a cargo of earth brought from the Holy Land, took the form of a huge Gothic cloister, whose arcades hold memorials and tombs. The entire space was frescoed during the 15th century, creating a building that was considered among the loveliest in Italy. In 1944 an Allied incendiary bomb set fire to the roof, and molten lead poured down the walls, destroying almost all the frescoes. An exhibition room displays photos of the Camposanto as it once looked.

✉ Piazza del Duomo, 56126 Pisa ☎ 050 560547 ⏰ Apr–end Sep daily 9–7; Mar, Oct daily 9–6.30; Nov–end Feb daily 10–4.30 💶 Adult €5, under 10 free

MUSEO DELL'OPERA DEL DUOMO

This museum displays religious statuary, paintings, vestments and other treasures from the Duomo's long history. There's superb sculpture by the Pisano family, including the ravishing *Madonna del Colloquio* by Giovanni (active c1265–1314), and the Pisan Cross, which was carried by the Pisan knights during the First Crusade. Other works include Islamic pieces that throw light on Byzantine influences on Pisan art, and a fine collection of Etruscan and Roman sculpture.

✉ Piazza del Duomo, 56126 Pisa ☎ 050 835010/560547 ⏰ Nov–end Feb daily 10–5; Mar daily 9–6; Apr–end Sep daily 8–8; Oct daily 9–7 💶 Adult €5, child (under 10) free

MORE TO SEE

PIAZZA DEI CAVALIERI

This lovely square, the heart of medieval Pisa, was transformed in the 16th century. The Palazzo dei Cavalieri was the headquarters of the Knights of St. Stephen and is decorated with sgraffito, in which the top layer of plaster is cut away to reveal a contrasting layer beneath.

MUSEO NAZIONALE DI SAN MATTEO

This museum has most of the major artworks from Pisa's churches.

✉ Piazza San Matteo in Soarta, 56123 ☎ 050 541865 ⏰ Tue–Sat 8.30–7.30, Sun 8.30–1 💶 Adult €5, combined ticket with Museo Nazionale di Palazzo Reale €8, under 18 free

MUSEO NAZIONALE DI PALAZZO REALE

Once a residence of the Medici and of the dukes of Lorraine and Savoy, the palace contains objects and paintings from their collections.

✉ Piazza Carrara, Lungarno Pacinotti 46, 56123 ☎ 050 926511 ⏰ Mon–Fri 9–2.30, Sat 9–1.30 💶 Adult €5, combined ticket with Museo Nazionale di San Matteo €8, under 18 free

SANTA MARIA DELLA SPINA

This Pisan-Gothic oratory was built in 1323 to house one of the thorns from Christ's Crown of Thorns. It once stood close to the river and was moved in 1871 to save it from flooding.

✉ Lungarno Gambecorte ☎ No phone ⏰ Apr–end Oct Mon–Fri 10–1.30, 2.30–6, Sat, Sun 10–1.30, 2.30–7; Nov–end Mar closed one hour earlier 💶 Adult €1.10

MUGELLO

www.mugellotoscana.it

Lying hard against the Apennines on Tuscany's border with Emilia-Romagna, the Mugello is a lushly fertile area densely planted with olive groves and vineyards. Away from the cultivated land around the Mugello, there are thick forests of oak and chestnut trees that form a backdrop to the scenic villages. The main town is Borgo San Lorenzo, but if you are planning a stay, it's better to head for one of the villages—perhaps Vicchio, birthplace of Fra Angelico, or Barberino di Mugello, a market town with an attractive central piazza. Barberino is on the way to Passo della Futa, a pass at 900m (2,950ft), from where there are superb views.

➕ 278 H3 🛈 Via P. Togliatti 45, 50032 Borgo San Lorenzo ☎ 055 845271 🕐 Tue, Thu 9–1, 3–6, Mon, Wed, Fri 9–1 🚊 Borgo San Lorenzo

PISA

▷ 140–143.

PISTOIA

www.pistoia.turismo.toscana.it

Pistoia sits at the foot of the Apennines, 47km (29 miles) east of Lucca (▷ 136–139). Its name probably derives from the Latin *pistores*, meaning 'bakers', as it was a town that supplied provisions to the Roman troops. Today much of the city's trade is based on plants and flowers (▷ 15). Pistoia's heart is Piazza del Duomo, with its 14th-century baptistery and sumptuous cathedral, and there are several other churches, as well as a museum. Every Wednesday and Saturday morning one of Italy's largest markets is held on the piazza.

The cathedral has a striking silver altarpiece, the *Dossale di San Jacopo*, made between 1287 and 1456, and found in the Cappella di San Jacopo. It is covered in a vast number of figures, some of which were carved by Filippo Brunelleschi. The 14th-century Baptistery of San Giovanni has a font made in 1226 and a 16th-century, gold-painted wooden altar. The church of San Giovanni Fuorcivitas is proud of its terracotta *Visitation* by Luca della Robbia. The Museo Civico's collection includes paintings ranging from Romanesque to 19th-century works.

➕ 277 F4 🛈 Palazzo dei Vescovi, Piazza del Duomo 4, 51100 Pistoia ☎ 0573 21622 🕐 Sep–end May Tue–Sat 9–1, 3–6; Jun–end Aug also open Mon and 2nd and 4th Sun of month 🚊 Pistoia

PRATO

www.prato.turismo.toscana.it

Romantics might be attracted to Prato by the story that this is where the monk and artist Fra Filippo Lippi met and fell in love with a nun, Lucrezia Buti, whom he later married. Prato means 'meadow', but today the town is surrounded by industry. It has a long association with textile manufacturing and has been famous for its fabrics since the 13th century. Most of the sights are within the medieval walls. The mighty, turreted walls of the Castello dell'Imperatore were built by Emperor Frederick II between 1217 and 1248, a time of huge developments in literature, science and poetry.

The cathedral (daily 7.30–12, 3.30–7) was built in the 12th century. *The Pulpit of the Sacred Girdle* by Michelozzo and Donatello graces a corner of the façade, and inside are frescoes by Filippo Lippi, including a famous depiction of Salome dancing at Herod's feast. You can see more works from the cathedral in the Museo dell'Opera del Duomo (Mon, Wed–Sat 9.30–12.30, 3–6, Sun 9.30–12.30). The church of Santa Maria delle Carceri, built in the form of a Greek cross, is regarded as a masterpiece of Renaissance architecture and contains terracotta works by Andrea della Robbia.

➕ 278 F4 🛈 Piazza Santa Maria delle Carceri 15, 59100 Prato ☎ 0574 24112 🕐 Mon–Fri 9–1.30, 2.30–6, Sat, Sun 9–1, 3–6; Apr–end Oct closes one hour later 🚊 Prato

SAN MINIATO

www.cittadisanminiato.it

San Miniato overlooks the Arno plain and has wide views of the valley. The lower part of the town is busy with leather workshops—something for which the town is now famous. Bombing during World War II destroyed much of the old town, but the tower built by Emperor Frederick II was rebuilt. Head up to San Miniato Alto to take in the best of the sights, spread between the Piazza del Popolo and the Piazza della Repubblica up the hill. The cathedral (daily 9–1, 3–5) has a Romanesque façade and a fine bell tower known as Matilda's Tower, after Matilda of Tuscany, who was born here in 1046. Farther up is the Rocca (castle), to which you can climb for extensive views of the surrounding countryside.

➕ 281 E5 🛈 Piazza del Popolo 3, 56027 San Miniato ☎ 0571 42745 🕐 Apr–end Oct daily 9.30–1, 3.30–7.30; Nov–end Mar 9–1, 3–7.30 🚊 San Miniato Basso

VIAREGGIO

www.aptversilia.it

Visitors come to Viareggio for its beach. This is the largest resort on Tuscany's Riviera, and as it is only an hour's drive from Florence, it attracts large numbers of day-trippers from the city. It is on the coast of northwestern Tuscany, squeezed between the chic resort of Forte dei Marmi to the north and Torre del Lago to the south. Much of the large sandy beach is divided into *stabilimenti balneari* (bathing concessions, ▷ 259), which means you have to pay to use it, but this does ensure that it is kept clean. The beach is edged by an elegant boulevard with several art nouveau buildings along it. The town's streets have plenty of hotels, pizzerias and shops.

Be sure to visit the Villa Puccini (Dec–end Mar Tue–Sun 10–12.30, 2.30–5.30; Apr, May 10–12.30, 3–6; Jun–end Oct 10–12.30, 3–6.30; closed Nov), south of Viareggio in Torre del Lago. Home of the opera composer Giacomo Puccini from 1891 to 1921, it has been preserved as it was during his lifetime, with period furniture and personal memorabilia. A bus service runs regularly from Viareggio—ask at the tourist office.

✚ 276 C4 🚹 Viale Carducci 10, 55059 Viareggio ☎ 0584 962233 🕒 Mon–Sat 9–2, 3–7.30, Sun 9–1; also Sun 4–7 in Jul and Aug. Closed 2nd and 3rd Mon of the month 🚉 Viareggio

VILLA MEDICI DI POGGIO A CAIANO

This is the best known of the country residences owned by the Medici family. Not only is it a superb building, inspired by ancient Rome and surrounded by parkland, it is also steeped in Italian history. Lorenzo il Magnifico (▷ 32) purchased a farmhouse on the site in 1480 and commissioned Giuliano da Sangallo to rebuild it. It became his preferred country hideaway and the place where he wrote his sonnets. His descendants added to the original structure with the entrance loggia and the splendid curving double stairway. Francesco I died here, allegedly poisoned, and Vittorio Emanuele II often used it as a love nest.

The interior of the villa is very striking and its main focus is the double-height Salone, created by Sangallo from the courtyard that occupied the space between the two blocks of the original farmhouse. The 16th-century frescoes that cover the ceiling include a superb depiction of *Caesar Receiving the Egyptian Tribute* by Andrea del Sarto and Pontormo's *Vertumnus and Pomona*, a sun-drenched, mellow painting of two Roman rural deities, that perfectly evokes the fruitfulness of Tuscany in summer. The frescoes can also be read as a tribute to the Medici family, who appear among the figures, and have references to the life of Lorenzo de'Medici—look out for the giraffe in the *Egyptian Tribute* which was presented to Lorenzo by the Sultan of Egypt. The villa is surrounded by parkland, laid out in a 19th-century English landscaped style, and shelters behind high walls.

✚ 278 F4 🚹 Piazza de' Medici 12–14, 59016 Poggio a Caiano ☎ 055 877012 🕒 Nov–end Feb daily 8.15–3.30; Mar, Sep, Oct 8.15–4.30; Apr, May 8.15–5.30; Jun–end Aug 8.15–6.30 💶 Adult €2, under 18 free 🔶 Accompanied (not guided) visits every hour on the half hour 🗓

VINCI

www.comune.vinci.fi.it
www.museoleonardiano.it

Vinci is the birthplace of the artist, architect, inventor and all-round genius, Leonardo da Vinci. This pleasant little town is surrounded by slopes thickly clad with olive groves. It's a quiet place mostly free from crowds of visitors, but there is enough in the little town to occupy you for several hours.

The greatest attraction is the Museo Leonardiano (Mar–end Oct daily 9.30–7; Nov–end Feb daily 9.30–6), in a castle from the early Middle Ages. It contains fascinating scale reproductions of the machines and models that Leonardo invented. The terrace beside the museum has superb views over the hills. You can also visit Chiesa di Santa Croce (check with the tourist office), the church where Leonardo was baptized. The town has some good bars and cafés where you can relax after your sightseeing.

Just 3km (2 miles) from Vinci is the Casa Natale di Leonardo (same hours as museum), the house where Leonardo was born in 1452. There's little to see inside, but the surrounding countryside is attractive.

✚ 277 F5 🚹 Via della Torre 11, 50059 ☎ 0571 568012 🕒 Mar–end Oct daily 10–7; Nov–end Feb 10–6

Opposite *Although less well-known to visitors, Mugello's landscape rivals that of Chianti*
Left *The little town of Vinci, birthplace of the famous artist*

THE GARFAGNANA

This drive takes you through the cool mountains of the Garfagnana, the region north of Lucca that stretches between the rugged country of the Parco Regionale delle Alpi Apuane in the west and the softer slopes of the Riserva Naturale dell'Orecchiella in the east. Towns and villages are sprinkled about the hills, and there are plenty of paths if you feel like stopping and exploring on foot.

THE DRIVE

Distance: 170km (106 miles)
Allow: 8 hours
Start/end at: Lucca

★ Leave Lucca (▷ 136–139) through the Porta San Donato and pick up the SR12 going towards Abetone. At the next exit follow the signs for Castelnuovo di Garfagnana. After 4km (2.5 miles) you will see the Lucchesi hills in front of you. Shortly after this, turn left at the brown signpost indicating 'Garfagnana' (▷ 135) and cross the bridge over the Serchio river onto the road that runs parallel to the SR12 on the river's opposite bank. Pass through two tunnels and, after about 4km (2.5 miles), turn left again. Stay on this road, which goes through Diecimo; papermaking factories bear witness to an old local industry. Drive on to the village of Borgo a Mozzano, where there is a bell tower on the left-hand side. Just

after this you'll see a sign saying 'Barga 18'; go over a bridge. The Ponte del Diavolo is to your right, but you can't drive over it.

❶ The distinctive Ponte del Diavolo (The Devil's Bridge), as it's locally known, dates from the 12th century. According to legend, the builder sought help from the Devil to build it and in return the Devil demanded the soul of the first being to cross the river. The builder is said to have outwitted the Devil by making sure that a dog went over the bridge first.

After about 8km (5 miles) take a right-hand turn towards Barga, cross the river, turn left into Calavorno, then continue through Piano di Coreglia to reach Fornaci di Barga. Just at the entrance to this village take the right-hand fork to Barga; the road climbs and the scenery becomes craggier and more alpine in appearance.

❷ Barga is a hilltop town with a lovely Romanesque cathedral that towers over the village (▷ 133). Don't miss the panoramic views of the Alpi Apuane mountains from the terrace by the cathedral entrance.

Continue through Barga and follow the sign for Castelnuovo di Garfagnana. Cross another river and drive through Castelvecchio Pascoli; near the village is the house of poet Giovanni Pascoli (1855–1912). Continue through Ponte di Campia and follow the SR445 for about 9km (6 miles) through thickly wooded hills to reach Castelnuovo di Garfagnana (▷ 135). This is the largest town in the area, and has an office of the Parco Regionale degli Alpi Apuane providing regional maps and books. When you reach the crossroads take the SP72 signed for San Pellegrino in Alpe. Drive through Campori.

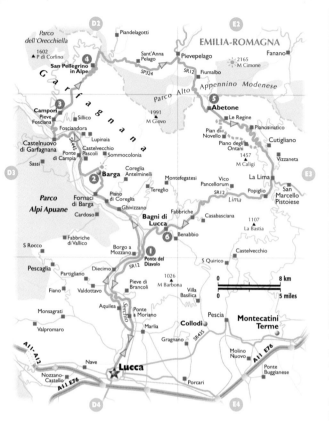

Clockwise from left *The Ponte del Diavolo, just outside Borgo a Mozzano; Barga's Romanesque Duomo; countryside near Bagni di Lucca*

❸ As you leave Campori, the road begins to wind steeply upwards, cutting through hills cloaked with chestnut trees. For many years the economy of the Garfagnana depended on chestnuts, cheese and spelt (a type of wheat).

After 13km (8 miles) you will reach San Pellegrino in Alpe.

❹ San Pellegrino is a little mountain village that has attracted pilgrims and artists for centuries. It is a good spot for a walk (▷ 149) and a bite to eat, and is also the home of the Museo Etnografico Provinciale, an excellent folk museum.

Drive on from San Pellegrino and join the SP324. Follow the road as it passes through Sant'Anna Pelago and Pievepelago. At the crossroads, turn right, taking the SR12 towards Abetone. Here you cross the river and start to climb again. Drive for 7km (4 miles) until you reach Abetone.

Above *Detail of the 13th-century carved pulpit in Barga's cathedral*

❺ From Abetone the SR12 winds down to Le Regine. You can continue on the SR12 here, or take an alternative route through the mountain woods and villages by turning off to the right just outside Abetone, at the brown sign indicating 'Piano degli Ontani'. Drive along this quiet road for about 2km (1 mile), then take the left-hand fork and continue through the woods to reach Pian di Novello, a small skiing village. From here the road twists steeply downhill, through Piano degli Ontani, eventually rejoining the SR12, where you turn right and follow the road to La Lima. Bear right in La Lima, still on the SR12, then drive through Popiglio, following the road for 17km (11 miles) until you reach Bagni di Lucca. Cross the bridge on the right-hand side to reach the town centre.

❻ Bagni di Lucca gained a reputation as a spa town in the 19th century, attracting many illustrious visitors who came to take the waters, including the poets Lord Byron, Shelley, and Robert and Elizabeth Barrett Browning. Cross back over the bridge and continue along the SR12, which passes the Ponte del Diavolo and takes you back to Lucca.

WHEN TO GO

Spring and autumn are the best times to visit; August is the most crowded time, and in winter snow and ice can make driving hazardous.

WHERE TO EAT
CAFFÈ CAPRETZ

Close to Barga's Tourist Information Office, this historic café is an ideal place to sit outside on a sunny day and enjoy a cappuccino and a pastry. ✉ Piazza Salvo Salvi 1, Barga ☎ 0583 723001 🕐 Closed Mon

ALBERGO L'APPENNINO
DA PACETTO

This relaxed family restaurant and inn at San Pellegrino in Alpe and its sister café on the other side of the road serve homemade food, ranging from cakes and pasta to bread and jam. ✉ Piazza San Pellegrino 5 ☎ 0583 649069 🕐 12–3, 6.30–9.30

There are also several places in Bagni di Lucca where you can grab a quick coffee.

PLACE TO VISIT
MUSEO ETNOGRAFICO PROVINCIALE

✉ Via del Voltone, San Pellegrino in Alpe ☎ 0583 649072 🕐 Jul, Aug daily 10–1, 2–6.30; Jun, Sep Tue–Sun 10–1, 2–6.30; Oct–end Mar Tue–Sat 9.30–1, Sun 10–1, 2–6.30; Apr–end May Tue–Sun 10–1, 2–4.30 💶 €2.50

Opposite *Landscape around San Pellegrino in Alpe*

THE PILGRIM TRAIL FROM SAN PELLEGRINO

This is an easy, but rewarding, circular walk high in the mountains of the Garfagnana. It starts and ends in the hamlet of San Pellegrino in Alpe, which grew up around the relics of St. Pellegrino and has attracted pilgrims for centuries. You can enjoy striking views over the mountains at several points along the trail.

THE WALK
Distance: 4km (2.5 miles)
Allow: 1 hour
Start/end at: Middle of San Pellegrino in Alpe, with the L'Appennino da Pacetto inn on your left and the museum on your right

★ Begin in the square between the museum and the inn. With the museum on your right, walk forward until you find a sign on the side of a building with the words 'In giro Monte Spicio' (roughly meaning 'this way to walk round Monte Spicio'). Go up the steps. Pass the mobile phone mast on the right and follow the wide, wooded path for just over 1km (0.5 miles).

❶ The landscape now begins to open up, taking on the appearance of moorland. On clear days there are some good views to the right.

Continue to follow the main trail, ignoring any side routes, until the path intersects with a wide gravel trail. A green post marks the point where the paths cross. If you turn right here you come to a building known as the Cappella di San Pellegrino.

❷ Pellegrino came to this area on a pilgrimage in the seventh century and stayed to provide refreshment and accommodation for other pilgrims.

To return to the main route, turn left and follow the wide trail. Continue until you reach a bend in the path.

❸ On the left-hand side of this bend is a rocky outcrop with an excellent viewpoint demonstrating just how high up you are.

Continue following the wide trail, down to a tarred road. At this point you are on the border between Tuscany and Emilia-Romagna. Turn left and continue downhill along the tarmac road. It's generally quiet, but still keep a lookout for any passing cars. Follow this road all the way to San Pellegrino. There are some exceptional views of the mountains as you approach the village.

WHEN TO GO
This area can be covered with snow early in the winter so, despite the easy trails, you should do this walk only in good weather.

WHERE TO EAT
ALBERGO L'APPENNINO DA PACETTO
✉ Piazza San Pellegrino 5 ☎ 0583 649069
🕐 Daily 12–3, 6.30–9.30

WALK

THE HEART OF LUCCA

This walk takes you through the beautiful heart of Lucca, a sublime town completely enclosed by its medieval walls. On streets that still follow the ancient plan of the old Roman colony on the site, it visits many of the small Romanesque churches for which the town is famous, as well as buildings and monuments that span some 2,000 years of history.

THE WALK
Distance: 2km (1.2 miles)
Allow: 2–3 hours
Start at: Piazzale Giuseppe Verdi
End at: Piazza San Michele

★ Begin in Piazzale Giuseppe Verdi, just inside the walls in the west of the town. Lucca is mostly pedestrian-only, and this is a good place to park your car. The piazza also has one of the town's two tourist offices. Walk east out of the piazza, away from the walls, on Via San Paolino.

❶ If you wish to visit the Museo Nazionale di Palazzo Mansi (▷ 138), take the first left, Via Galli Tassi. The museum is a few moments' walk on the left, and contains a picture gallery with works by Tintoretto and Bronzino among others, and is

housed in a sumptuous 17th-century palace. Otherwise, continue east on Via San Paolino, passing the church of San Paolino e Donato on the right, begun in 1522, probably on the site of vast Roman temple. Continue along the street until you come to Piazza Cittadella on the left.

❷ At the centre of the square, close to his family home, is a contemporary statue of the opera composer Giacomo Puccini (1858–1924), Lucca's most famous son.

Walk down Via di Poggio, which frames a beautiful view of San Michele in Foro, Lucca's loveliest church.

❸ The building and its dazzling façade (▷ 137) are revealed in their full glory when you emerge into

Piazza San Michele, the site of the old Roman forum (*foro*), from which the church takes its name. Admire the exterior, full of capricious details, and then look inside. At first the interior seems bare—most of the funds for the building were lavished on the exterior—but the transept contains a major work by the 15th-century Florentine painter Filippino Lippi (*c*1457–1504), *SS. Girolamo, Sebastiano, Rocco and Elena*.

Facing the church, walk to the far right corner of the square and take Via Roma and then turn left on Via Fillungo, Lucca's main north–south thoroughfare.

❹ A busy but attractive street, Via Fillungo is lined with shops and cafés, many of them with historic period interiors and façades. One of the best, on the right at No. 58, is the Caffè di Simo, once patronized by Puccini and other of the town's artists and intellectuals.

Follow Via Fillungo as it curves to the right, passing Via A. Mordini on the right. About 100m (110 yards) later a piazza opens up on the left, Piazza San Frediano.

5 The piazza is home to San Frediano (▷ 137), the second of Lucca's major churches. Admire the distinctive 13th-century mosaic of the Ascension fronting the church, then explore its interior, which is rich in important sculpture and paintings. Highlights include the sculpted font (on the right, near the south wall, as you enter); the Cappella Trenta (the last chapel on the opposite, left side of the church), where you'll see a superb sculpted altarpiece dating from 1422 by Jacopo della Quercia; and the Cappella di Sant'Agostino (the second chapel on the left, two down from the Cappella Trenta), which is covered in frescoes by Amico Aspertini (c1474–1552) that depict, among other things, the arrival of the Volto Santo (▷ 137) in Lucca, and San Frediano saving the town by miraculously diverting the waters of the Serchio river.

If you want to sample a little of the ramparts, this point of the walk is a good place to do so—walk right (north) from Piazza San Frediano down Via della Cavallerizza to Piazza Santa Maria, where there is a tourist office and several outlets that rent out bikes. From here you can easily walk or ride up to the walls.

To continue your town walk, return to Via Fillungo and pass through any of the little alleys immediately opposite Piazza San Frediano into Piazza Anfiteatro.

6 A magical but hidden square, Piazza Anfiteatro (▷ 138) is concealed within a ring of medieval houses, built over the site of the town's old Roman amphitheatre

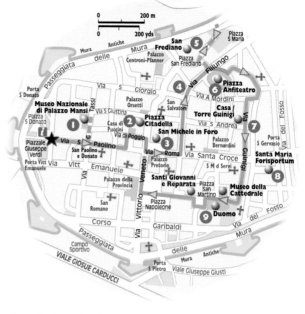

(anfiteatro), whose shape becomes obvious once you are standing in the airy, oval piazza.

Leave the piazza through one of the small alleys on the left (north) side and turn right into Piazza Pietro Somaldi, which takes its name from the church of San Pietro Somaldi, a pretty 12th-century Romanesque church on the left. Continue south past the church, past Via della Fratta on the left and curve right to take Via Guinigi on the left.

7 This highly attractive street takes its name from one of Lucca's most powerful medieval families, whose large former home and tower, the Casa and Torre Guinigi (▷ 139) you pass on the right.

Continue down Via Guinigi until Via Santa Croce on the right.

8 Opposite, on the left, is the Romanesque church of Santa Maria Forisportum, so called because when it was built in the 13th century it lay outside (fori) the then city walls and gate (portum).

Follow the continuation of Via Guinigi, Via Arcivescovado, south

until you come to the rear of the Duomo (▷ 137).

9 Walk to the front and visit the interior and—if you have time—the cathedral museum and Sant Giovanni e Reparata closeby (▷ 139).

From the cathedral square, you can return to Piazza San Michele either via Piazza Napoleone and Via Vittorio Veneto to the west, or the quieter Via Cenami or Via Beccheria north to Via Roma.

WHEN TO GO

Avoid mid-afternoon, when many of the shops and museums and churches on the walk will be closed. This part the afternoon is a good time to walk or cycle along the tree-shaded walls.

WHERE TO EAT

There are plenty of places to pause your walk. Piazza San Michele and Piazza Anfiteatro have cafés and bars with outside tables in good weather. Try Caffè di Simo at Via Fillungo 58 (▷ 159).

Opposite *Elegant Palazzo Controni-Pfanner is close to the church of San Frediano*

ALPI APUANE
GROTTA DEL VENTO
www.grottadelvento.com
This cave is one of the openings to the complex underground system that runs under the Alpi Apuane Nature Reserve. A guided tour takes in stalactites, stalagmites, small lakes and underground rivers.
✉ Grotta del Vento, 55020 Vergemoli
☎ 0583 722024 🕐 Apr–end Sep daily 10–6; Oct–end Mar Sun 10–6 💷 Adult €7.50, under 10 €5, for one-hour tour
🚌 SS12 from Lucca to Borgo a Mozzano, then left onto SS445 to Gallicano, from here turn off to Fornovolasco

BAGNI DI LUCCA
TERME JEAN VARRAUD
www.termebagnidilucca.it
One of the most popular of the springs in this spa town, known since the 13th century for its therapeutic waters. The best things about Terme Jean Varraud are its two natural steam grottoes, each at a stable temperature of between 40°C (102°F) and 47°C (115°F).
✉ Piazza San Martino 11, 55021 Bagni di Lucca ☎ 0583 87221 🕐 Nov–end May Mon–Sat 8.30–12.30; Jun–end Oct Mon–Sat 8.30–12.30, 2.30–6 💷 Treatments from €9.50; swimming pool from €10 (€12 on Sat)

CASENTINO
CASENTINESI
www.parks.it
This national park, the Parco Nazionale delle Foreste Casentinesi, is on the Apennine ridge between Tuscany and Emilia-Romagna. It has a wide choice of walking, cycling and horseback-riding routes. Among the beech and silver fir forests are buildings of religious and historical interest such as the Camaldoli monastery. There are 11 visitor offices around the park.
✉ Headquarters: Via G. Brocchi 7, 52015 Pratovecchio ☎ 0575 50301
🕐 Headquarters: Mon–Fri 9–1, also Tue, Thu 3–5.30 🚗 Take the Incisa Valdarno exit on A1, then SS69 following signs to the national park

COLLODI
PARCO DI PINOCCHIO
www.pinocchio.it
This park brings the story of the famous wooden puppet alive, with mosaics, statues and fountains incorporating all the story's characters. Attractions include puppet shows, a maze, a playground, exhibitions and a children's restaurant. Credit cards are not accepted.

Above *The small town of Altagnana, perched on a hillside in the foothills of the Alpi Apuane*

✉ Via San Gennaro 3, 51014 Collodi
☎ 0572 429342 🕐 Daily 8.30–dusk
💷 Adult €11, child (3–14) €8, under 3 free

GARFAGNANA
IL CORNIOLO
www.ilcorniolo.it
This country estate in the Parco dell'Orecchiella makes an ideal base for excursions on foot, by bike or on horseback. Sergio is an English-speaking qualified riding instructor who teaches and accompanies groups (direct number 340 350 2796). There are various schedules on offer. Accommodation is available as the estate is an *agriturismo* (▷ 266). Children under 7 are not accepted.
✉ Località Le Prade 25, 55033 Castiglione di Garfagnana, Lucca ☎ 0583 68705
🕐 By arrangement 💷 €25 for 2 hours; €60 for day excursion

GARFAGNANA ADVENTURES
www.garfagnanaadventures.com
This company, run by a married couple, will get you moving. It offers a number of tours of the area by

mountain or road bike, will take you kayaking on lakes, hiking or skiing over mountain tops. There are also some tours of the towns.

✉ Braccicorti, Località Braccicorti, Pontecosi, Pieve Fosciana 55036, Lucca
☎ 0583 649195 🕐 By arrangement
🚲 Half-day bike tour €65

PARCO ALPI APUANE
www.garfagnanavacanze.it
The visitors' office is an essential stopping place for advice on walking, rock climbing and mountain biking in the area. Maps are available and you can tailor activities to suit your abilities and schedule—anything from a short stroll to a 10-day circular walk among the surrounding mountains, staying in refuges.

✉ Piazza delle Erbe 1, 55032 Castelnuovo di Garfagnana, Lucca ☎ 0583 65169
🕐 Jun–end Sep daily 9–1, 3–7; Oct–end May Tue–Sun 9–1, 3–5.30

LUCCA
LA CACIOTECA
A tiny food shop selling a host of local and traditional seasonal produce. Staff are friendly and helpful, even if your command of Italian is weak. Try the ham, goat's cheese, olives and Lucchese wines for a quick picnic.

✉ Via Fillungo 242, 56100 Lucca ☎ 0583 496346 🕐 Mon–Sat 7–1.15, 3.30–7.30; Apr, Sep, Dec open Sun; Jan–end Mar, May–end Aug, Oct–end Nov occasional Sun opening

CARLI
First opened in 1655 and furnished as it was in the 18th century, Carli is one of Lucca's oldest jewellers. Visit for antique watches and silver, or just to see the high-vaulted room frescoed in 1800.

✉ Via Fillungo 95, 56100 Lucca ☎ 0583 491119 🕐 Tue–Sat 9.30–1, 3.30–7.30, Mon 3.30–7.30

CERAMISTI D'ARTE
The Tuscan artists Stefano Seardo and Fabrizio Falchi sculpt and paint at this workshop. Visit to pick up hand-painted decorative tiles, terracotta sculptures and marble

mosaics made from the prized Massa Carrara marble. Everything is produced according to ancient Italian ceramic techniques.

✉ Via Mordini 74/78, 56100 Lucca
☎ 0583 492700 🕐 Mon–Sat 10–1, 4–8

CIOCCOLATERIA CANIPAROLI
Chocolates from Lucca's most innovative chocolate maker are too delicious to pass up. The range combines traditional shapes and indulgent flavours. Be sure to sample the popular *praline di cioccolato* (chocolates with soft fillings).

✉ Via San Paolino 96, 56100 Lucca
☎ 0583 53456 🕐 Tue–Sun 9–1, 3.30–8. Closed Jul, Aug

ENOTECA VANNI
www.enotecavanni.com
Enoteca Vanni has been supplying Lucca and its visitors with typical local foods since 1965 and has some of the best wines, spirits and extra-virgin olive oils in the region. There is nowhere better to stock up on gourmet gifts or picnic items.

✉ Piazza del Salvatore 7, 55100 Lucca
☎ 0583 491902 🕐 Tue–Sat 9–1, 4–8, Mon 4–8

GALLERIA VANNUCCI
Among the best of Lucca's antiques shops, Galleria Vannucci has local 17th- and 18th-century furnishings and drawings in its two rooms. The records for some of the goods are particularly interesting, as they can be traced back to Lucca's busy period of antiques dealing in the 18th century.

✉ Via del Battistero 50/52, 56100 Lucca
☎ 0583 955815 🕐 Tue–Sun 9–1, 3–7, Mon 3–7

THE GOLDEN FOX
www.thegoldenfox.it
This establishment so prides itself on being an English pub that it imported its entire interior from England. English, Scottish and Irish beers are on tap. Credit cards are not accepted.

✉ Via Regina Margherita 207, 55100 Lucca
☎ 0583 491619 🕐 Tue–Sun 8pm–1am

LA GROTTA
Lucca is at the heart of countryside renowned for producing some of Tuscany's best olive oils, most of which can be bought in the town's many good food shops. La Grotta, a few paces from Piazza del Anfiteatro, is one of the best. The shop also sells cheese, ham, salami, honey and other Italian staples, plus gastronomic treats to take home.

✉ Via dell'Anfiteatro 2, 56100 Lucca
☎ 0583 467595 🕐 Mon–Sat 9.30–1, 3.30–7.30

LUCCA IN TAVOLA
Visiting connoisseurs love this wine shop, one of the most popular in the city. Drop by for a wine tasting, if not to buy a few cases to take home (they will organize shipment if you want to do this). The famed DOC Vino Rosso delle Colline Lucchesi is a good choice. They also stock olive oils, herbs and other delicacies typical of the region.

✉ Via San Paolino 130–132, 56100 Lucca
☎ 0583 581022 🕐 Mar–end Oct daily 9.30–7.30; Nov–end Feb Tue–Sun 9–1, 3.30–7.30

MARSILI COSTANTINO
Marsili gives you a tasty introduction to Lucca's local vineyards, with some lesser-known but delicious wines as well as famous varieties like Brunello, Rosso di Montalcino, Montecarlo and Colline Lucchesi. Take time to try some of the many herb liqueurs and digestivi that are produced, following traditional local recipes.

✉ Piazza San Michele 38 and Via del Moro 18–22, 56100 Lucca ☎ 0583 491751
🕐 May to mid-Nov Mon–Sat 8.30–1, 3.30–7.30; mid-Nov to end Apr Tue–Sat 9–1, 3.30–7.30, Mon 3.30–7.30

MCCULLOUGHS
Stop by for a Celtic or Gaelic-themed evening with live music and dancing. This lively Irish pub has Guinness on tap as well as a good selection of Irish and Scottish whiskies. Credit cards are not accepted.

✉ Piazza Curtatone 135, 55100 Lucca
☎ 0583 469067 🕐 Daily 8pm–1am

REGIONS NORTHERN TUSCANY • WHAT TO DO

MERCATO D'ANTIQUARIO

This large antiques market has a wide range of furnishings, rare coins and old jewellery on the 3rd Sunday of every month. On the 3rd Saturday and 4th Sunday of the month, there is a crafts market.

✉ Piazza San Giusto, Piazza Antelminelli and surrounding streets 🕔 9am–7pm

MERCATO DEI LIBRI

Behind the church of San Giusto and running towards both Piazza Napoleone and Piazza San Michele, Lucca's book stands sell anything and everything that is printed. Look for old prints, modern postcards and even comic books in all sorts of languages.

✉ Via Beccheria, 56100 Lucca 🕔 Daily 10–6

MERCATO DI LUCCA

Just inside the city's walls, between the San Jacopo and Elisa gates, Lucca's market sells clothing, flowers, food, table linen and household implements. Clothes and shoes are especially good value. Get here early for the best bargains.

✉ Via dei Bacchettoni, 56100 Lucca 🕔 Wed, Sat 9–1

NICOLAS

Known for its live music, Nicolas gives local musicians the chance to perform to an audience. The play list has everything from jazz and blues to pop and reggae as well as traditional Italian singers. Credit cards are not accepted.

✉ Viale S. Concordio 887, 55100 Lucca ☎ 0583 582378 🕔 Tue–Sun 8pm–2am

OSTERIA DEL NENI

This traditional wine bar gives you a family-run introduction to the best Chianti and Lucca regional wines. A wide range of snacks is available.

✉ Via Pescheria 3, 55100 Lucca ☎ 0583 492681 🕔 Tue–Sun 12–3, 7.30–11

PASTICCERIA TADDEUCCI

Popular for its delicious *buccellato* (sweet aniseed-flavoured bread with raisins), Pasticceria Taddeucci has been producing this classic Lucchese delicacy for four generations without change. It gets its name from the Latin *buccellatum* ('sailor's cookie'). It's best eaten at breakfast or for an afternoon snack.

✉ Piazza San Michele 34, 56100 Lucca ☎ 0583 494933 🕔 Apr–end Sep daily 8.30–8; Oct–end Mar Fri–Wed 9–1, 3–7

TEATRO ASTRA

Showing the most up-to-date cinematic releases in Lucca, Teatro Astra's one screen is popular among students. It also takes pride of place in Lucca's film festivals. Credit cards are not accepted.

✉ Piazza del Giglio 7, 55100 Lucca ☎ 0583 496480 🕔 Closed Thu 💵 Adult €7, child €5, gallery seats €8, reduced price of €5 for all on Wed

TEATRO DEL GIGLIO

www.teatrodelgiglio.it
From September to the end of November this 19th-century opera house stages classical dramas. Dance, opera and classical music performances take place from November to the end of March. It also houses the Centro Studi G. Puccini (The Puccini Studies Centre). Credit cards are not accepted.

✉ Piazza del Giglio 13/15, 55100 Lucca ☎ 0583 467521 💵 Adult €25, child €12

TORRE GUINIGI

Climb the 40m (130ft) Guinigi tower, which was built by the family of the same name, once one of the richest in Lucca. The tower was part of their 14th-century villa that now houses the Guinigi Museum. On top, there's an ancient oak tree and great views. Credit cards are not accepted.

✉ Via Sant'Andrea, 55100 Lucca ☎ 336 203221 🕔 Jul to mid-Sep 9am–11pm; mid-Sep to end Oct 9–7; Nov–end Feb 9.30–5; Mar 9–6.30, Apr–Jun 9.30–6.30 💵 Adult €5, child €4

MONTECATINI TERME

TERME EXCELSIOR

www.termemontecatini.it
There are nine different spas here, but this is the central one and open all year. The emphasis is on health and wellbeing, with a medical team available to give advice before starting treatments. Patients with liver and rheumatism problems are said to benefit from taking the waters, and you can indulge in a wide range of beauty treatments.

✉ Viale Verdi 61, 51016 Montecatini Terme, Pistoia ☎ 0572 778487 🕔 Therapy Centre: Easter–end Oct daily 8–12.30, 4–7; Nov–Easter 8–12.30. Beauty Centre: Mon–Sat 8.30–8, Sun 9–2 💵 Massages from €50

MUGELLO

AUTODROMO DEL MUGELLO

www.mugellocircuit.it
Motorsports events are staged regularly at this historic track owned by Ferrari. The biggest motorcycle races, including the Italian Grand Prix for 125cc and 250cc bikes, as well as the Superbike World Championships, draw large crowds who fill the natural amphitheatre around the track, which is one of the most scenic in the world. Credit cards are not accepted.

✉ Autodromo del Mugello, Mugello ☎ 055 849 9111 🕔 Contact for latest meetings 💵 Prices vary 🚗 Take 302 Faentina road passing Scarperia for Mugello or A1 (Bologna–Firenze) motorway and exit at Barberino di Mugello

PECCIOLI

PARCO PREISTORICO

www.parcopreistorico.it
The medieval town of Peccioli, above the Era Valley, is not just olive groves, vineyards and grassy hills. It is known for its prehistoric park, complete with reproductions of dinosaurs, cavemen and their habitats. There is also a large picnic area. Credit cards are not accepted.

✉ Via dei Cappuccini 20, 56037 Peccioli ☎ 0587 636030 🕔 Daily 9am–dusk. Closed Christmas and New Year 💵 Adult €4, child €4 (child 0–12 years €3 Sep–end Mar) 🚗 Take the Altopascio exit on A11 motorway, then follow signs to Peccioli

PIETRASANTA

TRENINO DELLE VACANZE

This *trenino delle vacanze* (holiday train) has fantastic views of the Versilia Coast, as it runs from the town along the coast of Marina di Pietrasanta during summer. The hour-long route takes in the towns of Le Nocette, Motrone, Tonfano, Fiumetto and Pietrasanta. You can buy tickets on board. Credit cards are not accepted.

✉ 0584 747737 (Fratelli Verona)
🕐 Jun–end Sep daily at 5.30pm and 9pm
✋ Adult €5, child €3

PISA

ARSENALE
www.arsenalecinema.it
This is an art-house cinema with four daily showings of two films, with an extensive library of old cinema and video. All screenings are in the original language. Credit cards are not accepted.
✉ Vicolo Scaramucci 4, 56127 Pisa ☎ 050 502640 ✋ Adult €5

BORDERLINE
www.borderlinepisa.it
This pub, part of a chain, has a good reputation for live music. Popular with the university crowd, the bar hosts live performances (mostly rock, blues and folk) most nights.
✉ Via G. Vernaccini 7, 56100 Pisa ☎ 050 580577 🕐 Mon–Sat 9.30pm–2am

CINEMA TEATRO NUOVO
Popular with visitors and locals, this art-house cinema has one screen showing films in their original language. Occasionally, films are not subtitled. Credit cards are not accepted.
✉ Piazza della Stazione 1, 56127 Pisa ☎ 050 41332 🕐 Closed mid-Jun to end Aug ✋ Adult €6.70, child €4.60

FEDERICO SALZA
www.salza.it
This Pisan outlet of a popular Turin confectioner sells beautifully fashioned chocolates and pastry goods. Look for the chocolate Leaning Tower of Pisa. It is a stone's throw from the Campo dei Miracoli and a must for any sweet-toothed visitor.
✉ Borgo Stretto 46, 56100 Pisa ☎ 050 580244 🕐 Jun–end Oct daily 8am–8.30pm; Nov–end May Tue–Sun 8am–8.30pm

GALLERIA BARSANTI
Galleria Barsanti is both an art gallery and a sculpture studio. Items are made of local marble and alabaster, and you can buy anything from kitsch unicorn sculptures to delicate copies of Etruscan masks. It's a huge shop, a short stroll from the Leaning Tower of Pisa.
✉ Piazza del Duomo 6, 56100 Pisa ☎ 050 560535 🕐 Daily 9–7.30

GASTRONOMIA CESQUI
Pisa's central food market is held in Piazza delle Vettovaglie, a square that also contains a variety of delicatessens. Cesqui is the most tempting, thanks to a wonderful selection of cheese, pasta, ham, oil and wine, many of them from local producers.
✉ Piazza delle Vettovaglie 38, 56100 Pisa ☎ 050 580269 🕐 Mon, Tue, Thu–Sat 7–1.30, 4–8, Wed 7–1.30

LANTERI
This big-screen cinema mostly shows the latest releases. Films are screened in the original language with Italian subtitles. There is free parking next door. Credit cards are not accepted.
✉ Via San Michele dei Scalzi 46, 56127 Pisa ☎ 050 577100 ✋ Adult €7, child €5

LENZI GHINO GIACOMO
www.ceramichelenzi.it
In this factory shop selling classic Tuscan ceramics, they pride themselves on producing basins, vases and pottery the traditional way. The beautifully decorated items make great gifts.
✉ Via Provinciale Vicarese 371, 56010 San Giovanni alla Vena, Pisa ☎ 050 799015 🕐 Mon–Sat 9–1, 3.30–7.30
🚗 Follow directions west out of Pisa towards Vicopisano and Cascina; San Giovanni alla Vena is midway between the two

LIBRERIA FOGOLA
This neat, tiny bookshop has very helpful staff as well as internet access. Books covering every subject under the sun are either on the shelves or can be ordered.

English-language books and tourist information available.
✉ Corso Italia 82, 56100 Pisa ☎ 050 502547 🕐 Mon–Sat 9–1, 4–8

LA LOGGIA
www.barlaloggia.com
This ice-cream shop, frequented by visitors and locals, becomes a bar at night, known for its international beers. After 7pm, drop by for some tasty Tuscan cooking.
✉ Piazza Vitt. Emanuele II 11, 56100 Pisa ☎ 050 991 1407 🕐 Daily 7am–4am. Closed first 2 weeks in Jan

ODEON
www.multisalaodeon.com
A modern multiplex showing the latest releases on four screens. Films are shown in the original language. Credit cards are not accepted.
✉ Piazza San Paolo all'Orto 18, 56127 Pisa ☎ 050 540168 ✋ Adult €7.50, child €5, reduced price of €5.50 for all on Fri

OFFSIDE
Themed evenings here range from Friday's gay and lesbian night to live music gigs on Wednesday and Saturday nights. Cocktails and dance club are on Sundays, and karaoke—the best night—is on Thursday. Credit cards are not accepted.
✉ Ospedaletto, Uscita Pisa Nord Est, Via Emilia, 56100 Pisa ☎ 338 852 6924 🕐 Mon, Wed–Thu 8pm–2am, Fri, Sat 8pm–4am, Sun 6pm–4am

PAOLO CAPRI
Designer Paolo Capri's showroom is a popular outlet for jewellery, watches and frames, most of them created by Florentine silversmiths. There is also a wide range of giftware inspired by local culture.
✉ Via di Marino 2, 56100 Pisa ☎ 050 577111 🕐 Tue–Sat 9.30–1, 4–7.30, Mon 4–7. Closed Jul Sat pm

PARCO REGIONALE DI MIGLIARINO-SAN ROSSORE-MASSACIUCCOLI
www.parks.it
Walking and biking routes in this national park along the coast include

16th-century pine forests, rich in wildlife. There's good birdwatching at Lake Massaciuccoli.

✉ Via Aurelia Nord 4, 56122 Pisa ☎ 050 525500 ✋ Free 🚗 From Pisa follow signs to Gombo and take the Viale delle Cascine to San Rossore; then the Viale dei Pini to Migliarino and head to Massaciuccoli for Lake Massaciuccoli

PAUL DEBONDT

A Dutch artisan and former Artistic Chocolate World Champion, Paul Debondt creates custom chocolate designs for clients. This Pisa outlet has everything from animal-shaped chocolates filled with almond paste to simple, rich truffles. The *ganascia* chocolates, made with fresh cream and butter, are what Debondt is known for. The shop is closed during the hot summer months.

✉ Via Turati 22, 56125 Pisa ☎ 050 501896 ◉ Oct–end Apr Tue–Sat 10–1, 4–8

I PISANI

www.ipisani.it

This delicatessen sells a selection of food produced by the best local artisans. Shop for truffles, olive oils, cheeses, salami, sauces and much more. The English-speaking staff can provide recommended recipes and cooking advice.

✉ Via di Signano 25/A, 56017 San Giuliano Terme, Pisa ☎ 050 817025/815013 ◉ Mon–Fri 9–1, 2–6 🚗 7km (4 miles) from Pisa on the Brennero Road (SS12) towards Lucca

SAN GIULIANO TERME

www.bagnidipisa.com

This 18th-century building, once used by the Grand Dukes of Tuscany, is set in the Pisan foothills. The spa is known for its facial and body treatments as well as regimes to revitalize the respiratory and immune systems. The hotel has a bar and restaurant.

✉ Largo Shelley 18, 56017 San Giuliano Terme ☎ 050 88501 ◉ Mon–Sat 8–1, 3–6 ✋ 50-minute massage €60 ; day spa use of pool €10; half-day Spa Experience €65; wide range of treatments available 🚗 7km (4 miles) from Pisa on the Brennero Road (SS12) towards Lucca

TEATRO SANT'ANDREA

www.teatrosantandrea.it

The attractive Romanesque Chiesa di Sant'Andrea was converted into a theatre in 1986. You can see local and touring performances here. Credit cards are not accepted.

✉ Via del Cuore, 56127 Pisa ☎ 050 542364 ◉ Season: Nov–end May ✋ Adult €5–€25, child €3–€18

TEATRO VERDI

www.teatrodipisa.pi.it

Inaugurated in 1867, this theatre is one of the most beautiful in central Italy and has a notable ceiling fresco. See opera, drama and dance in the 900-seat auditorium.

✉ Via Palestro 40, 56127 Pisa ☎ 050 941111 ◉ Season: Sep–end May ✋ €6–€50

TENNIS CLUB PISA

www.tennisclubpisa.it

This club has five outdoor clay courts, three of which have lighting for night games, and two indoor courts. The clubhouse has a bar, changing facilities and shop. You must book a court the day before.

✉ Piazzale dello Sport 7, 56122 Pisa ☎ 050 530313 ◉ Daily 9am–10pm ✋ €7.50 per person per hour

PISTOIA
BRUNO CORSINI

They have been making chocolates here since 1918 and there's a tempting range to try, including chocolates with chili peppers. Handmade Easter eggs can be ordered, and you can watch Corsini's hedgehog confetti or snowballs being made from hard spun sugar.

✉ Piazza di San Francesco 42, 51100 Pistoia ☎ 0573 20138 ◉ Mon–Sat 9–1, 4–7.30. Closed Jul–Sep Sat pm

FIASCHI

Pistoia is famous for its textiles and Fiaschi has a wide range of household linens with fine hand-embroidered tablecloths, napkins and silk and pure cotton nightgowns. Children's clothes are available too, and a selection of boxes decorated with lace and ribbons. Nearly all the stock is made locally.

✉ Via Atto Vannucci 20, 51100 Pistoia ☎ 0573 31701 ◉ Mon–Sat 9–1, 3.30–7.30. Closed Mon am in winter, Sat pm in summer

TIRRENIA
CICLILANDIA

www.ciclilandia.it

Ciclilandia (Cycleland) is one of Tuscany's more unusual amusement parks: mountain bikes, cycle-carriages, cycle go-carts and cycling lessons for youngsters, all watched over by traffic police. The Pirates' Castle has a different kind of fun with its tunnels, bridges and slides. Credit cards are not accepted.

✉ Piazza dei Fiori, 56018 Tirrenia ☎ 050 33573 ◉ Mid-Jun to mid-Sep Mon–Sat 4–7.30pm, 9pm–midnight, Sun 10–12.30, 4–7.30, 9pm–midnight; mid-Sep

Below *Head out in the evening and relax with a cocktail after a long day's sightseeing*

PARCO GIOCHI FANTASILANDIA

Split into two sections, Fantasy Land has a free area with electric car track, miniature train and mechanical bull. The other section has waterslides and swings. There's also a park specifically equipped for young children, with a range of toys including tricycles and pedal cars, and picnic tables. Credit cards are not accepted.

✉ Viale Tirreno, 42, 56018 Tirrenia
☎ 050 30326 ◉ Mar–end Sep Mon–Fri 2.30–dusk, Sat, Sun 8.30–dusk ✋ Paying section: Joint adult and child €4 🚗 Take the Pisa Centro exit on A12, then follow signs to Tirrenia

VIAREGGIO

GABRIEL CRYSTALS

www.gabrielcrystals.com
A dazzling collection of glass and crystal is displayed in this large showroom, with a fountain in the middle. There's beautiful hand-blown glass from Murano and crystal from France and Bohemia.

✉ Viale Carducci 23b, 55049 Viareggio
☎ 0584 430335 ◉ Jun–end Oct daily 10–1, 5–12; Nov–end May Tue–Sat 9.30–1, 3.30–8, Sun 3.30–8

MERCATO DI VIAREGGIO

This large, partially covered market has a fresh fish section with produce straight from the Riviera di Versilia. Stands in the central covered section sell a selection of shoes. Most stands are there daily, but the main market day is Thursday.

✉ Piazza Cavour, 55049 Viareggio
◉ Daily dawn–dusk

VIAREGGIO BEACH

There are miles of sandy beach at Viareggio, and the long promenade has plenty of places to buy a refreshing ice cream. Take refuge from the sun in the pine-shaded park, Pineta di Ponente (▷ 145 and 259 for more information).

◉ Daily dawn–dusk ✋ Charges to use certain areas of the beach apply

FEBRUARY/MARCH

VIAREGGIO CARNEVALE

www.viareggio.ilcarnevale.com
Viareggio's carnival is among Italy's biggest and best, with spectacular floats that wend their way along the waterfront four Sundays in a row. It's all accompanied by music, dancing and food.

✉ Piazza Mazzini 22 c/o Palazzo delle Muse, 55049 Viareggio ☎ 0584 184 0750
◉ 4 Suns in Feb–Mar ✋ Free 🚆 Trains run from Pisa to Viareggio every hour
🚗 Take the Versilia exit off A12

JUNE/JULY/AUGUST

A CORTO DI CINEMA

www.cinefestival.it/acortodicinema
This festival of short films is open to professional and amateur film directors of all nationalities, with a €600 top prize. All films have English subtitles and the shortlisted films are shown at the Cinema Italia before the winner is announced.

✉ Cinema Italia, Via Biscione 32, 55100 Lucca ☎ 0583 467264 ◉ 2nd week in Jun ✋ Free

PALIO DI SAN RANIERI

www.comune.pisa.it
A boat race held in honour of Pisa's patron saint. The teams consist of eight oarsmen, a cox and a climber who races to the top of a 10m-high (33ft) mast at the finish. The race can be seen along the Arno between the railway bridge and the Palazzo Medici. Try to get a spot at the Palazzo Medici for the mast-climbing finale.

☎ 050 560464 (Tourist board) ◉ 17 Jun

LUMINARIA AND G IOCO DEL PONTE

Pisa's main festival focuses on tug-of-war games between 12 teams, who push a 7-ton carriage over the Ponte di Mezzo. The highlight of the Luminaria are the blazing torches that light the houses and streets on either side of the river.

◉ Last Sunday in Jun

OPERA, THEATRE AND MUSIC FESTIVAL

www.ccmoperalucca.org
Lucca's squares, churches and halls are filled with sounds by amateur and semi-professional singers and musicians from around the world. It is sponsored by the Music College of the University of Cincinnati.

☎ 0583 493040 ◉ 15 Jun to 15 Jul
✋ Most concerts free; opera €15

SUMMER FESTIVAL LUCCA

www.summer-festival.com
Past acts at this Festival, one of Tuscany's most popular, have included Paul Simon, David Bowie, Oasis and Rod Stewart. There are plenty of Italian bands too.

✉ Piazza Napoleone and Piazza Anfiteatro, 55100 Lucca ☎ 0584 46477
◉ Jul ✋ Ticket prices vary. Tickets from TicketOne, ☎ 892101, www.ticketone.it

FESTIVAL PUCCINI

www.puccinifestival.org
This opera festival draws 40,000 spectators a year to its performances of Puccini classics.

✉ Viale Puccini 257/A, 55048 Torre del Lago Puccini, Lucca ☎ 0584 359322
◉ Jul, Aug ✋ €29–€95 🚗 A20, just outside Lucca on A11/SS1

BARGA JAZZ FESTIVAL

www.barganews.com/bargajazz.com
This international festival revolves around a jazz orchestra competition. Performances are held in Barga, Lucca and Castelnuovo di Garfagnana.

✉ Barga and Lucca ☎ 0583 711044
◉ Last week in Aug ✋ Adult €10, child €7.50 🚗 Barga

SEPTEMBER

LUMINARIA DI SANTA CROCE

Lucca's treasured Volto Santo (▷ 137) is carried in procession through the town's candlelit streets. The whole town turns out in homage to the effigy.

◉ 13 Sep

PRICES AND SYMBOLS

The restaurants are listed alphabetically (excluding La, Il, Le and I). The prices given are the average for a two-course lunch (L) and a three-course dinner (D) for one person, without drinks. The wine price is for the least expensive bottle. All the restaurants listed accept credit cards unless otherwise stated.

For a key to the symbols, ▷ 2.

BARGA
OSTERIA ANGELIO

If you are a jazz fan, you'll love this intimate restaurant, which serves rustic country fare at reasonable prices. The menu has few dishes and rotates seasonally, but usually includes grilled meats, cold cuts and some vegetarian pasta dishes. Reservations are recommended during the jazz festival (▷ 157).
✉ Piazza Angelio, 55051 Barga ☎ 0583 724547 🕐 Daily 12–3, 6–11 🍴 L €11, D €17, Wine €8

CAMAIORE
RISTORANTE LA MEA

This large, family-run place serves a variety of home-made Tuscan dishes with produce fresh from the local market. Popular dishes include *crostini alla toscana* (hot chicken liver and wild boar pâtés on toasted crusty bread), *ravioli con funghi* (wild mushroom ravioli) and a range of grilled and roasted meats, such as guinea fowl. Save some room for

the *dolci della casa*—desserts made to traditional family recipes. Credit cards are not accepted.
✉ Viale Provinciale, Valpromaro 1, 55041 Camaiore ☎ 0584 956047 🕐 Jun–end Sep daily 12–2, 7–10; Oct–end May Fri–Wed 12–2, 7–10 🍴 L €11, D €22, Wine €5

FAUGLIA
LA GATTAIOLA

You can see as far as Pisa's Leaning Tower and Lucca's city walls from the small hill town of Fauglia. Local Tuscan cuisine is served and the house specials come recommended by the friendly staff: wild mushroom risotto, roast lamb with garlic and a range of home-made pastas sprinkled with truffle shavings. Reservations are advisable.
✉ Vicolo San Lorenzo 2–4, 56043 Fauglia ☎ 050 650852 🕐 Tue–Sun 12.30–3, 7.30–10.30 🍴 L €25, D €33, Wine €8
🚗 From Pisa, take the Collesalvete/ Rome road, SS206; follow the signs to Fauglia (18km/11 miles from Pisa)

GARFAGNANA
ALBERGO L'APPENNINO DA PACETTA

www.albergolappennino.com
This friendly, family-run hotel has been receiving visitors since 1221. Everything in its excellent restaurant is home-made. Good, hearty mountain food includes *polenta con cinghiale* (ground maize cooked to a thick porridge served with a wild boar sauce).

Above *People in Tuscany, as in the rest of Italy, are passionate about good-quality food*

✉ Piazza San Pellegrino 5, 55035 San Pellegrino in Alpe, Lucca ☎ 0583 649069 🕐 Daily 12–3, 6.30–9.30 🍴 L €17, D €22, Wine €5.50 🚗 From Castelnuovo di Garfagnana follow SP72, and signs for San Pellegrino in Alpe

ALBERGO RISTORANTE DA CARLINO

Carnivores will find they are pampered here with generous hunks of freshly grilled meats appearing on wooden platters. There's local trout on the menu, and the vegetable soufflé will please vegetarians. Credit cards are not accepted.
✉ Via Garibaldi 15, 55032 Castelnuovo di Garfagnana, Lucca ☎ 0583 644270 🕐 Daily 12–3, 7.30–midnight. Closed Mon in winter 🍴 L €12, D €28, Wine €5

OSTERIA VECCHIO MULINO

Owner Andrea is part of the Italian Slow Food movement—suppliers of organic food, produced using traditional methods. His *osteria* is tiny and usually packed, so you might consider stopping for an early lunch or to buy ingredients for a picnic. If you eat in, wave after wave of delicious dishes are brought on wooden platters. These might include slivers of *bazzone* (local ham from pigs that forage in the woods) or *pane di patate* (bread made with potatoes). Shelves line the crowded walls with a large selection of wines.

✉ Via Vittorio Emanuele II 12, 55032 Castelnuovo di Garfagnana ☎ 0583 62192 🕐 Tue–Sat 10–8.30, Sun 11–8 🖐 L €14, Wine €5

LUCCA

BARSOTTI DA GUIDO

This small *trattoria*, a few paces from Piazza San Salvatore, serves predominantly Tuscan and Lucchese cuisine with the usual mixture of cold cuts, grilled meats (including wild boar sausage, beef and veal), roasts and home-made pastas. Light salads play a key role. There is no English version of the menu but staff are happy to translate. Small but well-chosen wine list.

✉ Via C. Battisti 28, 55100 Lucca ☎ 0583 467219 🕐 Mon–Sat 12–3, 7–11 🖐 L €17, D €28, Wine €7

BUCA DI SANT'ANTONIO

www.bucadisantantonio.com
One of the oldest restaurants in Lucca, Buca di Sant'Antonio is also one of the most popular. The menu is all à la carte, with an emphasis on Lucchese cuisine, and changes with the seasons. Dishes generally include grilled and roasted meats such as stuffed oven-cooked rabbit and pork with rosemary and garlic. The waiters can provide you with recommendations from the wine list, which is extensive. Reservations are advisable for dinner.

✉ Via della Cervia 3, 56100 Lucca ☎ 0583 55881 🕐 Tue–Sat 12.30–2.30, 7.30–10.30, Sun 12.30–2.30. Closed for a period in Jan and Jul 🖐 L €22, D €33, Wine €10

CAFFÈ DI SIMO

Lucca's loveliest old café is a belle époque gem, with polished brass, marble and ornate mirrors. It lies on the town's main shopping street, close to a cluster of other historic stores with wonderful shop fronts and interiors. In the past, it was magnet for literary and other figures, including the composer Puccini, and although it retains a traditional air, the atmosphere is anything but formal. Shoppers and visitors still

flock here for a restoring coffee, its delicious cakes and pastries, or some of the home-made ice cream, which is among the best in Lucca. Alternatively, you can have a light lunch, or supper in summer, of traditional regional dishes in the restaurant area.

✉ Via Fillungo 58, 55100 Lucca ☎ 0583 496234 🕐 Bar: Tue–Sun 8.30–8. Restaurant: summer Thu–Sat 12.30–2.30, 7–10, Sun–Tue 12.30–2.30; winter Thu–Sat 12.30–2.30 🖐 L €18, D €25

OSTERIA IL PERGOLONE

www.ilpergolone.com
There's an emphasis on home cooking at this family-run *osteria* on the edge of a small lake. In the compact dining room you can choose predominantly Lucchese dishes from either of the two menus (one meat, one fish). Taking pride of place on the meat menu are wild boar starters and rabbit stew. The fish menu varies according to the season, but tends to include lobster, langoustines and a variety of freshly caught seafood.

✉ Via di Tiglio 622, Località Palaiola, Pieve di Compito, 55012 Cappanori, Lucca ☎ 0583 960089 🕐 Thu–Tue 12.30–2.30, 7–11 🖐 L €10, D €17, Wine €6.50 🚗 Take the SS439 from Lucca towards Pontedera

RISTORANTE CANULEIA

A small and friendly restaurant that is within walking distance of the amphitheatre. It specializes in Italian fast food, or what the owners like to call 'spaghetti express'. It also has a generous *menù turistico*. Reservations are recommended.

✉ Via Canuleia 14, 55100 Lucca ☎ 0583 467470 🕐 Mon–Sat 12–2.30, 7.45–9.30 🖐 L €20, D €33, Wine €8

RISTORANTE CELIDE

Just outside Lucca's city walls, Ristorante Celide specializes in seafood caught fresh off the nearby Versilia Coast. House dishes such as lobster with seafood and vegetables come with wine recommendations and the bar is well stocked with after-dinner digestifs.

✉ Viale Giusti 7, 56100 Lucca ☎ 0583 91091 🕐 Mon–Sat 12.30–3, 7.30–11 🖐 L €19, D €33, Wine €6

RISTORANTE GAZEBO

www.locandalelisa.it
In the conservatory of the Locanda l'Elisa hotel (▷ 162), the Gazebo prides itself on using local produce in its classic regional dishes. The food is delicious and it makes a good choice for a romantic meal. Main courses like lamb cutlet with rosemary served on mashed potato with truffles reflect the chef's aim to serve traditional country food. Reservations essential.

✉ Via Nuova per Pisa 1952, 55050 Massa Pisana, Lucca ☎ 0583 379737 🕐 Mon–Sat 12.30–2.30, 7.30–10. Closed Jan 🖐 L €20, D €55, Wine €20 🚗 Take the A11 from Lucca, leave at the Lucca exit and follow the SS12 towards San Giuliano Terme/Pisa (3km/2 miles from Lucca)

RISTORANTE LA MORA

www.ristorantelamora.it
Although it is 10km (6 miles) from the city, this is one of Lucca's best-known and most expensive restaurants. Based on local Garfagnanan and Lucchese cuisine, dishes include oven-cooked pasta stuffed with meats, cheese and vegetables and rabbit stewed with rosemary and garlic. Reservations are required.

✉ Via Lodovica 1748, 55029 Sesto di Moriano, Lucca ☎ 0583 406402 🕐 Tue–Thu 12–2.30, 7.30–10. Closed for periods in Jan and Jun 🖐 L €17, D €39, Wine €10 🚗 Take the SS12 from Lucca towards Abetone

TRATTORIA DA LEO

www.trattoriadaleo.it
At this popular family-run *trattoria* you can eat on the shaded terrace. The menu includes dishes such as Tuscan bean soup, roast veal with roast potatoes and home-made spinach pasta.

✉ Via Tegrimi 1, 55100 Lucca ☎ 0583 492236 🕐 Sep–end Jun Mon–Sat 12.30–2.30, 7.30–10.30, Sun 12.30–2.30; Jul, Aug daily 7.30pm–10.30pm 🖐 L €11, D €22, Wine €10

MONTECATINI TERME

ENOTECA GIOVANNI

Many visitors come to Montecatini Terme for health reasons, and there is a fresh, light approach to food at this elegant restaurant. The menu has a good selection of fish, vegetable and meat dishes. There is also a comprehensive wine list. You can eat outside in the square in the summer. Reservations are recommended if you wish to eat here in the evening.

✉ Via Garibaldi 25/27, 51016 Montecatini Terme, Pistoia ☎ 0572 71695 🕐 Tue–Sun 12.30–2.30, 8–10. Closed 2 weeks from 14 Feb and from 15 Aug 👆 L €22, D €66, Wine €16

RISTORANTE LA TORRE

There is a funicular that will take you from Montecatini Terme to Montecatini Alto and this restaurant. It is in the pretty little main square with outside seating. There's a good Tuscan menu: try the hearty bean soup or the mixed grilled meats. The wine list has more than 400 different wines from which to choose. Inside there is a tower dating back to 1100, with space only for a candlelit table for two: a reservation for this is essential.

✉ Piazza Giusti 8, Montecatini Alto, 51016 Montecatini Terme, Pistoia ☎ 0572 70650 🕐 Wed–Mon 12–3, 7–11 👆 L €13, D €33, Wine €13 🚌 Follow signs for Montecatini Alto and wind uphill for 3km (2 miles)

PISA

BENY

A small restaurant that specializes in fish bought fresh from the market that morning. The chalkboard menu depends on the season, but generally includes langoustines, sea bass and various seafood pastas. The restaurant sees an increasing number of foreign visitors, but no English is spoken, so bring your dictionary if you want a translation of the ingredients.

✉ Piazza Chiara Gambacorti 22, 56100 Pisa ☎ 050 25067 🕐 Mon–Fri 1–2.30, 8–11, Sat 7.30–11. Closed 1 week in Aug 👆 L €25, D €44, Wine €13

LA BUCA

www.labuca.org

Within walking distance of Campo dei Miracoli, La Buca is in a popular spot in the heart of Pisa. It draws the crowds with its pleasant outdoor terrace and the set-price lunch menu, which offers Tuscan cuisine at a reasonable price. Dinner is a little more formal with à la carte menus and attentive waiters, but the dishes are nothing unusual for Pisa with lots of pizza and pasta choices.

✉ Via G. Tassi 6/B, Via S. Maria 171, 56100 Pisa ☎ 050 560660 🕐 Sat–Thu 12–3, 7–11 👆 L €14, D €22, Wine €9

DA BRUNO

www.pisaonline.it/trattoriadabruno

The self-proclaimed best restaurant in Pisa, Da Bruno is a long-established *trattoria* serving traditional Pisan cuisine. The menu includes rustic country dishes such as salt cod cooked with leeks and tomatoes and a variety of grilled fish dishes. Reservations advisable.

✉ Via Luigi Bianchi 12, 56100 Pisa ☎ 050 560818 🕐 Wed–Mon 12–3, 7–11 👆 L €22, D €28, Wine €18

DA UGO

A popular restaurant just outside the city, serving Italian and Tuscan meat and fish dishes. What's on offer depends on the market, but generally includes pasta, rice dishes, such as risotto with porcini mushrooms, and a range of home-made desserts. A good wine list complements the dishes. Reservations are advisable.

✉ Statale Aurelia 1, Migliorino Pisano, 56100 Pisa ☎ 050 804455 🕐 Tue–Sat, 12–3, 7.30–10.30, Sun 12–3 👆 L €17, D €28, Wine €6 🚌 Take Via Aurelia towards Genova; 10-minute drive from Pisa

OSTERIA DEI CAVALIERI

This small, whitewashed *osteria*, close to the university quarter, is popular with visitors and locals for its generously priced menu and friendly welcome. The cuisine is Tuscan and Lucchese with dishes such as *ribollita* (bean soup), *tortelli lucchese* (oven-cooked pasta stuffed with meats, cheese and vegetables) and a range of *grigliata* (grilled wild boar sausage, chicken, beef or veal). Vegetarian dishes are available on the à la carte menu. Reservations may be necessary in high season.

✉ Via San Frediano 16, 56100 Pisa ☎ 050 580858 🕐 Mon–Fri 12.30–2, 7–11.30, Sat 7.45–10. Closed 1 week in Aug and a period in Jan 👆 L €14, D €30, Wine €8

OSTERIA LA MESCITA

www.lamescita.org

Influenced by seasonal and local produce, this family-run restaurant and wine bar serves light but traditional Tuscan cuisine. The menu changes weekly dependings on what's on offer in the market. The wine cellar stocks more than 300 varieties.

✉ Via Cavalca 2, 56100 Pisa ☎ 050 957019 🕐 Tue–Fri 12.30–2.15, 8–10.30, Sat–Sun 12.30–2.15. Closed 3 weeks in Aug 👆 L €17, D €39, Wine €12

OSTERIA DEL PORTON ROSSO

Central and convenient, the informal, family-run Porton Rosso is seconds from Lungarno Pacinotti and the river and just three minutes' walk south of the main Piazza dei Cavalieri. Situated in a 12th-century townhouse and tower, it lies in one of the most characteristic corners of what remains of old Pisa. Menus change regularly, but there is always a fine selection of fish and seafood, though meat and other dishes are available. Desserts are home-made—if it's available, try the little pear and Parmesan pudding (*il budino di pere e parmigiano*).

✉ Vicolo Porton Rosso 11, 56100 Pisa ☎ 050 580566 🕐 Tue–Sun 12.30–2.30, 7.30–10.30. Closed Tue and a period in Aug 👆 L €20, D €25, Wine €15 🚌 Off Lungarno Pacinotti between Piazza Garibaldi and Via Curtatone e Montanara

PASTICCERIA SALZA

This, the oldest, most celebrated and most frequented of Pisa's smart cafés, has been in the same family since the 1920s. The double-fronted shop is on the city's main shopping street and is ideal for coffee, sandwiches (more than 40 varieties), cakes, snacks or an evening aperitif. There is also a confectionary section. Hot sandwiches and a few simple pasta dishes are available in separate waiter-service room to the rear.

✉ Borgo Stretto 46, 56100 Pisa ☎ 050 580144 🕐 Tue–Sun 7.45am–8.30pm 🍴 L and D €15

LA PERGOLETTA
La Pergoletta occupies one of the most attractive medieval towers in a street famous for its beautiful towers. The menu gives the best of Tuscany's rustic cuisine a modern twist. Dishes include soup with farro grain, roast lamb with rosemary and garlic and a fresh fish of the day. Reservations recommended.

✉ Via delle Belle Torri 36, 56127 Pisa ☎ 050 542458 🕐 Tue–Sun 1–2.30, 8–10.30. Closed 1st 2 weeks in Aug 🍴 L €17, D €33, Wine €8

RISTORANTE EMILIO
Close to the Campo dei Miracoli, this is a good place to stop for lunch. On a hot day the two dining rooms feel fresh with their whitewashed walls, wooden furnishings, marble flooring and leafy plants. The cuisine is mostly Tuscan with both fish and meat playing an important role. There is also a good local wine list. Reservations recommended; open for dinner by prior arrangement only.

✉ Via Cammeo 44, 56100 Pisa ☎ 050 562141 🕐 Daily 12–3.30pm 🍴 L €17, Wine €5.20

RISTORANTE SANTA MARIA
The Santa Maria has a well-priced but straightforward menu of pizzas, cold cuts, grilled meats and seasonal Tuscan dishes. The restaurant is split between a self-service area and a pizzeria in a dining room with arched doorways. The wine list is varied.

✉ Via Santa Maria 104/106, 56100 Pisa ☎ 050 561881 🕐 Daily 9–4, 6–12.30 🍴 L €16, D €40, Wine €7

LO SCHIACCIANOCI
A tiny *trattoria* specializing in fish from the nearby coast, pasta and

traditional Tuscan meat dishes. It's simple, old-fashioned and relaxed, with seafood pasta, grilled meats or fish. Other dishes include thick bean soup and mushroom ravioli. The wine list has labels from all over Italy.

✉ Via Vespucci 104a, 56125 Pisa ☎ 050 21024 🕐 Mon–Sat 12–3, 7.30–10.30 🍴 L €10, D €22, Wine €8

PISTOIA
TRATTORIA DELL'ABBONDANZA
Here swags of dried flowers and fruit hang from white-painted beams, and the tile-topped tables are covered with dark green mats. There's a definite bustle about the place, as a team of cooks prepares fried chicken, roasted rabbit and tripe cooked in the Florentine way. In fine weather tables are put outside.

✉ Via dell'Abbondanza 10, 51100 Pistoia ☎ 0573 368037 🕐 Fri–Tue 12.15–3, 7.15–10, Thu 7.15–10. Closed 1st 2 weeks in May and in Oct 🍴 L €10, D €22, Wine €4

VIAREGGIO
GIORDANO BRUNO
Former soccer player Bruno Giordano owns this combination of wine bar and pizzeria in a building with views to the sea and the mountains behind. Giordano organizes wine tastings from his selection of more than 1,300 different labels, of which 500 are non-Italian. Afterwards you can enjoy a pizza cooked in a wood-burning oven or sample some of the menu's other delights.

✉ Viale Europa 7, 55049 Viareggio, Lucca ☎ 0584 392201 🕐 Daily 8pm–2am 🍴 D €35 (Pizza €8), Wine €12

RISTORANTE PIZZERIA LEONE
Away from the activity of the seafront you can sit outside here and watch the bustle of the old port. Although the pizzas are excellent, fish is the priority here and locals pack in to eat the changing dishes of the day. The surroundings are simple, so all the attention is on the food and welcoming, helpful service. A delicious Prosecco (sparkling white wine) from the Veneto area

marries well with the food.

✉ Via della Foce 23–27, 55049 Viareggio, Lucca ☎ 0584 32198 🕐 Summer daily 7pm–midnight; winter Tue–Sat 7pm–midnight, Sun 12–3pm 🍴 D €33, Wine €8

TRATTORIA LA DARSENA
Hidden away on a backstreet in the less glamorous part of Viareggio, La Darsena is a popular family-run fish restaurant; booking is essential. The fish and seafood are always very fresh and prepared in a typically no-nonsense way. Start your meal with the endless stream of house antipasti. Follow this with a *spaghetti alle vongole* (with clams), *allo scoglio* (with mixed seafood) or with red mullet sauce. Main courses include octopus and potato stew and *fritto misto* (mixed, deep-fried seafood). The wine list is dominated by whites; the *vino della casa* is inexpensive and cheerful.

✉ Via Virgilio 150, 55049 Viareggio, Lucca ☎ 0584 392785 🕐 Mon–Sat 12–3.30, 7.30–10.30 🍴 L and D €17, Wine €8

Below *Bottled wines are usually locally produced, except in smarter restaurants*

PRICES AND SYMBOLS

The prices are the lowest and highest for a double room for one night including breakfast, unless otherwise stated. All the hotels listed accept credit cards unless otherwise stated. Note that rates can vary widely throughout the year.

For a key to the symbols, ▷ 2.

CARRARA

MICHELANGELO

www.rivieratoscana.com

Carrara is a working town, but has an attractive historic heart, home to this mid-range hotel, largely dating from the 1970s, which makes a good base for exploring the area's mining heritage and mountainous hinterland. The rooms are relatively plain, but clean, comfortable and with TVs and private bathrooms.

✉ Corso Fratelli Rosselli 3, 54033 Carrara ☎ 0585 777161 🖐 €80–€100 🛏 30 🕙 Closed mid-Dec to mid-Jan

CASTELNUOVO DI GARFAGNANA

DA CARLINO

www.dacarlino.it

Despite its growing popularity, the Garfagnana is still short of hotels. Da Carlino, in the centre of the region's main town of Castelnuovo, provides one of the few bases not only for the Serchio valley, but also for the Alpi Apuane and Orecchiella mountains to the east and west. Although a relatively modest modern hotel, the welcome is warm, and the large, co-owned restaurant-pizzeria (with summer terrace) offers excellent local cooking, including a selection of rustic local pastas you won't find elsewhere in Tuscany.

✉ Via Garibaldi 15, 55032 Castelnuovo di Garfagnana ☎ 0583 644270 🖐 €60–€70 🛏 32

LUCCA

ALBERGO CELIDE

www.albergocelide.it

Celide sits just outside the city's ramparts. The guest rooms here come with a range of modern facilities such as internet connection and cable TV. Downstairs is an intimate café-bar and upstairs the roof garden has panoramic views. Facilities also include a TV room, a courtesy bus into town, and 24-hour reception. There's a cocktail bar and restaurant next door.

✉ Viale Giusti 25, 55100 Lucca ☎ 0583 954106/7/8 🖐 €140–€190 🛏 58 🔵

ALBERGO SAN MARTINO

www.albergosanmartino.it

This three-star hotel in Lucca's old town is only a brief stroll from the cathedral. The bedrooms are well furnished and have a TV and refrigerator. An English-speaker comes to the hotel at 6pm every day to give guests a talk on what to see and do in Lucca. Parking and bicycle rental available.

✉ Via della Dogana 7/9, 55100 Lucca ☎ 0583 469181 🖐 €80–€110 🛏 9 🔵

HOTEL ILARIA

www.hotelilaria.com

The rooms here are modern, with bright tiling or carpets, pastel walls and beamed ceilings. Each has a private shower or bath. The large apartment is suitable for groups and for longer stays. Both bar and restaurant serve traditional cuisine. Private parking is available.

✉ Via del Fosso 26, 55100 Lucca ☎ 0583 47615 🖐 €200 –€230 🛏 40 🔵

HOTEL LOCANDA L'ELISA

www.locandalelisa.it

In attractive mountainous surroundings, the Hotel Locanda l'Elisa (pictured on page 164) is in a converted 18th-century villa thought to have been built under the direction of Napoleon's sister, Elisa Baciocchi. The 10 suites are decorated with period furnishings and lavish fabrics, and feel surprisingly intimate after the grandeur of the entrance. The stately conservatory houses the well-reputed Ristorante Gazebo (▷ 159). Guests have use of the lush, scented flower garden, bar, conference hall and laundry service.

✉ Via Nuova per Pisa 1952, 55050 Massa Pisana, Lucca ☎ 0583 379737 🖐 €260–€300 🛈 10 🌐 🏊 Outdoor 🅿 Follow the blue signs marked Pisa on SS12; the hotel is on the left, 5.5km (3.5 miles) from Lucca

NOBLESSE

www.hotelnoblesse.it

Until 2006, Lucca lacked a central hotel of the highest class, but in the Noblesse, converted from a 17th-century palazzo, is has acquired a superb luxury hotel. Ideally situated between Piazza San Michele and the Duomo, it is intimate and stylish, with oriental rugs on the terracotta floors and antiques, period furniture and rich fabrics in the rooms and public spaces. It also has parking and a pleasant outdoor area.

✉ Via Sant'Anastasio 23, 55100 Lucca ☎ 0583 440275 🖐 €390–490 🛈 15 🌐

PICCOLO HOTEL PUCCINI

www.hotelpuccini.com

This small, friendly, three-star hotel is in the very heart of Lucca. The guest rooms, although small, are well priced. Each bedroom has a TV, telephone, hairdryer and safe. Parking is available by arrangement. Courtesy car for trips to and from the airport or train station.

✉ Via di Poggio 9, 55100 Lucca ☎ 0583 55421 🖐 €92 🛈 14

LA ROMEA

www.laromea.com

Bed and breakfast is provided here on the first floor of a late 14th-century palace, just a short walk

from the Torre Guinigi. All rooms have TV and hairdryer. Private parking is available.

✉ Via Sant'Andrea, 56127 Lucca ☎ 0583 464175 🖐 €110–€130 (suites €120–€160) 🛈 3 rooms, 2 suites 🌐 🏊 Outdoor

VILLA LA PRINCIPESSA

www.hotelprincipessa.com

This four-star hotel at the base of the hills surrounding Lucca, just 3km (2 miles) from the city, is one of the most elegant lodgings in Tuscany. The luxurious guest rooms are decorated with antiques and have telephone, satellite TV and minibar. There is a lounge, bar and restaurants.

✉ Via Nuova per Pisa 1616, 55050 Massa Pisana, Lucca ☎ 0583 370037 🖐 €194–€299 🛈 42 🌐 🏊 Outdoor 🅿 On the SS12, follow the blue signs for Pisa, the hotel is on the right after 3.5km (2 miles)

VILLA ROMANTICA

www.villaromantica.it

A few minutes' walk from the city walls, Villa Romantica is a grand art nouveau townhouse surrounded by trees and flower-filled urns. Rooms have bright walls and busy fabrics. For a romantic experience, reserve the suite with four-poster bed. There's a bus service to central Lucca (four times an hour), free private parking and bicycles for rent.

✉ Via Barbantini 246, 55100 Lucca ☎ 0583 496872 🖐 €98–€130 🛈 6 🌐 🏊 Outdoor

MONTECATINI TERME
GRAND HOTEL DU PARK ET REGINA

www.regina-hotel.it

Shades of the Belle Époque are in evidence at this stately old spa hotel. Close to the thermal spas (▷ 134). There are spacious public rooms, a restaurant serving both Tuscan and international cuisine, a garden and parking. Sauna, massages and solarium are also available.

✉ Viale Diaz 8, 51016 Montecatini Terme, Pistoia ☎ 0572 79232 🖐 €150 🛈 78 🌐 🏊 Outdoor

MUGELLO
VILLA CAMPESTRI

www.villacampestri.it

The wild Mugello region has relatively few hotels, but this is one of the best, a pleasing 19th-century villa 5km (3 miles) from Vicchio, birthplace of the painter Fra Angelico and one of the area's most attractive villages. The rooms have plenty of antiques, paintings and other period details, along with terracotta floors and beamed ceilings. There is a good restaurant, L'Olivaia, and excellent wine list, with bottles kept in the medieval cellars of an earlier villa on the site.

✉ Via di Campestri 19/22, Località Campestri, 50039 Vicchio ☎ 055 849 0107 🖐 €144–€210 🛈 22 🌐 🏊 Outdoor

PIETRASANTA
ALBERGO PIETRASANTA

www.albergopietrasanta.com

This handsome hotel, just inland from the popular Versilia beaches, is in a 17th-century palazzo. The elegant interior (fine plasterwork, chandeliers, vast fireplaces and antique furniture) is a good backdrop for the owner's collection of modern Italian art. The comfortable bedrooms have warm parquet floors and smart fabrics; those at the top have round windows and are particularly attractive. Breakfast is served in a big conservatory and there is a pretty garden, as well as a Turkish bath.

✉ Via Garibaldi 35, 55045 Pietrasanta, Lucca ☎ 0584 793726 🚫 Closed early Jan–end Mar 🖐 €320–€400 🛈 19 🌐 🍽

PISA
GRAND HOTEL DUOMO

www.grandhotelduomo.it

This hotel is just a step away from the Leaning Tower. The roof garden has splendid views over the monuments on Campo dei Miracoli. Guest rooms are spacious and clean, with satellite TV. The restaurant serves Tuscan dishes, and there's a bar and private parking.

✉ Via Santa Maria 94, 56100 Pisa ☎ 050 561894 🖐 €130–€180 🛈 93 🌐

HOTEL FRANCESCO
www.hotelfrancesco.com
This small hotel close to the Leaning Tower has whitewashed rooms, with wooden furnishings and—in most cases—panoramic views. Breakfast is served on the main terrace. Bedrooms have TV and minibar. Facilities include a pizzeria, bicycle rental and airport shuttle.
✉ Via Santa Maria 129, 56126 Pisa ☎ 050 555453 🖐 €80–€130 ⓘ 13 🔄

HOTEL RELAIS DELL'OROLOGIO
www.hotelrelaisorologio.com
Wooden-beamed ceilings, spacious sitting rooms, antique furnishings and original fireplaces typify the interior of this old manor house, yet the guest rooms have every modern convenience. There's a well-regarded restaurant. An airport bus service is available on request.
✉ Via della Faggiola 12/14, 56126 Pisa ☎ 050 830361 🖐 €300–€490 ⓘ 21 rooms, 2 suites, 2 junior suites 🔄 📺 Solarium

HOTEL ROSETO
www.hotelroseto.it
This hotel, near the rail station, is brightly decorated, and large windows and high ceilings give the rooms an airy, spacious feel. The leafy roof garden, with space for some guests to take breakfast and for evening drinks, is one of the biggest attractions. There's also a breakfast room and bar.
✉ Via Pietro Mascagni 24, 56100 Pisa ☎ 050 42596 🖐 €60–78, excluding breakfast ⓘ 16 🔄

HOTEL VERDI
Small and friendly, this hotel lies within easy reach of Pisa's principal attractions. Its rooms are fresh and neatly furnished with some original touches. There is a lounge area with a bar, and free parking.
✉ Piazza Repubblica 5/6, 56100 Pisa ☎ 050 598947 🖐 €75–€125 ⓘ 32 🔄

ROYAL VICTORIA
www.royalvictoria.it
The Royal Victoria first opened in 1837, when the Piegaja family (whose descendants still run it) bought an old medieval tower and turned it into a hotel. It has expanded since then, and the hotel's history, frescoed ceilings and near-original furnishings ensure that the visitors' book is always full. The hotel has a bar, concierge service, free parking and bicycle rental.
✉ Lungarno Pacinotti 12, 56100 Pisa ☎ 050 940111 🖐 €77–€128 ⓘ 48 🔄 20 rooms

VILLA KINZICA HOTEL
www.hotelvillakinzica.it
Within walking distance of the Leaning Tower, the Villa Kinzica still charges reasonable rates. In a renovated Italian villa, the hotel has modern furnishings and pastel-hued decorations. Some rooms have views over the Campo dei Miracoli. There's a restaurant, concierge and room service.
✉ Piazza Arcivescovado 2, 56100 Pisa ☎ 050 560419 🖐 €95–€108 ⓘ 30 🔄

Above In a converted 18th-century villa, Hotel Locanda L'Elisa lies in attractive, mountainous surroundings just 5km (3.5 miles) from Lucca

PISTOIA
LEON BIANCO
www.hotelleonbianco.it
One of Pistoia's best-priced mid-range hotels, the Leon Bianco, part of a 15th-century palazzo, is at the heart of the pedestrian-only area of the town's historic centre. Rooms, although not big, are all comfortable and clean, with adjoining bathrooms. There is no restaurant, but a buffet breakfast is served.
✉ Via Panciatichi 2, 51100 Pistoia ☎ 0573 26675 🖐 €75–€100 ⓘ 27 🔄

PATRIA
www.patriahotel.com
In the south of the city's central historic district, close to the old walls, the Patria makes a good mid-price base for sightseeing. Vehicle access is difficult, but the hotel provides passes for those with cars. A buffet breakfast is served, but there is no restaurant.
✉ Via Crispi 8, 51100 Pistoia ☎ 0573 25187 🖐 €80–€115 ⓘ 28 🔄

VILLA CAPPUGI
www.hotelvillacappugi.com
This rural villa sits in open countryside at the foot of the Colli Pistoiesi, or Pistoian Hills, offering a pretty and tranquil alternative to the hotels in the town. It also provides a wide range of facilities, including tennis courts, gym, sauna and outdoor swimming pool.

✉ Via di Collegigliato 45, 51100 Pistoia ☎ 0573 450297 💶 €175–€195 🛏 70 💳 🏊 Outdoor ♨

SAN CASCIANO IN VAL DI PESA
VILLA IL POGGIALE
www.villailpoggiale.it
The Villa Il Poggiale occupies a beautiful Renaissance villa and retains the feeling of a private house. A pastel interior keeps things cool throughout the spacious and elegant public rooms and the individually furnished bedrooms. There are family portraits, antiques and (modern) four-poster beds, chandeliers and filmy white curtains. Outside, you can relax under the loggia at the front of the villa, on the west-facing terrace or by the swimming pool.

✉ Via Empolese 69, 50026 San Casciano in Val di Pesa, Firenze ☎ 055 828311 🕐 Closed Feb 💶 €150–€240 🛏 21 💳 🏊 Outdoor 🚗 2km (1.2 miles) from San Casciano on Empoli road

SANTA MARIA DEL GIUDICE
HOTEL VILLA RINASCIMENTO
www.villarinascimento.it
This hotel is a great choice, but visitors need to have their own cars as it's perched above the village. Guests can choose between rooms in the restored Renaissance stone villa and those in the wooden chalets. The whitewashed guest rooms have beamed ceilings and wooden floors. A bar is also available.

✉ Via del Cimitero 532, 55058 Santa Maria del Giudice, Lucca ☎ 0583 378292 💶 €130–€155 🛏 31 💳 17 rooms 🏊 Outdoor 🚗 On SS12, 8km (5 miles) from Lucca

SAN MINIATO
VILLA SONNINO
www.villasonnino.com
The central part of this peaceful old villa 4km (2.5 miles) east of San Miniato dates from the 16th century, and is surrounded by centuries-old parkland. The lovely rooms have plenty of period touches. The attractive Castelvecchio restaurant serves accomplished Mediterranean cooking.

✉ Via Castelvecchio 9/11, Località Catena, 56028 San Miniato ☎ 0571 484033 💶 €98–€155 🛏 13 💳

TIRRENIA
GRAND HOTEL GOLF
www.grandhotelgolf.it
The hotel is named after its two golf courses, which are open all year. The hotel and its vast grounds also have plenty for non-golfers, including a stretch of private beach, a piano bar and a restaurant. Balconied bedrooms have good panoramas over the coast and pine forests.

✉ Via dell'Edera 29, 56018 Tirrenia, Pisa ☎ 050 957018 💶 €140–€175 🛏 77 rooms, 18 suites 💳 🏊 Outdoor 🚗 Take the Pisa Centro exit on the A12 and follow signs for Tirrenia

HOTEL MEDUSA
www.hotelmedusa.com
Just a 30-minute drive from Pisa but beside the sea, the Medusa has the best of both worlds. It has a comfortable feel with soft sofas in the lounge area and chairs out on the terrace. Good Tuscan cooking is served in the restaurant. The hotel also has a bar, parking and beach chair reservations.

✉ Via Oleandri 37/39, 56018 Tirrenia, Pisa ☎ 050 37125 💶 €70–€104 🛏 32 💳 🚗 Take the Pisa Centro exit on the A12 and follow signs for Tirrenia

VIAREGGIO
GRANDE HOTEL PRINCIPE DI PIEMONTE
www.principedipiemonte.com
Renovation has restored the reputation of the central Principe di Piemonte as the finest hotel on the Versilia coast. The main building

is a Liberty-style (art deco) gem, while the rooms offer a variety of decorative styles. One of the two restaurants, the elegant Il Piccolo Principe, is open to non-residents.

✉ Piazza Giacomo Puccini 1, 55049 Viareggio ☎ 0584 4011 💶 €260–€450 🛏 91 (15 suites) 💳 🏊 Indoor and outdoor ♨

HOTEL MIRAMARE
www.miramarehotel.net
This hotel is extremely good value for one that is right on the waterfront. Bedrooms on the higher floors have the best views and are quieter. Parking is available in a nearby garage for €15 per day. The hotel also has a beach concession for €5–€8 per person per day. The restaurant is open July to end September.

✉ Lungomare Carducci 27, 55049 Viareggio, Lucca ☎ 0584 48441/2 💶 €77–€130 🛏 26 💳

HOTEL PLAZA E DE RUSSIE
www.plazaederussie.com
Built in 1871, the luxurious Plaza e de Russie retains some original marble floors and Murano glass chandeliers. The roof restaurant has spectacular views of the sea, mountains and coast. You can use the facilities of the adjacent beach concession, which has a seawater swimming pool.

✉ Piazza d'Azeglio 1, 55049 Viareggio, Lucca ☎ 0584 44449 💶 €158–€210 🛏 50 💳 🏊 Outdoor

VINCI
DA VINCI
www.hotelda-vinci.it
A favourite among business travellers, the Da Vinci also makes a good alternative for casual visitors who do not want to stay in Florence. The rooms are bright and spacious, with modern, up-to-the-minute facilities (including in-room internet access). The restaurant, the Osteria Ripa d'Arno, offers a mixture of traditional and more innovative Tuscan cuisine.

✉ Viale Togliatti 157, 50059 Vinci ☎ 0571 90941 💶 €42–€190 🛏 68 💳

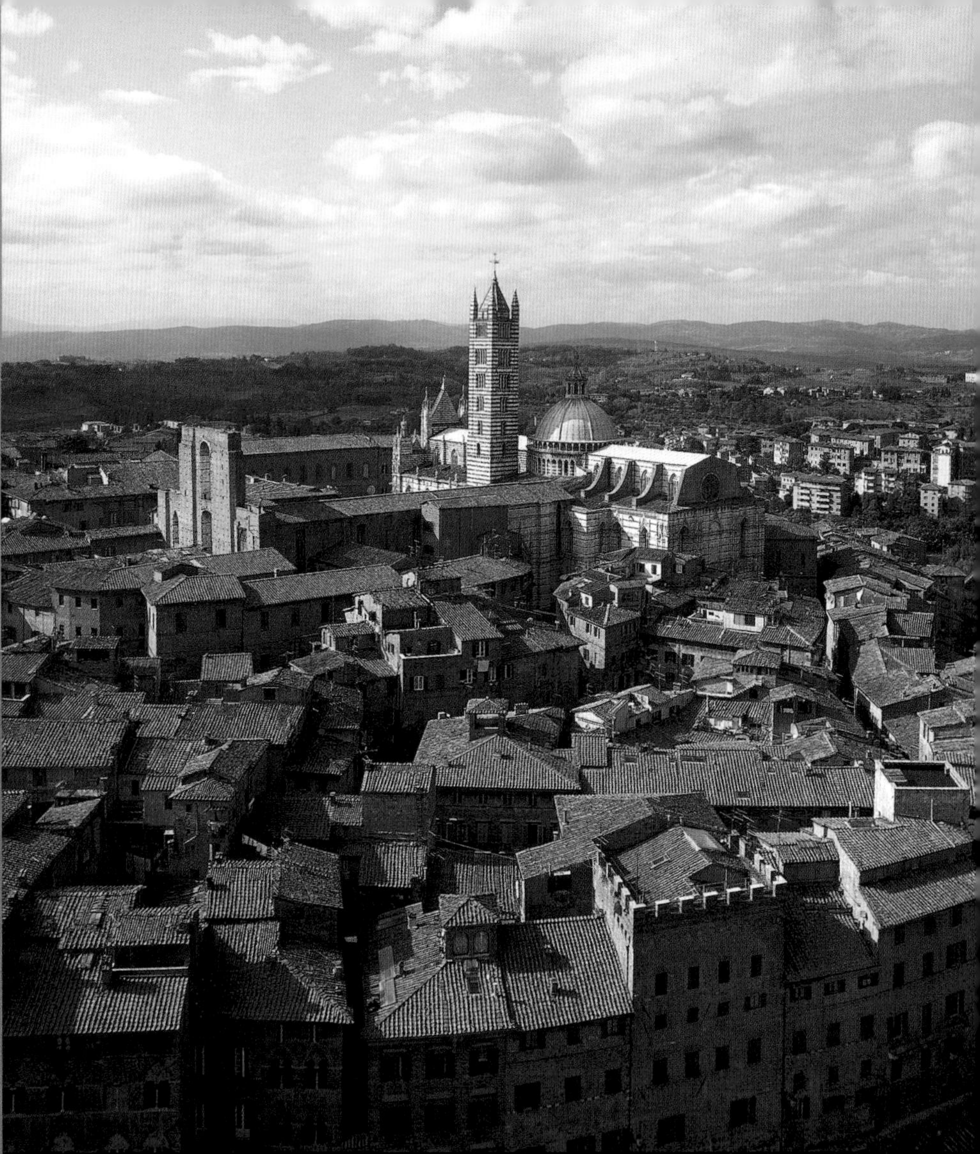

S Dalmazio

SP408

674

SIENA

Museo dell'Opera del Duomo

Duomo · · / · **Il Campo**

Pinacoteca Nazionale

Santa Maria della Scala ·

SP73

674

SP73   E78

Costalpino

Cerchiáia

SIENA

Italy's most perfect medieval city has two focal points: the shell-shaped Campo, one of the world's most beautiful squares, and the Duomo, a superb Gothic building. Around these two are art-filled churches and public buildings, picturesque streets that burst into life for the Palio horse-race, and tempting shopping and dining. This lies at the convergence of the three main streets, the Banchi di Sopra, the Banchi di Sotto and the Via di Città. Each runs along a ridge through the city's three medieval *terzi* (thirds, or districts), the Terzo di Città to the southwest, the Terzo di San Martino to the southeast and the Terzo di Camollia to the north. This central core was closed to traffic in the 1960s, making exploration more pleasurable and straightforward. To get your bearings use the Campo as your starting point, and then head west and uphill to the Duomo. The Torre del Mangia in the Campo and the Panorama dal Facciatone in the Museo dell'Opera del Duomo are ideal viewpoints for seeing the layout of the city. Central Siena is surprisingly small; you'll be able to walk to all the noteworthy sights in well under half an hour. If it's your first visit, include a night's stay; the city has a whole new perspective once the crowds of day visitors have left.

Siena was founded by the Etruscans and then became a Roman city, Saena Julia. In the Middle Ages it grew to be an independent republic and by the 14th century was one of Europe's major cities, a rich banking hub with an important wool industry, whose wealth paid for the construction of great buildings and funded major artists. The Black Death in 1348 brought Siena's prosperity came to an end; the population dropped from 100,000 to around 30,000. In 1557 Siena became part of the Medici Grand Duchy of Tuscany, emerging in the years that followed as little more than a minor provincial town. The upside of this was the preservation of its medieval core, with little building or demolition after the early 1400s. As a backwater, Siena was untouched during World War II and only saw regeneration as tourism developed during the second half of the 20th century, years that also saw the Monte dei Paschi di Siena, the city's oldest bank, become one of Italy's major financial players.

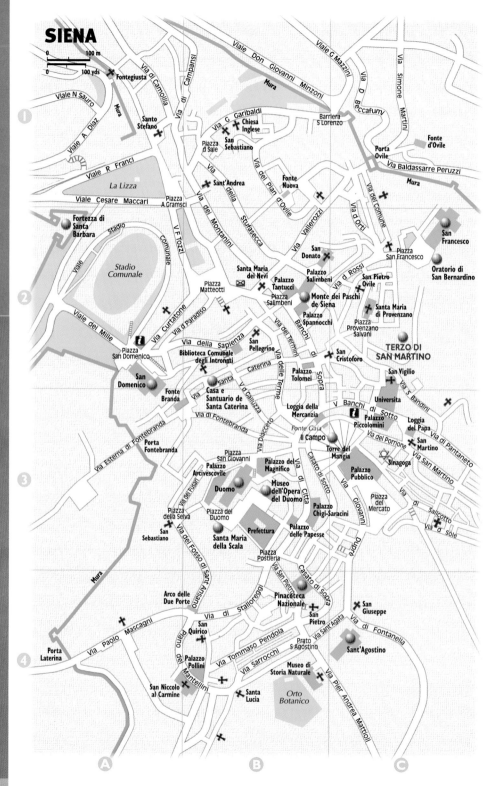

SIENA

0 —— 100 m
0 —— 100 yds

Fontegiusta

Viale Don Giovanni Minzoni

Viale G Mazzini

Via Simone Martini

Via di Camollia

Via di Campansi

Mura

Via D Beccafumi

Viale N Sauro

Santo Stefano

Via G Garibaldi

Chiesa Inglese

Barriera S Lorenzo

Viale A. Diaz

Mura

Piazza d'Sale

San Sebastiano

Porta Ovile

Fonte d'Ovile

Via Baldassarre Peruzzi

Viale R Franci

Sant'Andrea

Via della Stufasecca

Fonte Nuova

Via del Pian d'Ovile

Mura

La Lizza

Viale Cesare Maccari

Piazza A Gramsci

Via del Montanini

Via Vallerozzi

Via del Comune

San Francesco

Fortezza di Santa Barbara

Stadio

V F Tozzi

Piazza Matteotti

Santa Maria dei Nevi

San Donato

Palazzo Salimbeni

Via d'Orti

Piazza San Francesco

Oratorio di San Bernardino

Stadio Comunale

Viale Comunale

Palazzo Tantucci

Piazza Salimbeni

Via d' Rossi

San Pietro Ovile

Santa Maria di Provenzano

Viale dei Mille

Via Curtatone

Via d'Paradiso

Palazzo Spannocchi

Monte dei Paschi de Siena

Piazza Provenzano Salvani

Via della Sapienza

San Pellegrino

Via di Termini

Via Banchi di

San Cristoforo

TERZO DI SAN MARTINO

Piazza San Domenico

Biblioteca Comunale degli Intronati

Caterina

Via delle Terme

Via d Sopra

Palazzo Tolomei

San Vigilio

Via s Bandini

San Domenico

Santa

V d Galluzza

Casa e Santuario de Santa Caterina

Fonte Branda

Loggia della Mercanzia

Universita

Loggia del Papa

Via di Pantaneto

Via di Fontebranda

Via Diacceto

V Banchi di Sotto

Palazzo Piccolomini

Porta Fontebranda

Fonte Gaia

Il Campo

Via del Porrione

San Martino

Via San Martino

Via Esterna di Fontebranda

Piazza San Giovanni

Palazzo del Magnifico

Torre del Mangia

Sinagoga

Palazzo Arcivescovile

Duomo

Museo dell'Opera del Duomo

Via di Città

Palazzo Pubblico

Piazza del Mercato

Via di Salicotto

Piazza del Duomo

Palazzo Chigi-Saracini

Casato di Sotto

Via di Giovanni

Via d' Sole

Piazza della Selva

San Sebastiano

Via del Fosso di Sant'Ansano

Prefettura

Santa Maria della Scala

Palazzo delle Papesse

Piazza Postieria

Mura

Arco delle Due Porte

Via di Stalloreggi

Pinacoteca Nazionale

San Pietro

San Giuseppe

Via di Fontanella

Casato di Sopra

Via San Pietro

Via Paolo Mascagni

San Quirico

Prato S Agostino

Via Sant'Agata

Sant'Agostino

Porta Laterina

Piano del Mantellini

Palazzo Pollini

Via Tommaso Pendola

Via Sarrocchi

Museo di Storia Naturale

Via Pier Andrea Mattioli

San Niccolo al Carmine

Santa Lucia

Orto Botanico

A   B   C

SIENA STREET INDEX

REGIONS SIENA • CITY MAPS

169

IL CAMPO
▷ 172–175.

CASA E SANTUARIO DE SANTA CATERINA

St. Catherine of Siena lived as a Dominican tertiary—that is, a member of the Dominican order but living outside it—in her family home just south of the church of San Domenico (▷ 183), and you can visit the house today. Caterina Benincasa, as St. Catherine, is joint patron saint of Italy with St. Francis. She was canonized as much for her political as for her mystical role. Born in 1347, the daughter of a dyer and one of a reputed 23 children, she experienced visions from a very early age and became a nun at 16 contrary to the wishes of her parent and in the face of strong family opposition. In the aftermath of the Black Death of 1348, when Siena's population was devastated, she tended the poor and sick, but increasingly saw her God-given role as that of political mediator. She was instrumental through her letters in persuading Pope Urban V to return to Rome from Avignon, having first prevented the Sienese, Pisans and Florentines from rising against him, and afterwards worked tirelessly to reconcile the resulting schism between popes and anti-popes. Her later life was one of visions and prayer—she received the stigmata (marks that correspond to those left on Christ's body after the Crucifixion) in a vision. She died in 1380 and was canonized in 1460.

Her home has been altered over the centuries and now has a Renaissance loggia and a series of oratories—one on the site of her cell. In the adjoining church of San Domenico you can see the crucifix in front of which she is said to have received the stigmata, while the Oratorio di (chapel of) Santa Caterina contains frescoes by Il Sodoma and a fine 15th-century statue of the saint by Niccolò di Bartolomeo.

🕂 168 B2 ✉ Costa San Antonio 6, 53100 ☎ 0577 44177 🕒 Daily 9–12.30, 3–6; Chapel of the Crucifix 9–12 💵 Free

Above *From the Fortezza there are fine views of Siena*
Opposite *Nicola Pisano's octagonal pulpit in the Duomo is a masterpiece of Gothic sculpture*

DUOMO
▷ 176–179.

FORTEZZA DI SANTA BARBARA
www.enoteca-italiana.it

On the northwest edge of the old city looms the Fortezza di Santa Barbara, a huge square fort with massive corner bastions. Initially built by the Holy Roman Emperor Charles V in 1554, it was attacked and destroyed by a mob and rebuilt under Cosimo I in 1561 as a garrison. You can go inside and climb up for great views of the city and hills beyond, but most people visit to sample the wines at the Enoteca Italiana, a state-run enterprise inside the Fortezza. It stocks virtually all of Italy's 1,000-plus wines, more than 400 of which originate in Tuscany. You can sample many by the glass at the bar, and all are on sale to take with you. The Fortezza comes into its own in summer, when it becomes a venue for concerts. Just to the north are the gardens of La Lizza, laid out in the 18th century and still a green haven in this part of town. The gardens are the scene on Wednesdays of Siena's huge weekly market, one of the largest in Tuscany.

🕂 168 A2 ✉ Fortezza di Santa Barbara, 53100 ☎ Enoteca: 0577 288811 🕒 Tower: Daily 24 hours; Enoteca: Mon 12–8, Tue–Sat noon–1am 💵 Free

MONTE DEI PASCHI DE SIENA

Siena's early medieval wealth was based largely on banking, its financial dynasties dating back to the 12th century. The Monte dei Paschi de Siena was founded later, in the 15th century, but it is the world's oldest operating bank and plays a pivotal role in the social, cultural and economic life of the city. It was established as a charitable institution, lending money to the poor. Since the 15th century its headquarters have been two palazzi: the Spanocchi, a Renaissance palace, and the Salimbeni, a superb Gothic structure. In 1972 the architect Pierluigi Spadolino was commissioned to update the complex, which involved the construction of an ultramodern interior within the historic shell. This has created the perfect background for the bank's art collection, most of which is kept in the deconsecrated church of San Donato, reached by an underground passage from the main building. Here you will see some of Siena's finest Gothic masterpieces on display, including a crucifix by Pietro Lorenzetti (active 1320–48) and a jewel-like Madonna by Giovanni di Paolo (1403–82).

🕂 168 B2 ✉ Piazza Salimbeni 3, 53100 ☎ 0577 294599 🕒 By written request

IL CAMPO

INTRODUCTION

It is hard to imagine a more beautiful square than the Campo, the great scallop-shaped piazza at the heart of Siena. No matter how many times you visit the city, the sudden view of its graceful curves, ring of palaces and the great open space as you emerge from the surrounding narrow, stepped alleys still enthrals. At the Campo's lowest point is the Palazzo Pubblico, and, alongside it, the Torre del Mangia, a colossal civic bell tower intended to rival the height of the cathedral campanile nearby, which was built at the city's highest point. The Palazzo has long housed the city's civic authorities—and continues to do so to this day—but part of the vast building is also given over the Museo Civico, one of the city's highlights. It contains numerous beautifully frescoed rooms, as well as several of Tuscany's most celebrated paintings, notably Simone Martini's *Maestà* and a fresco cycle by Ambrogio Lorenzetti. Allow an hour or more for a tour. Once out, cross the courtyard to the entrance to the Torre del Mangia; master its 388 steps and you will be rewarded with superb views across the city and surrounding countryside from the top. Plan to leave enough time for a drink at one of the cafés around the Campo, perfect for people-watching. Prices are predictably high, but worth paying this once, just to enjoy one of Europe's great views. If you want to eat, however, you'll do better away from this visitor hub.

Il Campo (literally, The Field) occupies a site at the convergence of the three hilly ridges, the *terzi* (thirds, or districts), into which Siena is divided. Also intersecting here are the boundaries of the city's fiercely competitive *contrade* (parishes), making this area the only neutral patch of ground within the city. Here stood the Roman forum, which by the 13th century had become the city's main marketplace, earmarked by the city council in 1293 for expansion into a new public square. To enable construction of the surrounding buildings, a huge buttress was built beneath the lower half of the site, acting as the foundation

TIPS

» The Campo is best seen before the bus tours arrive, so get there early.

» Summer evenings are perfect for a stroll in the Campo.

» Check at the tourist office for details of the occasional summer concerts held in the square.

» If you're planning to attend the Palio, arrive early. You won't be able to leave the Campo for at least 2 hours after the race, so be prepared to do without shade, lavatories or refreshment for as much as 6 hours.

» Contrade feast days see flag-throwers and drummers in medieval costume processing through the Campo—check times with the tourist office.

Above *Horseriders compete in the* Palio, *the high-speed, bareback race around the Campo that takes place in July and August*

Opposite *The Palazzo Pubblico and Torre del Mangia lie at the base of the Campo*

for the Palazzo Pubblico, the future seat of the city government and financial offices. The Campo was completed by 1349, by which time the Palazzo Pubblico had also almost acquired its present form. The elegant palace is still home to the Sienese council, which occupies the upper floors of the building; the original council chambers, frescoed during Siena's medieval zenith, have been converted into the Museo Civico.

WHAT TO SEE

PALAZZO PUBBLICO

The halls and chambers in the Palazzo Pubblico—or town hall—comprise the Museo Civico and give a superb overview of Sienese painting. Here Sienese power, virtue and achievement from its medieval heyday are all proudly celebrated. Everything you see was once the backdrop to council meetings and decisions of state, a reminder of the former importance of the city and its government. After the tour it's worth heading back through the museum to climb the stairs to the rear loggia, which overlooks the Piazza del Mercato and has a superb view towards the countryside to the southeast.

✚ 168 C3 ✉ Piazza del Campo, 53100 ☎ 0577 292232 🕐 Mid-Mar to end Oct daily 10–7; Jan to mid-Feb, late Nov–end Dec daily 10–5.30; mid-Feb to mid-March, early Nov daily 10–6.30 ✋ Adult €7, under 18 free ❓ Combined ticket with the Torre del Mangia available: Adult €12

The Front Rooms

The Sala dei Priori (or Sala di Balia) has a series of scenes from the life of the Sienese-born Pope Alexander III, painted around 1407 by Spinello Aretino. The focus is on Alexander's struggles with Frederick Barbarossa, the German Holy Roman Emperor, and there's a splendid naval battle scene. The next room, the Anticamera del Concistoro, where there are Madonnas by Ambrogio Lorenzetti and Matteo di Giovanni, leads into a trio of rooms, one a richly embellished chapel. Highlights include a gilded bronze *She-Wolf Suckling Romulus and Remus* (Siena was allegedly founded by a son of Remus, ▷ 27) and Gothic frescoes by Taddeo di Bartolo dating from 1407–14. Off the Anticamera is the Sala del Concistoro, its ceiling a riot of writhing Mannerist forms and vivid tones, painted between 1529 and 1535 by Domenico Beccafumi.

Below *A view of the stunning scalloped-shaped Campo from the Torre del Mangia*

Sala del Mappamundo

The Sala del Mappamundo (Room of the World Map), which gets its name from a now-faded circular map, has two remarkable frescoes. Simone Martini's stupendous *Maestà*, a quintessential Sienese Gothic piece, richly decorative in style with an almost translucent quality, was commissioned by the comune (city government) in 1315. The *Equestrian Portrait of Guidoriccio da Fogliano*, long believed also to be by Martini—an attribution now disputed—shows a sturdy, mounted knight setting out to besiege a hill town, and encapsulates the late medieval dream of chivalry. The academic quarrel over its artist continues. Some argue that it is a genuine Martini (even if overpainted), while other experts say it is a 16th-century fake. Whatever the truth, it remains one of the most beguiling frescoes in Siena.

Sala della Pace

A doorway leads from the map room into the Sala della Pace (Room of Peace), with Ambrogio Lorenzetti's *Allegory of Good Government* and *Allegory of Bad Government* (1338). These were commissioned to remind the councillors of their duty, making clear how their government would affect Siena's citizens. The detail of everyday life in both is more compelling than the complexities of the allegorical iconography. The walled city depicted is clearly Siena. Country life, complete with hawking and pig-droving, is going on outside the walls while maidens dance inside.

CAMPO

Since the Middle Ages the Campo has been the focus of Siena's civic and social life. It is a gently sloping, rose-red, shell-shaped square, surrounded by a broad arc of palazzi, almost all of which date from the 14th to early 15th centuries, with the Palazzo Pubblico on the southeast side providing the focal point. The pavement is divided into nine segments, both to commemorate the rule of the Council of Nine, the medieval governing body, and to represent the folds of the Virgin's cloak. At ground level virtually every palazzo around the square is a café, bar, restaurant or gift shop, but the upper floors are still occupied by Sienese residents, who rent their windows to spectators at *Palio* time (▷ 187). Apart from the Palazzo Pubblico and Torre del Mangia (▷ below), the square has two other main features. The first is the Cappella di Piazza, a stone loggia close to the entrance to the Palazzo Pubblico. It was built to fulfil a vow made by the city authorities to commemorate the passing of the plague in 1348. The second is the Fonte Gaia, the fountain at the piazza's highest point, which was designed and sculpted in 1419 by Jacopo della Quercia. The present statues are 19th-century copies (the originals are now in Santa Maria della Scala).

✚ 168 B3

TORRE DEL MANGIA

Built by the *comune* between 1338 and 1348, the Torre del Mangia soars 97m (318ft) above the Campo. It was built as a campanile, whose bell marked the working hours of the day for all citizens. It was rung to mark the opening of the city gates at dawn, again to signal the workers' break for lunch, then to mark the end of of the working day, and finally to order the closing of the city gates. The name goes back to the first watchman, Giovanni di Balduccio, who was renowned as a *mangiaguadagni* (eater of profits). There are 388 steps to the top, the reward being great—if vertiginous—views. The tower was the last major project undertaken in the city before the Black Death of 1348, an event that wiped out a third of the population and casued an economic crisis.

✚ 168 C3 ✉ Piazza del Campo, 53100 ☎ 0577 292232 ⏱ Mid-March to end Oct daily 10–6.15/7; Nov to mid-March daily 10–4 💶 Adult €10, under 18 free; includes entry to Palazzo Pubblico; entry to tower alone €7

Above *Detail of a statue of a young girl in the Campo*

DUOMO

INFORMATION

www.operaduomo.siena.it

✚ 168 B3 ✉ Piazza del Duomo, 53100
☎ 0577 283048 ⏱ Duomo: Mar–end
May, Sep, Oct Mon–Sat 10.30–5.30,
Sun 1.30–5.30; Jun–end Aug Mon–Sat
10–8, Sun 1.30–6; Nov–end Feb Mon–Sat
10.30–6.30, Sun 1.30–5.30. Baptistery:
Jun–end Aug daily 9–8; Sep–end May
9.30–7 💶 Duomo: €3 (late Aug–late
Oct €6); Battistero: €3 🚉 Siena
🎧 Audioguide for €5 📖 Guidebook
for €10 🎁 Sells large range of books,
postcards, posters and gifts

Above *Beautiful frescoes adorn the
ceiling of the Libreria Piccolomini*

INTRODUCTION

Siena's Duomo, or cathedral, is one of Italy's greatest, on a par with the
cathedrals of Florence, Milan and the similar cathedral just over the Umbrian
border in Orvieto. Built on the city's highest point, and on a site probably
occupied by a Roman temple, it can be seen from far and wide, its distinctive
black-and-white striped campanile one of the city's most familiar landmarks.
Recent cleaning has restored the façade's rich medley of coloured marbles
and mosaics, along with its wealth of columns, sculptures, pillars and other
intricate decoration.

The building, predominantly Romanesque and Gothic in style, was more or
less its present size by the first quarter of the 13th century, the start of Siena's
period of greatest power and wealth. With money to spare, the authorities
visualized expanding the size of the cathedral, and in the 14th century built
the Baptistery on the slope at the rear of the cathedral. This was intended to
support an entirely rebuilt nave, but proved not strong enough. Plans were
then drawn up to completely reorientate the Duomo, converting the existing
building into the transept and constructing an enormous new nave northwards
in the direction of the Campo—you can still see the obvious remains of the
project on the right as you face the building. If achieved, it would have greatly
exceeded the size of Florence's cathedral and been only a little smaller St
Peter's in Rome. In 1348, however, the Black Death effectively ended Siena's
prosperity and the scheme for the Duomo Nuovo (New Cathedral) was
abandoned, leaving a tantalising few fragments that only hint at the scale of
the proposed extension.

Start your visit in the piazza, where you can admire the Duomo's façade
and see the remnants of the unfinished 14th-century nave extension. Inside,
spend time examining the marble flooring before moving around the cathedral

to take in the altars, chapels and sculptures. Many treasures were added to the interior of the Duomo over the years—it is far richer and more decorative than the Duomo in Florence—despite the crisis of 1348. The most notable was the Libreria Piccolomini in 1492, beautifully frescoed by the Umbrian painter Pintoricchio (*c*1454–1513) with scenes from the life of Pope Pius II, part of the Piccolomini family, a prominent Sienese dynasty. Enter the library through the entrance halfway down the nave on the left, and note the sculptures just left of the entrance on the Altare Piccolomini, some of which are early works by Michelangelo. Then see the interior's other highlight, Nicola Pisano's sculpted pulpit (1238), just to the left of the high altar.

Finally, don't miss the Baptistery and crypt. To reach these, go outside and walk down the right-hand side of the Duomo, through the arch and down the steps to the left. The crypt is on the left at the bottom of the first flight; the Baptistery is right at the bottom.

TIPS
» A maximum of 35 people are allowed on each crypt visit, so book in advance to ensure a place.
» No shorts or sleeveless tops are allowed in the Duomo.
» Only 700 people are allowed in the Duomo at one time, so you may have to be patient at peak times.
» A combined ticket , valid for 3 days, is available for the Battistero, Cripta, Museo dell'Opera del Duomo, Museo Diocesano and the Oratorio de San Bernardino for €10.

WHAT TO SEE

DUOMO PAVEMENT
The Duomo's marble paving is one of its greatest treasures, a series of 56 decorative and narrative panels produced between 1369 and 1547. Practically every well-known artist of the day was involved at some stage in their design, the result being a technically superb history of the development of Sienese art. The subject matter is an eclectic mix incorporating allegories, biblical scenes and geometric patterns, and decorations include simple sgraffito (with details engraved) and the variegated marble used for intricate designs. Be aware that during much of the year, some panels will be covered to protect them from visitors' feet.

Left *The Duomo's black-and-white striped Campanile is one of the city's most familiar landmarks*
Below *A bronze from the 15th-century Baptistery font*

PULPIT AND STATUES

The Duomo's pulpit is the work of Nicola Pisano, and was created in 1268, soon after his completion of the pulpit for the Baptistery at Pisa (▷ 143). This masterpiece of Gothic sculpture is octagonal, the sculpted panels following a similar design to those at Pisa, but executed in a freer and more realistic style. The high relief figures seem to burst from the marble—best seen in the *Last Judgement* panel. A work by Michelangelo is on the Piccolomini Altarpiece in the left aisle. He was commissioned to carve 15 statues, but only four were completed—Saints Peter, Paul, Pius and Gregory—before he was tempted to Florence to work on the *David* (▷ 70–71).

LIBRERIA PICCOLOMINI

This magnificent Renaissance library was built in the 1490s by the future Pope Pius III to hold the collection of books amassed by his uncle, Pius II, Aeneas Silvius Piccolomini. Pius II was the quintessential Renaissance man: well read, open-minded, and with a deep love of the classics, nature and travel. Before becoming pope he travelled widely, and his nephew commissioned the painter Pintoricchio to decorate the library with scenes from his uncle's travels. Vividly glowing and enclosed in classically inspired borders, each fresco depicts an episode from Pius' life, shown against superbly rendered architecture and realistically observed nature and landscape. We see Pius in Switzerland, Scotland and Germany, being made a cardinal and crowned pope, and officiating at the canonization of Catherine of Siena (▷ 171). Part of the cycle's charm lies in the wealth of detail, the expressions of the crowds, the lovely Tuscan landscape in the background, and the intricate decorative scheme around each panel. The library contains a Roman statue of the Three Graces and illuminated Renaissance books and manuscripts.

Above *A panel from the marble flooring depicting the She-Wolf, part of the legend of Acius and Senius, which gave Siena its name*

Opposite *A detail of the main entrance to the cathedral, one of three arched doorways on its façade*

BATTISTERO DI SAN GIOVANNI

The Baptistery's chief treasure is the early Tuscan Renaissance baptismal font, commissioned by the cathedral chapter and completed between 1416 and 1434. Jacopo della Quercia was responsible for the overall design, but the authorities also involved two of the major artists of the day: Lorenzo Ghiberti, who produced the *Baptism of Christ* and *John in Prison* panels, and Donatello, who carved Herod's Feast. Their work is full of drama, technically superb, and overshadows to some extent Jacopo della Quercia's niche statues and surmounting tabernacle.

CRIPTA

The crypt, once part of an entrance to the Duomo, was walled up when the Baptistery was built, and its interior filled with builders' rubble. In 2003 workmen cleared this and opened up the space, discovering a series of wall paintings dating from the 1270s. This was an artistic find of immense importance, as the style of the paintings is far in advance, in terms of movement, fluidity and spatial depth, of anything previously known from that date. Covered for so many centuries, the brown and yellow tones, tawny reds and glowing, deep blues are as fresh as when they were painted.

INFORMATION

www.operaduomo.siena.it

✚ 168 B3 ✉ Piazza del Duomo, 53100
☎ 0577 283048 🕐 Jun–end Aug daily
9.30–8; Mar–end May, Sep–end Oct
daily 9.30–7; Nov–end Feb daily 10–5
✋ Adult €6 🅿 Siena 🎧 Audiotours €5
📖 Official guidebook €6

TIP

» A combined ticket is available for the
Battistero, Cripta, Museo dell'Opera del
Duomo, Museo Diocesano and Oratorio di
San Bernardino for €10.

MUSEO DELL'OPERA DEL DUOMO

The Museo dell'Opera occupies a 15th-century building on the site of
what had been intended as the right aisle of the Duomo Nuovo (▷ 176).
Since the 19th century it has exhibited works of art from the decoration and
furnishings of the Duomo and is administered by the cathedral authorities.
Visiting the Museo dell'Opera is easy—follow the signs on the designated
route through the museum. At busy times, you may have to wait to get a
good look at the *Maestà*.

MAESTÀ

Duccio di Buoninsegna painted the *Maestà* over a four-year period from 1308.
It was commissioned as the altarpiece for the high altar of the Duomo and
portrays the Virgin, patron of Siena, as Queen of Heaven surrounded by her
court of saints. Duccio painted it on both sides, one side with the Virgin's
image, the other with a series of small panels telling the story of Christ's
Passion. When finished it was the most expensive picture ever to have been
commissioned. It remained at the Duomo until 1507 when, out of fashion, it
was relegated to a storeroom. Now one of the city's most prized possessions,
this glowing masterpiece is rich in intricate detail and brilliant tones standing
against a gold ground. Duccio's achievement was to retain this very Sienese
style yet abandon the stiffness of his predecessors' work—the *Maestà* is full of
movement, accurately observed light and spatial awareness. You can see this
at its best in the narrative panels, where the story of the Crucifixion is told for
an illiterate population as clearly as it might be in a modern comic strip.

MADONNA DEGLI OCCHI GROSSI

This haunting and primitive *Madonna with the Large Eyes* was the altarpiece
of the Duomo before the completion of the *Maestà*. The style is Byzantine,
but you can see the beginning of the transition into what was to become
Siena's own particular style in the statue's huge eyes. The work is by an
unknown artist.

PANORAMA DAL FACCIATONE

Above *The cathedral's museum holds
the greatest of all Sienese masterpieces,
Duccio's* Maestà

A narrow passage and steep stairway at the end of the top floor lead you
to a high lookout point, which gives a splendid view over the city and the
countryside beyond.

PINACOTECA NAZIONALE

The Sienese style of painting is a unique form of Gothic, a genre that owes much to Byzantine art and is typified by stylized and static composition, intense colours, intricate detail and burnished gold backgrounds. While Florence eagerly embraced the naturalism of the Renaissance, Siena continued to emulate older styles, and artists produced paintings with gold backgrounds well into the late 15th century. By the 1490s Florentine influence was stronger, and perspective became increasingly realistic. Eventually Mannerism, a 16th-century style that used distorted perspective and bright hues, brought Siena's artists into the mainstream of European painting.

THE ARTWORKS

The altarpiece by Simone Martini depicts scenes from the life of the local saint Agostino Novello and was probably painted in 1324. The central panel is of the saint, an Augustinian monk, while the side ones show four of the miracles he performed. The scenes take place in or around Siena itself; the rocks and woodlands, and the scene showing him conversing with an angel, reflect the fact that Agostino was a hermit. The miracles mainly involve children rescued from accidents, subjects chosen to appeal to the peasant congregation.

The Lorenzetti brothers, Pietro and Ambrogio, were prolific artists, innovative in that they explored the possibilities of perspective and greater realism within the conventions of Sienese Gothic. The lovely *Annunciation* by Ambrogio was executed in 1344, and exemplifies these developments: The Virgin's chair is firmly placed in three-dimensional space, rather than appearing flat, and the receding black-and-white pavement adds depth to the composition. Look for two tiny panels by the same artist, *City by the Sea* and *Castles by a Lake*; they are thought to be the first landscapes ever painted.

The *Fall of the Rebellious Angels* by Domenico Beccafumi is a perfect example of the dramatic Mannerist style, of which Beccafumi was the chief Sienese exponent. He painted this in the 1540s and it is heavily influenced by Michelangelo, whose *Last Judgement* in Rome's Sistine Chapel had just been completed. The serpentine figures, unbalanced composition and livid tones are all typical of Mannerism, in contrast to the serene figures of Gothic art.

INFORMATION

➕ 168 B4 ✉ Via San Pietro 29, 53100
☎ 0577 281161; ticket office 0577 46052 🕐 Mon 8.30–1.30, Tue–Sat 8.15–7.15, Sun 8.30–1.15 💶 Adult €4, concessions €2.50 🎧 Audioguide for €4
📖 A range of guidebooks is available from €8 🏪 Shop sells art books, pictures, posters, prints and postcards

Below *The altarpiece showing Agostino Novello by Martini is one of the Pinacoteca's treasures*

INFORMATION

www.santamaria.comune.siena.it
🕂 168 B3 ✉ Piazza del Duomo,
53100 ☎ 0577 224835; ticket office
0577 224828 🕐 Mid-Mar to end Oct
daily 10.30–6.30; Nov to mid-Mar daily
10.30–4.30 🎟 Adult €6, child (11–18)
€3.50, under 11 free 📖 Guidebooks
available in English, German and Italian
for €10 ☕ Small café-bar 🎪 Shop
selling mostly books

SANTA MARIA DELLA SCALA

This compelling complex was Siena's hospital for more than 800 years and is now being developed as a cultural focus for the city. A lively fresco cycle illustrates 15th-century daily life. The building was founded in the 11th century as a resting place for pilgrims on the Via Francigena, the route between Rome and northern Europe which skirted Siena. It evolved from this into both a charitable institution, helping Sienese citizens in times of crisis, and a full-scale orphanage and hospital. Richly endowed, the foundation was able to spare funds in the 15th century to decorate its church as well as the halls and wards. It became Siena's main hospital and was in use as such until 1995, when a new one opened. The frescoes were put on public view, and there's a plan to establish the huge complex as Siena's foremost museum and cultural space: It is already home to the Museo Archeologico and stages temporary exhibitions.

SALA DEL PELLEGRINAIO

This huge hospital ward, built around 1380, was frescoed in the 15th century with scenes telling the history of the original Ospedale and illustrating its role as a charitable institution. The artists were Lorenzo di Pietro, known as Vecchietta, and Domenico di Bartolo. There are eight main frescoes, four down each side wall, and three subsidiary ones across the end. Their content is almost entirely secular, extremely rare at that date, and they are crammed with wonderful details of everyday Sienese life. The left wall is devoted to the Ospedale's history, and on the Scala (ladder) leading to heaven from which the hospital took its name. The right wall depicts scenes illustrating the Ospedale's charitable functions.

CAPPELLA DEL SACRO CHIODO

The hospital chapel, painted by Vecchietta between 1446 and 1449, is named after the *chiodo* (nail) said to be a relic of the Crucifix that was once held here. The subject matter of the paintings is somewhat abstruse, with scenes from the Old Testament illustrating Christain teaching. The frescoes are unusual in Siena in not concentrating on the Virgin Mary, but she is not totally absent from the chapel. The altarpiece is a *Madonna della Misericordia* by Domenico di Bartolo, with the Virgin portrayed sheltering Siena's citizens beneath her cloak.

Opposite *The church of San Domenico, on the outskirts of the city*
Below *Frescoes dating from the 15th century decorate the walls of the Sala del Pellegrinaio*

ORATORIO DI SAN BERNARDINO

The entrance to the Oratorio di (Oratory of) San Bernardino, a Sienese-born preacher saint, is to the right of the church of San Francesco. The Oratorio has two chapels, the upper decorated with scenes from the life of the Virgin, the lower with episodes from the saint's life. Artistically, it is the upper chapel that enthrals, a Mannerist tour-de-force painted between 1496 and 1518 by Il Sodoma and Beccafumi. Below, San Bernardino is portrayed on his preaching travels.

➕ 168 C2 ✉ Piazza San Francesco ☎ 0577 283 0481 🕐 Mid-Mar to end Oct Mon–Sat 10.30–1.30, 3–5.30 ✋ Adult €3; combined ticket available, see Museo dell'Opera del Duomo (▷ 180)

SANT'AGOSTINO

Wander down the hill from the Pinacoteca Nazionale (▷ 182) and you'll come to the church of Sant'Agostino. It was built in the 13th century and extensively altered between 1747 and 1755, making it one of Siena's few neoclassical buildings. The 19th-century portico leads into a luminous interior, paved in majolica and containing some excellent paintings. Highlights are a resplendent Crucifixion (1506) by Perugino on the second altar in the south aisle, and two lunette medallions by Luca Signorelli (c1441–1523) in the Cappella Bichi in the south transept. Best of all is the Cappella Piccolomini, which contains a lunette fresco by Ambrogio Lorenzetti and Il Sodoma's *Adoration of the Magi*—there is no better illustration of the range of

Sienese art than in these two works, separated by over two centuries. Outside, the church's piazza is a pleasant space, close to the Orto Botanico, a cool, little-visited garden run by the University that contains every species found in Tuscany and plenty of exotics besides.

➕ 168 C4 ✉ Prato di Sant'Agostino, Via Sant'Agata ☎ 0577 226785 🕐 Mid-Mar to early Nov daily 11–1.30, 2–5.30; mid-Nov to mid-Mar by arrangement ✋ €2.50 ☛ By arrangement

SAN DOMENICO

The Dominicans founded their monastery in Siena in 1125. A preaching order, they spread God's word through fiery sermons and relied on vast, plain churches to hold the crowds they attracted. Gothic, brick-built San Domenico is such a structure, standing on the outskirts of the city with a good view of the Duomo (▷ 176–179). It was begun in 1226 and its history is entwined with the cult of St. Catherine of Siena, whose shrine (▷ 171) is nearby. The church has some notable paintings in the chapels. St. Catherine's chapel, halfway down the right side of the church, was built in 1488 and lavishly decorated by Il Sodoma. The marble altar (1466) includes a tabernacle that contains the saint's head, while the side walls were painted by Il Sodoma with depictions of Catherine. Back in the main church, the chapels on either side of the high altar have pictures representing the best of local talent: There's a Matteo di Giovanni triptych of the *Madonna and Child with St. Jerome and John the Baptist*

to the right, and in the second chapel to the left, the same artist's *St. Barbara, Angels and Saints Mary Magdalene and Catherine*, considered to be one of his most outstanding works.

➕ 168 A2 ✉ Piazza San Domenico ☎ 0577 280893 🕐 Daily 7–1, 3–6.30 ✋ Free

SAN FRANCESCO

If San Domenico is the church of St. Catherine, Siena's other great preaching stronghold, the Franciscan powerhouse of San Francesco, is linked to San Bernardino. Like San Domenico, the church stands on the edge of the city. It was completed in 1482, but badly damaged by fire in 1655. It was rebuilt in the 19th century. What you see today is a bit of a jumble, but there are fragments of frescoes by Pietro and Ambrogio Lorenzetti in two chapels to the left of the high altar, and a superb, glittering polyptych by Lippo Vanni in the sacristy. The church also has some noble marble tombs, including those of the Tolomei family, one of the city's powerful medieval clans.

➕ 168 C2 ✉ Piazza San Francesco ☎ 0577 289081 🕐 Daily 8–12, 3–7 ✋ Free

TERZO DI SAN MARTINO

The ward of the Terzo di San Martino, home to Siena's university, lies east of the Campo (▷ 172–175), a low-key, uncrowded area. The main street is the Banchi di Sotto, which passes the vast Palazzo Piccolomini, commissioned in the 1460s by Pius II. It's home to the Archivio di Stato, the city's archives, where visitors are welcome to inspect documents dating back to the 13th and 14th centuries.

The *terzo* has two main churches: San Martino, with a stunning *Nativity* by Domenico Beccafumi (1486–1551), and Santa Maria dei Servi, a lovely Renaissance church with some fine artwork and a great view of the city. Beyond here is the Porta Romana, the massive southern gateway into Siena.

➕ 168 C2

THE HEART OF SIENA

Siena is small enough for you to gain a rapid understanding of the city's layout. This walk takes you through the less-visited southern parts of the city, passing most of the main sights, and finishes at Piazza San Domenico, on the outskirts of the city.

THE WALK

Distance: 2.8km (1.7 miles)
Allow: 2–3 hours
Start at: Piazza del Duomo
End at: Piazza San Domenico

★ Start your walk on Piazza del Duomo, where you'll find the Duomo (▷ 176–179), the Museo dell'Opera del Duomo (▷ 180) and Santa Maria della Scala (▷ 181).

❶ The Duomo has a spectacular marble floor made up of 56 panels. In the aisles on either side of the nave are the *Ten Sibyls* by various artists, and earlier panels showing an *Allegory of Virtue* by Pintoricchio (c1454–1513); a *Wheel of Fortune* can be seen in the nave. Best of all are the panels in the central hexagon and the floor in front of the high altar. These are mainly the work (1518–47) of Domenico Beccafumi and depict scenes from the Old Testament.

The Piazza del Duomo is the first of two adjoining squares; from here walk down the steps to the rear right of the cathedral to enter Piazza San Giovanni with the Battistero di San Giovanni (▷ 179). Face the Baptistery and take the road to the right of it, Via dei Fusari, and then continue, where the road name changes to Via Girolamo. At the intersection with Via del Fosso di San Ansano is Piazza della Selva. Turn left onto the Via del Fosso di San Ansano until you reach an archway.

❷ The Arco delle Due Porte formed part of the city's 11th-century walls. Turn left at the arch onto Via di Stalloreggi and look for the house (No. 91–93) where over a four-year period Duccio di Buoninsegna (c1255–1319) painted his glorious *Maestà*, now on display at the Museo del Opera dell'Duomo (▷ 180).

At the intersection with Via San Pietro turn right. On your left are the Pinacoteca Nazionale (▷ 182) and the church of San Pietro. Continue down Via San Pietro and turn left onto Via Sant'Agata. Cross the gravel area to your right.

❸ The 13th-century church of Sant'Agostino (▷ 183) contains two splendid examples of Sienese painting by Giovanni Sodoma (1477–1549) and Ambrogio Lorenzetti (active 1319–48).

Back on Via Sant'Agata, walk as far as the intersection with Via Giovanni Dupré and turn left onto that road—it has attractive alleyways branching off to either side. Keep your eyes open for Via del Mercato, which will curve away to your right, and Piazza del Mercato. Take Via Malcontenti out of the square and onto Via di Salicotto, and turn left. Turn right onto Vicolo delle Scotte.

4 The Sinagoga, Siena's synagogue, is on your left. The Jewish ghetto was founded by Cosimo I de' Medici in 1571 and the Sinagoga was once at the heart of the city.

Cross Via del Porrione, so named after the Latin emporium or market place, referring to the Roman markets that stood close by. On the right is Loggia del Papa (Loggia of the Pope). Walk to the end of the road and turn left onto Banchi di Sotto. On your left stands the Palazzo Piccolomini. Look for Vicolo dei Pollaiuoli or Via dei Rinaldini on the left; either will bring you to Piazza del Campo.

5 Linger awhile in the Campo, simply to admire the views or to visit the Museo Civico in the Palazzo Pubblico (▷ 173, 174).

Leave the Campo by Via di Città and turn right, where you will see the Gothic Loggia della Mercanzia (1428–44). Continue past the intersection with Banchi di Sotto and onto Banchi di Sopra, a major

street that follows the path of the Via Francigena, an old pilgrim route between Rome and northern Europe. You will pass the Palazzo Tolomei along this road to your left.

6 Palazzo Tolomei is part of the original fortress-home of the Tolomei family, one of a number of powerful medieval banking families. There is also a statue of the she-wolf that suckled Romulus and Remus (▷ 27). Opposite is the Romanesque church of San Cristoforo in Piazza Tolomei.

Continue up Banchi di Sopra; ahead is Piazza Salimbeni.

7 Piazza Salimbeni has three fine palaces: Palazzo Tantucci (to the left, 1548); the 14th-century Palazzo Salimbeni (to the rear); and Palazzo Spannocchi (to the right, 1470). The Salimbeni family were prominent bankers and silk and grain traders, while Ambrogio Spannocchi was treasurer to the Sienese Pope Pius II. They now house the bank Monte dei Paschi di Siena (▷ 171). Leave the piazza on Via della

Sapienza. Along this road you will pass the church of San Pellegrino alla Sapienza and the Biblioteca Comunale degli Intronati. Via della Sapienza leads to Piazza San Domenico.

8 Piazza San Domenico is home to the church of San Domenico, notable for its associations with St. Catherine of Siena, whose shrine is nearby, and its frescoes by Sodoma (▷ 183).

WHEN TO GO
Early morning or after 4pm are the best times, as the city fills with visitors during the middle of the day. Note that the Sinagoga is only open on Sundays.

WHERE TO EAT
CAFFÈ NANNINI
▷ 188.

BAR IL PALIO
This pleasant bar on the Campo is a good place to take a break.
✉ Piazza del Campo ☎ 0577 282055
🕐 Daily 8am–2am

PLACES TO VISIT
SINAGOGA
✉ Via delle Scotte 14 ☎ 055 234 6654
🕐 Sun 10–1, 2–5 ✋ Free

SAN CRISTOFORO
✉ Piazza Tolomei ☎ 0577 282135
🕐 Daily 9–7 ✋ Free

SAN PELLEGRINO ALLA SAPIENZA
✉ Via della Sapienza 🕐 Daily 5–7
✋ Free

BIBLIOTECA COMUNALE DEGLI INTRONATI
✉ Via delle Sapienza 5 ☎ 0577 282972
🕐 Mon–Sat 9–6 ✋ Free

BATTISTERO DI SAN GIOVANNI
✉ Piazza San Giovanni ☎ 0577 283048

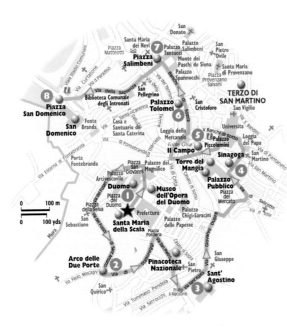

Opposite *Wander through Siena's narrow streets and you will see a different side to the city*

SHOPPING

ANTICHITÀ MONNA AGNESE
One of Siena's better antiques stores, stocking furniture and silver amid other items. A smaller shop on the opposite side of the street at No. 45 deals in antique jewellery.
✉ Banchi di Sopra 72, 53100 ☎ 0577 280205/282288 ⏰ Mon–Sat 10–1, 4–7.30

CERAMICHE ARTISTICHE SANTA CATERINA
This family business produces ceramics in the traditional Sienese style, using black, white and burnt sienna glazes. Their art is inspired by the local architecture, especially the Duomo. Watch them at work in their studio at Via Mattioli 12.
✉ Via di Città 74–76, 53100 ☎ 0577 283098 ⏰ Daily 10.30–8

CORTECCI ABBIGLIAMENTO
www.corteccisiena.it
The two branches of this shop stock men's and women's designer labels including Gucci, Armani, Yves Saint-Laurent, Christian Dior, Roberto Cavalli and Dolce & Gabbana. This branch has the more classic collections, while the other branch, at Piazza del Campo 30, stocks labels aimed at a younger market.
✉ Via Banchi di Sopra 27, 53100 ☎ 0577 280096/280984 ⏰ Mon–Fri 9.30–8, Sat 9.30–1

DROGHERIA MANGANELLI
A must for gourmets. It is a member of the Slow Food Movement, an organization that promotes organic food, grown and cooked using traditional methods. Drogheria Manganelli has been selling local produce since 1879, including cured meats, cheeses, vinegars, wine, olive oil, *ricciarelli* (almond cookies), home-made cakes and pasta sauces.
✉ Via di Città 71, 53100 ☎ 0577 280002 ⏰ Mon–Sat 9–8

LIBRERIA SENESE
Libreria Senese has a good selection of English-language books and magazines, including local guides. For a memento of your visit, you might want to pick up one of the many glossy picture books on Tuscany and Italy.
✉ Via di Città 62–66, 53100 ☎ 0577 280845 ⏰ Mon–Sat 9–8, Sun 10–8

OPIFICIO DEL BOSCO DI GROSSO MARIA
www.opificiodelbosco.com
This family-run business in the Chianti hills, just off the road to Follonica, produces jams, oils and spirits. Using traditional methods and local ingredients, many of which are gathered from the local woods, the products are wholesome and delicious. The store is also a member of the Slow Food Movement (see Drogheria Manganelli). Sample the food in the adjacent restaurant.
✉ Podere Porcignano 100, 53030 Radicondoli ☎ 0577 793134 ⏰ Wed–Mon 9–9 🚌 In the Parco delle Carline on SS73 west of Siena towards Follonica

PANIFICO IL MAGNIFICO
It's worth coming to this bread shop and delicatessen just behind the Duomo simply for the smell of fresh bread. You can buy *panini* made on the spot to take away, as well as well-priced *panforte*, a rich, chewy cake and Sienese specialty. Take a ticket when you enter to reserve your place in the queue.
✉ Via de' Pellegrini 27, 53100 ☎ 0577 281106 ⏰ Mon–Sat 7.30–7.30 (sometimes Sat 5pm in summer)

PASTICCERIA LE CAMPANE
A bakery known for its Sienese cakes and sweets: The fragrant, freshly baked *ricciarelli* (almond cookies) are the star attraction. From September to the end of November the family bakes *pan co'santi* (fruitcake); their excellent *cantucci* (almond cookies traditionally served with sweet wine) are enjoyed year round.
✉ Via delle Campane 9, 53100 ☎ 0577 282290 ⏰ Mon–Tue, Thu–Sat 8–1.30, 5–8, Wed, Sun 8–1.30

SIENA RICAMA

This embroidery and needlepoint shop is run by Signora Fontani, who makes all the goods herself. Drawing inspiration from medieval designs, local art, frescoes and manuscripts, the embroidered items include clothing, soft furnishings, lampshades and tapestries.

✉ Via di Città 61, 53100 ☎ 0577 288339 🕐 Mon–Fri 9.30–1, 2.30–7, Sat 9.30–1

TESSUTI A MANO

Drop into this workshop and boutique to pick up beautiful, hand-woven accessories and fashionable garments. Designer Fioretta Bacci can often be found sitting at a pair of large looms, weaving her incredible, much sought-after scarves, shawls and items of clothing.

✉ Via San Pietro 7, 53100 ☎ 0577 282200 🕐 Mon–Sat 10.30–1, 4–7

ENTERTAINMENT AND NIGHTLIFE

AL CAMBIO

Central Siena has only a handful of bars and clubs for a late-night drink or dance—most of the bigger clubs are out in the suburbs. Al Cambio is one of the exceptions, just five minutes east of the Campo on the street that leads to the church of Santa Maria dei Servi. With a dark, moody interior, it offers good, middle-of-the-road dance music (and live music some nights). It's popular with local students, and gets particularly lively at weekends.

✉ Via di Pantaneto 48, 53100 Siena 🕐 Daily 8pm–2am

BIRRERIA IL BARONE ROSSO

www.barone-rosso.com
Providing food, drink and live music in the heart of Siena's medieval streets, lively Il Barone Rosso is a popular haunt for Sienese beer drinkers, with Guinness on tap. Credit cards are not accepted.

✉ Via dei Termini 9, 53100 ☎ 0577 286686 🕐 Daily 9pm–3am

ENOTECA I TERZI

Lively bar in a gorgeous building that attracts the crowds all afternoon

JULY/AUGUST
SETTIMANE MUSICALE

www.chigiana.it
During this prestigious classical music festival, concerts take place all over the city. The festival usually includes a major opera production.

✉ Via di Città 89, 53100 ☎ 0577 22091 🕐 Jul

IL PALIO

www.ilpaliodisiena.com
The Palio—a high-speed, bareback horse race around the Campo in Siena—is arguably Italy's most famous festival. The event evokes

and evening. There's a small but comprehensive selection of Italian and international wines, a lunch menu and snack food.

✉ Via dei Termini 7, 53100 ☎ 0577 44329 🕐 Mon–Sat 12.30–3, 6–11

MODERNO

This single-screen cinema shows the latest releases in their original language. Most films come from Hollywood and are screened in English. There is no bar or refreshments, and credit cards are not accepted.

✉ Via Calzoleria 44, 53016 ☎ 0577 289201 🕐 Closed Jul, Aug 👋 Adult from €7, child €5

TEATRO DEI ROZZI

www.comune.siena.it
This restored theatre in the Accademia Rozzi stages dance, opera and drama productions during the winter season, November to the end of April. Credit cards are not accepted.

✉ Piazza Indipendenza 15, 53100 ☎ 0577 46960 👋 €5–€40

SPORTS AND ACTIVITIES
PISCINA DI SIENA

This is an open-air pool where you can cool off after a hard day's sightseeing.

great passion among the Sienese and it takes weeks to prepare the accompanying pageantry.

✉ Piazza del Campo, 53100 Headquarters: Piazza Gramsci 7, 53100 ☎ 0577 280551 🕐 2 Jul and 16 Aug 👋 Free

SIENA JAZZ

www.sienajazz.it
Siena Jazz presents jazz performances, seminars and master classes. Concerts are held in Piazza il Campo, Enoteca Italiana and Piazza Jacopo della Quercia.

✉ Fortezza Medicea Anfiteatro, 53100 ☎ 0577 271401 🕐 Late Jul 👋 Free

✉ Località Acquacalda, 53100 ☎ 0577 271567 🕐 Jun–end Aug daily 9.30–7 👋 Adult €5.50, child €3.50

STADIO COMUNALE

www.acsiena.it
Crowded with passionate residents on match days, this soccer ground is home to AC Siena. The less expensive seats are in the Curva Robur and Curva San Domenica—the two 'curves' or stands at the end of the stadium behind the goals.

✉ Via Mille 3, 53100 ☎ 0577 280937 🕐 Season: end Aug–end May 👋 Men from €22, women €16.50, child (10–14) €16.50, under 10 free; most expensive seat is €190

FOR CHILDREN
MUSEO DEL BOSCO DI ORGIA

Children enjoy Siena's Museum of the Woods, with its presentation of items used by the people who once lived in the nearby woodlands and their folk stories. Walks and trails provide an introduction to the animals and vegetation of the forest. Credit cards are not accepted.

✉ Località Borgolozzi, Fraz. Orgia, 53010 Sovicille ☎ 0577 342097 🕐 Fri, Sat 9.30–12.30; other days by request only 👋 Adult €2, child €1 🚗 15-minute drive from Siena on SS73, then onto SS37 and SP52 to Sovicille

PRICES AND SYMBOLS

The restaurants are listed alphabetically (excluding La, Il and Le and I). The prices given are the average for a two-course lunch (L) and a three-course dinner (D) for one person, without drinks. The wine price is for the least expensive bottle. All the restaurants listed accept credit cards unless otherwise stated.

For a key to the symbols, ▷ 2.

AL MANGIA

www.almangia.it
Al Mangia occupies a great spot overlooking the Piazza del Campo. The restaurant is now run by the fourth generation of the Senni family. Tastefully decorated, Al Mangia serves typical local meat and fish dishes, including quail's egg salad with palm hearts and smoked duck breast with *crostini* (toasted crusty bread). Reservations are recommended.
✉ Piazza del Campo 42–46, 53100 Siena ☎ 0577 281121 🕐 Daily 12–3.30, 7–10 ✋ L €39, D €50, Wine €16

AL MARSILI

www.ristorantealmarsili.it
This restaurant is in a building dating from the 14th century. Besides the large main dining area there are smaller brick niches, with banqueting tables for larger parties. The Tuscan cuisine includes *gnocchetti* (little potato dumplings) with duck, home-made *crespelle* (crêpes) and vegetarian options. The wine bar is in a cellar carved out of rock below the Marsili Palace. Reservations are advisable.
✉ Via del Castoro 3, 53100 Siena ☎ 0577 47154 🕐 Tue–Sun 12.30–2.30, 7.30–10.30 ✋ L €17, D €33, Wine €12

ANTICA OSTERIA DA DIVO

This eatery is celebrated as much for its architecture as for its food: The medieval building is very striking. You may find the back and basement rooms (former Etruscan tombs) a little morbid, but the romantic hidden corners and tunnels make the place popular. Try the pasta with rabbit sauce or duck with saffron croquettes.
✉ Via Franciosa 29, 53100 Siena ☎ 0577 284381 🕐 May–end Oct Mon–Sat 12–2.30, 7–10; Nov–end Apr Wed–Mon 12–2.30, 7–10 ✋ L €14, D €39, Wine €14

ANTICA TRATTORIA BOTTEGANOVA

www.anticatrattoriabotteganova.it
This popular restaurant lies 2km (1 mile) outside the old town walls. There's a *menù degustazione* that allows you to sample a number of dishes. Otherwise you can settle for fresh pasta, grilled or roasted meat and fish, and Italian classics such as a guinea fowl terrine with Sicilian pistachios and a chestnut-honey sauce. Vegetarian dishes available.
✉ Strada Chiantigiana 29, Frazione di Bottegnova, 52025 Siena ☎ 0577 284230 🕐 Mon–Sat 12.30–2, 8–10. Closed 1 week in Jan, period in Jul, Aug ✋ L €30, D €61, Wine €18 🚗 From the Porta Ovile in Siena, follow the SS408 towards Montevarchi

BUCA DI PORSENNA

Buca di Porsenna, named after an Etruscan king, is in a medieval building with the restaurant spread out over three levels. The secluded tables in the cellars are best. The connection to medieval times extends as far as the menu, which includes old recipes alongside modern Tuscan food. Reservations are recommended.
✉ Via delle Donzelle 1, 53100 Siena ☎ 0577 44431 🕐 Wed–Mon 12–2.30, 7.30–10.30 ✋ L €14, D €28, Wine €6

CAFFÈ NANNINI

Popular with visitors and locals, Caffè Nannini is a richly decorated café serving coffees and teas, ice cream, sandwiches, cakes, almond cookies, Sienese marzipan cakes, *panforte* (rich fruit cake) and more.

✉ Banchi di Sopra 22–24, 53100 Siena
🕐 Daily 7.30am–11pm ✋ L €12, coffee €1, cakes from €2.50

IL CAMPO

This is a great spot for people-watching, day or night. A consequence of this is that service may suffer at very busy times. The menu is a mix of Italian and European cuisine. No reservations, so just hang around until a table is free.

✉ Piazza del Campo 50–51, 53100 Siena
☎ 0577 280725 🕐 Daily 12–10.30 ✋ L €14, D €33, Wine €10

CANE & GATTO

This small restaurant seating just 24 is renowned for its service and food. There is no written menu: You just sit down and wait to be served several courses of traditional cuisine, including antipasti, soup, pasta, risotto, meat, salad, dessert and fruit. Each course comes with a wine to complement it. Special requests are also taken. Reservations are essential. Cane e Gatto will open at lunchtime if reservations are made in advance.

✉ Via Pagliaresi 6, 53100 Siena ☎ 0577 287545 🕐 Fri–Wed 8pm–10.30pm
✋ D €66, Wine €14

MEDIO EVO

www.medioevosiena.com

This family-run restaurant in a 13th-century house in the heart of Siena serves Tuscan dishes based on local produce, including meat, game, mushrooms, pasta and desserts. The wine list has more than two dozen local wines. Reservations recommended in high season.

✉ Via dei Rossi 40, 53100 Siena ☎ 0577 280315 🕐 Fri–Wed 12.30–3, 7.30–10
✋ L €25, D €36, Wine €8

OSTERIA CASTELVECCHIO

You will find Osteria Castelvecchio halfway up a steep incline in a palace dating from the eighth century. The menu changes daily, and includes modern interpretations of local dishes, as well as some historic recipes. Reservations are advisable.

✉ Via di Castelvecchio 65, 53100 Siena
☎ 0577 49586 🕐 Mon–Sat 12–2.30, 7.30–9.30 ✋ L €14, D €25, Wine €8

OSTERIA LA CHIACCHERA

The simple but filling dishes at the 'Chatterbox' are redolent of the area's peasant heritage. This is one of the least expensive places to eat in Siena and is also one of the few where you can eat late into the evening. The wine list is short and inexpensive. Reservations advisable. Credit cards are not accepted.

✉ Costa di Sant'Antonio 4, 53100 Siena
☎ 0577 280631 🕐 Wed–Mon 12–3, 7–12
✋ L €10, D €17, Wine €10

OSTERIA LE LOGGE

In a former medieval pharmacy, this charming restaurant is just off the Campo. The menu is full of simple, classic Tuscan dishes, such as ricotta and spinach dumplings in a cream sauce, and roast duck with fennel. Reservations are advised.

✉ Via del Porrione 33, 53100 Siena
☎ 0577 48013 🕐 Mon–Sat 12.30–2.30, 7.30–10.30. Closed periods in Jun and Nov
✋ L €22, D €44, Wine €10

RISTORANTE ENZO

This smart restaurant has a modern, creative approach to food. The menu's highlights include a good selection of fish, tasty yellow pumpkin and potato dumplings with porcini mushrooms and truffles, and a delicious terrine of nettles. Reservations are recommended.

✉ Via Camollia 49, 53100 Siena ☎ 0577 281277 🕐 Mon–Sat 12.30–2.30, 8–10.30. Closed last 2 weeks in Jul ✋ L €25, D €33, Wine €12

RISTORANTE GUIDO

www.emmeti.it/guido

Close to Piazza del Campo, Ristorante Guido is well liked for its superb food. Dishes include home-made pasta with asparagus, truffles and fresh mushrooms, fillet steak with asparagus and porcini mushrooms, and locally reared veal. Reservations are advisable.

✉ Vicolo del Pettinaio 7, 53100 Siena
☎ 0577 280042 🕐 Daily 12.30–2.30, 7.30–10 ✋ L €19, D €39, Wine €15

RISTORANTE PIZZERIA EZIO

The menu here includes pizza and traditional Italian meats and fish as well as international dishes and good vegetarian options. The cakes and desserts are all home-made and there's a good selection of wines.

✉ Via V. Emanuele II 32, 53100 Siena
☎ 0577 48094 🕐 Thu–Tue 12–2.30, 7–11
✋ L €12, D €28, Wine €11

SAPORDIVINO

www.ghcs.it

Dine beneath a crystal ceiling in the courtyard of the Palazzo Gori, in the Grand Hotel Continental (▷ 190). The traditional menu uses local ingredients and has a large selection of cheeses and cold meats, plus an extensive wine list. wine-tasting sessions are held regularly.

✉ Via Banchi di Sopra 85, 53100 Siena
☎ 0577 56011 🕐 Daily 12–2.30, 7–10.30
✋ L €28, D €55, Wine €25

LA TAVERNA DI SAN GIUSEPPE

www.tavernasangiuseppe.it

A lively group of young people runs this trattoria. It specializes in classic Tuscan food, with an emphasis on meat, although vegetarians are well catered to. Meals end with a delicious selection of desserts.

✉ Via Giovanni Duprè 132, 53100 Siena
☎ 0577 42286 🕐 Mon–Sat 12.15–2.30, 7–10. Closed last 2 weeks in Jan and Jul
✋ L €11, D €28, Wine €8

LA TORRE

Just off Piazza del Campo, La Torre is highly recommended. It has an open-plan kitchen so customers can watch their food being prepared. Home-made pasta comes with a choice of sauces, with well-prepared Tuscan standards such as oven-baked pigeon to follow. Reservations are essential.

✉ Via Salicotto 7, 53100 Siena ☎ 0577 287548 🕐 Fri–Wed 12.15–3, 6.45–9.15
✋ L €13, D €22, Wine €8

PRICES AND SYMBOLS

The prices are the lowest and highest
for a double room for one night including
breakfast, unless otherwise stated. All the
hotels listed accept credit cards unless
otherwise stated. Note that rates can vary
widely throughout the year.

For a key to the symbols, ▷ 2.

ALBERGO CANNON D'ORO

www.cannondoro.com
A good choice if you are on a budget
as it is within the walls of the old
city, and inexpensive by Sienese
standards. The bedrooms, on the
two floors above (no elevator), are
simply furnished but spotlessly
clean and reasonably quiet. The
hotel is reached via a quiet alley off
the busy shopping street, just off
the Campo.
✉ Via Montanini 28, 53100 Siena ☎ 0577
44321 🛗 €99 ❶ 30

ANTICA TORRE

www.anticatorresiena.it
This independent three-star hotel
gets its name from the 16th-century
medieval tower it occupies. The
rooms and corridors can seem
claustrophobic, but are full of
medieval charm. The breakfast room

is in a brick-lined 600-year-old former
pottery, and the best rooms are on
the top floor, up the steep, narrow
staircase, with views over Siena to
the green hills beyond.
✉ Via di Fieravecchia 7, 53100 Siena
☎ 0577 222255 🛗 €90–€120, excluding
breakfast ❶ 8 🔄

GRAND HOTEL CONTINENTAL

www.royaldemeure.com
A former noble house with
magnificent frescoes, this hotel is
a part of Siena's cultural heritage. A
covered courtyard is now a winter
garden and you can eat in style
at the Sapordivino restaurant. Full
leisure facilities are available at the
nearby Park Hotel via a courtesy
bus service.
✉ Via Banchi di Sopra 85, 53100 Siena
☎ 0577 56011 🛗 €200–€910 ❶ 51 🔄

GRAND HOTEL VILLA PATRIZIA

www.villapatrizia.it
The pale yellow villa has a
Renaissance garden with a tennis
court. The hotel has a restaurant
and meals are served in the garden
when the weather is good. Inside
are several large, comfortably
furnished reception rooms, and the
bedrooms are very well equipped.

The hotel is on the northern edge of
the city.
✉ Via Fiorentina 58, 53100 Siena ☎ 0577
50431 🛗 €170–€290 ❶ 33 🔄 ♨

HOTEL ARCOBALENO

www.hotelarcobaleno.com
Arcobaleno is a family-run three-star
hotel in a 19th- century Tuscan
country villa just outside the city
walls. Breakfast is served on a
covered terrace or in the hotel's
restaurant. All guest rooms have
private bathroom, TV, telephone and
internet connection.
✉ Via Fiorentina 32/40, 53100 Siena
☎ 0577 271092 🛗 €160 ❶ 19 🔄

HOTEL ATHENA

www.hotelathena.com
This four-star hotel in a quiet area
close to the Duomo contains a
curious mix of 1960s and 70s
design, with a classical Etruscan
pillar in the middle of the lobby. Its
rooms with three or four beds are
great value for groups who don't
mind sharing. Relax and enjoy the
views in the tranquil terrace bar and
restaurant. Free parking is available.
✉ Via P. Mascagni 55, 53100 Siena
☎ 0577 286313 🛗 €95–€220 ❶ 100
🔄

Left *The Campo, focus of the city's social life*

HOTEL CHIUSARELLI
www.chiusarelli.com
Visitors have been coming here since the 1860s. There are spacious public rooms and a large veranda room overlooking the garden where a generous buffet breakfast is served. Bedrooms have simple modern furnishings; those at the back are quieter. No elevator.
✉ Viale Curtatone 15, 53100 Siena ☎ 0577 280562 💶 €95–€125 🛏 49 🛗

HOTEL DUOMO
www.hotelduomo.it
This 17th-century palace is now a three-star hotel in a quiet part of the old town and is just a 5-minute walk from the Piazza del Campo. The bedrooms are modern, but the dining room has retained more of the building's original character. All guest rooms have private bathrooms. Free parking is available.
✉ Via Stalloreggi 34/38, 53100 Siena ☎ 0577 289088 💶 €150 🛏 23 🛗

HOTEL IL GIARDINO
www.hotelilgiardino.it
Il Giardino is a family-run hotel just outside the city walls on a hill in its own grove of olive trees. Well-kept, spacious rooms have period decorations and furnishings. There are great views over the city and surrounding countryside, and breakfast is served on the terrace. An extra bed can be put in your room for €25. Free parking.
✉ Via B. Peruzzi 33, 53100 Siena ☎ 0577 285290 💶 €130 🛏 27 🛗 🏊 Outdoor 🛗

HOTEL ITALIA
www.hotelitalia-siena.it
The bedrooms here are attractively furnished, and bathrooms have bright hand-painted tiles and a full range of accessories. There's a cheerful breakfast room, limited parking and helpful, friendly staff. It's a 10-minute walk into the old city.
✉ Via Cavour 67, 53100 Siena ☎ 0577 41117 💶 €95–€130 🛏 52 🛗

HOTEL MINERVA
www.albergominerva.it
A ten-minute walk from Piazza del Campo and the rail station, the three-star Hotel Minerva has views over the whole city and the hills beyond. The rooms are modern and fully equipped.
✉ Via Garibaldi 72, 53100 Siena ☎ 0577 284474 💶 €115 🛏 59 🛗

HOTEL SANTA CATERINA
www.hscsiena.it
This converted 18th-century villa still has much of its original decoration and furniture. The shady garden has fine views across to Monte Amiata. Ask for a room overlooking the garden as those over the street can be noisy. There is limited parking.
✉ Via E. S. Piccolomini 7, 53100 Siena ☎ 0577 221105 💶 €110–€175 🛏 22 🛗

HOTEL VILLA LIBERTY
www.villaliberty.it
This little hotel opposite the Medici fort is in a converted art nouveau villa. There is an intimate bar and sitting room on the ground floor and a small garden at the back. The bedrooms are comfortable, and the bathrooms are well equipped, clean and modern. There is ample free street parking.
✉ Viale Vittorio Veneto 11, 53100 Siena ☎ 0577 44966 💶 €90–€120 🛏 18 🛗

PALAZZO BRUCHI DI MASIGNANI
www.palazzobruchi.it
A bed-and-breakfast in an 18th-century building in the heart of Siena. There is a warm, relaxing atmosphere, the rooms are furnished with antiques, and large windows overlook the garden courtyard or the old city walls. The Bruchi is very good value. Credit cards are not accepted.
✉ Via Pantaneto 105, 53100 Siena ☎ 0577 287342 💶 €80–€150 🛏 9

PALAZZO RAVIZZA
www.palazzoravizza.it
This four-star pensione has been owned by the same family for more than 200 years. The 18th-

century palace was converted into a hotel in 1929 but it has kept its character through the likes of the checkerboard marble floors and columns. The guest rooms are furnished with antiques, and the best suites come with Jacuzzis.
✉ Via Piano dei Mantellini 34, 53100 Siena ☎ 0577 280462 💶 €130–€270 🛏 38 🛗

PICCOLO HOTEL ETRURIA
www.hoteletruria.com
This is a popular two-star hotel in the heart of Siena. The guest rooms are basic but all have telephone, TV, bathroom with shower and safe. Make your reservation as far in advance as you can.
✉ Via delle Donzelle 3, 53100 Siena ☎ 0577 288088 💶 €80, excluding breakfast 🛏 16 🛗

TRE DONZELLE
You find this well-run two-star hotel just a minute's walk from the Campo. Only four of the rooms have private bathrooms and there is no lift or breakfast, but the rooms are kept spotlessly clean and you couldn't be more central.
✉ Via delle Donzelle 5, 53100 Siena ☎ 0577 280358 💶 €40–€60 🛏 20

VILLA SCACCIAPENSIERI
www.villascacciapensieri.it
A colonial air pervades this four-star hotel in a grand 19th-century villa with high ceilings, beams and dark wooden furniture. It is on a hill 2km (1.25 miles) outside the city walls and there are panoramic views over Siena and the countryside from the hotel's well-designed gardens. Bicycles are available to rent, and a regular bus service from the gates makes this a good place to stay for anyone who prefers not to be in the heart of town. Tennis courts are available for rent.
✉ Via Scacciapensieri 10, 53100 Siena ☎ 0577 41441 🗓 16 Mar to 14 Nov 💶 €185–€245 (suite €305) 🛏 31 🛗 🏊 Outdoor 🚗 Take the Siena Nord and follow the signs for Nuovo Ospedale/ Policlinico Le Scotte and then follow signs for the hotel

SOUTHERN TUSCANY

When you imagine Tuscany, the chances are you imagine southern Tuscany, for this is the area that is filled with the region's classic landscapes—the cypress-topped hills, the poppy-filled wheat fields, the villas and rustic farmhouses, the silvery olive groves and the verdant vineyards of Chianti. It is also the region that contains Tuscany's most celebrated hill towns, its most beautiful abbeys and is where its most famous wines are produced.

Chianti, a large area of high wooded hills and pastoral vineyards between Florence and Siena, has been popular with visitors for centuries and is the perhaps the best-known area within southern Tuscany. For all its charms, however, Chianti is not blessed with many pretty towns and villages. For these you have to look elsewhere within the region. The picture-perfect village of San Gimignano is famous for its medieval towers, which create its captivating skyline, but also for its outstanding art-filled churches and museums. Less immediately striking, although far quieter, are Arezzo, which is noted for a superb fresco cycle by Piero della Francesca in the church of San Francesco, and Cortona, which seduces visitors with its pretty streets and sweeping views of the surrounding countryside.

Also outstanding are Pienza, a tiny village that has magnificent vistas and some good food shops, and the enchanting, art-filled hill towns of Montepulciano and Montalcino, also celebrated for their excellent wine. Not far from Montalcino are two of Italy's loveliest abbeys, the Abbazia di Sant'Antimo, a matchless Romanesque ensemble in glorious countryside, and Monte Oliveto Maggiore, distinguished by a major Renaissance fresco cycle.

More than elsewhere in Tuscany, this is a region with plenty of lesser-known small towns and villages that more than repay a visit—notably Colle di Val d'Elsa, Massa Marittima, Sansepolcro, Sovana, Pitigliano and Volterra—but also emerging areas like the Maremma, a coastal enclave noted for its fine wines and beautiful landscapes, the latter best seen on Monte Argentario and in the Parco Naturale dei Monti dell'Uccellina.

ABBAZIA DI MONTE OLIVETO MAGGIORE

This isolated but beautifully situated medieval abbey, still the home of a thriving Benedictine monastic community, stands on a hillside 9km (6 miles) northeast of Buonconvento (▷ 196). This is the heart of the Crete Senesi (▷ 200), the wild limestone landscape distinguished by scree and rock falls that lies south of Siena (▷ 166–191)—a landscape instantly appealing to medieval monastic orders seeking wilderness. The abbey itself, built of rosy brick, is surrounded by groves of olives, holm oak and cypress trees, first planted here by the early monks. It was founded by Bernardo Tolomei, a member of a wealthy Sienese family, and by the mid-15th century it was an immensely rich community with money to spare for artistic projects.

The monastery's highlight is the Chiostro Grande, which was frescoed between 1498 and 1508 with scenes from the life of St. Benedict—generally seen as the father of monasticism—by two of the outstanding artists of the day, Luca Signorelli (c1441–1523) and Giovanni Sodoma (1477–1549). The latter was an eccentric figure who kept an extraordinary menagerie of pets, including a talking raven and a badger, both of which appear in some of the fresco panels. The series starts on the east wall; follow it round to trace Benedict's life and enjoy the wealth of detail and the vivid hues. The monastery church has a 15th-century layout, with wooden choir stalls carved by Fra Giovanni da Verona. Upstairs there's a gorgeous Renaissance library. Today's monks have a library of 40,000 books and other documents, along with a workshop where they restore old books. They also produce wine, honey and olive oil, which you can buy at the monastery shop.

✚ 282 H8 ✉ 1 Località Monte Oliveto Maggiore, 53041 Asciano ☎ 0577 707611 🕐 May–end Sep daily 9.15–12, 3.15–6; Oct–end Apr 9.15–12, 3.15–5 🖐 Free
🖵 🏛

ABBAZIA DI SANT'ANTIMO

www.antimo.it

The honey-toned abbey church of Sant'Antimo, full of architectural appeal, stands untouched by time in a quintessential Tuscan landscape, 10km (6 miles) from Montalcino (▷ 203). Legend associates its foundation with Charlemagne (▷ 28), said to have built the abbey to thank God for saving his troops from a mysterious disease. In AD814 it was enriched with lands and privileges by Charlemagne's son. It became one of the richest abbeys in Tuscany, in part because it was on many important pilgrimage and trade routes. Parts of the complex are pre-Romanesque, though much of it dates to the 12th century, including the fine church, which has a layout unique in Tuscany, with a basilican plan and radiating chapels. The architecture has a distinctly French Romanesque touch, exemplified by the ambulatory (walkway) behind the main altar; this allowed pilgrims to walk as they prayed.

The abbey is now in the hands of French Augustinian monks, who celebrate mass, complete with Gregorian chants, several times daily. Don't rush a visit here—to appreciate the site, it's best to allow time to soak up the peace and serenity of the spot. If you are feeling energetic, it's a good starting point for a country hike (▷ 217).

✚ 282 H9 ✉ 222 Località Abbazia Sant'Antimo, Castelnuovo dell'Abate, 53024 Montalcino ☎ 0577 835659 🕐 Mon–Sat 10.15–12.30, 3–6.30; Sun 9.15–10.45, 3–5 🖐 Free

ABBAZIA DI SAN GALGANO

www.sangalgano.org

This huge ruined abbey (69m/226ft long and 29m/95ft wide), standing alone in the heart of the countryside, is one of the best examples of Cistercian Gothic architecture in Italy. The abbey dates back to the 13th century and was built in honour of St. Galganus (San Galgano), who lived on nearby Monte Siepi as a hermit in the 12th century and founded a small church there. It was once the largest Cistercian abbey in Tuscany and one of the two largest in Italy. The abbey's church was repeatedly sacked during the 13th century in inter-city Tuscan wars and gradually fell into disrepair, the roof finally collapsing in the 18th century. Today the walls and columns still stand, but it is open to the sky and little is left of the monastic buildings.

Close by, on a hill above the main abbey, you can see the Cappella di Monte Siepi, a domed rotunda that was once the saint's hermitage, transformed into a chapel between 1182 and 1185. Inside is the stone into which he is said to have thrust his sword as a symbol of his renunciation of worldly life.

Two more structures were later built here, a 14th-century Gothic chapel and an 18th-century rectory, forming an attractive rural ensemble. The side chapel of the rotunda contains some ghostly traces of frescoes by Ambrogio Lorenzetti; you can just make out Galgano offering his sword to St. Michael.

✚ 282 G8 ✉ San Galgano 53012, Chiusdino ☎ 0577 756738 🕐 Daily 24 hours 🖐 Free

Opposite and below *The Abbazia di Sant'Antimo, set in beautiful countryside near Montalcino*

ANGHIARI

www.anghiari.it

If you're exploring southeast Tuscany, Anghiari makes a pleasant stop. This little settlement, overlooking a fertile plain planted with tobacco and sunflowers, has all the charms of a typical Tuscan hill town, but with the added bonus of being well off the main visitor routes. Its chief claim to fame is as the scene of a 1440 battle between the Milanese and the Florentines, the subject of what is possibly the best known of all the great Renaissance works of art that have been lost: Painted by Leonardo da Vinci for the Palazzo Vecchio in Florence (▷ 86), this fresco was by all accounts a tour de force, depicting semi-naked warriors of breathtaking anatomical realism. Sadly, Leonardo's innovative fresco technique was a disaster and the work didn't survive. Anghiari has an exhibition that will tell you about the battle, but its main pleasures are to be found in exploring the steep streets and stepped alleyways at its heart.

✚ 283 K6 ℹ Corso Matteoti 103, 52031 Anghiari ☎ 0575 749279 🄯 Daily 9.30–12.30, 4.30–7.30 🚋 Sansepolcro

ASCIANO

Asciano has Etruscan roots, and its medieval history is as a town repeatedly fought over by Florence and Siena. It became permanently Sienese in the 13th century, and it was here that one of the city's greatest artists, Domenico di Bartolo, was born in around 1400. It is a beguiling little town, still partly enclosed within its walls. Of the three museums, one is devoted to Etruscan finds from the area, but of greater interest is the Museo d'Arte Sacra (Museum of Religious Art) in a palace in the middle of town. Its collection is surprisingly good for a town of this size and includes works by several major Sienese artists, among them Lorenzetti and Sano di Pietro. The area's artistic tradition kept going strong right through to the 19th century, and the town's third museum has works by local painter Amos Cassioli (1832–92). Make time to inspect the late 13th-century Romanesque-Gothic church of Sant'Agata.

✚ 282 H8 ℹ Corso Matteoti 18, 53041 Asciano ☎ 0577 719510 🄯 Mon–Sat 10–1, 3–6, Sun 10–1 🚋 Asciano

BAGNO VIGNONI

www.comunesanquirico.it

Bagno Vignoni is one of the region's most unusual sights: a village whose old stone buildings cluster around a large, open-air pool filled with water from natural hot springs. When the air is cool, a mist rises from the warm water and drifts over the village square. The spring was known in Etruscan times, and over the years the waters were enjoyed by Romans and popes, as well as by saints including Catherine of Siena (▷ 171). In medieval times the baths became a resting place for pilgrims on the Via Francigena, the pilgrims' route through Italy to Rome. This is still a great place to stop and rest, with plenty of restaurants; there's a playground near the parking area. You can't bathe in the pool in the square, but you can pay to enjoy the springs in an open-air hotel pool, or take a free dip by following the stream downhill to the pools formed at the confluence with the river down below.

✚ 282 J9 ℹ Strada di Bagno Vignoni, 53027, San Quirico d'Orcia ☎ 0577 888975 🄯 Wed–Fri 3.30–6.30, Sat–Sun 10.30–1, 3.30–6.30

BUONCONVENTO

This small, brick-built market town, about 27km (17 miles) south of Siena, was an important trading post in the mid-13th century. It has a well-preserved medieval core, surrounded by walls that were built between 1371 and 1381. The Museo d'Arte Sacra (Via Soccini 18; Mar–end Oct Tue–Sun 10.30–1, 3–7; Nov–end Apr Sat, Sun 10–1, 2.30–6) is a museum of religious art displaying Sienese paintings from the 14th to the 17th century, including an *Annunciation*. It also has displays of jewellery, wood and marble sculptures. Also worth seeing is the Museo della Mezzadria (Apr–end Oct Tue–Sun 10–1, 2–6; Nov–end Mar Tue–Fri 10–1.30, Sat–Sun 10–1, 2–6) in Piazzale Garibaldi, with varied displays on the region's rural and social history.

✚ 282 H8 ℹ Piazzale Garibaldi 2, 53020 Buonconvento ☎ 0577 807181 🄯 Tue–Sun 10–6 🚋 Buonconvento

AREZZO

This thriving provincial capital is best known to art lovers as the home of Piero della Francesca's greatest fresco cycle. You will also find excellent shopping and good food. Arezzo, crowned with a cathedral and fortress, descends in terraces down its hillside to a fertile plain near the River Arno. The town was founded by the Etruscans and grew in importance during Roman times, with a reputation for producing highly prized red-glazed vases. During the Middle Ages it thrived on gold and jewellery, and the old town from that time has survived. Arezzo remains a world leader in jewellery manufacture, and has a monthly antiques market. The town also hosts Arezzo Wave, one of Italy's biggest rock festivals (▷ 227).

THE LEGEND OF THE TRUE CROSS

One of Italy's most famous fresco cycles is in the church of San Francesco. Commissioned from Piero della Francesca by the Bacci family in the 1450s, the pictures tell the story of the Legend of the True Cross, which links the physical history of Christ's Cross—said to have been made from the Tree of Knowledge in the Garden of Eden, source of Eve's apple—to man's cycle of redemption. Such complicated iconography may not appeal, but the frescoes are sublime. The figures are solid, detached and static, the light translucent and the tones muted. Painted between 1453 and 1466, the frescoes deteriorated badly during the second half of the 20th century and only emerged from extensive restoration in the late 1990s. As a result, access is limited to small groups (▷ Tip).

OTHER SIGHTS

The Piazza Grande is the town's sloping main square, the scene of the *Giostra del Saracino* festival (Joust of the Saracen, ▷ 227). The alleys around it are full of dark workshops smelling of wood, where artisans restore antique furniture. Just off the southwest corner is the church of Santa Maria, with a superb 13th-century arcaded façade and shadowy interior. North from here, the cathedral, built over some 250 years from 1278, dominates the city (daily 7–12.30, 3–7). It contains a tiny fresco by Piero della Francesca and some fine stained glass. A short stroll away is the Passeggio del Prato, an attractive park overlooked by the Fortezza Medicea (1538–60), a castle built by the town's Medici rulers. The Museo Archeologico (daily 8.30–7.30), next to the Roman amphitheatre, has good collections of Roman and Etruscan bronzes and pottery.

INFORMATION

www.apt.arezzo.it

✚ 283 K6 🛈 Piazza della Repubblica 28, 52100 Arezzo ☎ 0575 377678
🕐 Apr–end Sep Mon–Sat 9–1, 3–7, Sun 9–1; Oct–end Mar Mon–Sat 9–1, 3–6.30
🚆 Arezzo

TIP

» Admission to the frescoes of the *Legend of the True Cross* (Apr–end Oct Mon–Fri 9–6.30, Sat 9–5.30, Sun 1–5.30; Nov–end Mar Mon–Fri 9–5.30, Sat 9–5, Sun 1–5) is strictly by timed ticket—only 25 people are allowed in every 30 minutes. Buy tickets (Adult €6) in advance at the ticket office ☎ 0575 352727, or buy online at www.apt.arezzo.it

Above *A detail from the* Legend of the True Cross *fresco cycle in the church of San Francesco*
Opposite *Piazza delle Sorgenti in Bagno Vignoni is filled with water from natural hot springs*

INFORMATION

www.chiantiechianti.it

✚ 282 G6 ℹ Viale Giovanni di
Verrazzano 59, 50022 Greve in Chianti,
☎ 055 854 6287 🕐 Easter–end Oct
Mon–Fri 10–1, 2.30–7, Sat 10–1, 2.30–5

TIPS

» You'll need a car to explore Chianti, as
public transport is limited.
» To get the best of the area make
frequent stops: Roads are winding and
thickly wooded and much of the appeal
lies in the villages and small towns.

CHIANTI

One of Tuscany's best-known and most popular areas, Chianti is noted for its
wooded hills, attractive villages and, especially, its vineyards and their fine red
wines. The Chianti region, between Florence and Siena, is generally explored
by driving along the Strada Chiantigiana (SS222), a designated wine road that
runs through the heart of the district. This seductive area of rolling hills has
produced wine since Etruscan times, and is still providing grapes for Chianti
wine. The landscape is likely to be familiar to you, even if you have never visited
the region: olive groves, farms, villas and vineyards, some offering tastings. The
small towns of the region are unassuming, but make rewarding stops.

CASTELLINA IN CHIANTI

The town was once of great strategic importance as it was on the border
between the territories of Siena and Florence. You can still see its fortress at
the top of the town and walk along the Via delle Volte, a tunnel-like road that
runs around the walls and was formerly used by soldiers. This is a good place
to buy both olive oil and wine.

RADDA IN CHIANTI

Radda in Chianti is a hilltop town with great views over the region and fine
buildings dating from the 15th and 16th centuries. During the Middle Ages it
was capital of the Lega di Chianti, a military league of local towns; the Palazzo
Comunale is decorated with local families' shields and faces the town church.

GREVE IN CHIANTI

Greve has plenty of wine shops and cobbled streets to explore. Piazza
Matteotti is the town's hub; the surrounding buildings have attractive arcades
and it's the scene of the weekly Saturday market. Look for the statue of local
hero Giovanni di Verrazzano, who in 1524 was the first European to enter New
York harbour.

BADIA A COLTIBUONO

Just 6km (4 miles) from Radda is the Badia a Coltibuono, an 11th-century
abbey, with the Romanesque church of San Lorenzo, one of the finest buildings
of that date in Tuscany. The abbey estate is now owned by one of Chianti's
biggest wine producers, which runs a restaurant (▷ 229) and a shop selling the
estate produce. You can walk along well-marked trails in the surrounding wood.

Above *Steep hillsides planted with rows
of vines create a typical Chianti landscape*

CORTONA

As one of the highest towns in Italy, Cortona has superb views over Tuscany and Umbria. It also has some great paintings by Fra Angelico and Luca Signorelli. A visit here provides good exercise as well as rewarding sightseeing, as Cortona is perched on the side of Monte Egidio, making its medieval streets extremely steep. Panoramic views take in the Valdichiana and the region south of here. Substantial parts of the town's Etruscan walls are incorporated into its predominantly medieval buildings, and there are churches and good museums to visit along the precipitous cobbled streets. The town's great works of art come from its associations with two painters: the monk Fra Angelico (1387–1455), who lived here for two years in the local Dominican monastery, and native son Luca Signorelli (c1441–1523), in his imaginative power the precursor of Michelangelo.

TWO IMPORTANT MUSEUMS

You'll find the Museo Diocesano (Easter–end Oct daily 10–7; Nov–Easter daily 10–5) on Piazza del Duomo. This is home to two masterpieces by Fra Angelico, an *Annunciation* and a *Madonna and Child with Saints*, along with works by Sassetta, Bartolomeo della Gatta and Luca Signorelli. Another highlight is a second-century Roman sarcophagus carved with scenes depicting Dionysus' battle with the Amazons.

The Museo dell' Accademia Etrusca e della Città di Cortona (MAEC, Apr–end Oct daily 10–7; Nov–end Mar daily 10–5) recalls the town's more distant past. It has a huge fifth-century bronze lamp, some exquisite jewellery, urns and vases, and an impressive ancient Egyptian collection.

Other places to see include the 14th-century church of San Domenico, with a fresco by Fra Angelico above the main door. The church of San Niccolò, approached through a small walled garden, contains a double-sided painting by Luca Signorelli. The Fortezza Medicea, a ruined Medici fortress, is at the northern end of town. The climb up to it is steep, but it's worth the effort for the views of Lake Trasimeno and Umbria. To enjoy the scenery less strenuously, head for the Giardini Pubblici at the end of Via Nazionale. This street has several smart shops as well as cafés where you can taste local delicacies.

INFORMATION

www.cortonaweb.net

➕ 283 K7 ℹ Via Nazionale 42, 52044 Cortona ☎ 0575 630352 ◷ May–end Sep daily 9–1, 3–7; Oct–end Apr Mon–Sat 9–1, 3–6

Below *A view over the rooftops of Cortona and the valley of Valdichiana*

SOUTHERN TUSCANY • SIGHTS

REGIONS

199

CHIANTI
▷ 198.

COLLE DI VAL D'ELSA
Colle di Val d'Elsa is a sleepy little town that is far more attractive than its rather unappealing modern suburbs lead you to expect. Relatively few visitors venture here, but for those that do the old part of town, Colle Alta, on the hill, has its rewards. It has retained much of its medieval layout, with quiet narrow lanes and little alleyways. The main street, Via del Castello, runs the length of the town's ridge, opening out midway into Piazza del Duomo, the main square. There's a small archaeological museum in the square with finds from local Etruscan tombs (May–end Oct Tue–Sun 10.30–12.30, 4.30–7.30; Nov–end Apr Tue–Fri 3.30–5.30, Sat, Sun 10–12, 3.30–6.30), and on Via del Castello is a palace containing the Museo Civico e d'Arte Sacra, with silverware, sculpture, and medieval and Renaissance paintings (Tue–Sun 10.30–12.30, 4.30–7.30).

Colle was a major manufacturer of paper from the Middle Ages. The crystal and glass-blowing industry was also important, and today 90 per cent of Italy's crystal is produced here. The Museo del Cristallo (Tue–Sun 10–12, 4–7.30) at Via dei Fossi 8a, in an old glass factory, documents the town's glass-making history.

✚ 282 G7 ℹ Via Francesco della Campana 43, 53024 Colle di Val d'Elsa ☎ 0577 922791 ✪ Daily 10–1, 3–6.30 🚃 Poggibonsi

CRETE SENESI
The Crete Senesi is the name given to a geological area south of Siena, which has some strange, crater-like landslides and bare slopes, where the pale fields of heavy clay are dotted with sheep and punctuated by pencil-slim cypresses. The heartland encompasses the town of Buonconvento (▷ 196), the abbey of Monte Oliveto (▷ 195) and the village of Asciano (▷ 196).

To see it at its best you should strike out on foot, preferably along one of the ridge routes, although the area still has plenty of quiet *strade bianche*, or white roads—unsurfaced dirt roads that are dusty and white in the summer. You could walk from tiny San Giovanni d'Asso, with its 11th-century church of San Pietro and 13th-century castle, all the way to Monte Oliveto.

✚ 282 H7 ℹ Corso Matteotti 18, Asciano, ☎ 0577 719510 ✪ Mon–Sat 10–1, 3–6, Sun 10–1 🚃 Asciano

GROSSETO
www.maremma.info.it
www.laltramaremma.it
Capital of its province, Grosseto is a functional administrative town. Although it suffered heavy bombing during World War II, its massive hexagon of town walls, built by Cosimo I (1519–74) after the Florentines took the town from the Sienese, were spared and are one of the highlights of a visit to this commercial metropolis. You can walk all the way round the walls in about 40 minutes, before inspecting the central Piazza Dante, the main remnant of the old town. It's home to the Duomo, originally 13th century, but heavily altered, both inside and out, during the 19th century. If you're heading into the Maremma (▷ 202), it's worth dropping into the Museo di Storia Naturale della Maremma (Tue–Sat 9–7), informative on the natural history of this low-lying area. The town's most notable church is San Francesco, which has some lovely cloisters.

✚ 284 G10 ℹ Viale Monterosa 206, 58100 Grosseto ☎ 0564 462611 ✪ Mon–Fri 8.30–6.30, Sat 8.30–1.30 🚃 Grosseto

ISOLA D'ELBA
www.aptelba.it
Many people visit the island of Elba to explore the place where Napoleon lived in exile from May 1814 to February 1815 (▷ 37), but even more come to enjoy the scenery, unspoiled beaches and bustling resort towns. There are plenty of sites to visit, including Napoleon's former villa as well as old, abandoned mines where semi-precious stones can still be found. The island is also an excellent place for walking.

About 10km (6 miles) west of the mainland and an hour's ferry ride from Piombino, Elba is a natural mosaic of coves, beaches, headlands, precipitous coastline, wooded mountains and terraced vineyards. It is the largest island in the Tuscan archipelago, a group of islands once described as the 'necklace that slid from the neck of Venus'. There are several walking trails as well as a cable car to the top of Monte Capanne (1,018m/3,340ft), from where you can enjoy excellent views of the archipelago.

In Portoferraio, the main town, you will find the Villa dei Mulini. This was Napoleon's home while he was exiled and is now a museum (Mon, Wed–Sat 9–7, Sun 9–1) containing furniture of the period and Napoleon's library. Porto Azzurro is a busy resort dominated by a huge fortress once used as a prison.

✚ 284 C10 ℹ Calata Italia 26, 193 Portoferraio ☎ 0565 914671 ✪ Easter–end Sep daily 8–8; Oct–Easter Mon–Sat 8–2, 3–6 🚢 From Piombino to Portoferraio

Opposite Landscape of the Crete Senesi, an area to the south of Siena
Below Boats line the harbour at Portoferraio, the principal town on the Isola d'Elba

ISOLA DI GIANNUTRI

If you're an island enthusiast, Giannutri makes a good day's excursion from Giglio or, in summer, Porto Santo Stefano. It's Tuscany's southernmost island, a flat semi-circular expanse easily walked in a couple of hours, and is part of the Parco Nazionale Arcipelago Toscano, Europe's largest protected marine park. There's little to see on the island except the ruins of a Roman villa at Cala Maestra, but the island has clear waters and excellent scuba diving. Giannutri is privately owned, so there is no accommodation or visitor facilities.

➕ 285 G13 ℹ Archetto del Palio 1, 58019 Porto Santo Stefano ☎ 0564 814208 🕐 Easter–end Oct daily 9–1, 4–7; Nov–Easter 9–1 🚢 From Porto Santo Stefano to Giannutri

ISOLA DEL GIGLIO

www.isoladelgiglio.biz

The lovely island of Giglio lies 15km (9 miles) across the sea from Monte Argentario (▷ 204). Packed in summer with people on holiday, it is best visited outside July and August, when the coast and villages are less crowded. If you do visit in high season, you can escape the crowds by heading into the unspoiled interior, a beguiling mix of woodland and barren rocks, which you can explore by rented bicycle or moped—ideal if you don't want to bring a car. It has three main villages: Giglio Porto, where the ferry docks, Giglio Castello, high in the hills 6km (4 miles) from the coast, and Giglio Campese, although the main holiday bases are by the sea. Beaches on Giglio tend to be small, tucked at the bottom of precipitous cliffs; if you're looking for sand, head for Campese, blessed with a 2km (1-mile) sickle of smooth beach. If you want to sightsee, there are castle ruins at Castello, but most people come simply to enjoy the good seafood restaurants, clear sea and glorious surroundings.

➕ 284 F12 ℹ Via Provinciale 9, Giglio Porto, 58012 Isola del Giglio ☎ 0564 809400 🕐 Jun–end Aug Wed–Mon 8.30–1.30, 5–8; May, Sep 9–12.30, 4–7; Oct–end Apr 10–12 🚢 From Porto Santo Stefano to Giglio Porto

LUCIGNANO

www.comune.lucignano.ar.it

Lucignano is a prosperous, tidy town built around the main church, which is approached by a double stairway. Behind it, you can visit the Museo Comunale, which contains a piece of 14th-century jeweller's work, a reliquary known as the *Albero di Lucignano* (Tree of Lucignano). One glance explains its name—sinuously tree-like in form, glittering with gold and silver, it has crystal and enamel leaves suspended from coral branches. Next door is the church of San Francesco, frescoed during the 13th and 14th centuries.

➕ 283 J7 ℹ Piazza del Tribunale 22, 52046 Lucignano ☎ 0575 838001 🕐 Mar–end Sep Tue, Thu–Sun 10–1, 3–6.30; Oct–end Apr Tue, Thu–Fri, 10–1, 2.30–5.30, Sat, Sun 10–1, 2.30–6 🚆 Monte San Savino or Arezzo

MAREMMA

www.parcomaremma.it

The Maremma is the name given to the coastal plain that stretches from Cecina (south of Pisa) to Civitavecchia in Lazio. Unspoiled coastal areas with wide, sandy beaches dominate the western part, while the interior consists of wild, marshy tracts of *maquis*—fragrant scrub containing a variety of herbs, wild flowers and low bushes. The Etruscans started draining the region, but it reverted to malarial swamp until it was finally drained by the Fascist regime under Mussolini. The area between Principina a Mare and Talamone on the Tyrrhenian coast is a nature reserve. The park visitor office is in Alberese, south of Grosseto (▷ 206). The region also now produces some of Tuscany's most expensive wines, notably from the area on the coast near Bolgheri. Sassicaia is the best known, its blend of local and French grape varieties having started the trend for 'Super Tuscan' wines.

➕ 285 G11 ℹ Parco Regionale della Maremma, Via del Bersagliere 4/6, 58010 Alberese ☎ 0564 407098 🕐 Mid-Jun to mid-Sep daily 7.30–6; mid-Sep to mid-Jun hours vary 🚆 Alberese

MASSA MARITTIMA

www.commune.massamarittima.gr.it

This old town has owed much of its prosperity since medieval times to the mining of various minerals in the surrounding metal-rich hills. Today it rewards visitors with some worthwhile artworks, an archaeological museum, another museum commemorating the town's mining history, and a fine 12th-century cathedral. Some 40km (25 miles) south of Volterra (▷ 213), Massa Marittima overlooks the Pecora valley.

The town is divided in two: The lower town, Città Vecchia (Old Town), has a striking, sloping medieval square, dominated by the cathedral, while the upper town, Città Nuova (New Town), has a 13th-century tower with extensive views. The 13th-century Palazzo della Podestà (Apr–end Oct Tue–Sun 10–12.30, 3.30–7; Nov–end Mar 10–12.30, 3–5) houses the museum of archaeology, with many Etruscan finds, and a small collection of medieval works of art, including a superb Maestà by Ambrogio Lorenzetti (active 1319–48).

➕ 281 F9 ℹ Via Todini 3–5, 58024 Massa Marittima ☎ 0566 902756 🕐 Mar–end Oct Mon–Sat 9.30–12.30, Sun 10–1, 3.30–6.30; Nov–end Feb Mon–Fri 9.30–12.30, 3.30–6.30 🚆 Follonica

MONTALCINO

This is an exceptional hill town in a dramatic position at the heart of one of Tuscany's most important wine regions, producing the much-admired Barolo and Brunello reds. Hilltop Montalcino, 40km (25 miles) south of Siena, overlooks some of southern Tuscany's most ravishing countryside. It's a pleasing town, with narrow streets, a warren of alleys and steps and a central piazza, and it is attracting increasing numbers of visitors. Allow a day to explore the town thoroughly, taste the wine and do some shopping. After your visit, you could drive 20 minutes farther to take in the superb Abbazia di Sant'Antimo (▷ 195).

THE TOWN

From afar, Montalcino appears to be dominated by its photogenic Rocca, a 14th-century fort (Apr–end Oct daily 9–8; Nov–end Mar Tue–Sun 9–6) built by the Sienese, which stands just inside the town walls. You can climb its high walls, ramparts and towers to enjoy the panorama over Tuscany—Siena should be visible on a clear day. The Rocca's interior is now a park, and there's an *enoteca* (wine shop, ▷ 186) where you can sample and buy Montalcino's famous Brunello wine and local foods.

Walk downhill from here, through Piazza Garibaldi and into Piazza del Popolo, the town's main square. Here are the Palazzo Comunale (town hall), built in 1292, and the Fiaschetteria Italiana (▷ 231), a pleasingly old-fashioned café and enoteca established in 1888, complete with red velvet seats, marble tables and ornate mirrors. Uphill from here is the Museo di Montalcino (Apr–end Oct Tue–Sun 10–1, 2–5.50; Nov–end Mar Tue–Sun 10–1, 2–5.40), the town's principal museum, in the former convent of Sant'Agostino. Highlights include medieval and late Gothic artworks, wood sculptures from the 14th and 15th centuries and a collection of majolica (a style of glazed pottery that originated during the Renaissance) jugs.

THE WINE

Montalcino produces Brunello, along with Barolo, Italy's premier wine, an intense single-grape wine produced within a tiny area around the town. Brunello, a strong and complex wine, commands huge prices; the lighter and younger Rosso di Montalcino, made with the same grape, is a less expensive option. Also worth trying is the fragrant Moscatello di Montalcino. Wine is on sale all over the town, but you are likely to get the best prices at outlying supermarkets.

INFORMATION

www.prolocomontalcino.it

➕ 282 H8 ℹ️ Via Costa del Municipio 8, 53024 Montalcino ☎ 0577 849331 🕐 Apr–end Oct daily 10–1, 2–7; Nov–end Feb 10–1, 2–5.45 🚌 Buonconvento

TIPS

» Try to park outside the city walls, where there are a number of free spaces (those marked with white lines); from there it's a short walk to the town.

» Montalcino is a good base for exploring the Abbazia di Sant'Antimo and the villages of the Val d'Orcia.

Above *Views from the Rocca, Montalcino's 14th-century fort, are spectacular*
Opposite *Long-horned cattle grazing on the Maremma*

MONTE AMIATA

www.amiataturismo.it

At 1,738m (5,702ft) Monte Amiata is the highest point in southern Tuscany. The mountain is part of an extinct volcano and has a distinctive pyramid shape, visible from many parts of the region. In the past it was renowned for its mines, in particular its mercury mines (now closed), which brought posperity to the area's many small villages. You can go and see the hot springs that gush from its rocks by taking a drive up the winding mountain roads, or by walking through the woodlands along a section of the Anello della Montagna, a marked trail that completely encircles the mountain with views all the way. In winter, it's possible to ski.

There are several small towns across its slopes, including the unofficial capital, Abbadia San Salvatore, a medieval town named for its Benedictine abbey (daily 7.45–6). It was founded in the eighth century and is one of the oldest abbeys in Tuscany. The present abbey church, consecrated in 1036, is Romanesque in style, with a long single nave and raised chancel. Don't miss the crypt, a cavernous space supported by fluted columns whose lintels are superbly carved with Byzantine/Lombard figures, unique in this part of Tuscany.

From Abbadia a road runs virtually to the mountain's summit for magnificent views. The Parco Faunistico del Monte Amiata (daily dawn to dusk), near Arcidosso, is a specially designated nature reserve, where you might see deer, mouflon (a breed of wild sheep) and the Amiata mouse-grey donkey.

Also worth exploring are Piancastagnaio, south of Abbadia, dominated by a superb 14th-century Aldobrandeschi fortress; Santa Fiora to the west, with remnants of another fortress and two fine churches; and Castel del Piano, the area's commercial hub.

⊹ 285 J9 🔢 Via Adua 25, 53021 Abbadia San Salvatore ☎ 0577 775811 🕐 Mon–Fri 8.30–1 (also Tue, Fri 3–5)

Above *The harbour at Porto Ercole, on the Monte Argentario promontory*

MONTE ARGENTARIO

www.comune.monteargentario.gr.it
www.lamaremma.info

The mountainous promontory of Monte Argentario rears up southwest of Grosseto (▷ 200). A one-time island, it became part of the mainland when its shallow waters silted up and a causeway was formed. You can now reach the mainland through the lagoons of Orbetello. The interior is steep and wooded, while its coast is a succession of headlands, tiny coves and hidden beaches. The promontory has long had a reputation as a chic holiday area, and you'll still see plenty of luxury villas, but prices have dropped and it's not as exclusive as it once was. There are two resorts: the more fashionable and developed Porto Santo Stefano, with its expensive yachts and beautiful people, and Porto Ercole, which still retains its old quarter, its fishing harbour and two Spanish fortresses. From here you can walk up Il Telegrafo, at 635m (2,083ft) Argentario's highest point. The area was once owned by the Spanish and became part of Tuscany in the 19th century, more than 200 years after the painter Caravaggio died of malaria on one of its beaches. Away from the coast, the high rocky terrain makes for superb walking.

⊹ 285 G12 🔢 Corso Umberto 55,

Archetto del Palio 1, 58019 Porto Santo Stefano ☎ 0564 814208 🕐 Easter–end Oct daily 9–1, 4–7; Nov–Easter 9–1 🚉 Orbetello

MONTE SAN SAVINO

www.comune.monte-san-savino.ar.it

On the opposite side of the Valdichiana from Cortona (▷ 199), Monte San Savino is a market town that once marked the border between Florence, Siena and Arezzo. Unlike many places in the area, San Savino has few visitors. This means that, although it is not in the top flight of hill towns, it is remarkably untouched by modern tourism. It has a mix of medieval and Renaissance buildings, local shops, and a bustling air of provincial small-town life that has its own appeal. The town has been associated with majolica (a style of glazed pottery that originated during the Renaissance) production for centuries; you'll see plenty on sale and there are examples in the small ceramic museum. Other sights include the 14th-century Sienese castle, the church of Santa Chiara (there's some fine majolica here too) and the Loggia dei Mercanti, designed by Sansovino (1460–1529), a native-born son of the town.

⊹ 283 J7 🔢 Corso Sangallo 73, 52048 Monte San Savino ☎ 0575 849418 🕐 May–end Sep Mon–Wed, Thu–Sat 9–1, 4–7, Sun 9–1; Oct–end Apr Fri–Sun 9–1

MONTEPULCIANO

This dream of a Tuscan hill town is renowned for its red wine. Wander the steep streets to discover fine palaces, intimate corners and tiny squares with lovely views.

THE TOWN

Montepulciano is one of Tuscany's highest hill towns, built along a narrow ridge with alleys dropping steeply away from the central main street. It owes its appearance to the 1511 treaty signed with Florence after long years of Sienese dominance. The Florentines sent Antonio da Sangallo to rebuild the gates and walls, a mission so successful that it provided the impetus for more extensive building by the same architect. The main square is Piazza Grande, near the town's highest point. It is dominated by the 16th- to 17th-century cathedral (summer daily 9–12, 3.30–7; winter 3–6), with an altarpiece of the Assumption (1401) by Taddeo di Bartolo, a superb, glowing treatment of a frequently recurring Sienese subject. In the baptistery are numerous reliefs, terracottas and other sculptures by various medieval and Renaissance artists. Also on Piazza Grande is the Palazzo Comunale, a 13th-century Gothic palace with a striking resemblance to Florence's Palazzo Vecchio (▷ 86); you can climb the tower for great views. Down the hill, the Museo Civico (Apr–end Jul, Sep–end Oct Tue–Sat 10–1, 3–7; Aug daily 10–7; Nov–end Mar Tue–Sat 10–1, 3–6) has a good collection of pottery, medieval sculpture, Etruscan tombs and funerary urns, along with paintings by Sienese artists.

Though not of the quality of Brunello (▷ 203), the wine of Montepulciano is still a treat. The so-called Vino Nobile was judged so fine by a 16th-century pope that he 'ennobled' it. Sample it in one of the wine shops and restaurants in town, including the elegant Caffè Poliziano with its art nouveau interior (▷ 231). Montepulciano plays host to various cultural events, especially in summer.

SAN BIAGIO

Outside the walls stands the pilgrimage church of San Biagio, Sangallo's greatest commission and one of Tuscany's most harmonious Renaissance buildings. Approached by an avenue of cypresses, the church occupied Sangallo from 1518 to his death in 1534 and illustrates all the elements that mark Renaissance architecture. The dome, the use of the three orders of classical columns and the freestanding towers all make this a superbly satisfying building, whose surroundings do much to contribute to its appeal. If you don't have a car, however, you might find the walk there and back a bit far.

INFORMATION

www.prolocomontepulciano.it
🞤 283 J8 🛈 Piazza Don Minzoni 1, 53045 Montepulciano ☎ 0578 757341 🕓 Easter–end Oct Mon–Sat 9–12.30, 3–8, Sun 9–12.30; Nov–Easter 9.30–12.30, 3–6, Sun 9–12.30
🚆 Montepulciano or Chiusi

Below The pilgrimage church of San Biagio lies outside the walls of Montepulciano

MONTERCHI

www.comunemonterchi.it

Monterchi lies between Arezzo (▷ 197) and Sansepolcro (▷ 211) in the upper Tiber Valley. A small walled village perched on a hilltop, it has great views towards Umbria and over the surrounding countryside. Small as it is, Monterchi does possess one highly significant work of art: the fresco of the *Madonna del Parto*, painted by Piero della Francesca in the mid-15th century. This depiction of a heavily pregnant, weary-looking Madonna, one of the most unusual portrayals of her in Western art, was once a focus of pilgrimage for pregnant women. It was painted in a nearby chapel, but was removed to an exhibition room on the Via Reglia following restoration (Apr–end Oct Mon–Fri 9–1, 2–7; Nov–end Mar daily 9–1, 2–5).

⊞ 283 L6 🛈 Piazza Umberto 1, 52035 Monterchi ☎ 0575 70092 🕙 Mon–Sat 8–2 🚇 Città di Castello

MONTERIGGIONI

www.monteriggionicastello.it

Driving south to Siena it's not easy to miss Monteriggioni, a tiny, perfectly preserved hill town still entirely enclosed by its medieval walls. You have to walk up the hill and through the towered gateway to enter the heart of the village, where you can recover your breath sitting at a café on the spacious square, while contemplating the small church there. Monteriggioni's main draws are its ramparts and its position, set on its hill like a granite crown. It was founded by the Sienese in 1203 to defend the northern approach to Siena from the Florentines. The circular walls were built between 1213 and 1219, destroyed in 1244 by invading Florentines, and rebuilt between 1260 and 1270. The 14 towers were described in Dante's Inferno as resembling giants. Today, Monteriggioni makes its living from tourism.

⊞ 282 G7 🛈 Largo Fontebranda 5, 53035 Castello di Monteriggioni ☎ 0577 304810 🕙 Daily 11–7

MURLO

www.comune.murlo.siena.it

The beguiling medieval *borgo* (fortified village) of Murlo lies to the south of Siena amid hilly countryside of a stark beauty. Its ring of medieval houses and steep streets leads up to the town hall and church, and it has a first-rate Etruscan museum that displays finds from the sites in the area, particularly from nearby Poggio Civitate. The museum is in the old castle, and its treasures include statues, terracotta tombs and metalwork.

⊞ 282 H8 🛈 Piazza delle Carceri 17, 53016 Murlo ☎ 0577 814099 🕙 Mar–end Oct Tue–Sun 10–1, 3–7; Nov–end Feb Mon–Fri 10–1, Sat–Sun 10–1, 3–5

PARCO REGIONALE DELLA MAREMMA

www.parks.it/parco.maremma

This area of protected parkland, literally the 'mountains of the little bird', allows you to experience a microcosm of classic Maremma scenery: extensive pine forests and endless, sandy beaches. This little-known western part of Tuscany takes in the Uccellina mountains, the Marina di Alberese pinewood, the mouth of the River Ombrone and the Trappola marsh. It is part of the wider Maremma region (▷ 202). The inland waters are a great place for spotting migratory birds and the characteristic *bovini maremmani*, long-horned cattle that roam the land. Other wildlife to look for includes wild boar, deer, porcupines, pine martens and wildcats. The park is an area to explore at leisure and on foot. There is a 5km (3-mile) walk through the park to the ruined abbey of San Rabano, and other footpaths will take you along the wild coastline or to watchtowers. There are magnificent views from the 15th-century fortress in Talamone.

⊞ 285 G11 🛈 Park visitor office, Via del Bersagliere 4/6, 58010 Alberese ☎ 0564 407098 ❓ Entry is at Alberese on SS Aurelia 1; at busy times, entry to the park is restricted

PITIGLIANO

www.collidimaremma.it

A volcanic ridge, riddled with caves used since Etruscan times, rises dramatically where two rivers meet, and on top is Pitigliano's jumble of mellow-toned buildings. This medieval town was once owned by the powerful Orsini family, and the main attraction here is the family residence, the 16th-century Palazzo Orsini (Apr–end Oct Tue–Sun 10–1, 2–7; Nov–end Mar Fri–Sun 10–1, 3–7), which has an excellent collection of Etruscan finds in its finely decorated rooms. Outside, you can explore the cobbled streets and inviting alleyways, admire the main square and enjoy the views of Monte Amiata (▷ 204). Look for the remains of a 14th-century aqueduct in the middle of town, and take in the cathedral, with its lovely baroque façade and medieval belfry. Pitigliano was home to a thriving Jewish community until World War II.

⊞ 285 J11 🛈 Piazza Garibaldi 51, 58017 Pitigliano ☎ 0564 617111 🕙 Easter–end Oct daily 9.30–1, 3–8; Nov–Easter Mon–Sat 9.30–1, 3–7

PIENZA

This miniature Renaissance city is set in southern Tuscany's most ravishing landscape, in rolling countryside in the southeast corner of the region. A compact town, it consists of a maze of small lanes that radiate from the main square. Once within its ancient walls, you will fall under the spell of its timeless atmosphere and crisp beauty, qualities recognized by UNESCO when Pienza was made a World Heritage site in 1996. It also has plenty of tempting shops and restaurants.

HISTORY

Tiny Pienza was the birthplace of Aeneas Silvio Piccolomini (1405–64), and he had a vision of his hometown as a model for Renaissance urban planning and architecture. When he became Pope Pius II in 1459, he put his ambitious plan into action, but he died before the project could be completed. As a result, only a handful of buildings, including the cathedral, was finished.

THE SIGHTS

Piazza Pio II has all Pienza's important religious and secular buildings. The cathedral (daily 8–1, 3–7), on the south side, has a number of tall windows that allow light to flood in. They illuminate altarpieces by five prominent Sienese artists commissioned by Pope Pius II, including Vecchietta's *Assumption* (1461–62). The Palazzo Piccolomini (mid-Mar to mid-Oct Tue–Sun 10–6.30; mid-Oct to mid-Mar Tue–Sun 10–5. Closed 2 weeks Feb, Nov) is just to the right of the cathedral, where members of the Piccolomini family lived up to the mid-1960s. You must take a guided tour to see the sumptuous state apartments and the Sala d'Armi (armoury room), bristling with all manner of fearsome medieval weaponry. Equally memorable are the views from the rear loggia. The Museo Diocesano (mid-Mar to mid-Oct Wed–Mon 10–1, 3–7; Nov to mid-Mar Sat–Sun 10–1, 3–6) brings together paintings, sculptures, tapestries and other medieval and Renaissance artworks from various churches in the area. Its most important pieces include a 14th-century cope that belonged to Pius, a wooden altarpiece by Pietro Lorenzetti (active 1320–48), and a 12th-century painted Crucifix. The other building on the square is the Palazzo Comunale (town hall). There are great views towards Monte Amiata (▷ 204) from the lanes along the top of the walls; Pieve di Corsignano is a 10th-century church that escaped Pius' redevelopment.

INFORMATION

www.comunedipienza.it

✚ 282 J8 ℹ Corso Rossellino 30, 53026 Pienza ☎ 0578 749905 🕐 Daily 9.30–1, 3–6.30

TIPS

» Leave your car outside the city walls—you will not be able to park inside the city.

» Try to arrive about 9am or after 4pm if you want to avoid tour buses from Siena in the peak summer months. Wednesdays and Thursdays also tend to be quieter than other days of the week.

» Look out for local pecorino (sheep's milk) cheese available in the city's delicatessens.

Above *Pienza's cathedral can be seen along the city walls*
Opposite *The hilltop village of Monterchi*

INTRODUCTION

San Gimignano is a picture-perfect medieval village dominated by a wonderful crop of towers that lend it one of the country's most evocative skylines. Its attractiveness inevitably means that it becomes very busy, especially in summer, and it repays an overnight stay, which will allow you to enjoy some of its genuine charm, free of the many thousands of day trippers.

The village was probably founded by the Etruscans, but enters recorded history in the 10th century, when the first feudal castle was built. This fortress provided the kernel for a settlement, which, by the 13th century, had acquired a set of walls. The town grew rich on agriculture and as a result of its position on the Via Francigena, the pilgrim and trade route to northern Europe. Its weakness was the propensity of its chief families for feuding. During the years of conflict, the families built 72 protective towers, 14 of which survive. Squabbles continued during the 13th and 14th centuries, only ending with the 1348 Black Death, which wiped out much of the population and crippled the economy. In 1353 San Gimignano became subject to Florentine rule and embarked on centuries of existence as a rural backwater. It was only the advent of post-war tourism and the revival of the town's wine industry that brought renewed prosperity.

The village is surprisingly small—it's possible to walk from one end of town to the other in 15 minutes—but there is still an extraordinary amount to see. Start your visit at the south gate, the Porta San Giovanni (there is a large parking area beyond this to the south, outside the walls), from where Via San Giovanni leads uphill to the interlocking main squares that form the hub of the town. Piazza della Cisterna, named after the 13th-century public well in the middle, is surrounded by a diverse selection of *palazzi*, towers and mansions. Pass through to Piazza del Duomo with its Collegiata, a superbly frescoed church, and the excellent museum and art gallery, which also includes access to the one tower open open to the general public. From Piazza del Duomo, Via San Matteo runs to the Porta San Matteo, the north gate. Beyond this lies the church of Sant'Agostino, famous for more wonderful frescoes.

WHAT TO SEE

COLLEGIATA

Little on the Collegiata's plain brick façade prepares you for the interior, covered with dazzling frescoes enhanced by the zebra- striped marble arcades. On the rear wall your attention is grabbed by Benozzo Gozzoli's 1465 fresco of St. Sebastian. The side walls have scenes from the Old and New Testaments, executed in the mid-14th century. The Old Testament scenes are particularly lively, packed with quirky detail and incidents. There's more spirituality in the New Testament scenes—look for the *Kiss of Judas* and *Christ Carrying the Cross*. Don't miss the Renaissance Cappella di Santa Fina in the right aisle, which is dedicated to San Gimignano's own saint.

✉ Piazza del Duomo ☎ 0577 940316 🕓 Apr–end Oct Mon–Fri 9.30–7.10, Sat 9.30–5.10, Sun 12.30–5.10; Mar, Nov–end Jan Mon–Sat 9.30–4.40, Sun 12.30–4.40; Feb services only 💷 Adult €3.50, child (6–18) €1.50

PALAZZO COMUNALE

The Palazzo Comunale (or Palazzo del Popolo) still houses the council offices, but also contains the Museo Civico, the town's main museum. Here too is the access to the Torre Grossa, the only one of the 14 surviving towers you can climb, with the Pinacoteca (art gallery) in the upper rooms. Climb up from the courtyard to reach the Sala del Consiglio, also called the Sala di Dante. It was

INFORMATION

www.sangimignano.com

➕ 281 F6 ℹ️ Piazza del Duomo 1, 53037 San Gimignano ☎ 0577 940008 🕓 Mar–end Oct daily 9–1, 3–7; Nov–end Feb 9–1, 2–6 💷 Combined tickets for the Palazzo Comunale, Pinacoteca, Museo Archeologico and Torre Grossa, Spezeria di Santa Fina, Museo Ornitologico and Galleria d'Arte Moderna: adult €7.50, child (6–18) €5.50

Opposite and below *Tall towers, a legacy of the town's feuding medieval families dominate San Gimignano's skyline*

here that Dante, as a Florentine diplomat, met members of San Gimignano's
council. The room contains Lippo Memmi's splendid gold-ground *Maestà*
(1316). Upstairs again are paintings by Florentine, Umbrian and Sienese artists.
Look for the 14th-century frescoes of wedding scenes in the little room off the
stairs, which include a vignette of lovers enjoying a bath before they go to bed.
✉ Piazza del Duomo ☎ 0577 990312 🕐 Mar–end Oct daily 9.30–7.30; Nov–end Feb 10–5.30
🖐 Adult €5, child (6–18) €4

SANT'AGOSTINO
Sant'Agostino was built in the 13th century and is renowned for its fresco
cycle on the life of St. Augustine by Benozzo Gozzoli (c1421–97). There's also a
magnificent marble altar (1495) by Benedetto di Maiano in the Cappella di San
Bartolo on the rear wall of the church, and a serene Renaissance cloister. The
frescoes, 17 in all, adorn the walls surrounding the high altar. Painted between
1463 and 1467, they trace Augustine's life from his childhood and schooling,
through his conversion to Christianity to his career as one of the most
important of the early Fathers of the Church. Augustine's life was spent in the
Middle East and Rome, but Gozzoli portrays it against a Florentine background,
with a mass of detail that gives a remarkably clear picture of everyday life in
the 15th century.
✉ Piazza Sant'Agostino ☎ 0577 940008 🕐 Apr–end Oct daily 7–12, 3–7; Nov–end Mar
7–12, 3–6 🖐 Free

ROCCA DI MONTESTAFFOLI
In 1353 the inhabitants of San Gimignano were ordered by the Florentines to
build a fortress at the town's expense 'to remove every cause of evil thinking'.
Massive walls, 283m (308 yards) in length, enclosed a pentagonal space
and a series of towers at the highest point in the town. By 1558 the Rocca
had served its purpose and was largely dismantled, leaving just one tower
standing. Today it's the public park, a lovely place for a picnic with the best
views in town. Climb the tower for a superb outlook over San Gimignano's
central cluster of towers, or walk the walls to view the landscape.
✉ Rocca 🕐 Daily 24 hours 🖐 Free

PIAZZA DELLA CISTERNA
The triangular piazza is a sweeping space paved with herring-bone brick, a
superb contrast to the narrow surrounding streets. The well (*cisterna*) in the
middle of the piazza gives it its name. The square is surrounded by palaces
and dominated by the soaring cluster of towers in the northwest corner. The
two most prominent are the twin Ardinghelli towers, guarding the entrance to
the adjacent Piazza del Duomo. The northeast corner is home to the Torre del
Diavolo, named after its owner attributed its height to the devil's work.
✉ Piazza della Cisterna 🕐 Daily 24 hours 🖐 Free

Above *The Renaissance cloister at
Sant'Agostino*

SANSEPOLCRO

This handsome, prosperous little town in the upper valley of the Tiber is a must for followers of the Piero della Francesca trail. At the foot of the Apennine mountains in the Tiber Valley, 8km (5 miles) northeast of Anghiari (▷ 196), Sansepolcro is said to have been founded by two 10th-century monks returning from the Holy Land with relics of Christ's tomb. This pleasant provincial town has one of Italy's biggest pasta factories, but the *centro storico*, its historic heart, is unspoiled. There's a handsome main piazza and on it a fine Romanesque-Gothic cathedral. In the shadowy interior, dimly lit by the alabaster glazing of a rose window, is a 10th-century *Volto Santo* (Holy Face) showing Christ as a patriarchal figure.

PIERO DELLA FRANCESCA

Most people come to Sansepolcro on the trail of Piero della Francesca, one of the Renaissance's most enigmatic and memorable artists. He was born in the town around 1420 and, despite absences to work on commissions in Florence, Urbino and Rome, lived the majority of his life here. He worked extremely slowly, his father having occasionally to apologize to his patrons for the length of time his son took, and his painting career was cut short by failing eyesight. Piero's latter years were occupied with writing two treatises, *On Perspective in Painting* and *On the Five Regular Bodies*, which laid out the mathematical theories that lie behind his work.

MUSEO CIVICO

The Museo Civico (Jun–end Sep daily 9–1.30, 2.30–7.30; Oct–end May 9.30–1, 2.30–6) in the old town hall has several of Piero della Francesca's paintings, including two of the most important: the *Madonna della Misericordia* and the *Resurrection*. The *Madonna*, Piero's earliest known painting, was commissioned by the charitable institution Compagnia della Misericordia, which is still in existence. It depicts the Virgin spreading her cloak to shelter a cross-section of humanity. On the wall at a right angle to this painting is the great *Resurrection*, dating from the 1450s. Revolutionary in style when it was painted, it depicts Christ emerging triumphant and muscular from the tomb. The background, a mix of bare and green-leafed trees, alludes to the cycle of death and resurrection. The museum also has a fine banner by Luca Signorelli, a bloodthirsty *Martyrdom of St. Quentin* by Pontormo and an archaeological collection.

INFORMATION

✚ 279 L6 🛈 Piazza Garibaldi 2, 52037 Sansepolcro ☎ 0575 740536 🕐 Apr–end Sep daily 9–1, 3.30–7; Oct–end Mar daily 9.30–12.30, 3.30–5.30; Sun in winter 9.30–12.30 only 🚊 Sansepolcro

Below *Sansepolcro is a pleasant provincial town, famed as the home of the Renaissance artist Piero della Francesca*

SAN QUIRICO D'ORCIA

www.comunesanquirico.it

You will find San Quirico d'Orcia 10km (6 miles) west of Pienza. The village once stood on the Via Francigena, the pilgrim route to Rome, and you can see the resulting economic growth this brought in the fine medieval houses that line Via Poliziano. However, you will also find some post-World War II housing sitting alongside the village's 16th-century gardens and exquisite medieval churches.

The main attraction is the Collegiata, a 12th-century church off Piazza Chigi, built on the ruins of an eighth-century church. There are exceptional Lombard-influenced carvings around the doors, and the interior highlights include inlaid Renaissance choir stalls and a *Virgin and Child Enthroned with Four Saints* by Sano di Pietro. On the edge of the village are the peaceful Horti Leonini. These gardens, laid out in 1580, consist of a flower garden and a natural woodland area. If you have time to wander around this partly walled village, you could take a look at the Palazzo Chigi, decorated with Roman frescoes.

✚ 282 J8 ℹ Via Dante Alighieri 33,

Below *Visitors to the spa town of Saturnia relax in its thermal waters*

53027 San Quirico d'Orcia ☎ 0577 897211 🕐 Apr–end Oct and 19 Dec–6 Jan daily 10–1, 3.30–6.30

SAN VINCENZO

www.comunesanvincenzo.li.it

South of Livorno (▷ 134) a string of resorts lines the coast. Still farther south, pine forests take over from hotels, and beaches become less crowded. The best stretch is at Bolgheri, an internationally important nature reserve that is a microcosm of the area's habitats. If you want to visit the region, San Vicenzo, 20km (12 miles) to the south, makes a good base. It's a fast-growing resort, with a black-sand beach and a clutch of older buildings to add to its charms. The coast is well wooded with pines, and the beach is big enough to allow you to escape the crowds.

✚ 281 D8 ℹ Via Beatrice Allata 4, 57027 San Vincenzo ☎ 0565 701533 🕐 Jun–end Sep Mon–Sat 9–1, 4.30–8, Sun 10–12.30; Oct–end May Mon–Sat 9–1

SATURNIA

If you are feeling stressed or tired, head for this spa town in the inland, hilltop region of the Maremma (▷ 202). Saturnia was named by the Romans after Saturn, the father of the gods, because they believed it to be one of the oldest settlements in Tuscany. It is famous for the sulphurous, hot, blue-green waters of the Gorello falls, which fume and bounce off natural basins of white stone. You can bathe in the waters for nothing, or book into one of the chic hotels to try various treatments such as mud baths.

✚ 285 H11 ℹ Piazza Garibaldi 51, 58017 Pitigliano ☎ 0564 617111 🕐 Easter–end Oct daily 9.30–1, 3–8; Nov–Easter Mon–Sat 9.30–1, 3–7

SORANO

Etruscan roads cut through the tufa all around Sorano, a village 9km (6 miles) northeast of Pitigliano (▷ 206), and the hillsides are riddled with caves and tombs, causing the landslides that have made parts of Sorano uninhabitable. The old part of the village spreads down a steep cliff above a spectacular gorge. It's full of odd corners and workshops carved out of the living rock, with serendipitous discoveries lying around every corner. Above medieval Sorano looms the 18th-century Masso Leopoldino quarter, worth the climb for the views. Visit the Fortezza Orsini, once an Aldobrandeschi family stronghold, for its 16th-century military engineering. Sorano has a number of artisan workshops and a small ceramic industry.

✚ 285 J11 ℹ Piazza Garibaldi 51, 58017 Pitigliano ☎ 0564 617111 🕐 Easter–end Oct daily 9.30–1, 3–8; Nov–Easter Mon–Sat 9.30–1, 3–7

SOVANA

On the border with Lazio, the sleepy little town of Sovana has several striking reminders of an illustrious past. It was once a significant Etruscan town and you will see a number of Etruscan, Roman and medieval relics on your visit here. It was also the birthplace of Hildebrand, who became Pope Gregory VII in 1073.

The village is really only a couple of streets. The main street, Via di Mezzo, has the ruins of a medieval fortress at one end. There is a fine Romanesque/Gothic cathedral, which has an even older crypt. One of the town's highlights is the 13th-century parish church of Santa Maria on the Piazza del Pretorio. It has a Romanesque exterior, frescoes by the Sienese school, and a carved ciborium, or altar canopy, dating from the eighth or ninth century. The limestone cliffs that surround Sovana are dotted with tombs and there are a number of signposts for you to follow. Tuscany's most important and elaborate Etruscan tomb, the Tomba Ildebranda, dates from the third century BC. It was discovered in the 1920s and is on the outskirts of the village.

✚ 285 J11 ℹ Piazza Garibaldi 51, 58017 Pitigliano ☎ 0564 617111 🕐 Easter–end Oct daily 9.30–1, 3–8; Nov–Easter Mon–Sat 9.30–1, 3–7

VOLTERRA

Volterra is an unspoiled hilltop town rich in mementos of Etruscan, Roman and medieval times. Its best buy is alabaster, a millennia-old mainstay of the town's economy. High in the volcanic hills west of Siena, Volterra was one of the Etruscans' largest settlements, the focus of their mining region. The Romans mined here too, ensuring the town's survival as a wealthy settlement into the Middle Ages. Besieged by the Florentines, Volterra lost its independence in 1472 and slid slowly into obscurity. Today, the medieval town remains virtually intact and the town is an agreeable place, still relatively little visited.

THE TOWN

Volterra's medieval heart is the Piazza dei Priori, site of a splendid ensemble of medieval buildings that includes the massive battlemented Palazzo dei Priori, the first town hall to be built in Italy (1208–54), the Palazzo Pretorio, and the Palazzo Vescovile, the bishop's palace. The latter is home to the Museo d'Arte Sacra, where the highlight is the wonderful *Madonna di Villamagna* (1521) by the Mannerist Rosso Fiorentino. Behind the piazza are the 12th-century black-and-white cathedral and a freestanding 13th-century baptistery. Northwest from here, at the bottom of steep streets and outside the medieval walls, are the remains of the Roman theatre, while farther down the hill a narrow country lane runs through the Porta Diana, a third-century BC city gateway. Across town, over the hill, the Parco Archeologico is more like a park than an archaeological site, a lovely green space on hot afternoons. It is overlooked by the Rocca (fort), built by the Medici after they sacked the town.

THE MUSEUMS

Volterra has two unmissable museums: the Museo Etrusco Guarnacci (Via Don Minzoni 13; mid-Mar to end Oct daily 9–7; Nov to mid-Mar 8.30–1.30; combined ticket with Pinacoteca), one of Italy's most important archaeological museums, and the Pinacoteca Comunale (Via dei Sarti; mid-Mar to end Oct daily 9–7; Nov to mid-Mar 8.30–1.30; combined ticket with Museo Etrusco), a fine painting collection in a lovely old palazzo. Etruscan fans should allow a good two hours for the Guarnacci's huge collection, which includes more than 600 funerary urns dating from the fourth to first centuries BC and some extraordinary bronze sculptures. The Pinacoteca presents a good overview of Sienese and Florentine painting. Its highlight is Rosso Fiorentino's *Deposition* (1521), one of the most compelling of all Mannerist works.

INFORMATION

www.provolterra.it

✚ 281 F7 ℹ Via Giusto Turazza 2, 56048 Volterra ☎ 0588 86159 or 0588 86150 ◑ Apr–end Oct daily 10–1, 2–7; Nov–end Mar 10–1, 2–6 ⛟ Saline di Volterra

Above *The ruins of the Roman theatre*

SIENA AND SOUTHERN TUSCANY

From Siena, this drive takes you south past the ancient abbeys of Sant'Antimo and Monte Oliveto Maggiore and the hilltop towns of Pienza, Montepulciano and Montalcino. Some of Italy's finest wines are produced in this region, so look for wine bars and shops where non-drivers can try a glass or two.

THE DRIVE

Distance: 190km (118 miles)
Allow: 11 hours (spread over 2 days, staying at Pienza or Montepulciano)
Start/end at: Siena

★ Leave Siena on the bypass, or *tangenziale*, heading south towards Rome, and take the last exit onto Via Cassia. In 3km (2 miles) you will see signs indicating 'Buonconvento 25'. After another 8km (5 miles) turn left, staying on the SR2 for Buonconvento. When you come to a crossroads, stay on the SR2. Bear right after the bridge to enter the town.

❶ The market town of Buonconvento (▷ 196), unusual in this area in that it is not perched on a hill, has a medieval old town and a small museum, the Museo d'Arte Sacra. It was once an important stop on the Via Francigena, the pilgrims' route that stretched from Canterbury to Rome.

Leave Buonconvento, following the SR2 through the town's outskirts. Turn right and take the SP45 towards Montalcino. The scenery becomes more pleasing and you will soon see the town on the hill ahead of you. Signs for *enoteche* (wine bars and shops), many of which offer free tastings, abound.
    After about 9km (6 miles), bear right at the top of the hill and join the SP14, following signs for Montalcino. With the city wall to the right you arrive at the roundabout

(traffic circle) at the top of the hill. There is free parking on the left and pay parking to the right, next to La Fortezza.

❷ Montalcino (▷ 203) is famous for its Brunello wine, characterized by an intense aroma and delicate, warm flavour with a hint of vanilla.

After exploring Montalcino, head for the Abbazia di Sant'Antimo by following the brown signs from the roundabout (traffic circle) at the top of the hill and getting on the SP55. The road now starts to wind downhill and in about 2km (1 mile) you should spot the abbey, nestling below the hills on the right-hand side. Turn right to reach the abbey.

Opposite *The Abbazia di Sant'Antimo*

❸ Abbazia di Sant'Antimo (▷ 195), set in a serene Tuscan landscape almost untouched by time, was once one of the richest abbeys in Tuscany. If you are feeling energetic it is a good starting point for a walk (▷ 217).

From here, return to the road and drive up the hill to Castelnuovo dell'Abate. Turn right at the top of the hill, following the sign indicating 'Stazione Monte Amiata' on the SP22. You will now pass the Val d'Orcia, from where the road begins to twist downhill. Pass over a level crossing (grade crossing) by Monte Amiata station and cross the River Orcia before coming into the hamlet of Monte Amiata, after which the road begins to climb again. When you reach the intersection, go to the left towards Castiglione d'Orcia. From here the road climbs even more steeply, with rewarding views. When you come to an intersection, take a left turn and pick up the SR323. Continue towards Castiglione d'Orcia.

❹ Castiglione d'Orcia has two churches worth seeing: the Romanesque church of Santa Maria Maddelena, and the church of Santo Stefano with its 16th-century façade and Madonnas by Simone Martini (1284–1344) and Pietro Lorenzetti (active 1320–48). At the heart of town is Piazza Vecchietta, named after the artist Lorenzo di Pietro (1412–80), who was known as Il Vecchietta and is claimed as a son by the town. It is overlooked by the Palazzo Comunale, where there's a fresco of the Madonna and Child with two saints in the Sienese school style, taken from the nearby village of Rocca d'Orcia.

Drive through the village, then head downhill. After 5km (3 miles) turn left at the intersection to take the SR2. Continue until you reach the intersection for Bagno Vignoni. Park just outside town, on top of the hill.

❺ Bagno Vignoni has been used as a spa since Etruscan times and is dominated by an enormous outdoor pool of warm, sulphurous water (▷ 196).

Go back downhill from the town, turn left at the end of the road and then take the next right onto the SP53 for Pienza. Turn left onto the SP18 and drive uphill, and you will see the red sandstone town of Pienza (▷ 207). Park at the bottom of the hill.

❻ Pienza is a UNESCO World Heritage Site. Its focal point is the Piazza Pio II, bordered by the Palazzo Piccolomini, the Palazzo Borgia and the cathedral. The cathedral has a pure Renaissance exterior and late-Gothic style interior, and contains several altarpieces by Sienese masters.

Leave Pienza and continue uphill until you come to an intersection. Turn right here for the SP146 and Montepulciano. Follow the road until you reach the town and park outside the walls.

❼ The picturesque hill town of Montepulciano (▷ 205) has sweeping views and a maze of steep, winding streets and alleyways. Besides the Renaissance church of San Biagio, the town has many wine shops where you can purchase bottles of Vino Nobile, the famous local wine, which has a delicate bouquet with violet scents. From Montepulciano, drive downhill. Turn right for Pienza on the 146 and after 7km (4 miles) turn right onto the SP15, a twisting road heading towards Torrita di Siena. Turn left just in front of a bar on the corner to join the SP57. Follow the road to an intersection where you take a sharp left past Petroio and then drive on for another 4km (2.5 miles), after which you turn right for Montisi. The road now descends in tight bends, passing through the woods until you reach an intersection. Turn left here and follow the SP14 through Montisi and on to the outskirts of San Giovanni d'Asso. When you come to the next intersection, turn right towards the Abbazia di Monte Oliveto Maggiore. Follow this road to Montefresco,

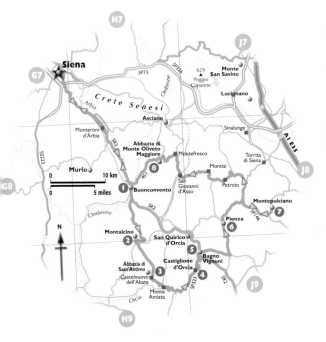

then turn left at the intersection and drive for another 3km (2 miles). At the next intersection go left, then quickly turn off to visit the late 13th-century abbey.

❽ The Abbazia di Monte Oliveto Maggiore (▷ 195), a Benedictine abbey, stands in a wooded park on a scenic rise and is still inhabited by monks. Pause to admire the famous frescoes in the main cloister.

WHEN TO GO
You can do this drive any time of year, but July and August are the hottest and busiest months, while the countryside is at its best in spring and autumn.

Below *A pretty courtyard in Pienza*

WHERE TO STAY
RELAIS IL CHIOSTRO DI PIENZA
▷ 237.

IL MARZOCCO
▷ 237.

WHERE TO EAT
FIASCHETTERIA ITALIANA
This lovely old café in Montalcino serves coffee, light meals and wine.
✉ Piazza del Popolo 6, Montalcino ☎ 0577 849043 🕐 7.30am–midnight

LA PARATA
La Parata, in Bagno Vignoni, serves *panini* and cakes, along with local cheese and olive oil. You can sit outside on fine days.
✉ Piazza Moretta 40, Bagno Vignoni ☎ 0577 887508; 🕐 Thu–Tue 10.30–2.45, 7.30–9.30

CAFFÈ POLIZIANO
Enjoy cakes, snacks or a glass of wine at this art nouveau café in Montepulciano. Meals are served in its restaurant.
✉ Via di Voltaia nel Corso 27–29, Montepulciano ☎ 0578 758615 🕐 Daily 7am–midnight

PLACES TO VISIT
MUSEO D'ARTE SACRA
✉ Via Socini 18, Buonconvento ☎ 0577 807181 🕐 Apr–end Oct Tue–Sun 10–1, 3–6; Nov–end Mar Sat–Sun 10–1, 3–5 ✋ €3.50

ABBAZIA DI SANT'ANTIMO
✉ Castelnuovo dell'Abate, Siena 53024 ☎ 0577 835659 🕐 Mon–Sat 10.15–12.30, 3–6.30; Sun 9.15–10.45, 3–5 ✋ Free

AROUND THE ABBAZIA DI SANT'ANTIMO

This walk starts at the serene Abbazia di Sant'Antimo, one of the finest Romanesque churches in Italy, dating back to the ninth century. It takes you past quiet woodlands and olive groves to the lovely hamlet of Villa a Tolli, where time seems to have stood still for centuries.

THE WALK

Distance: 6.4km (4 miles)
Allow: 1.5–2 hours
Start/end at: Abbazia di Sant'Antimo, near Castelnuovo dell'Abateo

From the parking area, walk towards the abbey. When you are in line with the abbey entrance, you will see a large brown sign on the right-hand side with details of this walk. Turn right and follow the wide track that was once the main Roman road.

After about 300m (330 yards) you'll come to a small stone hut where the path forks. There is a red-and-white mark painted on the hut, and this sign is used to denote the correct trail throughout the walk. Take the left-hand fork and continue ahead. If you are on the walk in spring this path will be laced with wild flowers. The landscape now closes in and your path is surrounded by woodland, with a farm on the left-hand side.

Keep following the trail, watching out for patches of heather where trees have been cut down. This was used locally to make brooms and is still commonly known as broom (*scopa*) in Italian.

Continue until you reach another fork and take the right-hand path. You will be walking through denser woodland now, full of glossy Mediterranean trees such as juniper. The path begins to climb and becomes rockier underfoot. Follow it to another fork, where again you will take the right-hand path. You should see a sign that points to Villa a Tolli.

Wind uphill, watching for the occasional red-and-white mark on the trees. This is a steep climb, which will eventually bring you to an olive grove on the left-hand side, and then to a broad trail.

On your left is a farmhouse, La Magia. Turn right, following the wide gravel trail. Eventually the trail winds to the right and you will see the tiny church and bell tower at Villa a Tolli.

Walk into the village, where there are workers' cottages and several wineries, where you maybe able to buy a bottle of wine.

From the village it is possible to continue following the trail all the way to Montalcino. Otherwise, retrace your steps to walk back to the abbey, turning left at La Magia, left at the next trail, then taking the right-hand fork to walk downhill.

From here you get superb views of the abbey.

WHEN TO GO

The best time to go is late spring or early summer (late April, May or early June) as many of the wild flowers will be in bloom. Alternatively, go in September or October to see the wine harvest.

WHERE TO EAT

There are a number of cafés in Castelnuovo and Montalcino, but you won't be able to get anything to eat or drink on the route itself, so take a picnic.

Above *Quiet woodlands and pastures surround the ninth-century Abbazia di Sant'Antimo*

217

SIENA, VOLTERRA AND SAN GIMIGNANO

This drive is through the kind of rolling countryside that typifies Tuscany. You travel along quiet roads through gently undulating hills, past olive groves, cypress trees and immaculately preserved hilltop towns and villages, many of which are generally overlooked by visitors.

THE DRIVE

Distance: 154km (96 miles)
Allow: 8 hours
Start/end at: Siena

★ From Siena, follow the bypass, or *tangenziale*, towards Florence. As the road climbs take the Siena Acquacalda exit and follow the road past some houses to a roundabout (traffic circle). Turn left here onto the Via Cassia to Monteriggioni.

❶ Monteriggioni's fortifications can be seen high on the hill. You have to park at the bottom of the town and continue on foot to the top. It's worth the climb to see this extraordinarily well-preserved medieval fortified town, encircled by tower-studded walls (▷ 206). From Monteriggioni follow the signs indicating 'Firenze 46'. At the T-junction, turn left at the sign for Colle di Val d'Elsa.

❷ The landscape now becomes flatter and is covered with vineyards; this area is known as Chianti Colle Senesi. When you reach a roundabout (traffic circle) you will see a large sign on the left saying CALP, indicating the works of one of the world's biggest producers of rock crystal.

Drive into Colle di Val d'Elsa, going uphill to reach the Colle Alta, the old part of town. Follow the parking signs and park in Via della Porta Vecchia.

❸ Colle di Val d'Elsa (▷ 200) is defined by three levels: Borgo (Borough), Castello (Castle) and Piano (Plain). It is renowned for the production of fine, handcrafted crystal. Enter the Borough through the Porta Nuova, gateway to a string of fine 16th- and 17th-century noble houses: the town hall, Palazzo

Usimbardi, Palazzo Buoninsegni and the magnificent, but unfinished, Palazzo Campana, which marks the entrance to the castle, the oldest part of Colle di Val d'Elsa. The Piazza del Duomo is overlooked by the 14th-century Palazzo Pretorio, now seat of the Museo Archeologico (Archaeological Museum), the 17th-century cathedral, and the Bishop's Palace, housing the Museo Civico e d'Arte Sacra (Museum of Religious Art). Via delle Volte, the most attractive corner of the town, leads off the square.

From Colle take the SR68, following signs for Volterra. After 6km (4 miles) the road climbs into the heart of the country. Go through Castel San Gimignano, after which there are glorious views of vineyards, olive groves, dark cypresses and fields of sunflowers. In the distance is the thermal electric plant at Larderello, 33km (21 miles) from Volterra. Look for steam rising from the underground thermal springs that spurt from these hills. After about 8km (5 miles) you should begin to see Volterra on the horizon as you reach the top of the hill, and shortly after that (1km/0.5 mile) you reach the town.

4 Volterra (▷ 213) was founded by the Etruscans, and has splendid medieval buildings and a Roman theatre.

Leave Volterra and follow the signs for Pontedera. After 4km (2.5 miles) you will see a yellow sign on the left-hand side for San Cipriano.

5 Photographers will find this little church an ideal spot for capturing the extensive views.

Alternatively, keep going and follow the SP15 as it winds its way steeply downhill, taking the right-hand fork and going over a modern bridge, until you reach an intersection. Take the exit for Firenze and follow the SP4 for about 9km (6 miles). Turn right and follow the signs for San Gimignano. You will see the town perched on a hill in the distance; drive up and park outside the town walls.

6 San Gimignano (▷ 208–210) is frequently referred to as the medieval Manhattan, because of its striking crown of towers. It's worth stopping to spend some time wandering around the unspoiled (if busy) streets.

Leaving San Gimignano, drive around the town walls to reach an intersection, where you turn right for Poggibonsi. Go straight over the next round-about towards Poggibonsi.

7 When you reach the uninspiring industrial town, go left at the next roundabout (traffic circle), and get onto the Superstrada Firenze-Siena to return to Siena.

WHEN TO GO
The scenery is so lovely that this drive is good any time of the year, but to miss the crowds try to avoid summer, visiting in early spring or late autumn.

WHERE TO STAY
HOTEL SAN LINO
▷ 238.

WHERE TO EAT
TRATTORIA DA BADÒ
Head to this *trattoria* in Volterra to sample some typical Tuscan dishes.
✉ Borgo San Lazzero 9, Volterra ☎ 0588 86477 🕙 Thu–Tue 12–2, 7–9.30

VILLA PALAGIONE
This elegant villa, just outside Volterra, off the SR439, is a lovely rural spot for a meal.
☎ 0588 391129 🕙 Apr–end Oct daily 7.30pm–9pm, lunch by arrangement.

GELATERIA DI PIAZZA
Gelateria di Piazza in San Gimignano's Piazza della Cisterna serves some of the best ice cream in Italy.
🕙 Mid-Feb to mid-Nov daily 9am–11pm

PLACES TO VISIT
MUSEO ARCHEOLOGICO
✉ Piazza del Duomo, Palazzo del Duomo, 53034 Colle di Val d'Elsa 🕙 Apr–end Oct Tue–Fri 10–12.30, 4.30–7.30; Nov–end Mar Tue–Fri 3.30–7.30, Sat, Sun 10–12, 3.30–6.30 ✋ €3

MUSEO CIVICO E D'ARTE SACRA
✉ Via del Castello 31, 53034 Colle di Val d'Elsa ☎ 0577 923888 🕙 Tue–Sun 10.30–12.30, 4.30–7.30 ✋ €3

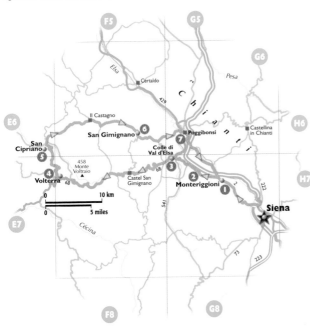

Above *Porta San Marco, historic gateway to the city of Siena*
Opposite *Hilltop Colle di Val d'Elsa*

SAN GIMIGNANO

The old hilltop town of San Gimignano, with its celebrated skyline, is one of the highlights of a visit to Tuscany. This walk introduces you to the town's main museums and churches, including the former cathedral. It also takes you off the well-trodden visitor route to explore some of the quieter streets where you can best soak up the town's medieval beauty.

THE WALK

Distance: 2.5km (1.5 miles)
Allow: 1–2 hours
Start/end at: Third (and last) parking area outside the city walls, called Parking No. 3 on Via Bagnaia

★ From the parking area, cross the road, go up some steps and enter the city walls. Turn right following Via Folgore da San Gimignano and Via XX Settembre. Turn left into Via San Matteo.

❶ Via San Matteo is surrounded by medieval palaces and towers. The same ornamental motifs appear on the façades: Window arches are decorated with friezes of arrowheads, and doors are framed by typically Tuscan arches, where the keystone is shaped like a teardrop. Halfway down the street on the left you pass the tiny Romanesque church of San Bartolo.

Continue along Via San Matteo to enter Piazza del Duomo.

❷ The piazza's beauty is striking, but the original purpose of the towers found here was grim. In medieval times, when inter-family conflict was rife, the towers were both status symbol and offensive and defensive fortress. Noble families, the *magnati*, crowned their palaces with these symbols of their wealth, each aiming to build higher than the next one. Today, just 14 of the original 72 towers survive.

Walk to the left-hand corner of the piazza and descend into Piazza della Cisterna.

❸ Piazza della Cisterna takes its name from the 13th-century well (*cisterna*) in the middle.

With your back to Piazza del Duomo,

leave Piazza della Cisterna by the right-hand corner, passing under the 12th-century Arco dei Becci. From here you can walk all the way down Via San Giovanni, which has some of the best shops, to the Porta San Giovanni.

❹ Porta San Giovanni is one of the city gates.

Turn right at the gate and right again at the sign for Madonna dei Lumi at the top of the steps on the left-hand side, where you will pass the Trattoria Chiribiri on the right. This means you are climbing back to the heart of San Gimignano along Via Berignano, a quiet residential street with unusual views of the towers crowning the highest point of the city. Here you will pass the La Mandragola restaurant (▷ 232). At the end of this street turn right then take the first left up Via della

Costarella. At the top, turn right through the archway leading into the frescoed courtyard of the Palazzo del Popolo.

❺ The Palazzo del Popolo, dating from 1323, contains the Museo Civico (▷ 209–210). The most beguiling exhibits are the wedding scene frescoes, dating from the 1320s, by Memmo di Filippuccio and his assistants. They show a happy couple taking a bath together and the groom stealing into bed alongside his sleeping bride. The energetic can climb the adjacent Torre Grosso for outstanding views.

Exit the Palazzo del Popolo and turn right, then immediately left under an arch into a small courtyard with the Collegiata on the right. This is Piazza Luigi Pecori.

❻ The Piazza has a loggia that is now the entrance to the Baptistery that shelters an *Annunciation* fresco by Ghirlandaio (1482). Musicians often perform on the opposite side of the square, next to the Palazzo della Propositura (Provost's house). There is also a small museum of religious art in the square.

Leave the square and turn left to reach the steps of the Collegiata (▷ 209) in Piazza del Duomo. Go through the Baptistery to enter the Collegiata.

❼ The Collegiata is modelled on the cathedral of Siena with its striped walls and star-covered vaults. The interior is a feast of frescoes. *The Last Judgement* scenes (1393–96) by Taddeo di Bartolo are the greatest attraction here since they depict a grotesque range of punishments being given to the damned by devils who are clearly relishing their task. Less gruesome are the scenes from Genesis (1367) by Bartolo di Fredi, which include an appealing depiction of the creation of Adam and Eve.

Turn left out of the Collegiata and left again at the church into Piazza

delle Erbe, and then walk along Via della Rocca. Look out for the signs to 'rocca e parco di Montestaffoli'. This will lead you to the Fortezza di Montestaffoli, which has good views of the city and surrounding countryside from its walls.

Backtrack to Piazza del Duomo, and leave by Via San Matteo. At the end you emerge by Porta San Matteo; turn right down Via Cellolese and left into Piazza Sant'Agostino.

❽ Sant'Agostino (▷ 210) is dominated by frescoes in the choir by Benozzo Gozzoli (*c*1421–97), illustrating the life of St. Augustine. They are fresh and vivid, full of the gentle landscapes that this painter so loved.

To return to your car, leave the square beside the church of San Pietro and walk back down Via Folgore da San Gimignano to

the gate in the city walls.

WHEN TO GO
Early morning and late afternoon are relatively quiet. Thursday, market day, is also a good time to visit.

WHERE TO EAT
OSTERIA DEL CARCERE
Choose from a range of simple, traditional dishes at this restaurant.
✉ Via del Castello 13 ☎ 0577 941905
🕐 Daily 12.30–2, 7.30–9.30)

GELATERIA DI PIAZZA
✉ Piazza della Cisterna 5 ☎ 0577 942244
🕐 Mid-Feb to mid-Nov daily 9am–11pm

PLACES TO VISIT
SANTO BARTOLO
✉ Via San Matteo 🕐 Daily 8–7 ✋ Free

SANT'AGOSTINO
🕐 Apr–end Oct daily 7–12, 3–7; Nov–end Mar 7–12, 3–6 ✋ Free

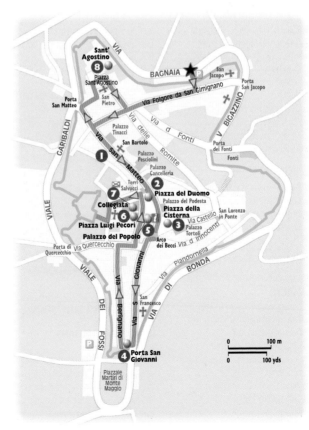

AREZZO

L'ALVEARE

This tiny store specializes in local produce. As its name suggests (*l'alveare* means 'the beehive'), the shop sells neatly packaged Aretine honey. Arezzo is part of a beekeeping region that stretches from Arezzo to Grosseto and produces honey of fine quality.
✉ Via Niccolò Aretino 19, 52100 Arezzo
☎ 0575 20769 🕐 Tue–Sat 9–12.30, 3.30–7.30, Mon 4–8

LA BELLE EPOQUE

La Belle Epoque deals in antique fabrics. The fragile laces and embroidered linens are dainty and make exquisite decorative items.
✉ Piazza di San Francesco 18, 52100 Arezzo ☎ 0575 355495 🕐 Mon–Sat 10–1, 5–8

DA ARETÈ

This busy ceramics shop sells a vast range of local terracotta, as well as arts and crafts. Look for the beautifully decorated, minuscule copies of Aretine buildings in terracotta, which make great gifts.
✉ Piazza Grande 38, 52100 Arezzo
☎ 0575 352803 🕐 Daily 10–7.30. Closed Jan

DE' CENCI

This is an excellent *pasticceria* (cake shop), and a great favourite among locals, especially on Sunday mornings, when they come to buy cakes and pastries to take to lunch with friends or relations. For excellent bread, also visit Boutique del Pane at Via Garibaldi 74 (tel 0575 354992; Mon–Sat 7.30–1, 5.30–7.30).
✉ Via de' Cenci 17, 52100 Arezzo ☎ 0575 231102 🕐 Tue–Sat 9–1, 4–8, Sun 9–1. Closed Aug

EDEN

This popular cinema is famous for its role in Roberto Benigni's 1997 film *La Vita é Bella* (*Life is Beautiful*) (▷ 252). Most films shown here are screened in their original language with subtitles. A bar sells drinks and snacks. Credit cards are not accepted.
✉ Via Guadagnoli 2, 52100 Arezzo
☎ 0575 353364 💷 Adult €7, child €5

LA FERROVIA ITALIANA

www.trenitalia.com
The LFI (La Ferrovia Italiana) railway, with its fleet of electric locomotives, links Arezzo with Stia, Bibbiena and Sinalunga. Take a ride for wonderful views over the surrounding countryside. If you are in the area at the right time, try to reserve seats on a steam train (tel 0575 300712, usually May and September, tickets cost €35).
✉ Piazza della Repubblica 1/a, 52100 Arezzo ☎ 0575 39881 🕐 Mon–Sat 16 services a day, Sun 4 services a day
💷 From €2, depending on distance

FIERA ANTIQUARIA

www.arezzofieraantiquaria.com
One of Italy's leading antiques fairs, the Fiera Antiquaria spills across Piazza San Francesco, Piazza Grande and the Logge Vasari. With more than 600 dealers, there are items ranging from 19th-century furniture to 17th-century glass and objects dating back to the Renaissance. The fair appeals to serious collectors as well as browsing visitors.
✉ Piazza di San Francesco, 52100 Arezzo
ℹ Via Cesalpina 28 ☎ 0575 377993
🕐 Apr–end Sep first Sun of the month 7.30–7; Oct–end Mar 7.30–3

GRACE

www.grace.it
Run by three friends, this trendy club and sushi restaurant has an interior verging on the kitsch, with art deco seating and 1970s lighting.

Opposite Bargain hunting at the Fiera Antiquaria in Arezzo's Piazza Grande

A variety of theme nights includes performances by local acts. Credit cards are not accepted.

✉ Via Madonna del Prato 125, 52100 Arezzo ☎ 0575 403669 ⏱ Fri midnight– 4am 🖐 From €15

GRACE GALLERY

The Grace Gallery has pride of place among the many antiques shops that line Arezzo's cobbled side streets. Specializing in furnishings and paintings, it also has a superb array of trompe l'oeil curiosities, bronzes and eccentricities. Browsers are welcome. There is also a second branch at Piazza Grande 30.

✉ Via Cavour 30, 52100 Arezzo ☎ 0575 354963 ⏱ Daily 9–12.30, 2.30–7

JOLLY

Jolly is a multi-screen cinema showing the latest blockbusters. Most of the films are screened in their original language with subtitles. There's also a bar serving drinks and snacks. Credit cards are not accepted.

✉ Via del Trionfo 27, 52100 Arezzo ☎ 0575 910395 🖐 Adult €7, child €5

MACELLERIA-GASTRONOMICA BARELLI

A *macellaria* is a butcher and Barelli is where the locals come to buy their *bistecca* (steak), among other excellent meats. The shop also sells a range of meat-dominated ready-made meals (useful if you are staying in a villa with a kitchen). If you just want a snack or choice of foodstuffs to take home, there is also a selection of olive oil and other general gastronomic treats.

✉ Via della Chimera 22/B, 52100 Arezzo ☎ 0575 357754 ⏱ Mon, Tue, Thu, Fri 8–1, 4–7, Wed, Sat 8–1 (also winter Sat 4–7). Closed 3 weeks in Aug

PANE E SALUTE

Come here for the bakery's *focaccia*, available in plain, wholegrain or olive. The deliciously light olive-oil bread is perfect for picnic lunches. A round,

flat loaf called *pane medievate* is the house classic.

✉ Corso Italia 11, 52100 Arezzo ☎ 0575 20657 ⏱ Mon–Sat 7.30–1.30, 4–8

SKATERPARK DI AREZZO

This skate park, 3km (2 miles) from downtown Arezzo, welcomes anyone who turns up. Locals come here to skateboard, rollerblade and BMX bike on the numerous multi-purpose ramps.

✉ Calamandrei Industrial Estate, Via Ferraris, 52100 Arezzo ⏱ Daylight hours 🖐 Free

TEATRO PETRARCA

Named after Arezzo's most famous poet and scholar, the Teatro Petrarca is renowned for its perfect acoustics and its performances of theatre, opera, ballet and classical music. Europe's largest choir competition, Guido d'Arezzo, takes place here at the end of August. Credit cards are not accepted.

✉ Via Guido Monaco 8/14, 52100 Arezzo ☎ 0575 23975 🖐 Adult €10–€30, child €9–€23

TESSITURA ARTIGIANA CASENTINESE

www.tacs.it

At this big retail outlet and factory you can purchase locally produced fashions made from Casentino (the mountainous area nearby) and textiles, and watch their 13 phases of production. The scarves make excellent gifts.

✉ Via Sanarelli 49, 52017 Stia ☎ 0575 583659 ⏱ Mon–Fri 8–12, 2–6, Sat 9.30–12 🚌 Take SS71 Umbria Casentinese road northwest towards Bibbiena, then follow signs for Stia

BUONCONVENTO
BOTTEGA DEL PANE

www.dolcezzedinanni.com

The staff here are proud to tell you how they supply the English Queen, Queen Elizabeth II, at Christmas with their freshly baked Tuscan goodies, such as *cantucci* (hard almond cookies for dunking in the sweet wine Vin Santo), *ricciarelli* (soft almond

cookies) and *panforte* (fruitcake) in various flavours. The unusual *amaretti* (macaroons) flavoured with lemon, orange or coffee are definitely worth a try.

✉ Via Roma 36, 53022 Buonconvento ☎ 0577 809016 ⏱ Mon–Sat 7.30–1, 5–7.30

IL POZZO DI SANTA LUCIA

A carefully chosen selection of household furnishings, super-sharp cooking knives, a variety of cooking utensils carved in olive wood, candles, tableware and bright ceramics can be found here: all perfect for gifts.

✉ Via Roma 42, 53022 Buonconvento ☎ 0577 809090 ⏱ Mon–Sat 9.30–1, 4–7.30

CHIANTI
ENOTECA DEL CHIANTI CLASSICO

www.chianticlassico.it

This well-established wine shop in Greve, capital of Chianti Classico, has a series of small rooms filled with bottles on wooden shelves. On display are 300 different examples of Chianti Classico, as well as a large selection of Super Tuscans and other Tuscan wines like the sweet Vin Santo.

✉ Piazzetta Santa Croce 8, 50022 Greve in Chianti ☎ 055 853297 ⏱ May–end Oct daily 9.30–1, 3–7.30; Nov–end Apr Thu–Tue 9.30–1, 3–7.30

MANIERA

www.maniera.net

American John Ryan and his Italian wife Daniela Tozzi display their fine handcrafted Tuscan goods in a converted old brick kiln—household linens, pottery, wooden furniture, glass, tableware, table silver from Florence, travertine marble plates and bowls, brass door knockers and fashion accessories. Special orders can be arranged.

✉ Fornace di Meleto, 53013 Gaiole in Chianti ☎ 0577 744023 ⏱ Mar–end Jan daily 10–6 🚌 1km (0.5 miles) from Gaiole just off the Siena road SS408; take turning to Rietine and Maniera is on the right after 500m (545 yards)

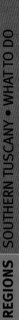

Above *Wine tasting at Enoteca La Fortezza in Montalcino*

CORTONA
IL COCCIAIO
www.terrabruga.com
One of Cortona's oldest and most creative ceramics shops is full of locally produced terracotta. The sunflowers that blanket the local fields in summer are rendered on the best-selling ceramic pieces.
✉ Via Nazionale 56, 52044 Cortona ☎ 0575 604405 🕐 Daily 9.30–1, 3.30–7.30

IL GIRASOLE
www.il-girasole.com
Owner Alessandra Federici scours the countryside to gather her stock of Tuscan arts and crafts. You will find ceramics, bronze and jewellery among the selection of gifts and houseware.
✉ Via Casali 2/4, 52044 Cortona ☎ 0575 601616 🕐 Daily 9.30–7.30. Closed Mon in winter

LORENZINI
A wonderful collection of hats for ladies and gentlemen—warm felts for the winter and straw hats for the summer. Many are by Borsalino, a famous name in Italy. You'll also find a big range of umbrellas and shoes.
✉ Piazza della Repubblica 18, 52044 Cortona ☎ 0575 603296 🕐 May–end Sep daily 9.30–8; Mar–end May, Oct–end Dec 10–1, 2.30–7.30. Closed Jan, Feb

ISOLA D'ELBA
GIANNINI
Elba is famous for its minerals, which are still mined and worked here. This big showroom displays an amazing collection of objects made from stones, crystals and semi-precious gemstones, including jewellery and ornaments such as little carved animals and trees made of crystal.
✉ Viale Italia 2, 57036 Porto Azzuro, Isola d'Elba ☎ 0565 95307 🕐 May to mid-Oct daily 9–midnight; mid-Oct to end Apr 9–1, 3–7

MUTI E LUPI
This is where you'll find the true original version of *schiaccia briaca*, an olive oil bread made with dried fruits and pine nuts, with the addition of some of the local wine, Aleatica, to give it its name and red appearance. The wine itself is also sold here, along with other home-made breads and cakes.
✉ Via Palestro 13, 57038 Rio Marina, Isola d'Elba ☎ 0565 962304 🕐 Jun–end Sep daily 7.15–1.30, 4–8.30; Oct–end May Mon–Sat 7.15–1.30

MONTALCINO
ENOTECA LA FORTEZZA DI MONTALCINO
www.enotecalafortezza.it
In this wine bar and shop inside the courtyard of the medieval fort, you can sample a glass of the famous local red wine, Brunello, with some simple food—cold meats or cheese with hunks of crusty bread—while gentle music plays in the background. More than 125 producers of Brunello are represented here, along with other Tuscan and national wines. Wine and olive-oil tastings can be arranged.
✉ Piazzale Fortezza, 53024 Montalcino ☎ 0577 849211 🕐 Apr–end Oct daily 9–8; Nov–end Mar 9–6

LE TELE ANTICHE
www.LeAnticheTele.com
Beautiful fabrics for household furnishings and linens are still handwoven in the traditional way in various parts of Tuscany, and here a tempting range is attractively displayed. Owner Alexia, a skilled needlewoman, will sew to order and ship worldwide.
✉ Via Mazzini 27, 53024 Montalcino ☎ 0577 849338 🕐 Easter–end Nov Tue–Sun 9.30–1, 4.30–8. Closed Sun Dec–Easter and 27 May–7 Jun

VILLA I CIPRESSI
www.villacipressi.it
Beekeeper Hubert Ciacci has beehives on his nearby estate, and his mother runs this retail outlet selling their products: honey, candles, cosmetics, soaps and various foods based on honey.
✉ Via Ricasoli 26, 53024 Montalcino ☎ 0577 848640 🕐 Mar–end Nov daily 10–8; Dec–end Feb Sat, Sun only

MONTEPULCIANO
BOTTEGA DEL RAME
www.rameria.com
Three generations of the Mazzetti family have been making copper kitchen utensils and decorative items—as you can see in their workshop near the shop at Piazza Teatro 4. They also sell lamps and walking sticks with unusual handles. Tax-free shopping and worldwide shipping can be arranged for non-EU customers.
✉ Via dell'Opio nel Corso 64, 53045 Montepulciano ☎ 0577 758753 🕐 Daily 9.30–1, 2.30–7.30

CANTINA DEL REDI
www.cantinadelredi.com
Look for the sign outside the Palazzo Redi on Via Ricci già della Mercanzia, which leads to the top entrance of this *cantina* (wine cellar). Follow the ramp winding through the cellars dating from 3,000 years ago, carved out of the rock. In the dim light you can see the huge oak barrels filled with the famous local wine—Vino Nobile di Montepulciano—which you can taste when you arrive at the bottom.
✉ Via di Collazzi 5, 53045 Montepulciano ☎ 0578 716092 🕐 Mar–end Dec daily 10.30–1, 3–7; Jan, Feb Sat, Sun 10.30–1, 3–7 🎟 Free

MALEDETTI TOSCANI
www.maledettitoscani.it
This spacious shop sells not only newspapers, but also outstanding leather goods: a big range of albums and assorted books bound in heavy leather and a collection of luggage to last a lifetime. It also sells pens, ink, seals and wax and photographs of the surrounding countryside.
✉ Via di Voltaia nel Corso 40, 53045 Montepulciano ☎ 0578 757130
🕐 Easter–end Oct daily 11–1, 3–7

MONTE SAN SAVINO
CERAMICHE ARTISTICHE LAPUCCI
The little town of Monte San Savino has been renowned for centuries for its ceramicware, with its distinctive floral decoration: You will see examples in the small Museo del Cassero on Piazza Gamurrini. Lapucci, a workshop in the historic centre, continues the tradition. The owner lives on the premises, so simply ring the bell if the shop seems shut.
✉ Corso Sangallo 8–10, 52048 Monte San Savino ☎ 0575 844375 🕐 Daily 9–12.30, 3.30–7.30

MONTEVARCHI
PRADA FACTORY OUTLET
Montevarchi is home to the Prada factory and its bargain outlet: bags, ties, lingerie and shoes at discounts of as much as 80 per cent. When you arrive, take a ticket from the machine and wait your turn to enter. If you can't find what you want in the Prada range, the store also stocks Miu Miu, Helmut Lang and Jil Sander.
✉ Località Levanella SS 69, 52025 Montevarchi ☎ 055 919 6528 🕐 Mon–Fri, Sun 10.30–8, Sat 9.30–8 🚗 Turn off A1 at junction Valdarno and follow the signs

PIENZA
BOTTEGA ARTIGIANA DEL CUOIO
Owner Valerio Truffelli sews all his leather goods by hand in his little shop. He makes almost anything to order, but you can buy ready-made belts, purses and notebooks. The cowhide skins come from near Pisa,

an area famous for tanning. A man's belt will cost you in the region of €27.
✉ Corso Il Rossellino 58, 53026 Pienza ☎ 0578 748730 🕐 Easter–end Nov Mon–Sat 9.30–1, 3–8, Sun 9.30–1; Dec–Easter daily 9.30–1

BOTTEGA DEL NATURISTA
You'll be offered tastings of pecorino in this shop, the locally produced cheese made with sheep's milk. There are many varieties, but look out for two in particular: a soft fresh type or a more mature one, sometimes seasoned in wine, or wrapped in walnut leaves and ashes. When you've made your selection, they'll vacuum-pack your purchases. There is also a tempting range of honey, dried herbs, vinegars and locally produced salamis and cured meats.
✉ Corse Il Rossellino 16, 53026 Pienza ☎ 0578 748081 🕐 Jun–end Aug daily 9.30–1, 3–8; Sep, Oct, Apr, May 9.30–1, 3–7. Closed Nov–Feb Wed

POPPI
PARCO ZOO DELLA FAUNA EUROPEA
www.parcozoopoppi.it
Opened in 1972 by vet Dr. Roberto Mattoni, this zoo exhibits specifically European animals, including deer, wolves, bears, birds of prey, and species in danger of extinction, such as the Asinara donkey. There are also pony rides, a botanical garden and a children's play area to add to the experience. A restaurant, bar, picnic area and free parking are available. Credit cards are not accepted.
✉ Zoo Fauna Europa, 52015 Poppi ☎ 0575 504541 or 504542 🕐 Daily 9–7 👉 Adult €6, child (3–11) €5 🚗 30–minute drive from Arezzo along SS71; follow signs for Bibbiena, then Parco Nazionale delle Foreste Casentinese or Parco Zoo Poppi

RAPOLANO TERME
ANTICA QUERCIOLAIA THERMAL BATHS
www.termeaq.it
Antica Querciolaia has been a spa resort since Etruscan times. Its spring provides thermal baths

and an adjoining park with three open-air pools. You can watch the water erupting from the famous intermittent fountain every 10 minutes and try a mud wrap or inhalation treatment.
✉ Via Trieste 22, 53040 Rapolano Terme ☎ 0577 724091 🕐 Daily 9–7
👉 Treatments from €21. Swimming pool: €11 Mon–Fri, €14 Sat, Sun 🚗 Rapolano is on the SS326; turn off at the A1 intersection Valdichiana and follow the signs

SAN GIMIGNANO
ANTICA LATTERIA
The friendly, family-run Antica Latteria (Old Dairy) is known for its regional gastronomic delicacies and locally produced wines. It's an excellent place to get goodies for a picnic or to pick up gourmet food to take home.
✉ Via San Matteo 19, 53037 San Gimignano ☎ 0577 941952 🕐 Daily 9–8

AVALON
www.avalon-pub.com
Avalon appeals to all tastes with its *birreria* (pub), *enoteca* (wine bar) and pizzeria, spread across three buildings in the old town. There is occasional live music and entertaining karaoke nights.
✉ Viale Roma 1/3/5, 53037 San Gimignano ☎ 0577 940023 🕐 Wed–Mon 12.30pm–2.30pm, 7pm–1.30am; pub only open 7pm–1.30am

BAR CAFFÈ GELATERIA COMBATTENTI
www.sangimignano.com
The self-proclaimed oldest bar in San Gimignano, this spot has been a bar, café and meeting place since 1924. Try the vintage grappa from beautiful hand-blown glass bottles.
✉ Via San Giovanni 124, 53037 San Gimignano ☎ 0577 940391 🕐 Mon, Wed–Sun 8am–midnight

BAZAR DEI SAPORI
Saffron was originally cultivated in various parts of the Siena province between the 12th and 15th centuries, but was eventually abandoned in favour of more profitable crops. This is one of 20

Above *A craftsman at work with alabaster in Volterra*

shops that make up Associazione Il Croco, an organization that promotes this precious spice. It is sold here in the raw form, along with other local produce such as ham.

✉ Via San Giovanni 8, 53037 San Gimignano ☎ 0577 942021 ◷ Feb–end Dec daily 9.30/10–6/8. Closed 10 days end Jan

CASE E COSE

On San Gimignano's main street, Case e Cose is filled with locally made arts and crafts. In addition to the ceramics, they sell bowls, chopping boards and other objects made from olive wood. The service is friendly and browsers are welcome.

✉ Via San Giovanni 99, 53037 San Gimignano ☎ 0577 942116 ◷ Apr–end Oct daily 9.30–7.30; Nov–end Mar 10–5.30/7

CINE ESTATE

On Saturdays and Sundays, and three nights a week, the public park hosts an outdoor cinema. Performances include Hollywood blockbusters and European art-house films in the original language.

✉ Rocca di Montestaffoli, 53073 San Gimignano ☎ 0577 940008 ◷ Jun–end Aug; days vary ⚏ Adult €6, child €5

COLLINE METALLIFERE

The Colline Metallifere hill range, named after the rich deposits of iron, lead, copper and pyrite that give the area its unusual colour, has various walking and cycling routes

that take you through gentle rolling countryside.

✉ Tourist office at Via Roncolla 38, 56045 Pomarance ☎ 0588 63187 ⬛ Take SS68 towards Volterra, turn right at Saline di Volterra onto SS439 towards Larderello

MUSEO CRIMINALE MEDIOEVALE

San Gimignano's Torture Museum is a rather gruesome presentation of a private collection of medieval instruments used for torture. All manner of items for all manner of misdeeds over the ages, including the Inquisition, are covered. Probably not for the fainthearted or very young. It's near the Piazza della Cisterna. Credit cards are not accepted.

✉ Via del Castello 1/3, 53037 San Gimignano ☎ 0577 942243 ◷ Mid-Mar to mid-Apr Mon–Sat 10–6, Sun 10–7; mid-Apr to early May daily 10–7; early May to mid-Jul daily 10–8; mid-Jul to end Aug daily 10–midnight; Sep, Oct daily 10–8; Nov to mid-Mar Mon–Fri 10–6, Sat 10–1, 2–6, Sun 10–1, 2–7 ⚏ Adult €8, child €5.50

MUSEO ORNITOLOGICO

This local ornithological collection showcases around 330 species of bird. It is particularly interesting for its presentation of extinct species and information on species on the verge of extinction. The owners have obviously put a lot of love and attention into this museum. Credit cards are not accepted.

✉ Chiesa di San Francesco, Via Quercecchio, 53037 San Gimignano ☎ 0577 941388 ◷ Apr–end Sep daily 11–5.30 ⚏ Adult €1.50, child €1

TENUTA TORCIANO

www.torciano.com

In the hills just outside San Gimignano, this shop is attached to a vineyard that has been run by the Giachi family since 1720. They have wine tastings and educational courses as well as selling their own olive oils. Try some local dishes with the excellent wine at the small restaurant.

✉ Via Crocetta 18, Ulignano, 53030 San Gimignano ☎ 0577 950055 ◷ Daily 9–8 ⬛ Exit Siena/Florence highway at

Poggibonsi Nord and follow signs for San Gimignano; once out of Poggibonsi look for the signs to Ulignano; after 6km (4 miles) there will be signs for the shop itself

TINACCI TITO & M. GRAZIA SNC

www.tinacci.com

You can choose from a wide range of Tuscan arts, crafts and design, ranging from expensive objects to inexpensive gifts, at a large showroom housed in renovated wine cellars in the old town. Take your pick from a wide range of ceramics, terracotta, wooden furniture and other items such as masks, religious articles and leather goods.

✉ Via San Giovanni 41/A, 53037 San Gimignano ☎ 0577 940345 ◷ Mar–end Oct daily 8–8; Nov–end Feb Tue–Sun 9–12.30, 2–6.30

SATURNIA
TERME DI SATURNIA

www.termedisaturnia.it

The thermal spring water feeding the pools at a constant temperature of 37°C (99°F) is said to benefit skin conditions, and joint and muscular aches. You can get treatments and medical advice. There is also a gym with trained staff, snack bar and changing rooms.

✉ 58050 Saturnia ☎ 0564 600111/600888 ◷ Pool: Apr–end Oct daily 9.30–7.30; Nov–end Mar 9.30–5.30. Treatment centre: daily 8am–9pm. Booking advisable Sat, Sun (☎ 0564 600301). Gym: daily 9–6.30 ⚏ Entry €22 per day; sunbed €7; full body massage €85

SINALUNGA
CIRO PINSUTI TEATRO

www.sinalunga.it/teatro

This small theatre, a copy of Milan's La Scala, is named after the best-known son of this well-preserved Etruscan town—the 19th-century composer Ciro Pinsuti. Local choirs, orchestras and jazz musicians perform here. Credit cards are not accepted, but you can reserve ahead.

✉ Via Umberto I, 53048 Sinalunga ☎ 0577 631200 ◷ Season: Nov–end Apr ⚏ Adult €10, child €5

TALLA

CASEIFICIO PRATOMAGNO
www.caseificiopratomagno.com

A scenic 30-minute drive from Arezzo, this shop in the town of Talla is worth the trip. It stocks a range of pecorini (sheep's milk cheeses; from €8), extra-virgin olive oils (from €6.50), honey (from €3.10), *prosciutto* (cured ham; from €10) and wines (from €3). Tours can be arranged.

✉ Via di Bicciano 29a, 52010 Talla ☎ 0575 597330 ⚀ Mon–Fri 9–12.30, 3–7.30, Sat 9–1.30 🚗 From Arezzo follow signs to Casentino then Talla, or from A1 intersection at Valdarno and again follow signs for Casentino then Talla

VOLTERRA

ENOTECA SCALI
www.enotecascali.com

Choose from one of over 700 wines, which range from top-of-the-line to a simple bottle of Chianti to drink with a picnic lunch. Also a wide selection of local cheeses, cured meats, salamis, fresh bread and other local specialties.

✉ Via Guarnacci 13, 56048 Volterra ☎ 0588 81170 ⚀ Mar–end Oct daily 9–8; Nov, Dec, Feb daily 9–1, 3.30–7.30

FABULA ETRUSCA
www.fabulaetrusca.it

Replicas of Etruscan gold jewellery, made on the premises. Custom-made designs can be commissioned or there is a wide range of ready-made items, with prices ranging from €50 for earrings.

✉ Via Lungo le Mura del Mandorlo 10, 56048 Volterra ☎ 0588 87401 ⚀ May–end Oct daily 10–7; Nov–end Feb Mon–Sat 9.30–1, 3–7.30 (open occasional Sun)

IL GIRASOLE

A gift shop with a great range of handcrafted and other gifts, from wooden toys to photo frames, quill pens and inks, seals and sealing wax, stencils, paper goods and a range of aromatherapy products.

✉ Via Buonparenti 15, 56048 Volterra ☎ 0588 85312 ⚀ Apr–end Sep daily 9–8; Oct–end May Mon–Sat 9–1, 3.30–7. Occasional Sun opening

FESTIVALS AND EVENTS

MAY

MOSTRA DEL CHIANTI
www.mostradelchianti.it

Montespertoli sits on a hill in the middle of the Chianti region and has spectacular views of Florence. One of the wine capitals of Tuscany, it is the perfect place to taste the best of the year's vintage. The Piazza San Pietro in the heart of the town is taken over by wine lovers and professional buyers who flock to this well-established event.

✉ Contact tourist office, Via Sonnino, 50025 Montespertoli ☎ 0571 657579 ⚀ One week, from last Sun in May

JUNE

ESTATE SAN GIMIGNANO
www.sangimignano.com

Arts festival with good music, including open-air opera recitals, classical concerts and film screenings in the ruins of the Rocca fortress. See Cine Estate (▷ 226).

✉ Piazza del Duomo 1, 53037 San Gimignano ☎ 0577 940008 ⚀ Mid-Jun to Aug 🎟 €14–€40

JULY

AREZZO WAVE
www.italiawave.com

Arezzo Wave is one of Italy's most important and enduring rock festivals, which explains the 250,000-strong audience it attracts. Around 150 different events take place during the week.

✉ Via Baronconte da Montefeltro 4/10, 52100 Arezzo ☎ 0575 401722 ⚀ First week in Jul 🎟 Free

ROSSI ALABASTRI
www.rossialabastri.com

Established in 1912, Rossi Alabastri is the oldest alabaster workshop in Volterra. Its stock ranges from simple dishes to large statues that show off the marvellous translucent quality of the stone. Worldwide shipping can be arranged.

✉ Via del Mandorlo, 56048 Volterra ☎ 0588 86133 ⚀ Apr–end Oct daily 9–1, 3–6; Nov–end Mar Mon–Fri 9–1, 3–6

VOLTERRA TEATRO
www.volterrateatro.it
www.boxol.it

Held in Volterra and the surrounding towns, this is Italy's leading avant-garde theatre festival. It includes experimental drama, dance and film, with a good variety of international acts performing in English.

✉ La Fortezza, 56048 Volterra ☎ 0588 80038/92736 ⚀ Mid- to late Jul 🎟 Tickets €22–€66

AUGUST/SEPTEMBER

BRAVIO DELLE BOTTE
www.valdichiana.it/montepulciano

This race, dating from 1372, sees a two-man team from each of Montepulciano's eight *contrade* (districts) rolling 80kg (176-lb) wine barrels, mainly uphill, through the town's streets to the Piazza Grande. Meanwhile there's plenty of dancing and drinking going on in the crowd that gathers to encourage the rollers.

⚀ Last Sun in Aug

GIOSTRA DEL SARACINO
www.giostradelsaracino.arezzo.it

A vibrant medieval celebration of chivalry and jousting that can be traced back to the 14th century, when Christian armies trained for the Crusades. The four opposing teams from the four quarters of Arezzo (Crucifera, Foro, Sant'Andrea, Santo Spirito) compete for the Lancia d'Oro (the Golden Lance) trophy.

✉ Piazza Grande, 52100 Arezzo ☎ 0575 377462 ⚀ Last Sun in Aug and first Sun in Sep 🎟 Free

PRICES AND SYMBOLS

The restaurants are listed alphabetically (excluding La, Il, Le and I). The prices given are the average for a two-course lunch (L) and a three-course dinner (D) for one person, without drinks. The wine price is for the least expensive bottle. All the restaurants listed accept credit cards unless otherwise stated.

For a key to the symbols, ▷ 2.

AREZZO

ANTICA OSTERIA L'AGANIA

www.agania.com

L'Agania looks the part of a traditional, old-fashioned *osteria*, decorated with an eclectic but pleasing mixture of old photographs, paintings and prints, wine bottles and strings of garlic and peppers. The menu offers simple, well-honed regional cooking, expertly prepared by a group of women, most of whom have worked at the restaurant for years.

✉ Via Mazzini 10, 52100 Arezzo
☎ 0575 295381 ⏰ Jul–end Aug daily 12–2.30, 7–10.30; Sep–end Jun Tue–Sun 12–2.30, 7–10.30. Closed a period in Jun
✋ L €18, D €27, Wine €13

Above *Atmospheric Buca di San Francesco, in the heart of Arezzo*

BACCO E ARIANNA

On the ground floor of an old building in the heart of town, Bacco e Arianna is a great wine bar, serving a good selection of food. Since the owner is an enthusiastic connoisseur, this is one of the best places in Arezzo for sampling local wines by the glass. Local cheeses and cured meats are served alongside Tuscan dishes and desserts.

✉ Via Cesalpeno 11, 52100 Arezzo
☎ 0575 299598 ⏰ Tue–Thu 10–7, Fri–Sat 10am– midnight, Sun 10–6 ✋ L €17, D €24, Wine €8

BUCA DI SAN FRANCESCO

www.bucadisanfrancesco.it

Right in the heart of Arezzo, this family-run restaurant is in the basement of a 14th- century medieval palace. The menu reflects the traditional cuisine of the area with dishes such as *ribollita* (a thick bean and cabbage soup) and Chianti beef stew. A list of famous patrons includes Charlie Chaplin, Salvador Dalì and President Truman. Reservations are advisable.

✉ Via San Francesco 1, 52100 Arezzo
☎ 0575 23271 ⏰ Wed–Sun 12–2.30, 7–9.30, Mon 12–2.30. Closed 2 weeks in Jul
✋ L €14, D €28, Wine €9

LA TORRE DI GNICCHE

This small bar seats just 30, but in the summer people spill out on to the terrace. A menu is available but regular customers here trust the knowledgeable staff to decide between the snacks, sandwiches and local main dishes that change regularly with the seasons. They have a good selection of local cheeses, and a wine list that includes the local Colli Aretini.

✉ Piaggia San Martino 8, 52100 Arezzo
☎ 0575 352035 ⏰ Thu–Tue 12–3, 6–1am
✋ L €8, D €22, Wine €12

BAGNO VIGNONI

IL LOGGIATO

Described as a wine bar, this establishment feels more like a farm kitchen of 100 years ago. Baskets and herbs hang from the ceiling and a big wooden bread chest stands in the corner. All dishes are fresh and home-made: warming soups, cakes, pastries, local meats and cheeses. Gentle jazz music plays softly in the background. Opening times tend to be as individual as the place.

✉ Piazza delle Sorgenti 36, 53020 Bagno Vignoni, Siena ☎ 0577 888973
⏰ Mar–end Dec Fri 6pm–midnight, Sat, Sun 9am–midnight ✋ L & D €14, Wine €10

OSTERIA DEL LEONE

This sophisticated restaurant serves delicious regional dishes such as light pastry topped with melted fresh sheep's cheese and generous helpings of local grilled meats. There's a dedicated menu for vegetarians and all the food is fresh and seasonal.

✉ Piazza del Moretto, 53020 Bagno Vignoni, Siena ☎ 0577 887300 🕐 Tue–Sun 12.30–2.30, 7–10. Closed periods in Nov and Feb ✋ L €13, D €28, Wine €10

BUONCONVENTO
RISTORANTE DA MARIO

This family-run *trattoria* is popular with locals, who come to enjoy the home cooking, and visitors are warmly welcomed. Try the freshly made Tuscan pasta or the soup made from spelt, a type of grain that was grown by the Etruscans. There's a little garden at the back for summer eating.

✉ Via Soccini 60, 53022 Buonconvento, Siena ☎ 0577 806157 🕐 Sun–Fri 12–2.30, 7.30–9.30. Closed Aug ✋ L €10, D €22, Wine €4

CERTOSA DI MAGGIANO
IL CANTO

www.certosadimaggiano.com
The celebrated restaurant of the Hotel Certosa di Maggiano (▷ 235) is in a former monastery dating from 1314. Meals are created from the hotel's farm produce. Visit the rustic kitchen for breakfast or sit by the pool in summer.

✉ Strada di Certosa 82, 53100 Siena ☎ 0577 288180 🕐 Thu–Mon 12.30–2.30, 8–10, Wed 8–10. Closed 10 Dec–10 Feb ✋ L €44, D €72, Wine €20

CAPRESE MICHELANGELO
BUCA DI MICHELANGELO

In an old stone house at Caprese Michelangelo, this eatery is in a quiet area with panoramic views over the Tevere Valley forests and is well suited to those who like a long walk to build up an appetite. The house where Michelangelo was born is only a brief stroll away. Tuscan dishes fill the menu, and on Sundays a hearty Tuscan multi-course lunch

is served. The wine list has a few local labels.

✉ Via Roma 51, 52033 Caprese Michelangelo ☎ 0575 793921 🕐 Jun–end Sep daily 1–2.30, 8–9.30; Feb–end May, Oct–end Dec Fri–Wed 1–2.30, 8–9.30 ✋ L €22, D €41, Wine €10 🚗 Take SS71 from Arezzo towards Bibbiena, turn right to Anghiari, then left to Caprese Michelangelo

CHIANTI
DELLA PIEVE

www.spaltenna.it
This is the restaurant of the Castello di Spaltenna hotel (▷ 235), a beautifully converted monastery on the outskirts of Gaiole in Chianti. The restaurant has a lovely setting, in the former monastery's cloister and dining outside by candlelight on a summer evening is a truly memorable experience. The menu is a sophisticated take on Tuscan staples, and changes with the season.

✉ Località Pieve di Spaltenna, 53013 Gaiole in Chianti ☎ 0577 749483 🕐 Easter–end Oct daily 12.30–2.30, 8–9.30 ✋ L €30, D €45

IL CARLINO D'ORO

The family have been running this little *osteria* for nearly 50 years; you can look into the kitchen and watch Mamma seasoning her chicken with local fresh herbs before spit roasting it on the big open hearth. It is always packed—mostly with locals. Arrive early to be sure of a table; otherwise reservations are essential. It is only open for lunch, except on weekends in the summer.

✉ Località San Regolo 33, 53013 Gaiole in Chianti, Siena ☎ 0577 747136 🕐 Tue–Sun 12–2 ✋ L €13, Wine €5 🚗 Follow SP484 between Radda in Chianti and Castelnuovo Berardenga. At Castello di Brolio take turning to Pianella—San Regolo is then less than 1km (0.5 mile)

RISTORANTE BADIA A COLTIBUONO

www.coltibuono.com
The Abbey of Coltibuono is the home of cookery writer Lorenza de' Medici, and her son Paolo Stucchi Prinetti runs this attractive

restaurant. Most of the recipes used are Lorenza's, with a lighter approach to traditional Tuscan cooking. Extra-virgin olive oil and Chianti wine also come from the family estates. It's worth making a reservation, as the restaurant is some distance from Gaiole, and very popular.

✉ 53013 Gaiole in Chianti, Siena ☎ 0577 749424/749031 🕐 May–end Oct daily 12.15–2.30, 7.15–9.30; Mar and early Nov Tue–Sun, 12.15–2.30, 7.15–9.30. Closed mid-Nov to Feb and Mon Mar, Apr ✋ L €18, D €40, Wine €8 🚗 Take SP429 from Radda in Chianti towards Montevarchi (6km/ 3.5 miles from Radda)

RISTORANTE DA ANTONIO

Crisp, snowy white is used throughout this elegant restaurant to create a cool, minimal atmosphere and show off the beautifully presented food and wine. The owners go daily to Viareggio to get their fish fresh from the market there and menus vary accordingly. No meat dishes are served. Reservations are advisable, especially for dinner.

✉ Via del Chianti 28/32, 53019 Castelnuovo Berardenga, Siena ☎ 0577 355321 🕐 Tue–Sat 1–2.30, 8–10.30, Sun 11–2.30. Closed Nov ✋ L €44, D €66, Wine €14 🚗 Follow the signs for Castelnuovo Berardenga on SP484, off the Siena/ Sinalunga road (SP326); it is on the road to San Giusme on the edge of town

TRATTORIA DEL MONTAGLIARI

www.montagliari.it
This *trattoria* is on an idyllic wine estate 5km (3 miles) from Greve. The menu's highlights include pasta ribbons with rich wild boar sauce, home-made ravioli and guinea fowl with an intense wine sauce. The estate produces Chianti Classico and Riserva, Vin Santo and Amaro— all of which you can buy in the estate shop.

✉ Via Montagliari 29, 50020 Panzano, Greve in Chianti, Firenze ☎ 055 852014 🕐 Tue–Sun 12.30–2.30, 7.30–9.30; open Mon on public holidays. Closed 10 Jan– 20 Feb ✋ L €14, D €28, Wine €7.50 🚗 On the SS222 from Siena to Florence

Above *Grappolo Blu restaurant, near the main square in Montalcino*

and many half-bottle options. The food embraces such key Tuscan staples such as *pappa al pomodoro*, *pappardelle sulla lepre* (pasta with a hare sauce) and wild boar, but with fine one-off dishes such as *tagliolini* (fine pasta) with a sauce of duck and wild fennel.

✉ Via Maffei 2, 52044 Cortona ☎ 0575 630556 🕐 Thu–Tue 12.30–2.30. 7.30–10.30. Closed 2 weeks in Nov ✋ L €25, D €32, Wine €13

COLLE DI VAL D'ELSA
L'ANTICA TRATTORIA
Despite a location in the more modern, lower part of the town, this restaurant stands in a pleasant square (you can dine outdoors in summer) and has a lovely, old-fashioned interior. Generally Tuscan in inspiration, the food often has a creative twist. The service is practised and pleasantly informal.
✉ Piazza Arnolfo 23, 53034 Colle di Val d'Elsa ☎ 0577 923747 🕐 Wed–Mon 12.30–2.30, 7.30–10.30. Closed Tue, mid-Dec to mid-Jan and a period in Aug ✋ L €28, D €35, Wine €13

ARNOLFO
www.arnolfo.com
The Arnolfo has maintained its reputation for excellent cuisine over many years. The setting, in a townhouse in the old, upper town, is elegant and the cooking is sophisticated—a main course might include *piccione in due cotture con fave di cacao e cipolline* (pigeon with cocoa beans and bay onions)—but remains true to Tuscan tradition and uses the best local ingredients. If you wish to stay, the restaurant also offers four pretty rooms from €180.
✉ Via XX Settembre 50/52, 53034 Colle di Val d'Elsa ☎ 0577 920549 🕐 Thu–Mon 12.30–2.30, 7.30–10.30. Closed Tue, Wed ✋ L €50,D €90, Wine €18

CORTONA
IL FALCONIERE
www.ilfalconiere.it
When you eat at this old country hotel, you can choose between the elegant period charm of the dining room, the wrought-iron and glass conservatory or the outdoor terrace with a view over the Val di Chiana. The modern Italian menu includes home-made pasta and locally produced olives and grapes. The wine list highlights the local Baracchi vineyard. Reservations advisable.
✉ Località San Martino 370, 52044 Cortona ☎ 0575 612679 🕐 Mar–end Oct daily 1–2, 8–10; Nov–end Feb Tue–Sun 1–2, 8–10 ✋ L €25, D €72, Wine €20
🚗 Just north of Cortona, on the main road towards Arezzo, is a turning on the right to San Martino

LA LOCANDA NEL LOGGIATO
A family-run restaurant, La Locanda nel Loggiato is in a pretty medieval lodge overlooking the little square in Cortona. Choose from indoor or outdoor dining. The high quality of the restaurant's local cuisine attracts people from the surrounding area as well as visitors, so reservations are necessary during the summer months.
✉ Piazza di Pescheria 3, 52044 Cortona ☎ 0575 630575 🕐 Thu–Tue 12.30–3, 7.15–11 ✋ L €11, D €19, Wine €6

OSTERIA DEL TEATRO
www.osteria-del-teatro.it
Small steps lead to this restaurant made up of three dining rooms, each different. Photographs of actors and actresses who have performed over the years at the nearby Teatro Signorelli adorn the walls. Wine is excellent, with over 600 labels from which to choose

ISOLA D'ELBA
LA CANOCCHIA
In the two simple rooms here, the rough whitewashed walls are hung with nautical prints and pictures. You will find classically cooked fish dishes using only the finest, freshest ingredients—food you can only find at a restaurant within striking distance of the sea. The island's wines make the ideal accompaniment. Reservations advisable in the evenings.
✉ Via Palestro 2/4, 57038 Rio Marina, Isola d'Elba, Livorno ☎ 0565 962432 🕐 May–end Sep daily 12.30–2.30, 7.30–midnight; Oct, Feb–end Apr Tue–Sun. Closed Nov–Jan ✋ L €13, D €33, Wine €12

STELLA MARINA
www.ristorantestellamarina.com
Long a popular choice in Elba's main town, Stella Marina has a good position on the port, with a plentiful supply of fresh fish and seafood. There is also an excellent selection of wines, grappa and other spirits and liqueurs. You can just have simply grilled fish if you wish, but the menu also offers more creative fish and seafood options.
✉ Via Vittorio Emanuele II 1, 57037 Portoferraio ☎ 0565 915983 🕐 Mid-Jun to end Sep daily 12–2.30, 7–10.30; Oct to mid-Jun Tue–Sat 12–2.30, 7–10.30 ✋ L €23, D €35, Wine €15

ISOLA DEL GIGLIO
DA MARIA
At the top of the hill at the far end of the medieval walled village, Da Maria has been a *trattoria* for three generations. In the tranquil white-walled rooms, you feel as though

you are a family guest rather than a customer. You get home cooking at its best, with freshly caught fish to the fore. The *trattoria* is small, so reservations are advisable.

✉ Via della Casa Matta, Giglio Castello, 58012 Isola del Giglio, Grosseto ☎ 0564 806062 ⏱ Thu–Tue 12.30–2.30, 7.30–9.30. Closed Jan–end Mar ✋ L €11, D €28, Wine €10

MONTALCINO
CASTELLO BANFI
www.banfi.it

Banfi, 19km (30 miles) southwest of Montalcino, is one of the main Brunello vineyards, and there is no mistaking the magnificent castle that sits at the heart of its domain. This is home to the multi-award-winning Castello Banfi restaurant and more informal Taverna Banfi. Both the setting—the castle lies in beautiful countryside—and the food are memorable, and merit the trip from Montalcino.

✉ Località Sant'Angelo Scalo, 52034 Montalcino ☎ 0577 816054 ⏱ Castello Banfi: Tue–Sat 7.30pm–11pm. Closed Sun, Mon, Jan and Aug. Taverna Banfi: Mon–Sat 12.30–3. Closed Sun, 2 weeks in Jan and Aug ✋ Castello Banfi: D €80, Wine from €15. Taverna Banfi: L €25, Wine from €15

FIASCHETTERIA ITALIANA
A local institution, this is the best and most conveniently situated of Montalcino's many cafés and wine bars, thanks to its 19th-century interior and central position on the town's main square. You can buy local wine by the glass or by the bottle, and there is a selection of *antipasti* and light meals.

✉ Piazza del Popolo 6, 53024 Montalcino ☎ 0577 849043 ⏱ Daily 7.30am–midnight. Closed Thu from Nov–Feb ✋ L and D €15, Wine from €3 by the glass

GRAPPOLO BLU
Down some steps from the main piazza is Luciano's great restaurant. Terracotta floors, scrubbed tables and rush-seated chairs marry happily with the white walls and beamed ceiling—true Tuscan style. Eat Tuscan bean soup, *crostini* with a

variety of different toppings, and shin of beef in balsamic vinegar—but leave room for the meltingly delicious lemon tart.

✉ Via Scale di Moglio, 53024 Montalcino, Siena ☎ 0577 847150 ⏱ Daily 12–3.30, 7.30–10. Closed period mid-Jan to mid-Feb ✋ L €14, D €25, Wine €8

OSTERIA AL GIARDINO
The air of cool modernity in this white-walled osteria contrasts with the hearty, warming Tuscan cooking. Dishes include home-made pasta with a spicy tomato sauce or the locally farmed rabbit in a special sauce. For dessert there's a tiramisu to die for.

✉ Piazza Cavour 1, 53024 Montalcino, Siena ☎ 0577 849076 ⏱ Thu–Tue 12.15–2.30, 7.30–9.45. Closed mid-Jan to mid-Feb ✋ L €17, D €39, Wine €15

TAVERNA DEI BARBI
www.fattoriadeibarbi.it

This smart restaurant is annexed to a Brunello vineyard 5km (3 miles) southeast of Montalcino. You can enjoy good local cooking and home-produced wines in a tasteful, rustic dining room dominated by a vast stone fireplace.

✉ Fattoria dei Barbi, La Croce, Località Podernovi, 52034 Montalcino ☎ 0577 847117 ⏱ 12.30–2.30. 7.30–10.30. Closed Tue pm, Wed (except Aug), Jan and 2 weeks in Jul. Opening times are subject to change ✋ L €20, D €27, Wine €15

MONTEPULCIANO
CAFFÈ POLIZIANO
This bar/café, with marble-topped tables and upholstered benches around the walls, seems to be in a time warp. It's been like this since 1868, serving hot chocolate and teas and the usual drinks. Light lunches of omelettes, pastas and salads are served in the spacious ground-floor rooms. Downstairs is an elegant restaurant open only in the evening for dinner.

✉ Via di Voltaia nel Corso 27–29, 53045 Montepulciano, Siena ☎ 0578 758615 ⏱ Daily 7am–midnight. Restaurant Mon–Sat 7pm–10.30pm. Closed Feb ✋ L €8, D €33, Wine €14.50

IL CANTUCCIO
www.ristoranteilcantuccio.com

This typically Tuscan restaurant serves straightforward food—mixed salami, *crostini*, grilled meats, sausages and gently simmered beans. Summer salad with bread, tomatoes and herbs and roast rabbit are sometimes on the menu. The house wine is fine, but you might prefer the Vino Nobile di Montepulciano on its home ground. For friendly service and good value, Il Cantuccio can't be beaten. It is very busy at lunchtime with day visitors but quieter in the evenings.

✉ Via delle Cantine 1, 53045 Montepulciano, Siena ☎ 0578 757870 ⏱ Tue–Sun 12–2.30, 7.30–10 ✋ L €17, D €28, Wine €9

LA GROTTA
This well-established restaurant has such delights as ravioli stuffed with pigeon in a saffron sauce and duck cooked with juniper berries and honey. Excellent service and a large wine list, including a good choice of the local Vino Nobile di Montepulciano. Reservations are advisable.

✉ Località San Biagio, 53045 Montepulciano, Siena ☎ 0578 757607 ⏱ Thu–Tue 12.30–2.15, 7.30–9.30. Closed Jan, Feb ✋ L €28, D €50, Wine €12

OSTERIA BORGO BUIO
www.borgobuio.it

Borgo Buio occupies 14th-century wine cellars and is decorated with numerous antiques. Expect simple Tuscan cooking, with dishes such as vegetable tartlets to start and *coniglio ripieno* (stuffed rabbit) and *polpettone* (meatloaf) to follow.

✉ Via di Borgo Buio 10, 53045 Montepulciano ☎ 0578 717497 ⏱ Daily 12.30–2.30, 7.30–10.30 ✋ L €20, D €28, Wine €12

MONTE SAN SAVINO
LA TERRASSE
www.ristorantelaterrasse.it

La Terrasse faces the main gateway into the medieval village of Monte San Savino, 19km (12 miles) from Arezzo. The menu includes local and national dishes, and the wine list is international.

✉ Via di Vittorio 2/4, 52048 Monte San Savino ☎ 0575 844111 ◷ Thu–Tue 12–2.30, 7–10.30. Closed 2–3 weeks in Nov ⊔ L €17, D €28, Wine €6

MONTERIGGIONI
RISTORANTE CASALTA
www.ristorantecasalta.it

A restaurant with a changing repertoire of basically Tuscan recipes in a light, modern style. Try grilled prawns on a white bean purée or breast of guinea fowl stuffed with spinach and foie gras. There is an extensive list of Italian and foreign wines. Booking for dinner is recommended.

✉ Via Matteotti 22, Strove, 53035 Monteriggioni ☎ 0577 301171 ◷ Thu–Tue 1–2, 8–10. Closed 10 Jan–10 Feb ⊔ L €22, D €50, Wine €15 🚗 Turn off the Florence/Siena superstrada at Monteriggioni; follow signs for Colle di Val d'Elsa; turn left through Abbadia Isola and on to Strove; it is just beyond the church on the right (15km/9 miles from Siena)

PIENZA
CAFFÈ DELLE VOLPE
The emphasis here is on natural, healthy food and drink. Fresh fruit or vegetable juices are served with filled crêpes or assorted *panini* (filled rolls). Also good ice creams and a big range of teas. Credit cards are not accepted.

✉ Via delle Case Nuove 7, 53026 Pienza, Siena ☎ 347 404 3450 ◷ May–end Sep daily 8–8; Oct–end Apr Tue–Sun 8–8 ⊔ *Panini* from €12

DAL FALCO
www.ristorantedalfalco.toscana.nu

There's a tree-shaded piazza outside Pienza's walls, from where an archway leads through to Falco. The terracotta floors, whitewashed walls and dark wood add charm, but the strip lighting detracts from the atmosphere. The food is truly Tuscan: expect *crostini* (toasted crusty bread) with liver, olives and tomato, steaming pasta and plainly grilled meat. They do great *salsicce* (home-made sausages) and delicious

formaggio al prosciutto (grilled cheese wrapped in parma ham).

✉ Piazza Dante 3, 53026 Pienza, Siena ☎ 0578 748551 ◷ Sat–Thu 12.30–3, 7–10 ⊔ L €11, D €22, Wine €10

LATTE DI LUNA
Roberto and his family own and run this popular restaurant famed for its *maialino* (roast sucking pig) and *semifreddo al aranci* (a soft ice cream with an intense orange taste). There is a small outside terrace. It's very lively and always packed, so reservations are definitely advisable.

✉ Via San Carlo 2, 53026 Pienza, Siena ☎ 0578 748606 ◷ Wed–Mon 12–2.30, 7.30–10. Closed periods in Feb and Jul ⊔ L €13, D €28, Wine €10

SAN GIMIGNANO
BAR LE TORRI
This is a large and airy café, but in good weather you can take advantage of the outdoor seating on the Piazza del Duomo. Light lunches are served, and the pastries here are highly recommended.

✉ Piazza del Duomo 10, 53037 San Gimignano ☎ 0577 940746 ◷ 7am–9.30pm. Open Mon on public holidays ⊔ L €6, D €6, Wine €10

BEL SOGGIORNO
www.hotelbelsoggiorno.it

Within the city walls, Bel Soggiorno shares a 13th-century building with a hotel of the same name. The restaurant has been run by the same family for five generations, who serve dishes following Etruscan and medieval recipes. Traditional furnishings and a glass wall giving views over the rolling hills add to the charm. Reservations advisable.

✉ Via San Giovanni 91, 53073 San Gimignano ☎ 0577 940375 ◷ Thu–Tue 12.30–2.30, 7.30–10. Closed mid-Feb to end Mar and late Nov–26 Dec ⊔ D €45, Wine €8

DORANDÒ
www.ristorantedorando.it

In a 14th-century building, the Dorandò lies between Piazza del Duomo and Piazza della Cisterna. Some of the menu's dishes are

based on Etruscan and medieval recipes, but each has a modern twist. The desserts are delicious. Reservations are essential.

✉ Vicolo dell'Oro 2, 53037 San Gimignano ☎ 0577 941862 ◷ Easter–end Oct daily 12.30–2.30, 7.30–9.30; Nov–Easter Tue–Sun 12.30–2.30 7.30–9.30. Closed mid-Jan to mid-Feb ⊔ L €28, D €44, Wine €8

LA GROTTA GHIOTTA
La Grotta Ghiotta specializes in produce from San Gimignano. It is recommended for the quality of the food, the low prices and the escape it provides from the bustle of the crowds. The menu includes wonderful cured hams, olives, local cheeses, honey and fresh bread, and there's also a good wine list.

✉ Via Santo Stefano 10, 53037 San Gimignano ☎ 0577 942074 ◷ Apr–Oct daily 12–8; Nov–Mar daily 9–3 ⊔ L €11, D €17, Wine €5

LA MANDRAGOLA
www.locandalamandragola.it

A large, busy restaurant, La Mandragola serves Tuscan dishes that include home-made breads and locally harvested mushrooms and truffles. Local wines fill the list, making the restaurant popular with visitors on wine tours. Reservations are advisable.

✉ Via Berignano 58, 53037 San Gimignano ☎ 0577 942110 ◷ Easter–end Oct daily 12–2.30 7.30–10; Nov–Easter Fri–Wed 12–2.30 7.30–10 ⊔ L €17, D €28, Wine €9

OSTERIA DEL CARCERE
The Slow Food movement has given its seal of approval to this tiny, 30-seat restaurant. The food is resolutely Tuscan, but has the occasional more unusual touch (such as guinea fowl with chestnuts). There are also inventive salads and several choices for vegetarians. The two young owners are sommeliers as well as cooks, so the 90-strong wine list is as good as the food.

✉ Via del Castello 13, 53037 San Gimignano ☎ 0577 941905 ◷ Mid-Mar to mid-Jan Fri–Tue 12.30–2.30, 7.30–10.30, Thu 7.30–10.30. Closed Wed ⊔ L €22, D €32, Wine €12

OSTERIA DELLE CATENE

The interior of Osteria delle Catene is an interesting mix of handmade medieval brickwork and contemporary paintings and lighting. The menu includes classic as well as unusual local dishes, with an emphasis on saffron, the spice on which San Gimignano built its wealth. Try the saffron soup or wild boar with black cabbage, accompanied by wine from their local selection. Advance reservations are needed in high season.

✉ Via Mainardi 18, 53037 San Gimignano ☎ 0577 941966 🕐 Thu–Tue 12.30–2, 7.30–9.30 🍴 L €17, D €29, Wine €8

IL PINO

www.ristoranteilpino.it

A family-run restaurant close to the Porto di San Matteo in the heart of the town, with brick arches and candlelit rooms giving it a medieval atmosphere. Classical San Gimignano dishes are prepared with locally sourced ingredients, including *bruschetta* with wild boar, *crostini* with salmon and mascarpone, saffron soup, and pork fillet with Chianti and juniper sauce. Local vineyards are represented on the wine list. Reservations are advisable.

✉ Via Cellolese 6, 53037 San Gimignano ☎ 0577 942225 🕐 Fri–Wed 12.30–2.30, 7.30–10. Closed 16 Nov to 16 Dec 🍴 L €28, D €44, Wine €9

LE TERRAZZE

www.hotelcisterna.it

This restaurant is in the Cisterna Hotel, and its main draw is the views over San Gimignano. Although there is no outdoor seating, one wall in the 14th-century dining room is all glass, providing the illusion of alfresco dining all year round—as well as magnificent, panoramic views. Traditional Tuscan and San Gimignano cuisine and a wide selection of wines, both local and national.

✉ Piazza della Cisterna 23, 53037 San Gimignano ☎ 0577 940328 🕐 Fri–Mon 12.30–2.30, 7.30–9.30, Wed–Thu 7.30–9.30 🍴 L €17, D €33, Wine €10

SAN VINCENZO
GAMBERO ROSSO

Fulvio Pierangelini's restaurant is one of only a handful in Tuscany to possess two Michelin stars. It is in a light, airy room overlooking the marina at San Vincenzo. Although the menu has some meat dishes, most people come here to sample the exquisite fish and seafood. The set, multi-course *menù degustazione* of Gambero Rosso classics (including a spicy seared tuna salad, velvety chick pea cream soup with prawns and fish sautéed with artichoke hearts) is excellent value at €85, or you can choose à la carte. Booking is essential.

✉ Piazza della Vittoria 13, 57027 San Vincenzo, Livorno ☎ 0565 701021 🕐 Wed–Sun 12.30–2.30, 7.30–10 🍴 L and D €48 (set menu), €55 (à la carte), Wine €20

SANSEPOLCRO
DA BEPPINO

Although Da Beppino is also a hotel, most people come here for the food, especially in summer, when you can dine outside in the garden. Try the tasty pizzas or the home-made pastas. Main courses often include fish, but classic meat dishes, such Chianana beef with Chianti, are usually best.

✉ Viale Diaz 12, 52037 Sansepolcro ☎ 0575 742287 🕐 Tue–Sun 12.30–2.30, 7.30–10.30. Closed Mon, period Jun–Jul 🍴 L €20, D €25, Wine €12

RISTORANTE VENTURA

This well-established *trattoria* is popular with locals. It serves traditional Tuscan food, such as hearty meat dishes, bean dishes, pasta and soups. The interior has a rustic style.

✉ Via N. Aggiunti 30, 52037 Sansepolcro, Arezzo ☎ 0575 742560 🕐 Tue–Sat 12.30–2.15, 7.30–9.30, Sun 12.30–2.15. Closed 3 weeks in Aug 🍴 L €17, D €33, Wine €12

SOVANA
HOTEL-RISTORANTE ETRUSCA

With 12 rooms , this mid-range hotel makes a delightful base in Sovana,

but even if you are just passing through, be sure to eat in the hotel's simple but beautiful dining room, part of a building at the heart of the village that dates from 1241.

✉ Piazza del Pretorio 16, 58017 Sovana ☎ 0564 616183/614193 🕐 Thu–Tue 12.30–2.30, 7.30–10.30 🍴 L €22, D €27, Wine €15

VOLTERRA
DA BADÒ

On the outskirts of Volterra, on the road from Colle di Val d'Elsa, Da Badò is a traditional *trattoria*, with just two small dining rooms and classic seasonal Tuscan cooking. Dishes might include local Volterran specialties such as pigeon or chick peas with pasta and sausages. The choice of local cheeses is especially good, as is the house wine.

✉ Borgo San Lazzero 9 ☎ 0588 86477 🕐 Thu–Tue 12.30–2.30, 7.30–10.30 🍴 L €22, D €28, Wine €12

L'INCONTRO

L'Incontro means 'the meeting' and this is where many locals and visitors gather. A glorious smell of chocolate and a tempting counter full of home-made pastries and chocolates greet you. There's a little wine bar at the back where simple meals are served: soups, salads, cold cuts and cheese.

✉ Via Matteotti 18, 56048 Volterra, Pisa ☎ 0588 80500 🕐 Daily 7am–1am 🍴 D €17, Wine €10

TRATTORIA IL SACCO FIORENTINO

The menu at this elegant restaurant has dishes to suit all tastes, but the emphasis is on fish and game: *bocconcini di cinghiale al Chianti* is wild boar stewed in a rich wine sauce. Vegetarians could choose *pecorino al forno con radicchio roso e noci* (red-leaved chicory covered with fresh pecorino cheese and walnuts cooked in a hot oven).

✉ Piazza XX Settembre 18, 56048 Volterra, Pisa ☎ 0588 88537 🕐 Thu–Tue 12–2.30, 7–9.30. Closed mid-Jan to mid-Feb and 1 week in Jun or Jul 🍴 L €10, D €22, Wine €8

PRICES AND SYMBOLS

The prices are the lowest and highest for a double room for one night including breakfast, unless otherwise stated. All the hotels listed accept credit cards unless otherwise stated. Note that rates can vary widely throughout the year.

For a key to the symbols, ▷ 2.

ANGHIARI
RELAIS LA COMMENDA

www.relaislacommenda.com
This bed-and-breakfast is just outside Anghiari, in a former monastery surrounded by cypress, oak, beech and olive woods. Rooms inside the stone interior are large and boldly decorated, with yellow walls, blue furnishings and red rugs. There are beamed ceilings, wooden floors and open fires in most rooms, including the large lounge for guests. The surrounding countryside is great for walkers, and there are a number of activities that can be arranged, such as archery, cooking courses, sailing and windsurfing.
✉ Località Commenda 6, 52031 Tavernelle di Anghiari, Arezzo ☎ 0575 723356 ✋ €160–€207 ❶ 4 suites, 3 apartments ⚊ Outdoor ❑ From Arezzo, take the SS Aretina until Ville, then follow directions to Anghiari. The Relais is on the right; 27km (17 miles) from Arezzo

AREZZO
HOTEL CONTINENTALE

www.hotelcontinentale.com
The hotel was built in 1948 and has bright furnishings, lavish bathrooms and a large panoramic roof garden. The guest rooms are modern and equipped with satellite TV and minibar. Breakfast is served on the roof terrace if the weather is fine. Other facilities include a restaurant and free parking.
✉ Piazza Guido Monaco 7, 52100 Arezzo ☎ 0575 20251 ✋ €108, excluding breakfast ❶ 76 ✿

HOTEL MINERVA

www.hotel-minerva.it
The Minerva has grown up around its traditional Tuscan restaurant, which was known as the Spiedo d'Oro when it first opened in 1968. It is in here that the buffet breakfast is served. There is also a courtesy airport shuttle service and parking.
✉ Via Fiorentina 4, 52100 Arezzo ☎ 0575 370390 ✋ €100–€135 ❶ 130 ✿ ❑ From the Autostrada A1 Arezzo exit, follow directions to the centre of Arezzo for 5km (3 miles) and then signs for the hotel

ASCIANO
BORGO CASABIANCA

There are several accommodation possibilities at this restored *borgo*

(fortified hamlet) in the heart of the Crete, approximately 10km (6 miles) east of Asciano. In the main 18th-century villa are three attractive rooms and six suites, while dotted around the grounds are 20 or so apartments and around a dozen more rustic *agriturismo* options. The extensive facilities include a restaurant, pool, tennis courts and gym.
✉ Località Casabianca, 53041 Asciano ☎ 0577 704362 ◷ Closed early Jan–late Mar. Restaurant closed Wed ✋ €290–€360 ❶ 39 ✿ ⚊ Outdoor 🎾

BAGNO VIGNONI
HOTEL POSTA MARCUCCI

www.hotelpostamarcucci.it
This peaceful spa hotel with old-fashioned comforts is set in the beautiful countryside of the Val d'Orcia. Guests can reach the large thermal pool by a passageway: Unwind under the stream of water as it enters the pool at 43°C (110°F), or sit on the benches in the water to relax. You can also indulge in a massage. There's a restaurant, and spacious public rooms. Two meals are obligatory on Saturdays and public holidays.
✉ Via Ara Urea 43, Bagno Vignoni 53027, San Quirico d'Orcia, Siena ☎ 0577 887112 ✋ €82–€102 ❶ 35 ✿

BUONCONVENTO
HOTEL GHIBELLINO
www.hotelghibellino.it
Although it is modern, this hotel is notable for the use of traditional local materials. The guest rooms have wooden floors and locally carved headboards. Subdued lighting throughout creates a calm environment, and there is a solarium/roof terrace.
✉ Via Dante Alighieri 1, 53022 Buonconvento, Siena ☎ 0577 809112 🖐 €85–€95 🛈 23 �

CERTOSA DI MAGGIANO
CERTOSA DI MAGGIANO
www.certosadimaggiano.it
In a former 14th-century monastery this is one of the most luxurious hotels close to Siena. Its rooms are lavishly furnished with rich linens and wall coverings, with 18th-century paintings in the public areas.
✉ Stada di Certosa 82, 53100 Siena ☎ 0577 288180 🖐 €400–€594 🛈 17 � ⛵ Outdoor 🛎

CHIANTI
ALBERGO DEL CHIANTI
www.albergodelchianti.it
This old hotel in an ancient building is on Greve's central piazza. Bedrooms are light and airy, with wrought-iron headboards and cool white draperies, while downstairs there are terracotta floors, white walls and a tasteful mix of the modern and antique. The vine-shaded eating area in the garden is a real bonus.
✉ Piazza G. Matteotti 86, 50022 Greve in Chianti, Firenze ☎ 055 853763 🕐 Closed Nov to mid-Dec and mid-Jan to end Mar 🖐 €90–€100 🛈 16 🔚 ⛵ Outdoor

ALBERGO LA FONTE DEL CIECO
www.lafontedelcieco.it
This hotel, in an early 20th-century townhouse, has seven bedrooms with wrought-iron bedsteads, terracotta floors and wooden beamed and tiled ceilings. The bathrooms are very well equipped, with plenty of soft towels. There is a small garden and a view onto the main square.
✉ Via Ricasoli 18, 53013 Gaiole in Chianti, Siena ☎ 0577 744028 🖐 €90–€120 🛈 8

CASTELLO DI SPALTENNA
www.spaltenna.it
Just outside Gaiole in Chianti, in classic Tuscan countryside, you'll find Castello di Spaltenna. It retains the wonderful medieval appearance and atmosphere of the fortified monastery from which it was converted. Modern facilities complement the period setting, and the outstanding recreational facilities include tennis courts, two pools, sauna, gym and Turkish bath. Dinner in the Della Pieve restaurant is especially memorable (▷ 229).
✉ Località Spaltenna 13, 53013 Gaiole in Chianti ☎ 0577 749483 🖐 €230–€360 🛈 37 🔚 ⛵ Outdoor 🛎

HOTEL VILLA LA GROTTA
www.hotelvillalagrotta.it
This four-star hotel is in a 19th-century villa, with more rooms in an adjacent farmhouse. Turkish bath and spa treatments are available, but the main attraction is the countryside, including the wine estate of Borro.
✉ Località Brolio, 53013 Gaiole in Chianti, Siena ☎ 0577 747125 🖐 €240–€280 (suites €340–€360) 🛈 12 🔚 ⛵ Indoor and outdoor 🚗 From the A1 exit at signs for Valdichiana, follow the signs for Siena, turn off and go through Castelnuovo Berendega and follow signs for Brolio

RELAIS FATTORIA VIGNALE
www.vignale.it
The Fattoria Vignale is one of Italy's top hotels. Expect traditional Tuscan architecture, well-polished antiques, huge fireplaces and opulent sofas. The bedrooms, some with private terraces, are luxurious, with service to match. The vaulted wine cellars house a taverna, and there's an elegant restaurant a short distance from the main building.
✉ Via Pianigiani 8, 53017 Radda in Chianti, Siena ☎ 0577 738300 🖐 €165–€260 🛈 37 🔚 ⛵ Outdoor

VILLA CASALECCHI
www.villacasalecchi.it
Some 2km (1.2 miles) south of Castellina in Chianti, this 19th-century villa lies in the heart of classic Chianti country, surrounded by vineyard-swathed hills. The rooms and few apartments are filled with antiques and have a rustic yet refined style. The frescoed restaurant is open to non-residents, and in summer guests can make use of tennis courts and a pool.
✉ Località Casalecchi, 53011 Castellina in Chianti ☎ 0577 740240 🕐 Closed Dec–Feb 🖐 €150–€245 🛈 16, 3 apartments 🔚 ⛵ Outdoor

COLLE DI VAL D'ELSA
RELAIS DELLA ROVERE
www.chiantiturismo.it
Colle di Val d'Elsa lacked for upmarket hotels until the opening of this restored townhouse, once part of a 12th-century abbey. The spacious, peaceful rooms display an eclectic mixture of modern and traditional styles. There are pleasant gardens (with a swimming pool) and in summer you can dine outside in Il Cardinale, the hotel restaurant.
✉ Via Piemonte 10, 53034 Colle di Val d'Elsa ☎ Hotel: 0577 924696. Restaurant: 0577 923707 🕐 Hotel closed early Nov–Mar. Restaurant closed at lunch, Wed and 2 weeks Nov–Dec 🖐 €229–€319 🛈 30 🔚 ⛵ Outdoor

CORTONA
CASA BELLAVISTA
www.casabellavista.it
This bed-and-breakfast is within easy reach of Cortona and Arezzo, with views of Monte Amiata. Here you can experience a traditional Tuscan home. Breakfast is served in the dining room. The public rooms include a library, study and lounge.
✉ Località Creti 40, 52044 Cortona ☎ 0575 610311 🕐 Closed Jan, Feb 🖐 €90–€115 🛈 4 ⛵ Outdoor 🚗 Take the Valdichiana exit from A1 and follow signs for Foaino della Chiana and then Fratta–S. Caterina; turn right next to the ruined building and follow the road uphill for 1km (0.5 miles); 35km (22 miles) from Arezzo, 12km (7 miles) from Cortona

IL FALCONIERE RELAIS

www.ilfalconiere.it

This luxury hotel, a converted 17th-century villa, stands in extensive grounds 4km (2.5 miles) north of Cortona. The elegant interior, with frescoed walls, canopied beds and precious paintings and antiques, has an aristocratic air. The delightful restaurant, set amid olive and cypress trees, is also outstanding.

✉ Località San Martino a Bocena, 52044 Cortona ☎ 0575 612679 ⬚ €270–€360 ❶ 19 ◆ ⬚ Outdoor

HOTEL ITALIA

The three-star Hotel Italia has modestly priced rooms in a palace dating from the 1600s, just a few steps from Cortona's main square. The hotel's restaurant serves typical Tuscan cuisine. The large roof terrace is a great place to enjoy the panoramic views.

✉ Via Ghibellina 5/7, 52044 Cortona ☎ 0575 630254/630564 ⬚ €100–€137 ❶ 26 ◆

RELAIS VILLA BALDELLI

www.villabaldelli.com

This 17th-century country villa is now a four-star hotel. It sits in peaceful parkland with a golf driving range. Rooms are simple but elegant with beamed ceilings, wrought-iron beds and wooden furnishings. There is a bar and wine-tasting room. Walks, horseback riding and excursions can be arranged and there is an on-site golf academy.

✉ San Pietro a Cegliolo 420, 52044 Cortona ☎ 0575 612406 ⬚ €220 –€350 ❶ 15 ◆ ⬚ Outdoor ⬚ Take the Valdichiana exit on A1 and follow signs for Cortona; at Camucia take SS71 in the direction of Arezzo; the Relais is on the right just after Sodo

RELAIS VILLA PETRISCHIO

www.villapetrischio.it

The 18th-century Villa Petrischio is set on a hill overlooking the Chiana valley about 10km (6 miles) west of Cortona. Oriental-style gardens, fountains, flowers and cypresses provide a ravishing setting. The elegant rooms and four suites are individually decorated, but all contain antique furniture and have exposed beams. In summer, you can dine outside in the restaurant close to the hotel pool.

✉ Via del Petrischio 25, 52042 Località Farneta ☎ 0575 610316 ⬚ Closed mid-Jan to mid-Mar ⬚ €195–€215 ❶ 14, 4 suites ◆ ⬚ Outdoor

GROSSETO

L'ANDANA

www.andana.it.

This beautiful hotel west of Grosseto is the first Italian project by the celebrated French hotelier and restaurateur Alain Ducasse. A former royal lodge on a large estate, it comprises a main villa in lovely grounds, surrounded by olives and vineyards. Rooms are spacious but understated. There is also an ESPA spa, and health club, with a golf course on the way. The restaurant, the Trattoria Toscana, is superb.

✉ Località Badiola, 58100 Grosseto ☎ 0564 944800 ⬚ Closed 6 Jan to mid-March ⬚ Doubles in high season from €638, Prestige Suite 4 €1,400. ❶ 20 (13 suites) ◆ ⬚ Indoor and outdoor ⬚

CASTELLO DI VICARELLO

www.vicarello.it

In remote Tuscan countryside off the SS223 road to Siena, Castello di Vicarello is less a hotel than a grand private residence, with just seven suites dotted around the grounds and 12th-century building. Communal dining heightens the house-party atmosphere (although meals can be taken in your room). The hotel is very peaceful, very chic, and very bohemian, but not for everyone. Boar and other hunting can be arranged in season.

✉ Poggio del Sasso, near Pagainico, 38km (23 miles) northeast of Grosseto ☎ 0564 990718 ⬚ Suites from €370. ❶ Seven suites ⬚ Outdoor

ISOLA D'ELBA

HOTEL VILLA OMBROSA

www.villaombrosa.it

Just over the headland from the port there is a fine pebble beach with clear blue water and, above it, this charming family-owned hotel. It's an ideal base for visiting the island without bringing a car. A room with a sea view costs a supplement, depending on the season, and you must pay for two meals daily in July, August and September.

✉ Via Alcide De Gasperi 9, 57037 Portoferraio, Isola d'Elba ☎ 0565 914363 ⬚ Closed mid-Oct to Mar ⬚ €190 ❶ 38 ⬚ Turn right from the ferry terminal and follow the port, then follow signs for Centro Storico and then signs for Spiaggia Le Ghiaie; the hotel is 460m (500 yards) along the bay on the left

VILLA OTTONE

www.villaottone.com

This white-fronted villa stands on the shoreline of the bay at Portoferraio, some 10km (6 miles) from the main town. The guest rooms are split between the villa and a newer building. Some rooms have Jacuzzis. The hotel has a private beach, restaurant, bar, gardens and tennis courts. The complex is well placed for touring the island.

✉ Località Ottone, 56037 Portoferraio, Isola d'Elba ☎ 0565 933042 ⬚ Closed mid-Oct to Mar ⬚ €142–€470 (half board only) ❶ 80 ◆ ⬚ Outdoor ⬚ From Portoferraio (10km/6 miles from the hotel), take the Porto Azzura road, turn left at the sign for Bagnaia Maggazina; the hotel is 4km (2.5 miles) along on the left

ISOLA DEL GIGLIO

IL SARACENO

www.saracenohotel.it

The granite building is set on rocks just above the sea with views to Monte Argentario. Steps lead down to the water, and you can sunbathe among the rocks. The restaurant has an outside terrace. Rooms are minimally furnished, with white walls. Parking is available.

✉ Via del Saraceno 69, 58013 Giglio Porto, Isola del Giglio ☎ 0564 809006 ⬚ Apr–end Sep ⬚ €75–€120 ❶ 44 ◆

LUPOMPESI

BOSCO DELLA SPINA RESIDENCE

www.boscodellaspina.com

Set in peaceful hills, the four-star

Bosco della Spina Residence is on the edge of the Maremma forest, and near the medieval village of Lupompesi. It makes a good base for exploring the smaller villages and archaeological sites of the province of Siena. The building is a successful mix of old and new. All the rooms have good views—those overlooking the gardens are best.

✉ Lupompesi Murlo, 53016 Siena ☎ 0577 814605 ⊘ Closed 7 Jan–14 Feb ⊌ €120–€180 ⬆ 14 suites ⬇ ⛱ Outdoor 🚗 20km (12 miles) south of Siena; from Siena, take the SS2 and follow signs for Rome/Buonconvento and then turn left for Murlo

MASSA MARITTIMA
VILLA IL TESORO
www.villailtesoro.com.
Like L'Andana (▷ 236) and Castello di Vicarello (▷ 236), this is one of several new-wave upmarket hotels opening in the Maremma as the region becomes better known and more popular with visitors. It is 3.5km (2 miles) northwest of Massa Marittima, with a wonderful rural setting, fine views and a striking circular pool, although the fastidious restoration and modern and *arte povera* décor in the 20 rooms may not be to all tastes. Request one of the four Superior Suites in the small, self-contained *villetta*, preferably those opening on to the garden.

✉ Località Valpiana, 58020 Massa Marittima ☎ 0566 92 971 ⊘ Il Fiore restaurant closed Wed. Hotel closed Nov to mid-Mar ⊌ €225–€360 ⬆ 20 ⬇ ⛱ Outdoor

MONTALCINO
CASTELLO DI VELONA
www.castellodivelona.it
In 2001, this isolated 11th-century castle, near Castelnuovo dell'Abate, south of Montalcino, was little more than a ruin. Now it is a superb luxury hotel. Views are superb, and rooms and public areas mix delightful period details with modern facilities. The restaurant, Le Colonne, offers refined Tuscan cooking. Staying here is a treat, as prices can be steep, though good internet deals are often

available and rates drop considerably outside high season.

✉ Località Velona, Castelnuovo dell'Abate ☎ 0577 800101 ⊌ €290–€390 ⬆ 24 ⬇ ⬛

DEI CAPITANI
www.deicapitani.it
Almost all the rooms in this beautifully converted late medieval building have sweeping views over the Val d'Orcia. Bedrooms are lofty, with cool tones, lovely beamed ceilings and plenty of space; some are in the annex to the main building. It's a family-run hotel that prides itself on personal service, so expect smiles and helpfulness. The breakfast buffet will keep you going all day, and if the private parking's full, the hotel staff will help you find a space in town.

✉ Via Lapini 6, Montalcino, 53024 Siena ☎ 0577 847227 ⊘ Closed 15 Jan to 15 Feb ⊌ €115 (apartments €165–€180) ⬆ 24 ⬇ ⛱ Outdoor

MONTE ARGENTARIO
HOTEL LA CALETTA
www.hotelcaletta.it
You'll get good value for money at this hotel, in a quiet position on the water's edge at the far end of town. The guest rooms are relaxing, with white walls and blue furnishings, and all look on to the sea. There is a small beach outside with sunbeds and parasols for guests, and a scuba-diving shop next to it. The hotel has an excellent restaurant. Parking is available nearby.

✉ Via Civinini 10, 58019 Porto Santo Stefano, Grosseto ☎ 0564 812939 ⊌ €62–€168 ⬆ 26 ⬇

IL PELLICANO
www.pellicanohotel.com
The guest accommodation at this luxury hotel is set among the pine trees in the expansive grounds. The terraced gardens are scented with Mediterranean plants and stretch down to the sea. Relax by the pool or down by the sea, or play tennis before a buffet lunch on the terrace. You can be pampered at the Beauty

and Spa Centre. The restaurant has an extensive wine list.

✉ Cala dei Santi, 58018 Porto Ercole, Grosseto ☎ 0564 858111 ⊘ Apr–end Oct ⊌ €388–€788 (sea view €450–€892) ⬆ 50 ⬇ ⛱ Heated outdoor ⬛

MONTEPULCIANO
ALBERGO DUOMO
www.albergoduomo.it
The Albergo Duomo is directly opposite the Duomo. the lovely old building has been sensitively restored in true Tuscan style. Room sizes vary; try for one of the huge first-floor rooms at the front.

✉ Via San Donato 14, 53045 Montepulciano ☎ 0578 757473 ⊌ €85 ⬆ 13

IL MARZOCCO
www.albergoilmarzocco.it
This Renaissance palace has spacious public rooms. The best bedrooms have terraces and marvellous views. Simple home cooking is served in the restaurant.

✉ Piazza Savonarola 18, 53045 Montepulciano ☎ 0578 757262 ⊌ €95 ⬆ 16

PIENZA
RELAIS IL CHIOSTRO DI PIENZA
www.relaisilchiostrodipienza.com
This beautifully restored 15th-century monastery offers 21st-century comfort. The bedrooms are big, the beds slumber-inducing, and antique pieces enhance the public areas. A good restaurant, dreamy terraces and cascades of geraniums add to the magic, and it's all a minute's walk from Pienza's main piazza.

✉ Corso Rossellino 26, 53026 Pienza ☎ 0578 748400 ⊘ Closed 7 Jan to 15 Mar ⊌ €220 ⬆ 37 ⬇ ⛱ Outdoor

SAN GIMIGNANO
ALBERGO RELAIS SANTA CHIARA
www.rsc.it
A short walk from the town, the four-star Relais Santa Chiara combines contemporary architecture with superb views. To ensure the best view, request a room with a balcony. The hotel has no restaurant, but a

generous breakfast is served. There is also a cocktail bar, a garden and parking. Guest rooms are equipped with satellite TV and minibar.

✉ Via Matteoti 15, 53037 San Gimignano ☎ 0577 940701 💶 €160 ⓘ 41 🔵 ≈ Outdoor

L'ANTICO POZZO
www.anticopozzo.com
This superbly restored 15th-century townhouse is now a three-star hotel in the heart of San Gimignano. The interior is medieval in character. There's a bar in the old brick cellar and the first-floor courtyard has great views of the town's stone towers and cobbled streets. Each room comes with satellite TV, minibar and safe.

✉ Via San Matteo 87, 53037 San Gimignano ☎ 0577 942014 ⓒ Closed Dec to mid-Jan 💶 €110–€135 (superior €160) ⓘ 18 🔵

HOTEL PESCILLE
www.pescille.it
The rolling countryside 3km (2 miles) from San Gimignano is home to an old farmhouse turned three-star hotel. The hotel garden is perfect for a pleasant evening stroll. The hotel also has a solarium, tennis courts, bar and internet access. Guest rooms are modern and sleek, while the building still presents a picture of authentic, old-fashioned Tuscany.

✉ Località Pescille, Strada Provinciale 47, 53037 San Gimignano ☎ 0577 940186 💶 €100–€130 ⓘ 50 🔵 ≈ Outdoor 🚍 From San Gimignano, take the road signed for Castel San Gimignano/Volterra; the hotel is on the left

SANSEPOLCRO
ALBERGO FIORENTINO
www.albergofiorentino.com
There's been a hotel here since 1807 and the public rooms are virtually unaltered. The modernized bedrooms are simply furnished and represent good value for such a central position. There is a restaurant and parking (€10 per day) but no elevator.

✉ Via Luca Pacioli 60, 52037 Sansepolcro, Arezzo ☎ 0575 740370 💶 €80 ⓘ 21

SATURNIA
HOTEL TERME DI SATURNIA
www.termedisaturnia.it
The baths of Rome live on in this luxury spa resort. Travertine marble on the walls and wooden floors create a cool, minimalist feeling. The huge adjoining thermal pool is fed by a sulphurous hot spring. The emphasis is on health and wellbeing with medical facilities on hand. The restaurant serves light, healthy food with local wines. There is also a golf driving range.

✉ 58050 Saturnia, Grosseto ☎ 0564 600111 💶 €400–€770 ⓘ 140 🔵 💶

SOVANA
SCILLA
www.scilla-sovana.it
Sovana is at its best in the evenings, so a stay at this charming hotel in the heart of the village is recommended, but book ahead. The building is old, so rooms tend to be small, but they are well equipped, furnished and decorated. The restaurant serves great food.

✉ Via di Sotto 3, Sovana, 58010 Grosseto ☎ 0564 616531 ⓒ Closed first 10 days in Feb and all Nov 💶 €65–€90 ⓘ 8 🔵

SUBBIANO
HOTEL RISTORANTE LA GRAVENNA
www.lagravenna.it
La Gravenna is a panoramic drive up to the mountain town of Subbiano. All guest rooms have private bathrooms, there's a bar and restaurant. Free parking is available. Walking treks and horseback riding can be arranged.

✉ Località Gravenna 101, 52010 Subbiano ☎ 0575 420682/48588 💶 €85 ⓘ 37 🚍 SS71 in the direction of Bibbiena and then follow signs for Subbiano and Gravenna; 12km (7 miles) from Arezzo

VOLTERRA
ALBERGO VILLA NENCINI
There are magnificent views from this hotel, a 17th-century villa just outside Volterra. Most of the bedrooms are comfortably furnished, with private bathrooms.

✉ Borgo Santo Stefano 55, 56048 Volterra, Pisa ☎ 0588 86386 💶 €83–€88 ⓘ 37 ≈

HOTEL SAN LINO
www.hotelsanlino.com
This agreeable hotel has bedrooms decorated in warm pastel shades. There is a restaurant where a buffet breakfast is served, a bar and internet access. The staff are a charming team.

✉ Via San Lino 26, 56048 Volterra, Pisa ☎ 0588 85250 ⓒ Closed for periods Nov–Jan 💶 €77–€140 ⓘ 43 🔵 ≈

PRACTICALITIES

Practicalities gives you all the important practical information you will need during your visit from money matters to emergency phone numbers.

WEATHER

CLIMATE

The best months to visit are May, June and September, when you should find long sunny days, but avoid the real heat of July and August. Winters are cold, with snow in the mountains. November can be dank and wet. Around Christmas, you can hope for some crystal-clear, cold, sunny weather.

WEATHER REPORTS

BBC World News, www.bbc.co.uk, and CNN, www.CNN.com, broadcast regular global weather updates in English. There are also a number of dedicated websites, such as Weather Channel at www.weather.com.

DOCUMENTS

PASSPORTS

All visitors to Italy need a passport, which should be valid for at least another six months from the date of entry into Italy. Officially, visitors from EU countries only need a national identity card (if your home country has them). In practice, you will need a passport. If you lose your passport, you should contact your embassy or consulate (▷ 248).

Keep a note of your passport number or make a photocopy of your passport's information page.

VISAS

If you are an EU national, or from Australia, Canada, New Zealand or the United States, you do not need a visa for stays of up to 90 days. To extend your visit you can, one time only, apply to any police station for an extension of a further 90 days. This extension cannot be used for studying or employment, and you will have to prove that you can support yourself financially. Contact the Italian embassy in your home country before travelling because visa rules can change at short notice. If you are a citizen of a country other than those listed, contact the Italian embassy in your country to check requirements.

TRAVEL INSURANCE

Take out your insurance as soon as you book your trip to ensure you are covered for delays. Most policies cover cancellation, medical expenses, accident compensation, personal liability and loss of personal belongings (including money). Your policy should cover the cost of getting you home in case of a medical emergency.

An annual travel policy may be the best value if you do a lot of travelling, but long trips abroad may not be covered. If you have private medical insurance, check your policy, as you may be covered while you are away.

TIME ZONES

CITY	TIME DIFFERENCE	TIME AT 12 NOON GMT
Amsterdam	0	noon
Auckland	+11	11pm
Berlin	0	noon
Brussels	0	noon
Cairo	+1	1pm
Chicago	-7	5am
Dublin	-1	11am
Johannesburg	+1	1pm
London	-1	11am
Madrid	0	noon
Montreal	-6	6am
New York	-6	6am
Paris	0	noon
Perth, Australia	+7	7pm
San Francisco	-9	3am
Sydney	+9	9pm
Tokyo	+8	8pm

Italy is one hour ahead of GMT. The clocks are moved forward an hour for daylight saving time on the last Sunday in March. The clocks go back an hour on the last Sunday in October. The chart shows the time differences from Italy.

FIRENZE

TEMPERATURE

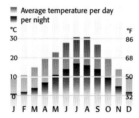

RAINFALL

GROSSETO

TEMPERATURE

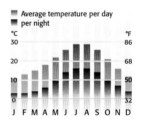

RAINFALL

HEALTH

» No vaccinations are necessary for a trip to Italy, unless you are coming into the country from an infected area. If you have any doubts, contact your doctor before you leave.

» You should always make sure you have adequate health insurance—see Travel Insurance on page 240.

» European citizens should carry a European Health Insurance Card (EHIC), available through post offices, health offices and social security offices. Italy has a reciprocal health agreement with the rest of the EU, Iceland, Liechtenstein and Norway, which allows free or reduced-cost dental and medical (including hospital) treatment on presentation of the EHIC.

» If you are on regular medication, you should ensure that you have adequate supplies for your trip. Make a note of the chemical name (rather than the brand name) in case you need replacement supplies.

» See pages 244–245 for more details on health matters.

WHAT TO TAKE

» Your driver's licence.

» Photocopies of all important documents: passport, insurance details, credit card, debit card, passport numbers and registration numbers for mobile phones, cameras and other expensive items.

» Alternatively, scan documents and send them to a web-based email account that can be accessed worldwide.

» Lightweight cottons and linens to wear during the summer, and depending on the time of year that you travel, rain-proof gear and an umbrella.

» Clothes that cover your shoulders and knees if you intend to visit churches or other religious buildings.

» Comfortable shoes for walking, especially in the hills.

» A torch (flashlight) and binoculars.

» An Italian phrase book—any attempt at Italian is appreciated (▷ 268–271).

» A first-aid kit.

CUSTOMS

The import of wildlife souvenirs from rare and endangered species may be illegal or require a permit. Before you make any such purchase, you should check customs regulations.

See below for more details on what can be brought through customs.

Below *The Duomo's campanile, Lucca*

DUTY-FREE AND DUTY-PAID GUIDELINES

Anything that is clearly for personal use can be taken into Italy free of duty, but it is worth carrying receipts for valuable items in case you need to prove that they were not bought in Italy.

Duty-paid allowances for US citizens

» 1 litre of alcohol	» 1 bottle perfume
» 100 cigars (non-Cuban)	(if trademarked in the US)
» 200 cigarettes	

You can take home up to $800 worth of duty-paid goods, provided you have been out of the country for at least 48 hours and have not made another international trip in the previous 30 days. This limit applies to each member of your family, regardless of age, and allowances may be pooled. For the most up-to-date information, see the US Department of Homeland Security's website: www.customs.treas.gov.

Duty-paid guidelines for EU citizens

You cannot buy goods duty-free if you are journeying within the EU. You can take home unlimited amounts of duty-paid goods, as long as they are for your own personal use. In the UK, H. M. Customs and Excise considers anything over the following limits to be for commercial use.

» 3,200 cigarettes	» 10 litres of spirits
» 3kg of tobacco	» 90 litres of wine
» 400 cigarillos	» 20 litres of fortified wine
» 200 cigars	(such as port or sherry)
» 110 litres of beer	

Whatever your entitlement, you cannot take home goods for payment (including payment in kind) or for resale. These goods are considered for commercial use and duty is payable. For the most up-to-date information, see the H. M. Customs and Excise website: www.hmce.gov.uk.

ITALIAN EMBASSIES AND CONSULATES ABROAD

COUNTRY	ADDRESS		
Australia	12 Grey Street, Deakin ACT 2600	tel 02-6273 3333	www.ambcanberra.esteri.it
Canada	275 Slater Street, 21st Floor, Ottawa (ON), KIP 5HP	tel 613/232-2401	www.ambottawa.esteri.it
Ireland	63/65 Northumberland Road, Dublin 4	tel 01 660 1744	www.ambdublino.esteri.it
New Zealand	34–38 Grant Road, PO Box 463, Thorndon, Wellington	tel 04 4735 339	www.ambwellington.esteri.it
South Africa	796 George Avenue, Arcadia 0083 Pretoria	tel 012 423 0000	www.ambpretoria.esteri.it
UK	14 Three Kings Yard, London W1K 4EH	tel 020 7312 2200	www.amblondra.esteri.it
USA	3000 Whitehaven Street NW, Washington DC 20008	tel 202/612-4400	www.ambwashingtondc.esteri.it

MONEY

Italians traditionally use cash, but this is changing. Credit and debit cards are widely accepted, but not for small sums. Food bought in a store is paid for in cash and market traders don't take cards.

BEFORE YOU GO

» It is advisable to use a combination of cash, traveller's cheques and credit cards rather than relying on any one means of payment during your trip.

» Check with your credit card company that you can withdraw cash from ATMs (cash machines). You should also check what fee will be charged for this and what number you should phone if your card is stolen (see panel).

» Traveller's cheques are a relatively safe way of carrying money, as you are insured if they are stolen. Remember to keep a note of their numbers separately from the cheques themselves.

EXCHANGE RATES

The exchange rate per euro for visitors from the UK, US and Canada is subject to daily fluctuation. At the time of printing €1 is worth approximately £0.95, US$1.28 and C$1.59.

CREDIT AND DEBIT CARDS

MasterCard, Diners Club and Visa are widely accepted in Tuscany, as well as Eurocheque cards, but some smaller establishments still do not take credit cards (carta di credito). Look for the credit card symbols in the shop window or check with the staff.

You can also use your credit card to make cash withdrawals, although your credit card company will charge

LOST OR STOLEN CREDIT CARDS

American Express
06 7228 0371
Diners Club
800 864064
MasterCard/Eurocard
800 870866
Visa/Connect
800 877232
American Express traveller's cheques
800 872000

it as a cash advance. Contact your company to get a PIN number.

ATMS

ATMs (cash machines), called bancomats in Italy, are plentiful, and many are accessible 24 hours a day. Most have instructions in a number of languages, including English. You avoid commission and the exchange rates are better when you withdraw cash with a debit card (Cirrus/Maestro/Delta) from an ATM rather than using a bureau de change. Check with your bank before leaving home that you will be able to take cash out with your card while in Italy.

TRAVELLER'S CHEQUES

Traveller's cheques are accepted almost everywhere. To avoid additional exchange rate charges, take cheques in euros, pounds sterling or US dollars.

CURRENCY EXCHANGE

Banks in your home country will have differing exchange and commission rates. Check for details and shop around before you buy.

In Italy, traveller's cheques, personal cheques and foreign money can be changed at banks, rail

stations and airports, and very often at major hotels (generally at a less attractive rate).

BANKS AND POST OFFICES

The largest banks in Italy are Unicredito and Intesa-BCI, and Monte dei Paschi di Siena is the largest in Tuscany. Most major banks have ATMs and exchange facilities, although they are often very busy. Banks are usually open from 8.30 until 1 or 1.30, and again for a short time in the afternoon. Some open on Saturday morning. Central post offices usually have a currency exchange that is open throughout the day until 7.

BUREAUX DE CHANGE

There are bureaux de change (cambio) in all the main cities, usually open throughout the day until around 7.30. They often change money commission-free, but the exchange rates are not as good as those from banks.

CURRENCY RESTRICTIONS

Import and export of local and foreign currency is unlimited, but check with your embassy before departure if you need to bring large sums into the country. Amounts greater than this should be declared and validated in Italy.

WIRING MONEY

Wiring money is a lengthy process and the bureaucracy involved means that it is probably not worthwhile unless you are planning to spend quite a long time in Italy. You can get money wired out to any bank from home, but if your bank is already in contact with certain banks in Italy it will make the process a lot easier. Ask your bank at home for a

BANKS IN MAIN TUSCAN TOWNS

Florence	Cassa di Risparmio di Firenze, Via Bufalini 6, 50122 Firenze	tel 055 26121	www.bancafirenze.it
	Banca d'Italia, Via dell'Oriuolo 37–39, 50122 Firenze	tel 055 245472	www.bancaditalia.it
	Banca Nazionale del Lavoro, Via Cavour 59, 50129 Firenze	tel 055 495340	www.bnl.it
Siena	Monte dei Paschi di Siena, Via Banchi di Sotto 41, 53100 Siena	tel 0577 281211	www.mps.it
Pisa	Cassa di Risparmio di Pisa, Lungarno Gambacorti 21, 56126 Pisa	tel 050 915423	www.carisimi.it
Lucca	Banca del Monte di Lucca, Piazza Martino 4, 55100 Lucca	tel 0583 48721	www.fondazioneblmlucca.it

10 EVERYDAY ITEMS AND HOW MUCH THEY COST

Sandwich	€2.50–€4.50
Bottle of water	€0.50–€2
Cup of tea or coffee	€1.50–€4
0.5 litre of beer	€3.20–€6.50
Glass of wine	€0.85–€4.50
Daily newspaper	€0.90–€3
Roll of camera film	€5
20 cigarettes	€3.80
An ice cream cone	€2
A litre of petrol (gas)	€1.53

list of affiliated banks. Always ask for a separate letter, telex or fax confirming that the money has been sent and ask that it be sent to Swift. It can take up to a week, sometimes more, for the money to transfer. American Express Moneygram and Western Union Money Transfer are faster from the US, but more expensive. Citibank can transfer money for a flat fee of $10 to anywhere in the world (www.c2it. com). Do not wire more money than you need; you can only export just over €10,300.

DISCOUNTS

» Seniors (over 65) can get discounts on some museum entry charges on production of an identity document, but this is often restricted to EU residents only (▷ 250).

» An International Student Identity Card (ISIC; www.isic.org) may help you obtain free or reduced entry to museums and attractions as well as other discounts.

» See pages 47 and 53–54 for information on transport passes.

TAXES

» Sales tax (IVA) is at 20 per cent. It is added to services such as meals you have in restaurants and hotel accommodation. This is non-refundable.

» Visitors from non-EU countries are entitled to a reimbursement of the 20 per cent tax paid on purchases to the value of more than €154.94, which needs to be spent in the same store.

» The store must provide a properly completed invoice itemizing all goods, the price paid for them, and the tax charged, as well as full address details of both the vendor and purchaser. The goods must then be taken out of the EU within three months.

» The goods and the invoice(s) should be taken to the booth at Italian customs on your departure from the EU, prior to checking in your baggage. This is where your claim will be processed.

» For further information visit www.aziendedogane.it

» Tax can also be reclaimed through Global Refund Tax Free Shopping, a service offered by major retailers worldwide. For more information visit their website at www.globalrefund.com

TIPPING

Italians do not tip heavily. Service is often included in your hotel or restaurant bill, although a little extra is appreciated if the service has been good. The following is a general guide:

Pizzerias or trattorias	round up to the nearest euro
Restaurant	10 per cent
Bar service	up to €0.25
Taxis	round up to nearest €0.50
Porters	€0.50 to €1 per bag
Chambermaids	€0.50 to €1 per day
Cloakroom attendants	€0.50
Toilets	€0.20–€0.50

HEALTH

HOW TO FIND A DOCTOR

» To get in touch with a doctor (*un medico*), ask at your hotel or consult the *Pagine Gialle* (Yellow Pages, www.paginegialle.it) under Unità Sanitaria Locale.

» If you need emergency treatment, go directly to the Pronto Soccorso (casualty department/ER) of the nearest hospital.

» If you are staying in Florence, you can contact the Tourist Medical Service, Via Lorenzo il Magnifico 59, tel 055 475411, www.medicalservice.firenze.it. Doctors here speak English, French and German, but the service is private. A visit will cost €45 and no appointment is necessary. They provide a drop-in service six days a week (Mon–Fri 11am–noon, 5–6, Sat 11am–noon) and a 24-hour callout service is available on the same telephone number.

» If you are staying outside Florence, your hotel or local tourist office will help you find a multilingual doctor.

EMERGENCY TREATMENT

The telephone number 118 is for the ambulance service. The number 112 is for help when you are anywhere in Europe—in Italy, you will be put through to the police (*Carabinieri*) (▷ 248).

HOW TO GET TREATMENT WITH THE EHIC

» If you need medical treatment while you are away, take your EHIC (▷ 241) to the Unità Sanitaria Locale (USL) office, which will give you a certificate of entitlement.

» Take this certificate to any doctor or dentist on the USL list to receive free treatment. If they need to refer you to a hospital, they will give you a certificate that entitles you to free treatment.

» If you go to hospital without being referred by a doctor, you should give the form to them.

» If you do not have a USL certificate, you will have to pay for treatment and it may be difficult to get the money back afterwards—and then you will probably only receive a partial refund.

» If you are charged in full for prescriptions, keep the price tags or receipts to claim a refund.

» It is advisable to make a photocopy of your EHIC form, as some doctors and hospitals will keep the original.

HOW TO GET TREATMENT WITH INSURANCE

» If you have health insurance at home it may cover you for medical treatment abroad. Check your policy before you leave home.

» Take a copy of your insurance documents to the doctor or hospital—they may be able to bill your insurance company direct.

» If you have to pay for treatment, keep all your receipts for your insurance claim.

PHARMACIES

Pharmacies (*farmacia*) sell toiletries as well as a wide range of over-the-counter medicines. Pharmacists are well trained and can give advice on minor ailments. Most pharmacies are open during normal shop hours, but a rotation system operates in major cities so that there is at least one open at all times—a copy of the rotation is displayed in pharmacy windows.

DENTAL TREATMENT

If you have an EHIC, contact the USL (▷ left). If you do not have one of these, contact a private dentist (look in the Yellow Pages under *Dentista*, or ask staff at your hotel to recommend one). Again, take a copy of your insurance details and keep your receipts.

OPTICIANS

Opticians can usually carry out minor repairs to your glasses, such as replacing screws, on the spot, for little or no charge. Lenses can often be replaced overnight. If you really cannot survive without your glasses or contact lenses, bring a copy of your prescription with you

Above *A green cross outside a shop indicates that it is a pharmacy*

SELECTED HOSPITALS WITH EMERGENCY DEPARTMENTS		
CITY	**ADDRESS**	**TELEPHONE**
Florence	Santa Maria Nuova, Piazza Santa Maria Nuova 1	055 27581
Grosseto	Misericordia, Via Senese 161	0564 485111
Lucca	Campo di Marte, Via del Ospedale 238	0583 955791
Pisa	Santa Chiara, Via Roma 67	050 992111
Poggibonsi, near San Gimignano	Località Campostaggia Via Senese 30	0577 586111
Siena	Policlinico Le Scotte, Via Mario Bracci 16	0577 586111

so that you can have replacements made up if necessary. If possible, pack a spare pair of glasses for emergencies.

FOOD AND WATER

Italy's tap water is generally safe to drink, but you should look out for signs that say *acqua non potabile*, which means the water is not drinkable. Local meat, dairy products, poultry, seafood, fruit and vegetables are all safe to eat.

SUNSHINE

From April to the end of September the sun is extremely strong and you will need to wear a high-factor (SPF) sunblock (factor (SPF) 15 or above is recommended).

HAZARDS

Insect bites are irritating rather than dangerous. There are no malaria-carrying insects in Italy, but there is an ongoing mosquito problem across the country, even in inland towns. Use plenty of insect repellent or a mosquito net at night in the summer months, and be vigilant near water and woodland areas.

COMPLEMENTARY MEDICAL TREATMENT

Alternative medicine, such as homeopathy and reflexology, is becoming increasingly popular. Local pharmacies can help you find practitioners in your area and most sell homeopathic remedies. It is not offered as part of the national health service and is not regulated, so be very careful in your choice.

Above *Travelling on long-haul flights can present health risks such as DVT*
Below *Call 118 for the ambulance service*

HEALTHY FLYING

» Visitors to Italy from as far as the US, Australia or New Zealand may be concerned about the effect of long-haul flights on their health. The most widely publicized concern is deep vein thrombosis, or DVT. Misleadingly called 'economy class syndrome', DVT is the forming of a blood clot in the body's deep veins, particularly in the legs. The clot can move around the bloodstream and could be fatal.

» Those most at risk include the elderly, pregnant women and those using the contraceptive pill, smokers and the overweight. If you are at increased risk of DVT see your doctor before departing. Flying increases the likelihood of DVT because passengers are often seated in a cramped position for long periods of time and may become dehydrated.

TO MINIMIZE RISK:

Drink water (not alcohol)
Don't stay immobile for hours at a time
Stretch and exercise your legs periodically
Do wear elastic flight socks, which support veins and reduce the chances of a clot forming

EXERCISES

1 Ankle Rotations
Lift feet off the floor.
Draw a circle with the toes, moving one foot clockwise and the other counterclockwise

2 Calf Stretches
Start with heel on the floor and point foot upward as high as you can. Then lift heels high keeping balls of feet on the floor

3 Knee Lifts
Lift leg with knee bent while contracting your thigh muscle. Then straighten leg pressing foot flat to the floor

Other health hazards for flyers are airborne diseases and bugs spread by the plane's air-conditioning system. These are largely unavoidable, but if you have a serious medical condition seek advice from a doctor before flying.

BASICS

ADDRESSES IN FLORENCE

Florence has a dual address system. Each street has a double set of numbers: A black or blue number denotes a private residence or hotel, and a red number indicates a shop, restaurant or business. In a written address, the letter 'r' after the street number stands for *rosso* (red) and means it's a business address. You may see 'Int' in an address. This stands for 'internal', and indicates a building that is inside a courtyard.

ELECTRICITY

The electric current in Italy is 240 volts, and appliances are fitted with sockets that have two round pins. If your appliances are manufactured for 240 volts, you just need a plug adaptor. If your voltage is different, as it will be from the US, you need an adaptor and transformer.

LAUNDRY

If you make use of the hotel laundry service, your clean clothes will be returned to your room and the (often high) charge added to your bill. Self-service launderettes (*lavandaria automatica*) are few and far between in Italy, but are emerging in the larger cities. A wash costs around €4. Dry cleaning (*lavasecco*) starts from around €3 for a shirt up to €7.50 for larger items, but the quality of the service varies immensely.

Below *An art nouveau-style house number*

LOCAL WAYS

» A few words of Italian will always go down well (▷ 268–271), even if you can only manage hello and goodbye. Use *buongiorno* for hello up to midday, and *buona sera* in the afternoon and evening.

» Italians tend to use please and thank you less frequently than other nationalities.

» Show respect and dress appropriately when visiting places of worship. Cover your shoulders and knees.

» Don't intrude on religious services unless you wish to take part.

» Before taking photographs in churches and museums, always check that it is permitted and never use the flash.

» Italians tend to drink alcohol only with meals, and public drunkenness is frowned upon.

» In cafés, never attempt to use the tables if you have paid bar prices.

» If you only want a one-course meal, eat in a pizzeria. It's considered bad form to eat fewer than two courses in a restaurant.

LOST PROPERTY

» A lost property office is an *ufficio oggetti smarriti*.

» In Florence:
ATAF city buses: Via Circondaria 17G, tel 055 235 2190, Mon–Fri 8–12.30, 4–6.
Trains: Santa Maria Novella, platform 16, tel 055 235 6120, daily 6am–midnight.

Florence airport: tel 055 306 1711, daily 8am–10pm.

» Siena rail station: tel 0577 207360, daily 8–8.

» Siena town: Via F. Tozzo 3, tel 0577 292588, Mon, Fri 11am–1.30pm, Tue, Thu 3–5pm

» Pisa rail station: tel 050 849400, daily 7am–10.30pm.

MEASUREMENTS

Italy uses the metric system. Distances are measured in metres and kilometres, fuel is sold by the litre and food is weighed by the kilogram. Italians also use the *ettogrammo* (100g), usually abbreviated to etto.

TOILETS

There are public toilets at rail stations and in larger museums, but otherwise they are rare. You will probably end up using the facilities in a bar or café. Owners may let you use their facilities if you are not a customer, but obviously they prefer you to buy something first. Many bars keep the toilets locked, so you will need to ask for the key. Facilities can be basic: Toilet paper may not be provided, and sometimes there is only one lavatory for both men and women. In some places there is a dish for gratuities—you should tip around €0.25. Where separate facilities exist, make sure you recognize the difference between *signori* (men) and *signore* (women).

PLACES OF WORSHIP

If you are Roman Catholic you will have no problem finding somewhere to celebrate your faith in Tuscany. There are Catholic churches in even the smallest towns and villages, and religious festivals are celebrated enthusiastically throughout the year.

» There is an Anglican church of St. Mark's at Via Maggio 16, 50125 Florence (tel 055 294764, www.stmarksitaly.com), which holds daily services.

» St. James is an Episcopalian church at Via Bernardo Ruccelai 9, 50123 Florence (tel 055 294417, www.dionet.it/stjames), where

Above *A priest outside San Miniato al Monte*

services are held on Sundays.
» To find synagogues and Jewish communities in Tuscany, go to www.kosherdelight.com or www.mavensearch.com
» There are few mosques in Italy. For information contact the Unione delle Comunità ed Organizzazioni Islamiche in Italia, www.islam-ucoii.it (UCOII; Via Padova 38, 20127 Milano, tel 02 8366 0253).

SMOKING

» Smoking is very common in Italy.
» Smoking in all public places was banned in 2005. This includes public transport, inside airport buildings and in public offices and buildings.
» Cigarettes and other tobacco products can only legally be sold in *tabacchi* (tobacconists) to those over 16. The stand-alone *tabacchi* are open during normal shop hours (▷ 250) and there are vending machines outside many *tabacchi*. Those attached to bars stay open longer.

VISITING WITH CHILDREN

Children are welcomed in almost all restaurants and at most hotels. Items such as baby food are available in many food stores or supermarkets. The lack of public toilets and changing facilities, however, can make things difficult for anyone with very young children.
» You should keep a particular eye on your children when wandering around Florence's busy streets.
» Italian children stay up late—if parents are eating out, the kids go too. This means that most hotels do not provide a baby-sitting service.
» Slap a high-factor (SPF) sunscreen on your children and keep them covered up in the sun.
» Children are susceptible to heat stroke, so seek shade in the middle of the day and keep their heads and necks well protected.
» Most hotels will put up to three or four beds in a room so families can stay together; the add-on cost is around 30 per cent of the original room price.
» Hotels are often unheated until the end of October.
» If you are bottle-feeding your baby, you might want to take the formula with you.
» Children aged 4 to 12 qualify for a 50 per cent discount on trains; those aged under 4 travel free.
» Entrance to state-run museums is free to EU citizens under 18 and over 60. But you must bring proof of identity, especially for children, to be eligible. If you don't, you'll have to pay the full charge.

VISITORS WITH A DISABILITY

Wheelchair access is improving in the larger cities, as it is in the smaller towns, where many of the museums have been adapted. It is always worth asking individual establishments what access is like. However, the narrow, cobbled streets and lack of pavements (sidewalks) in many of the old towns can prove difficult.
» Holiday Care in the UK publishes information on accessibility for visitors with disabilities (The Hawkins Suite, Enham Place, Enham Alamein, Andover, SP11 6JS, tel 0845 124 9971, fax 0845 124 9972, www.holidaycare.org.uk).

CONVERSION CHART		
From	**To**	**Multiply by**
Inches	Centimeters	2.54
Centimeters	Inches	0.3937
Feet	Meters	0.3048
Meters	Feet	3.2810
Yards	Meters	0.9144
Meters	Yards	1.0940
Miles	Kilometers	1.6090
Kilometers	Miles	0.6214
Acres	Hectares	0.4047
Hectares	Acres	2.4710
Gallons	Liters	4.5460
Liters	Gallons	0.2200
Ounces	Grams	28.35
Grams	Ounces	0.0353
Pounds	Grams	453.6
Grams	Pounds	0.0022
Pounds	Kilograms	0.4536
Kilograms	Pounds	2.205
Tons	Tonnes	1.0160
Tonnes	Tons	0.9842

» In the US, SATH (Society for Accessible Travel and Hospitality) has lots of tips for visitors with visual impairment or reduced mobility (www.sath.org).
» Tourist offices should be able to help you.
» See page 58 for more details for visitors with a disability.

Below *Access for wheelchair users may prove problematic in some Tuscan cities*

FINDING HELP

PERSONAL SECURITY

Tuscany is much like any other region in the West when it comes to crime. You should be safe against personal attack, but petty crime, especially pickpocketing, is fairly common. Visitors who are not on their guard are main targets, so take some sensible precautions:

» Take care around rail stations, on public transport and in crowded areas in the larger cities where pickpockets and handbag (purse) thieves may be operating. Be particularly wary of groups of children who may try to distract your attention while stealing from you.

» Passports, credit cards, travel tickets and cash should not be carried together in your bag or pocket. Only carry with you what you need for the day and make use of safe deposit facilities in hotels.

» An increasing number of robberies are taking place from cars at rest stops along main roads. You should treat with caution offers of help if you find yourself with a flat tyre, as sometimes the tyre will have been punctured deliberately.

» Lock your vehicle and never leave valuables in it even if you will only be away for a short time or are nearby.

» Never carry money or valuables in your back pocket. Always keep them secure in a money belt or similar.

» Do not flaunt your valuables; leave valuable jewellery in a hotel safe.

» Never put your camera or bag down on a café table or on the back of a chair, from where it could be snatched.

» Carry bags or cameras on the side of you that is farthest away from the road, to minimize the risk from scooter-borne bag snatchers.

» Wear your shoulder bag across your body rather than just over your shoulder, from where it can be easily snatched.

» If you have a safe in your hotel room, do not use your date of birth as the code. It is on your passport and your hotel registration.

LOST PROPERTY

ATAF has lost property offices for articles left on buses or trams, as do Trenitalia for anything left on their trains (▷ 54, 246).

» If you will be making an insurance claim, you need to report the loss to the police to get a statement (*denuncia*).

» If your passport is lost or stolen, report it to the police and your consulate. The whole process of getting a replacement is easier if you have kept a copy of your passport number or a photocopy of the information page in a safe place.

» If your credit or bank card is stolen, report it to the police and phone the appropriate emergency number to cancel your card (▷ 242). All are open 24 hours a day.

» If your traveller's cheques are stolen, notify the police, then follow the instructions given with the cheques.

REPORTING THEFT

Report thefts to a police station, where you will need to make a statement. It is unlikely that you will get your belongings back, but you need the statement (*denuncia*) to make a claim on your insurance. You can find the address and contact details of your nearest police station in the Yellow Pages (*Pagine Gialle*)

under Commissariato, Commando di polizia or Stazione dei carabinieri or online at www.paginegialle.it

POLICE

In Italy there are three branches of the police, any of whom should be able to help you if you are in need.

» The *carabinieri* are military police, easily recognizable by the white sash they wear across their bodies. They deal with general crime, including drug control.

» The *polizia* is the state police force, whose officers wear blue uniforms. They too deal with general crime, and if you are unfortunate enough to be robbed (or worse) they are the ones you will need to see.

» The *vigili urbani*, traffic police, wear dark blue uniforms and white hats.

EMBASSIES AND CONSULATES

Lists of embassies and consulates are available from tourist offices. You can also look under Ambasciate or Consolati in the phone book or visit www.embassyworld.com.

Below Carabinieri *are easily recognizable by the white sash on their uniforms*

COMMUNICATION

CALL CHARGES

Freephone numbers (*numeri verdi*) usually begin with 800; national call rate numbers begin with 848 or 199. Hotels tend to overcharge for long-distance and international calls, so it is best to make calls from a public phone, using a telephone card. Rates are lowest on Sunday throughout the day and between 10pm and 8am on weekdays and Saturday.

PUBLIC TELEPHONES

If you are calling from a public telephone you must deposit a coin or use a phone card to get a dialling tone. Note that some pay phones will only accept coins and others only phone cards. Phones that take only coins tend to be less reliable than phone-card phones. Call-centre phones are a better bet than the often poorly maintained public telephones. Here you are assigned a booth to make your call and you pay the attendant when you have finished.

PHONE CARDS

Prepaid *carte telefoniche* (phone cards) are used widely throughout Tuscany. You can buy them from post offices, tobacconists, newsstands and bars. To use, tear off the corner of the card and insert it in the slot of the public phone. When you dial, the amount of money on the card is shown in the window. After you hang up, the card is returned so you can use it until it runs out. The Time phone card is good value, allowing you to call Europe and the United States at about €0.30 per minute during peak time; however, if you are calling between 10pm and 8am, or all day Sunday, conventional phone cards are less expensive.

MOBILE PHONES

It can be very expensive to use your mobile phone abroad and you will often be charged to receive calls as well as to make them. If you travel abroad frequently and intend to use your phone, consider swapping your SIM card for a card from an alternative provider—either a foreign network or a dedicated provider of international mobile phone services. You can buy these at mobile phone shops before you leave.

Text messages can be cheaper than voice calls, but check your service provider's charges for making calls and text messages.

CALLING ABROAD

A call from outside Italy is dialled as 00 39 + 055 (code for Florence) + phone number.

A call from Florence to the UK is dialled as 00 44 + the area code omitting the first 0 (eg 01780 becomes 1780) + the number. A call from Florence to the US would be dialled as 001 + the area code + the number.

For all calls within Italy, local and long distance, dial the regional code (*prefisso*), which begins with 0—as 055 for Florence.

LAPTOPS

If you intend to use your own laptop in Italy, remember to bring a power converter to recharge it and a plug socket adaptor. A surge protector is also a good idea. To connect to the internet you need an adaptor for the phone socket.

If you use an international internet service provider, such as AOL or Compuserve, it's cheaper to dial up a local node rather than the number at home. Dial-tone frequencies vary from country to country, so set your modem to ignore dial tones.

INTERNET CAFÉS

You'll find internet cafés across Tuscany. They provide reasonably inexpensive internet access, usually costing around €5 an hour. You need a web-based email account if you want to send or receive email from abroad (gmail, hotmail, yahoo and many more).

POSTAL SERVICES

Poste Italiane have 14,000 post offices (*posta, ufficio postale* or *PT*) across Italy. These are usually open Monday to Friday 8.15–2, Saturday 8.15–12 or 2, with larger offices open until 7pm. In the past, mail services have been notoriously unreliable, but the introduction of a priority service (*posta prioritaria*) has provided a more efficient alternative, relieving the pressure on the old state mail service, which has also become more reliable.

Stamps (*francobolli*) are also sold at tobacconists denoted with an official *tabacchi* sign, a large 'T'. They can weigh letters but for heavy letters and a packages, it's best to go to a post office.

For information on all Italy's mail services, contact Poste Italiane (tel 800 222666, www.poste.it). In general, post offices are open Mon–Fri 8.15–2, Sat 8.15–12 or 2, or in larger towns and cities they are open until 7pm.

POSTCARDS

These are classed as low-priority mail and may well not be received until well after you have arrived home. If you want them to arrive at their destination within a couple of weeks, send them *prioritaria*.

AREA CODES FOR MAJOR CITIES	
Florence	055
Pisa	050
Siena	0577

COUNTRY CODES FROM ITALY	
Australia	00 61
Belgium	00 32
Canada	00 1
France	00 33
Germany	00 49
Greece	00 30
Ireland	00 353
Netherlands	00 31
New Zealand	00 64
Spain	00 34
Sweden	00 46
UK	00 44
USA	00 1

OPENING TIMES AND TICKETS

BANKS
Most are open Monday to Friday 8.30–1.30. Larger branches might open on Saturday.

CAFÉS AND BARS
The hours kept by cafés and bars vary between establishments and according to the season.

CHURCHES
Most churches open early in the morning for Mass, often around 7am. They close at lunchtime, opening again around 4 and closing at 7pm. Some of the larger churches are open all day, but some may be closed to visitors during services. Check the Sights section of this book for specific opening times, or contact the church.

MUSEUMS AND GALLERIES
Opening times for museums and galleries vary greatly, according to season and location. Many close one day each week, usually Monday. Check the Sights section of this book, or contact the museum or gallery for up-to-date information.

PHARMACIES
Pharmacies are usually open the same hours as shops, but take turns staying open during the afternoon and late into the evening. Look for the list in the shop window providing details of other pharmacies in the area and their opening times.

POST OFFICES
These are usually open Monday to Friday 8.15–2, Saturday 8.15–12 or 2. Larger offices are open until 7pm.

RESTAURANTS
Restaurants serving lunch open at 12 and usually close in the afternoon. They reopen, along with those that only serve dinner, some time after 7pm until late. Pizzerias usually only open in the evening. Many restaurants close for the whole month of August—look for the sign *chiuso per ferie*.

SHOPS
Traditionally, shops open in the morning between 8 and 9 and close for lunch at around 1. They reopen in the afternoon at 3.30 or 4 and close at 8. Most are closed Sundays and Monday mornings. Shops in larger cities increasingly stay open all day.

NATIONAL HOLIDAYS
Shops and banks generally close on public holidays when the road and rail networks are usually very busy. There is limited public transport service on 1 May (Labour Day) and the afternoon of Christmas Day. However, with the exception of Labour Day, 15 August (Assumption) and Christmas Day, most bars and restaurants remain open. See panel for other national holidays.

ENTRANCE FEES
Admission to churches is usually free. However, you may be asked for a small donation or charged a fee to see inside a church, or part of a church, that is of artistic or historic interest. You should expect to pay around €2, but it can be as much as €8. Museums charge for admission; entrance fees are usually €5–€10, but discounts are almost always available (see below). Entrance fees sometimes include a guided tour.

COMBINED TICKETS
Siena (▷ 166–191) has a ticket incorporating all of its museums, providing significant savings, as does Pisa (▷ 140–143) and San Gimignano (▷ 208–210). In Florence, the Palazzo Vecchio and the Cappella Brancacci have joint tickets and you can buy combined tickets for various museums at the Palazzo Pitti (▷ 84–85): a pass that covers all the Palazzo Pitti museums costs €11.50 for adults (except during special exhibitions) and is free to children aged under 18; a combined ticket for the Giardino di Boboli and Argenti, Costume and Porcellane museums costs €7 for adults, free for children aged under 18. Most major towns or regions have combined tickets for museums and areas of cultural

interest. Further details are available from tourist offices.

BOOKING TICKETS
You can buy tickets to a number of attractions in Florence from Firenze Musei (Via Ricasoli 7, tel 055 294883, Mon–Fri 8.30–6.30, Sat 8.30–12.30, www.firenzemusei. it). The service costs €3 and covers: Cappelle Medicee, Galleria dell'Accademia, Galleria degli Uffizi, Giardino di Boboli, Museo Archeologico, Museo Nazionale del Bargello, Museo di San Marco, plus the Galleria Palatina, Galleria d'Arte Moderna and Museo degli Argenti at the Palazzo Pitti. Tickets can be bought in various combinations.

DISCOUNTS
Where there is an admission charge for a church, discounts are rarely available, but all other museums and attractions have concessions for students (with an international student card), European Union citizens over 65, and children under 5 or 6, who are generally admitted free. Children under 10 may have free admission too. There tend to be discounts for those up to the age of 18 and this is sometimes extended to those under 20. Some attractions have free entry for visitors with a disability and a carer.

NATIONAL HOLIDAYS
If a public holiday falls on a weekend, it is celebrated on that Saturday or Sunday. If the holiday falls on a Tuesday or Thursday, many people take the Monday or Friday off to make a *ponte* (bridge) to the weekend. Saints' days are celebrated locally in individual cities, such as 24 June, St. John's Day, in Florence.

1 Jan	New Year's Day
6 Jan	Epiphany
Mar/Apr	Easter Monday
25 Apr	Liberation Day
1 May	Labour Day
2 Jun	Republic Day
15 Aug	Assumption of the Virgin (Ferragosto)
1 Nov	All Saints' Day
8 Dec	Feast of the Immaculate Conception
25 Dec	Christmas Day
26 Dec	St. Stephen's Day

TOURIST OFFICES

Most major towns have a tourist office and there are information desks at the airports. Known as Ufficio di Turismo, or Ufficio Turistico, they tend to keep normal shop opening hours (▷ 250). They have maps and information and provide help and advice in finding accommodation. They may also book accommodation and tours for you. The Aziende Promozione del Turismo (APT) and the Ente Provinciale per il Turismo (EPT) are usually devoted more to the bureaucracy of tourism rather than providing information for visitors. Villages sometimes have a small office known as a Pro Loco, but these often have limited opening hours. All cities have a central office with extended opening hours. The table below shows the addresses and Italian contact details for the main tourist offices overseas.

OVERSEAS TOURIST OFFICES

Italian State Tourist Offices Overseas (ENIT)	www.enit.it	
Australia	Level 4, 46 Market Street, Sydney NSW 2000	tel 02 9262 1666
Canada	175 Bloor Street E., Suite 907, South Tower, M4W 3R8, Toronto	tel 416 925 4882
UK	1 Princes Street, London W1 8AY	tel 020 7408 1254
US	630 5th Avenue, Suite 1565, Rockefeller Center, NY 10111	tel 212/245-5618

TOURIST OFFICES

Florence	Via Cavour lr	tel 055 290832	fax 055 234 6285	www.firenzeturismo.it
Lucca	Piazza S. Maria	tel 0583 919931	fax 0583 91663	www.luccatourist.it
Pisa	Piazza del Duomo 1	tel 050 560464	fax 050 831 0626	www.pisaturismo.it
Siena	Piazza del Campo 56	tel 0577 280 551	fax 0577 281041	www.terresiena.it

WEBSITES

www.aboutflorence.com
Plenty of information to help you plan your visit, or to use when you are there. There are maps and plenty of information to give you an insight to the city (in English, Spanish and Japanese).

www.cafe.ecs.net
A useful and interactive site that has a directory of internet cafés in Italy. You are invited to contact the site with comments (in Italian and English).

www.castellitoscani.com
Comprehensive information about all the castles in Tuscany, with maps and directions (in English).

www.firenze.net
Lots of information about Florence on a range of subjects such as museums, shopping, entertainment and restaurants (in English and Italian).

www.firenzemusei.it
This site encompasses the major museums in the city, with background on the collections as well as practical information (in English, Italian and Spanish).

www.firenzeturismo.it
The official site of the APT in Tuscany (in English and Italian).

www.florence.ala.it
Lots of information and links to accommodation sites and museums as well as maps and cultural details (in English).

www.Florence.hotelguide.net
www.Florence.hotelsfinder.com
Searchable databases of hotels and apartments for rent in Florence (in English).

www.fodors.com
A comprehensive travel-planning site that lets you research prices and book air tickets, aimed at the American market (in English).

www.museionline.it
This site covers museums all over Italy but allows you to search by different categories as well as by region (in English and Italian).

www.parks.it
A very useful site if you want to explore outside the cities, as it lists the parks, reserves and protected areas in the country, including Tuscany (in English, French, German and Italian).

www.theAA.com
If you are planning to drive to Tuscany or rent a car while you are there, visit this site for up-to-date travel advice (in English).

www.turismo.toscana.it
A very good site that covers all manner of things that you might want to do on holiday (in English, German and Italian).

www.welcometuscany.it
A good general website, with lots of information, particularly on themed topics, such as cooking courses, sports and romantic Tuscany (in English).

MEDIA

TELEVISION

Italy has three state-run television stations (RAI-1, -2 and -3), which broadcast some worthy entertainment, three stations run by Prime Minister Berlusconi's Mediaset group (Italia Uno, Rete Quattro and Canale Cinque), and a number of local channels. RAI-3 has international news broadcasts, including an English-language section. Most hotels, from mid-range upwards, have satellite television, so you can keep up to date with the news and sport on channels such as BBC World or CNN. There are few Tuscan channels.

RADIO

RAI Radios 1, 2 and 3 (89.7FM, 91.7FM and 93.7FM), the state-run stations, have a mixture of light music, chat shows and news—all in Italian. Radio Italia Network (90–108FM) is the best national radio station for dance music, and Radio Deejay (99.7–107FM) broadcasts a variety of popular music and chat shows. You can get BBC radio stations including Radio 1, Radio 2, 5 Live and 6 Music on the internet via www.bbc.co.uk. The BBC World Service frequencies in Italy are MHz 12.10, 9.410, 6.195 and 0.648. To find US radio stations online visit www.radio-locator.com.

NEWSPAPERS

You can buy major international newspapers such as *The Times*, *The Financial Times*, *The Guardian*, *The European*, *The New York Times*, *The Wall Street Journal* and *The International Herald Tribune*, though they are sold for three times their home cover price. They are usually available from about 2pm, the day after publication, at larger newsstands.

Florence's most popular paper is *La Nazione*. It publishes regional versions for most Tuscan towns. Other papers include *La Repubblica* and *Corriere della Sera*. There are two daily sports papers published in Italy—*La Gazzetta dello Sport* (printed on pink paper) and the *Corriere dello Sport*—mainly dominated by soccer and motor sport news.

MAGAZINES

English-language magazines are hard to find, but if you read a little Italian, *Panorama* and *L'Espresso* are good for news, while *Oggi* has more of a focus on celebrity gossip and lifestyle. *L'Espresso*, renowned for its restaurant reviews and accreditations, is highly respected in Italy.

Opposite *Keeping abreast of national and regional events*

FILMS AND BOOKS

FILMS

» *Hannibal* (2001), the sequel to *The Silence of the Lambs*, contains some scenes shot in Florence's palaces and along the banks of the River Arno.

» To get an idea of the rolling Tuscan countryside, watch Kenneth Branagh's adaptation of Shakespeare's *Much Ado About Nothing* (1993). Starring Branagh as Benedict and Emma Thompson as Beatrice, this play is brought to life in the hilltop Villa Vignamaggio, with its knot gardens and vineyards, typical of Greve in Chianti.

» *Under the Tuscan Sun* (2003) stars Diane Lane as a writer who visits Tuscany and decides to embrace the region's people and lifestyle. It was shot in various Italian locations, including Cortona and Florence. The film is based on the book of the same name by Frances Mayes.

» Set in 1930s Italy and shot in Terni in Umbria and Arezzo in Tuscany, *La Vita è Bella* (Life is Beautiful, 1997) is a dark yet heart-warming tale of a Jewish bookkeeper who struggles to hold his family together during German occupation and help his son survive the horrors of a Jewish concentration camp.

» Franco Zeffirelli co-wrote and directed *Tea with Mussolini* (1999). It follows the fortunes of a group of expatriates living in Florence at the start of World War II. The all-star cast includes Cher, Maggie Smith, Judi Dench, Joan Plowright and Lily Tomlin.

» Bernardo Bertolucci's *Stealing Beauty* (1995), with Liv Tyler, was filmed around Castelnuovo, Gaiole in Chianti and Siena.

» *The English Patient* (1996), directed by Antony Minghella, was partly shot around Siena, Pienza, Pisa and the Monastero di Sant'Anna in Camprena.

BOOKS

There are many god books covering Italy's long, eventful history.

» Anyone interested in Italian politics and society should read *The Dark Heart of Italy* (2003) by Tobias Jones, which discusses Italian life under Berlusconi's administration.

Above *Actor Anthony Hopkins on location in the Piazza della Signoria during the filming of* Hannibal

» E. M. Forster's novel *A Room with a View* (1908) is a critique of 19th-century middle-class Britons abroad in Florence. The author's *Where Angels Fear to Tread* (1905) is set in San Gimignano.

» *Up at the Villa* (1941) by W. Somerset Maugham follows the fortunes of an English widow in Florence.

» There is a huge number of travel biographies on the shelves, but particularly good is *Vanilla Beans and Brodo: Real Life in the Hills of Tuscany* (2002) by Isabella Dusi, which gives an insight into rural Tuscan life.

WHAT TO DO

SHOPPING

Shopping is taken seriously in Italy, and the provincial capitals of Florence, Siena, Arezzo and Grosseto all have their fair share of stylish shops, while you'll find some nice surprises in even the smallest towns. In design and fashion the big names have conquered the world, but there's more to retail therapy than haute couture and designer labels. Craftsmanship is highly valued and everything from furniture to underwear can be made to order. The backstreets are the places to find the tiny stores and workshops selling gifts and self-indulgent purchases.

Out-of-town shopping arcades, outlet stores and factory shops are slowly making an appearance, while towns traditionally associated with a particular product—ceramics, wine, jewellery—have a huge choice at excellent prices. Wine, food and olive oil are sold direct from the estates. In summer, you can taste and buy other local produce at the many *sagre*, food festivals (▷ 261).

MARKETS

There are daily food markets in most large towns. They generally take place in a purpose-built market hall or in a specific square or street, selling meat, groceries, fish, dairy produce, fruit and vegetables. Where there's a daily food market, the weekly market will be devoted to clothes, shoes, household goods, plants, flowers, toys, toiletries and fabrics. In Florence the most prominent markets are the Mercato Centrale (▷ 108), Mercato di Sant'Ambrogio (▷ 109) in the Santa Croce district and Mercato Nuovo (▷ 109), which is also known locally as Porcellino.

DEPARTMENT STORES

Department stores have been slow to catch on in Italy. However, in Tuscany you'll find branches of the big four: La Rinascente, Coin, Upim and Standa.

SUPERSTORES

Superstores are becoming much more widespread and generally concentrate on food, household items and linens. They are found on the outskirts of middle- to large-sized towns and cities, along with factory outlets.

picture frames, accessories and restored antique furniture.

Jewellery
Italy is one of the world's biggest jewellery manufacturers. Production is most prolific in Arezzo and there's a well-established tradition of in-house design across the country. Many jewellers make pieces to order.

Paper
Beautiful handmade paper, often marbled or block-printed, is a good buy across the region.

Shoes and Leather
You'll find shoes, belts, bags and accessories at both ends of the price range. The markets are great trawling grounds for bargains.

Clockwise from opposite Leather goods for sale in the Mercato Nuovo, Florence; daily food markets are held in most large towns in the region; fresh artichokes for sale

OPENING HOURS
These are fairly standard and apply for most of the year, but be prepared for erratic changes.
» Supermarkets, larger stores and visitor-oriented shops generally stay open all day (*orario continuato*)—that is, 9 or 10am to 7 or 7.30pm.
» Most other stores are open Monday to Saturday 8.30–1 and 4.30 or 5.30–7.
» Clothes shops may not open until 10am.
» Food shops are open on Monday mornings (unlike some stores) and they often close on Wednesday afternoons.
» Hours may change from mid-June until the end of August; some shops close completely when their owners are on holiday, while others stay open later for visitors.
» Small shops may close for anything from a week to a month during July and August.
» A pharmacy (*farmacia*) somewhere near your hotel will be open for prescriptions 24 hours a day; this is done on a rotation system and pharmacies post addresses and opening times in their windows.

WHAT TO BUY
Fashion
Fashion is the shopping focus in Italy, and you will find big names and chain stores in every major city and large town. Stores selling popular Italian exports generally carry a larger range than you'd find at home at more competitive prices. Smaller stores sell individual items with a distinct Italian twist.

Food and Wine
Every region has its own local food and wine, available in food stores, markets or delicatessens. Buy such items when you see them—move on a few kilometres and you may be out of the production area and they may not be available.

Handicrafts
Tuscany has a strong artisan tradition that continues to flourish. There is a huge range of regional handicrafts to seek out, such as olive-wood bowls and plates, alabaster ware and glassware, with many products only available in the area where they are made. Florence has an abundance of craft workshops specializing in

ENTERTAINMENT AND NIGHTLIFE

There is plenty to keep you entertained in the region, from cinema and theatre to classical music and opera. The university city of Florence is the liveliest in the region, with activity moving to the coastal resorts during the summer, when the open-air bars and clubs attract huge crowds. The university town of Siena has plenty going on during term-time, though it's primarily aimed at students. The other provincial capitals have a certain amount of nightlife; ask at the tourist offices or look out for fliers in bars. Throughout Tuscany you'll find out-of-town clubs in the midst of the countryside; they're generally open on weekends only.

CINEMA

Cinema is thriving in Italy, but the main problem will be language. It's acknowledged that Italian dubbing is the best in the world, so films are automatically dubbed rather than subtitled. In Florence, you should be able to find a cinema showing VO (*versione originale*) movies; elsewhere, outside film festivals, they are likely to be in Italian.

» Tickets normally cost around €7, with discounts for the early shows on Monday, Tuesday, Thursday and Friday and all day Wednesday.

» Very few cinemas accept payment by credit card.

» At busy times, some cinemas sell *posto in piedi* (standing only) tickets; there is no discount for these.

» Smoking is not allowed.

CLASSICAL MUSIC, BALLET AND DANCE

During the winter months most cities and towns of any size will have a regular schedule of classical and orchestral music, though you're unlikely to hear anything avant-garde or contemporary. The same is true of ballet and dance. The best time to see dance is during the summer festivals (see tourist offices for details, ▷ 251).

MUSIC IN CHURCHES

Concerts are staged in some of the region's most beautiful churches, where you can hear organ, orchestral and choral recitals in superb surroundings, often with acoustics to match. Look out for posters or ask at local tourist offices.

OPERA

Opera fans should not miss the opportunity to see Italian opera performed on home soil. It might not be what you are used to, as here it's popular entertainment with a great deal of audience participation: After arias shows can be held up for minutes at a time while the audience show their appreciation (or disapproval).

» The season runs from October to the end of March.

» Top names tend to sing for the first few nights only, so keep an eye on cast lists.

» Prices vary considerably depending on the venue and company.

» Smoking is not allowed inside the venues.

LIVE MUSIC

Big international bands and stars sometimes take in Florence on their tours. If so, the concerts will be well advertised by posters and tourist information offices will be able to help.

Tuscany hosts two major rock festivals: Arezzo Wave (▷ 227), one of Europe's biggest, in June, and Pistoia Blues in July.

If you're looking for the sounds of traditional Italy, head for the festivals, where there may be a chance to catch local bands and groups.

THEATRE

Unless you speak Italian it's unlikely you'll want to go to the theatre in Italy. Florence has a thriving theatre scene and most provincial capitals have a theatre, busiest during the winter season, from September to the end of April.

In summer, there are open-air festivals, taking place in classical theatres and arenas, or the courtyards and gardens of historic buildings—check with the tourist office for details.

LISTINGS

Local listings can be found in Friday editions of newspapers. Magazines in Florence will sometimes cover other events in the region, but your best option outside the city is the local tourist office. For Florence, look out for: *Firenze Oggi*, free in hotels and bars; *Firenze Spettacolo*, on sale Fridays from newsstands; *Informacittà*, on sale monthly and

free from tourist offices. The website is www.informacittafirenze.it.

TICKETS

Tickets for events in Florence are available direct from venues or from the company Box Office (Via Alamanni 39, Firenze, tel 055 210804) www.boxol.it.

For events around the region, including the *Maggio Musicale* (▷ 117), contact a central booking office: tel 199 112112 (inside Italy), tel +39 0424 600458 (outside Italy) www.firenzeturismo.it.

OPENING HOURS

Things start to heat up around midnight in Florence, but many bars have a prolonged happy hour from 7pm to 9pm, often accompanied by snacks. In smaller towns and rural areas, the opposite is the case, and you may struggle to find a bar open after 11pm.

BARS

Bars are open from early till late and serve everything from breakfast, coffee and snacks to beer, wine and aperitifs, with no licensing hours.

Outside Florence, bars are at their busiest between 6.30 and 9. Evening-only bars often have live music nights and guest DJs, but you'll only find these in Florence and the larger towns. Stylish hotels sometimes have bars that also offer music. Tuscans generally view bars as places to be seen and to meet their friends, and may happily nurse one drink for hours, and even at the hottest clubs relatively little alcohol is drunk.

CLUBS

» There is not much difference between bars with music and small clubs in Italy.

» Many clubs charge an entrance fee, which can include a free drink.

» Some clubs will ask you to buy membership (*tessera*), which can be purchased on the door. Prices vary and it may be free.

» If there is no entrance fee, you may receive a card, which is stamped when you buy drinks and totalled up when you leave.

» There are often set nights for particular styles of music.

» Check the local tourist office for details as nightclubs drop in and out of fashion and new venues regularly open while others close.

FLORENCE

Many central bars and clubs are underground and have no air-conditioning. Some close in summer, when the action moves to the coast; a special late train runs from Florence to Viareggio on weekends in summer and the journey takes a little over an hour. Opening times are erratic and, as everywhere, things can change without warning.

GAY AND LESBIAN NIGHTLIFE

Over the last 10 years Italians have become far more tolerant towards gay and lesbian relationships, but there's still a long way to go in rural areas, and the gay scene remains relatively low profile away from the larger towns. If you're looking for gay bars and clubs, head for the larger cities; Florence is particularly gay-friendly. In summer Torre del Lago, near Viareggio, is the place to go for a vibrant club scene.

» *Babilonia* is a monthly publication that has gay listings for all of Italy (available at most newsstands).

» Azione Gay e Lesbica publishes a gay and lesbian map of Tuscany.

» Log on to www.arcigay.it, the official site of Italy's foremost gay and lesbian network, or alternatively try www.gay.it/pinklily.

LISTINGS

Major cities have local listings magazines. Newspapers also have information, particularly for late-night music and the club scene. Tourist offices will be able to help, and bars are a good place to pick up fliers.

Opposite *Bars serve everything from coffee and breakfast to wines and aperitifs*

SPORTS AND ACTIVITIES

Italy's best-loved sport is soccer, passionately followed by millions of fans. Hot on its heels is basketball, introduced after World War II and now hugely popular. Baseball and American football have also crept in from across the Atlantic, while the Italian passion for cycling is totally home-grown. During the long, hot summers, swimming and watersports are popular. Upscale hotels have pools and tennis courts, and some will arrange a round of golf for you. Many *agriturismi* (▷ 266) organize activities such as horseback riding, mountain biking and walking.

CYCLING
Hundreds of local clubs take to the roads each weekend, and cyclists out en masse and spectators lining the streets are a common sight all over the country. The largest is the Giro d'Italia, an annual round-Italy race with several stages usually passing through Tuscany. It takes place in the second half of May, and attracts competitors from all over the world.

You can easily rent a bicycle to get around cities or venture out of town onto marked cycle routes—tourist offices provide maps of the trails. If you're in hilly country, think twice before embarking on what could be a tough day in high temperatures. The best cycling is in the province of Siena, where, particularly south of the city, the country is flatter and more open than the hills of Chianti. The Siena APT publishes an excellent free booklet packed with information and details of several attractive itineraries suitable for all levels of cyclists.

Renting a bicycle is quite straightforward; ask at local tourist offices, or consider an organized tour.

GYMS
Italian gyms are mainly private, so you'll need to take out temporary membership. Larger city gyms may have a sauna, Turkish bath and solarium and you can book a massage or hydrotherapy treatment.

HORSEBACK RIDING
You can enjoy riding all over Tuscany, either on a riding holiday, or simply by renting a mount from one of the many stables. You'll find stables all over the region, many offering lessons or organized excursions. Local tourist information offices all have details of what's available in their areas, as well as information on staying at *agriturismi* that offer riding.

SOCCER
» The soccer season runs from the end of August until June, with a two-week break from the end of December into January.
» Matches take place on Sunday afternoons.
» Ticket prices range from €15 to €85. The least expensive seats are in the *curva* (curve) at each end of the pitch (field) and the most expensive are along the side of the pitch, in the *tribuna* (stand).
» Tickets can be purchased from venues, merchandise outlets or agencies.
» General information is available online at www.lega-calcio.it; for details of fixtures for Florence's main team, Fiorentina, visit www.acfiorentina.it.

Above *Most towns and cities in the region have an indoor swimming pool*
Opposite *Take your sport further and go abseiling*

SWIMMING

Many small towns, especially those along the coast, have a public pool. In the main cities, where swimming pools are usually privately run, you may need to buy a temporary membership.

Italian resort beaches are divided into sections, each run as a *stabilimento balnearo* (bathing establishment). They are private, and you pay a hefty fee. This should cover the use of a changing cabin, sun lounger and parasol. Each *stabilimento* normally has showers, toilets and eating and drinking facilities.

Beach standards are high, with sand cleaned and raked overnight, but water cleanliness can vary. Sea water off major resorts, in remote areas and where the coast is rocky meets high international standards. Avoid swimming near major cities, ports or industrial coastal areas.

All Italian resorts have a legal obligation to allow free access to a section of the beach, so it is possible to avoid payment if all you want is a quick dip. However, these free-access areas are often small and the beaches unkempt.

Inland in Tuscany there are occasional stretches of river where you can swim. These can be idyllic and it's worth checking at tourist offices.

TENNIS

There are plenty of opportunities to enjoy a game of tennis, with courts frequently floodlit so you can play in the cooler evenings. Most towns have clubs where you can rent a court throughout the day.

WALKING AND HIKING

Tuscany provides some of Europe's most beautiful walking landscape, seen at its best from mid-April to early June. Don't plan any major hikes for July and August, when temperatures are high and the country dry. In September the weather cools. Access to the countryside is easy: Italy has no laws concerning trespassing so, as long as you follow a path and touch nothing, you can go pretty well anywhere. The major drawback to walking is the lack of well signposted trails or good maps. Notable exceptions are the trails marked out by the CAI (Club Alpino Italiano) that you'll find in the Alpi Apuane, the Orecchiella, the Val d'Orcia and parts of Elba. CAI paths are marked with red-and-white signs (usually painted on trees and rocks), but even with them, you'll need a map.

WATERSPORTS

You can rent windsurfers, small boats, catamarans and other equipment at the larger resorts along the Tuscan coast. If you're looking to jet- or water-ski, a resort hotel is probably your best bet, but it's expensive. Scuba divers and snorkellers will find plenty of choice around Monte Argentario and the islands—the main dive bases—where specialized firms offer accompanied day and night dives.

LISTINGS

Events are advertised in listings magazines, Italy's two daily sports newspapers, *La Gazzetta dello Sport* (printed on pink paper) and the *Corriere dello Sport*, and in Friday newspapers. Local tourist offices should be able to help you with any of these activites, or at least point you in the right direction.

HEALTH AND BEAUTY

Given those two major Italian obsessions, the *bella figura*, or looking good, and the digestive system, it's not surprising that Tuscany is well-equipped with spas, health and beauty centres. Recent years have seen the transformation of once serious and utilitarian bathing establishments into luxurious temples of the body, where it's possible to combine hydrotherapy of all sorts with some serious pampering in opulent surroundings.

SPAS

Tuscan spas are patronized by young and old right across the social spectrum, and 'taking the waters', whether it's immersing the body or delicately sipping a glass or two, is an integral part of everyday life, ensuring there's something for every taste and pocket.

Tuscany is blessed with mineral-rich, naturally heated springs, and there are *terme* (spas) all over the region, particularly around Chianciano (near Montepulciano) and Montecatini. Many spas still function purely as therapeutic clinics, where doctors will work out a regime for different medical conditions, but an increasing number of *centri benessere* (health and beauty centres) are geared to those who just want to be pampered in style. You'll also find free access to hot springs where the water emerges near the spas themselves: Bagno Vignoni (▷ 196) and Saturnia (▷ 212), both in southern Tuscany, are good places for a free swim.

FOR CHILDREN

Children are considered part of mainstream society in Italy and so you'll find few child-specific facilities and amusements, and Tuscan cities are not particularly child-friendly. There is still plenty to do, though, with the bonus that children are indulged, respected and integrated into whatever's going on.

FAMILY-FRIENDLY AREAS
Tuscany can keep most outdoor families occupied, from exploring tiny towns to cycling, hiking and horseback riding. Some children will be bored after a short time in Florence or the larger towns, so punctuate culture with time in the country or at the beach. Many families find a villa with a pool makes the ideal base, or you could vary your trip by mixing a few days in a city with time on an *agriturismo* (▷ 240); most have lots going on.

Good areas for children include the coast and southern Tuscany, while most age groups will enjoy a day out at the Parco di Pinocchio at Collodi (▷ 152).

BEACHES
The seaside holiday is a major part of Italian family life. Small children will be happy at resorts along the Tyrrhenian and Ligurian coasts of Tuscany, where sandy beaches with shallow bathing, beach games and playgrounds are interspersed with rockier stretches. Bear in mind that few *stabilimenti* (▷ 259) have lifeguards, so children should not be left unattended. Lovely as the islands are, they're not ideal for very young children, who find more to do along the string of broad sandy beaches in the Maremma (▷ 202).

You should also bear in mind the strength of the sun, particularly in the middle of the day, and follow the Italian habit of a long siesta in the shade. If your children are in and out of the water persuade them to cover up with a T-shirt, even when in the water.

ACTIVITIES
For older children there are activities galore in the countryside and along the coast, such as tennis, riding, sailing, swimming, bathing in hot mineral springs and hill walking. If you're near one of Tuscany's natural parks, it's worth checking out what outdoor organized activities are on during your stay; you'll find most on offer during school holiday times (www.parks.it).

For more information, check with the local tourist office.

PARKS
Although all the major cities have parks, only the biggest have grassy areas large enough for children to play games and run around in. However, many have playgrounds, with a selection of swings and slides, and they are good places for a picnic. Even small towns and villages have a few slides and swings to entertain children.

CITIES
Tourist information offices will be able to recommend attractions that are likely to appeal to children. Specific attractions in Florence include the Museo dei Ragazzi (the Children's Museum of Florence) and the other activities in the Palazzo Vecchio, Museo Stibbert and the Museo di Storia della Scienza.

In Siena, older children will be fascinated by the different aspects of the Palio (▷ 187) and will enjoy a visit to one of the contrade museums—the tourist office will be able to help. Most kids over five will happily spend time browsing in the markets.

DISCOUNTS
In Italy, admission prices for museums, galleries and other attractions are nearly always reduced for children, but you will need proof of identity to be eligible (▷ 250). Family tickets are increasingly available. Some museums are free to those under five or even up to 18. If prices are not displayed, it's always worth asking.

Clockwise from left *There are lots of shops that will attract children; the Marzocco outside the Palazzo Vecchio; Siena's Palio, an event rich in pageantry*

FESTIVALS AND EVENTS

There's no shortage of festivals celebrating religious holidays, the arts and gastronomic delicacies. Celebrations are organized by Italians for Italians, but they are open to anyone who's willing to participate in the right spirit. That spirit differs enormously according to each festival's focus, so be prepared for intense religious feeling or exuberant high spirits. Major festivals, such as Siena's *Palio*, attract visitors from all over the world, and it's important that you book your accommodation well in advance. You'll find low-key local events throughout the country during the summer. Keep an eye open for posters and ask at tourist offices. For an enthusiastic overview of Italian festivals visit www.hostetler.net.

RELIGIOUS FESTIVALS

These festivals are closely linked to the calendar of the Roman Catholic Church. In Tuscany Christmas is celebrated by elaborate *presepi* (cribs) set up in churches. The lead-up to Lent is the excuse for some serious Carnevale (carnival) partying in many towns, including Viareggio, which stages Italy's largest carnival outside Venice. Easter sees Florence's major festival, the Scoppio del Carro (explosion of the cart), when a cart of fireworks explodes during Easter Mass. Holy Week, the run-up to Easter, is celebrated with religious processions in many small towns—head for Castiglione Fiorentino and Buonconvento to catch the best. Corpus Domini, commemorating the cult of the Blessed Sacrament, and the August feast of the Assumption of the Virgin are celebrated across the region. The Day of the Dead (1 November) is when Italians return to their native towns and villages to tend their relatives' graves and reunite with their whole family. At local levels, every town and

village has its own patron saint, whose feast day is celebrated with processions and church services, culminating in late-night partying.

TRADITIONAL FESTIVALS

For an adrenaline rush head for Siena and the passion and spectacle of the *Palio*, a hair-raising bareback horse race preceded by a spectacular procession with flag-throwing. This is Tuscany's biggest festival, but Arezzo's *Giostra del Saracino* (The Saracen's Joust) along with *Il Gioco del Ponte* (The Bridge Game) and the *Luminaria di San Ranieri* (St. Ranieri's Illumination) in Pisa are historic events that attract thousands. Inhabitants of many small towns celebrate their history by dressing in traditional costumes and parading through the streets.

ARTS FESTIVALS

Italy has a lively arts festival scene, particularly in the summer, when amphitheatres, arenas, churches and piazzas are transformed into venues for cultural events. These festivals cover everything, including Greek

theatre, opera, dance, rock and jazz. Many run for well over a month.

Central Italy is particularly active, and if you're in Tuscany during the summer an evening dose of culture is easy to find. Look out for Florence's *Maggio Musicale Fiorentino*, which ranks high on the international circuit, as does the *Settembre Musica* series. Opera-lovers can hear Puccini performed at the composer's villa on the shores of Lago di Massaciuccoli, while farther south there's more opera at Batignano, near Grosseto.

FOOD FESTIVALS

For a true taste of Italy seek out the *sagre* (food festivals), where you can sample local produce. These small-town festivities provide an insight into rural Italian life. Eating and drinking are often accompanied by a brass band and dancing, rounded off with a firework display. Wine is often a major feature, as it is on *Cantine Aperte* (open wine cellars) day, a May Sunday when wine-producing estates throw open their doors for tastings.

Eating is definitely one of life's pleasures in Tuscany, as it is all over Italy. Tuscan food is fresh, seasonal and, above all, local. There's no such thing as Italian cooking, but rather regional cuisine, and generally you'll eat the best of Tuscan produce cooked to Tuscan recipes. Expect to find magnificent meat, beans, bread and fruity olive oil.

FRESH REGIONAL PRODUCE

Most Tuscan cooks are obsessed with freshness and food shopping is a daily social event in smaller towns. This is beginning to change in Florence and the larger towns, as huge supermarkets cater to an increasingly busy population. But even here you will notice the range, freshness and quality of what's available. Outside the big cities, you're also unlikely to find restaurants serving anything other than local food, so don't expect to find much in the way of specialties from other Italian regions, let alone any serving international cuisine.

BREAD AND BEANS

Bread is one of the traditional staples and features heavily in local cooking—served up as *crostini* (bread with a savoury topping) covered in olive paste, fresh tomatoes or drizzled with oil, adding body to old-fashioned soups such as *ribollita* (thick vegetable soup), and providing the perfect foil to locally cured *prosciutto crudo* (raw

cured ham) and *finocchiona* (fennel-flavoured salami).

Tuscans are dubbed *mangiafagioli* (bean-eaters) with some justification. Beans are very popular throughout the year, from the first tender broad beans eaten raw with pecorino (cheese made from sheep's milk) to the dried white beans with sage that accompany grilled meats.

MEALS

Many Italians eat breakfast (*prima colazione*) in a bar—a cappuccino, strong coffee with plenty of hot milk, and a sweet pastry. Hotels usually serve a buffet breakfast with fruit juice and a selection of cereal, cold meat and cheeses.

Lunch (*pranzo*) and dinner (*cena*) both follow the same pattern—though it's unlikely that you will want to tackle the full menu twice a day. The first course is the *antipasto* (starter, literally 'before the meal'), a selection of *crostini*, cold meats and salami, seafood or vegetable dishes. *Il primo* (first course) consists of pasta, soup

or risotto. This is followed by the *secondo* (second course), a portion of a meat or a fish dish, served on its own—if you want vegetables (*contorni*) or a salad (*insalata*) order them separately. This is followed by a selection of desserts (*dolci*) or cheese (*formaggio*). The former is often fruit, fruit salad (*macedonia*) or an ice cream (*gelato*), though more sophisticated places will have a wider range. There's no pressure to go through the whole menu, and it's acceptable to order a *primo* and salad, or an *antipasto* and *secondo*.

Italians drink water (*acqua minerale*) with every meal, either sparkling (*frizzante* or *con gas*) or still (*senza gas*), accompanied by a relatively modest amount of wine or a beer. Excessive drinking is frowned upon in Italy. Bread is included with every meal.

MEALTIMES AND SMOKING

If you are heading for breakfast in a bar, most open around 7–7.30am. Restaurants normally open for lunch around 12.30 or 1 and stop serving at 3; they reopen for dinner around 7.30–8pm.

Smoking is banned in all public places.

WHERE TO EAT

» *Trattorie* are usually family-run places. They are generally more basic than restaurants. Sometimes there is no written menu and the waiter will reel off the list of the day's specials. They usually open at lunchtime and in the evening.

» *Ristoranti* are not always open for lunch. The food and surroundings are usually more refined than those of a *trattoria*. Both *trattorie* and *ristoranti* add a cover charge (*coperto*), which includes bread and a service charge to the bill.

» *Pizzerie* specialize in pizzas, but often also serve simple pasta dishes. Look out for the sign *forno al legno*, meaning that the pizzas are cooked in a wood-fired oven.

» *Osterie* can either be old-fashioned places specializing in home-cooked food or extremely elegant, long-established restaurants.

PAYING THE BILL

» Request the bill (*il conto*) and check whether service is included.

» Scribbled bills on scraps of paper are illegal; if you don't get a proper one, say that you need a receipt (*una ricevuta*), which all restaurants, bars and shops are legally obliged to give. Both they and you can be fined if you do not take this with you.

» Smaller establishments normally expect to be paid in cash; you'll be able to use a credit card in more expensive establishments.

» If service isn't included, it's customary to leave a small tip—some loose change will do.

» Most restaurants have one official closing day a week, but many places open every day during the summer.

SNACKS AND ICE CREAM

» Bars serve hot and cold drinks, alcohol and snacks throughout the day. It's customary to eat or drink standing up; you will pay a surcharge if you sit down either inside or at

a table outside. In busier city bars make your request and pay at the cash desk, then take the receipt (*scontrino*) and go to the bar where you will be served.

» Snacks include *panini* (filled rolls), *tramezzini* (sandwiches made on soft white bread), mini-pizzas and toast (toasted sandwiches). Upscale bars will bring olives, crisps (chips) or nuts with your drink if you're sitting down.

» All bars have toilets (*bagni*) but you may have to ask for the key (*chiave*).

» *Alimentari* (general grocers) sell breads and will often make you up a *panino* (filled roll).

» Pizza is available everywhere and served by the slice from tiny *pizzerie* to take out—look for the sign *pizza al taglio*. There are also a few international pizza chains to be found around the region.

» *Tavole calde* are stand-up snack bars that serve freshly prepared hot food; some have seating as well.

» *Forni* (bakers) sell *foccacia*, a tasty flat oil and herb bread.

» *Rosticcerie* serve spit-roasted food, particularly chicken, pasta and vegetable dishes to eat in or take out.

» *Gelaterie* sell a range of ice cream, served in a cone (*cono*) or a tub (*coppa*) of varying sizes. The best ice cream is made on the premises, known as *produzione propria*.

» Larger towns and cities have outlets of McDonald's and Burger King.

» International cuisine is very limited in Italy. Chinese restaurants are becoming increasingly popular in some larger towns, but Florence is about your only option in Tuscany for a wider choice.

WHAT TO DRINK

» Coffee (*caffè*) is served in bars and cafés. Choose from a small black coffee (*caffè* or *espresso*), a cappuccino (with frothy milk), *caffè con latte* (very milky coffee), *caffè macchiato* (an espresso with a drop of milk) or a *caffè corretto* with a slug of spirits. If you want weaker coffee, ask for a *caffè lungo* or an *Americano*. Decaffeinated coffee

goes by the generic name Hag.

» Tea (*tè*) is generally served black; ask for *latte freddo* (cold milk) if you want milk. In summer *tè freddo* (iced tea) is popular.

» Hot chocolate (*cioccolata calda*), often served with whipped cream (*panna*), is popular during the winter.

» Beer (*birra*) is widely drunk, either bottled or draught (*alla spina*). Preferred Italian brands include Nastro Azzuro, Peroni and Moretti. Imported beers are widely available.

» Wine is served in bars as well as in restaurants. Ask for white (*bianco*), red (*rosso*) or the less common rosé (*rosato*). House wine is either *vino della casa* or *vino sfuso*, and can be very good. Bottled wines are locally produced, except in smarter restaurants; best are DOCG wines (Denominazione d'Origine Contollata e Garantita)—the label guarantees its origins. Many producers market some superb wines as *vino da tavola*, which are well worth sampling.

» Super Tuscan wines are made from non-traditional grapes. They are expensive, but highly regarded.

» Spirits are known by their generic names, and you will find all the usual ones on sale. Italians are also fond of *aperitivi* such as Martini, Campari, Cinzano and the artichoke-based Cynar, and firmly believe in settling the stomach after eating with a *digestivo*. Fiery grappa is the most common, but herb-based liqueurs (*amari*), such as Averna and Montenegro, are drunk everywhere and there are dozens of local varieties: Amaretto, based on almonds, Strega, made from herbs and saffron, and *limoncello*, a lemon liqueur. Stock and Vecchia Romagna are Italy's preferred brandies.

» Soft drinks such as cola and lemonade compete with others, such as *spremuta di arancia* (freshly pressed orange juice), *granita* (fruity crushed ice), *sugo di albicocca* (bottled apricot juice) and *frullato*, a type of milk shake.

Opposite *Stop at a* gelateria *for the perfect pick-me up*

To appreciate Tuscan cuisine fully you will need to venture away from the beaten track and sample local dishes. If you don't speak Italian this can be a daunting prospect, but knowledge of a few key words will help you to work out what's on the menu, order what you want and avoid any embarrassing blunders. This menu reader will help you to translate common words and familiarize yourself with dishes and ingredients that you are likely to see on a menu.

PIATTI – COURSES
antipasti starters
primi piatti first courses
secondi piatti main courses
contorni vegetables/side dishes
dolci desserts
spuntini snacks

CARNE – MEAT
agnello lamb
cacciagione game
cinghiale wild boar
coniglio rabbit
fegato liver
maiale pork
manzo beef
pancetta bacon
pollo chicken
prosciutto cotto cooked ham
prosciutto crudo cured raw ham, saltier and stronger than Parma ham
salsiccia sausage
tacchino turkey
trippa alla Fiorentina tripe with onions
vitello veal

PESCE – FISH
alici anchovy
baccalà dried salt cod
branzino sea bass
fritto misto mixed fried fish
merluzzo cod
sarde sardines
sogliola sole
tonno tuna
trota trout

FRUTTI DI MARE – SEAFOOD
aragoste lobster
calamari squid
canestrelli scallops
cozze mussels
gamberetti prawns (shrimps)
ostriche oysters
vongole clams

VERDURE – VEGETABLES
asparagi asparagus
carote carrots
cavolo nero strong dark cabbage used in Tuscan winter soups
cicoria bitter green leaves stewed with garlic and olive oil
cipolla onion
fagioli beans
fagiolini green beans
latuga lettuce
melanzane aubergines (eggplant)
patate potatoes
peperone red/green pepper (capsicum)
piselli peas
pomodori tomatoes
spinaci spinach
zuccha pumpkin

METODI DI CUCINA – COOKING METHODS
affumicato smoked
al forno baked
alla griglia grilled, often over an open wood fire
arrosto roasted
bollito boiled
casalinga home-made
cotto cooked
crudo raw
fritto fried
ripieno stuffed
stufato stewed

LA PASTA – PASTA
cannelloni baked meat- or cheese-filled tubes
fettucine wide strips
fusilli spiral shapes
lasagne layers of pasta, meat sauce and béchamel or tomato sauce
pappardelle rippled strips
penne quill shapes
ravioli pasta parcels filled with meat, cheese or spinach
tagliatelle thin ribbons or strips

tortellini little 'hats' with meat or cheese filling

SALSI/SUGI – SAUCES
amatriciana bacon, tomato, chilli and onion
arrabbiata tomato and hot chilli
brodo broth
burro e salvia melted butter, parmesan and sage
cacciatore sauce for meat: tomato, onion, garlic, mushrooms, wine
carbonara pancetta bacon, egg, cream and black pepper
passata sieved tomatoes
pesto basil, garlic, pinenuts, olive oil and pecorino
puttanesca tomato, garlic, hot chilli, anchovies, capers
ragù minced meat, tomato and garlic
salsa sauce
salsa verde parsley, garlic,

anchovies, capers, lemon juice, salt, pepper, olive oil
salsa di pomodoro tomato sauce
sugo another term for sauce

SPECIALITÀ – SPECIAL DISHES
acqua cotta thin vegetable soup, sometimes served with a poached egg
bistecca alla fiorentina thick steak grilled over a wood or charcoal fire
crostini rounds of toasted bread topped with olive oil, garlic and a variety of other toppings
fagioli al fiasco haricot beans stewed in olive oil
fagioli all'uccelletto beans stewed slowly with garlic, sage and tomatoes, and sometimes link sausages
pappardelle al sugo di lepre rippled strips of pasta with a hare sauce
peperonata sweet pepper and tomato stew
polpette meatballs
ribollito literally meaning 're-boiled', vegetable soup thickened with bread and served the day after it's prepared
scaloppini thinly sliced veal cooked in white wine
stracotto beef stew

CONTORNI – SIDE DISHES
insalata mista mixed salad
insalata verde green salad
pane bread
patate fritte chips (french fries)

ALTRI PIATTI – OTHER DISHES
antipasto misto mixed cold meats: salami, ham etc.
frittata omelette
gnocchi small dumplings made from potato and flour or semolina
minestrone thick vegetable soup with pasta
risotto rice cooked in stock
risotto alla Milanese risotto with saffron
zuppa soup

DOLCI – CAKES/DESSERTS
cantuccini crunchy almond biscuits, served with wine at the end of a meal

cassata Sicilian fruit ice cream
cioccolata chocolate
crema custard
gelato ice cream
macedonia fruit salad
panforte hard spiced fruit cake from Siena
panna cream
una pasta a cake/pastry
semifreddo chilled semi-frozen dessert
tiramisù chocolate/coffee sponge (ladyfinger) dessert
torta tart, often latticed and filled with jam
zabaglione egg, sugar and Marsala dessert
zabaione di Verduzzo custard pudding with Friuli wine
zuccotto ice cream cake
zuppa inglese trifle

FRUTTI – FRUIT
arancia orange
ciliege cherries
fragole strawberries
lamponi raspberries
mele apples
melone melon
pera pear
pesca peach
pesca noci nectarine
uve grapes

FORMAGGI – CHEESES
fontina smooth, rich cheese
un formaggio di capra goat's cheese
un formaggio nostrano local cheese
parmigiano parmesan
pecorino hard cheese made with sheep's milk

BEVANDE – DRINKS
acqua minerale mineral water
birra beer
caffè corretto coffee with liqueur/spirit
caffè freddo iced coffee
caffè con latte milky coffee
caffè lungo weak coffee
caffè macchiato coffee with a drop of milk
caffè ristretto strong coffee
digestivo after-dinner liqueur
frizzante fizzy

ghiaccio ice
liquore liqueur
porto port wine
secco dry
spumante sparkling wine
succo di arancia orange juice
tè tea
tè al latte tea with milk
tè freddo iced tea
vini da tavola table wines
vini pregiati quality wines
vino bianco white wine
vino rosato rosé wine
vino rosso red wine

CONDIMENTI – SEASONINGS
aglio garlic
aromatiche herbs
basilico basil
capperi capers
pepe pepper
peperoncino chilli
prezzemolo parsley
rosemarino rosemary
sale salt
salvia sage
senape mustard
zucchero sugar

Choose from world-class hotels in historic buildings, ultra-chic boutique hotels or family-run pensioni that haven't changed much in 30 years; or rent a villa, stay on a farm or track down a village room. On the whole, accommodation is more expensive in Tuscany than in many other parts of the country, and is in high demand from May until late September. So shop around, and book in advance for the best deals.

HOTELS

Tuscan hotels (*alberghi*) are graded by the regional authorities on a star rating of one to five. These refer to the facilities provided—air conditioning, telephone and television, elevator, swimming pool—rather than an establishment's character or its level of comfort.

» You can expect five-star hotels to be grand, with superb facilities and a high level of service.

» Four-star establishments will be almost as good as five-star.

» Three-star hotels are more idiosyncratic. Prices can vary enormously between them, as can the public areas, and staffing levels will be considerably lower, with often only one person manning the entire hotel. You can expect all three-star rooms to have a television, a telephone and sometimes air conditioning.

» One and two-star hotels are relatively inexpensive, but are clean and comfortable, and rooms almost always have private bathrooms in two-star places. Breakfast is usually included, but simpler hotels rarely have restaurants, and some do not provide breakfast. Breakfast can be very poor too, so consider a bar breakfast instead.

BED AND BREAKFASTS

Establishments offering bed and breakfast are becoming increasingly common across Italy. The trend began in 2000, when the government, fearful that there would be insufficient rooms to house the expected influx of visitors and pilgrims for the millennial celebrations, relaxed the rules for setting up these and other types of accommodation. Most tourist offices and official accommodation listings and websites now carry details of B&Bs, most of which are on a par with better one-star or most two-star hotels (including en-suite bathrooms). Bear in mind, though, that breakfast may sometimes amount to little more than a roll and coffee.

AGRITURISMI

The *agriturismo* trend was started to enable farmers and landowners to conserve redundant farm buildings by converting them into holiday accommodation. This can take the form of a small and luxurious hotel, an apartment, or simply a handful of rooms in a converted barn. Accommodation is often on a week-only basis, but many owners will rent rooms by the night, and meals can be provided. *Agriturismi* are often in beautiful surroundings and frequently provide activities such as riding, escorted walking and mountain biking. Many have swimming pools and serve their home-grown produce at meal times. The movement is particularly strong in Tuscany. You'll need a car as *agriturismi* can be well off the beaten track, and most require advance booking. All tourist offices carry a full list of *agriturismi* in the area.

INDEPENDENCE
Cooking for yourself is an excellent option for cutting costs and giving yourself freedom. In Tuscany there's both a range of city apartments and a great number of old farmhouses and villas to choose from. Tour operators sell villa packages, which include flights and car rental, but if you want to be independent, contact the local visitor offices well in advance, or look at their websites. There are also websites devoted to private house rentals. If you're using Italian internet sites do your research online, then phone to book.

RIFUGI
If you're in the mountains hiking or climbing, you can stay in a network of *rifugi*—mountain huts—owned by the Club Alpino Italiano. Most are fairly sparse, but all are very reasonably priced and surrounded by wonderful countryside with spectacular views. For further details contact local tourist offices or go to www.cai.it and click on rifugi.

ROOMS TO RENT
In popular areas you may see signs saying rooms, bed and breakfast, *camere* or *zimmer*. These are rooms to rent in private houses and are a good option if money is tight or you can't find a hotel. Local tourist offices keep a list.

VILLAS
Villas in Italy vary enormously in quality and price. A few really are villas—large, old and rather grand country houses. Most, though, are renovated rural homes, farmhouses, houses in restored hamlets or modern buildings on the coast or in a rural or semi-rural location. Be sure what you are

booking, and in particular check whether the property has its own, private swimming pool—often pools are shared, especially in villas comprising several self-contained apartments, and in converted hamlet or village 'complexes'. If there is a pool, check that it is functioning— many villa owners open their pools only in late June or July. If privacy is important, also check whether the owner lives on or close to the rental premises—many do. Check what the price includes (linen, oil or other heating, electricity and compulsory cleaning after your stay may all be extra). Also look at prices throughout the year. Peak season is usually in July and August, but even just a week outside these months, or outside school half-terms the rest of the year, can result in substantial savings. A growing trend among villa operators is to offer three- or four-day rentals (rather than a week or two weeks) in traditionally quieter periods of the year. This allows the possibility of taking a villa as part of a short break.

RESERVATIONS
Florence is so popular that you will need to book in advance at whatever time of the year you decide to visit. Elsewhere, Italians are on holiday during August, so remember you'll be competing with them for beds. If you're booking in advance from home, make certain you get written or printed confirmation and take it with you. Without this, you may turn up and find all knowledge of your booking denied.

FINDING A ROOM
» If you haven't made a reservation before you arrive, start your search around the main piazza or in the *centro storico* (old town). In hilltop villages and towns it is also worth looking outside the *centro storico* or town walls. The tourist information office will have lists and may be willing to make the reservationon your behalf.
» Yellow signs direct you to hotels both in the middle and on the

outskirts of towns and villages.
» Check-out time is normally noon, but hotels will usually store your luggage until the end of the day.

PRICING
» Italian hotels are legally required to post rates for high and low season on every bedroom door.
» You should agree on a price before making a reservation.
» Rates vary according to the season, sometimes by as much as 25 per cent. Some hotels have high (*alta*) and low season (*bassa stagione*) rates; others charge the same rate year round (*tutto l'anno*).
» Hotels often quote their most expensive rates. So if you want a particular hotel ask if they have a less expensive room.
» City hotels sometimes have reduced weekend rates.
» Smaller hotels can be open to gentle bargaining, particularly during quieter times. However, don't be surprised if you don't get anywhere.
» Hotels are often willing to put another bed in a room for an extra 35 per cent, ideal for families with children.
» Internet sites or hotel websites often have the best deals, special offers or last-minute prices.

FURTHER SOURCES OF INFORMATION

AGRITURISMI
There are numerous *agriturismo* rental companies and websites for all regions of Tuscany. Both www.agriturist.com and www.agriturismo.net sites provide extensive listings. **Touring Club Italiano** (TCI) publishes *Agriturismo e vacanze in campagna* annually at €40. Visit www.touringclub.it.

CAMPING
TCI (see above) publishes an annual guide to campsites, *Campeggio e Villaggi Turistici* (€20).

Opposite *Hotel Italia*, Cortona

Once you have mastered a few basic rules, Italian is an easy language to speak: it is phonetic and, unlike English, particular combinations of letters are always pronounced the same way. The stress is usually on the penultimate syllable, but if the word has an accent, this is where the stress falls.

Vowels are pronounced as follows:

a	casa	as in mat short 'a'
e	vero closed	as in base
e	sette open	as in vet short 'e'
i	vino	as in mean
o	dove closed	as in bowl
o	otto open	as in not
u	uva	as in book

Consonants as in English except:
c before **i** or **e** becomes **ch** as in church
ch before **i** or **e** becomes **c** as in cat
g before **i** or **e** becomes **j** as in Julia
gh before **i** or **e** becomes **g** as in good
gn as in onion
gli as in million
h is rare in Italian words, and is always silent
r is usually rolled
z is pronounced **tz** when it falls in the middle of a word

All Italian nouns are either masculine (usually ending in **o** when singular or **i** when plural) or feminine (usually ending in **a** when singular or **e** when plural). Some nouns, which may be masculine or feminine, end in **e** (which changes to **i** when plural). An adjective's ending changes to match the ending of the noun.

USEFUL WORDS

yes	sì
no	no
please	per favore
thank you	grazie
you're welcome	prego
excuse me!	scusi!
where	dove
here	qui
there	la
when	quando
now	adesso
later	più tardi
why	perchè
who	chi
may I/can I	posso

CONVERSATION

What is the time?
Che ore sono?

I don't speak Italian
Non parlo italiano

I only speak a little Italian
Parlo solo un poco italiano

Do you speak English?
Parla inglese?

I don't understand
Non capisco

Please repeat that
Può ripetere?

Please speak more slowly
Può parlare più lentamente?

Write that down for me, please
Lo scriva, per piacere

Please spell that
Come si scrive?

My name is
Mi chiamo

What's your name?
Come si chiama?

Hello, pleased to meet you
Piacere

This is my friend
Le presento il mio amico/la mia amica

This is my wife/husband/ daughter/son
Le presento mia moglie/mio marito/ mia figlia/mio figlio

Where do you live?
Dove abiti?

I live in ...
Vivo in ...

I'm here on holiday/vacation
Sono qui in vacanza

Good morning
Buon giorno

Good afternoon/evening
Buona sera

Goodbye
Arrivederci

How are you?
Come sta?

Fine, thank you
Bene, grazie

I'm sorry
Mi dispiace

SHOPPING

Could you help me, please?
Può aiutarmi, per favore?

How much is this?
Quanto costa questo?

I'm looking for ...
Cerco ...

Where can I buy ...?
Dove posso comprare ...?

How much is this/that?
Quanto costa questo/quello?

When does the shop open/close?
Quando apre/chiude il negozio?

I'm just looking, thank you
Sto solo dando un'occhiata, grazie

This isn't what I want
Non è quel che cerco

I'll take this
Prendo questo

Do you have anything less expensive/smaller/larger?
Ha qualcosa di meno caro/più piccolo/più grande?

Are the instructions included?
Ci sono anche le istruzioni?

Do you have a bag for this?
Può darmi una busta?

I'm looking for a present
Cerco un regalo

Can you gift wrap this please?
Può farmi un pacco regalo?

Do you accept credit cards?
Accettate carte di credito?

I'd like a kilo of ...
Vorrei un chilo di ...

Do you have shoes to match this?
Ha delle scarpe che vadano con questo?

This is the right size
Questa è la taglia (misura—*for shoes*) giusta

Can you measure me please?
Può prendermi la misura, per favore?

This doesn't suit me
Questo non mi sta bene

Do you have this in ...?
Avete questo in ...?

Should this be dry cleaned?
Questo è da lavare a secco?

Is there a market?
C'è un mercato?

NUMBERS

0	zero
1	uno
2	due
3	tre
4	quattro
5	cinque
6	sei
7	sette
8	otto
9	nove
10	dieci
11	undici
12	dodici
13	tredici
14	quattordici
15	quindici
16	sedici
17	diciassette
18	diciotto
19	diciannove
20	venti
21	ventuno
22	ventidue
30	trenta
40	quaranta
50	cinquanta
60	sessanta
70	settanta
80	ottanta
90	novanta
100	cento
1,000	mille
million	milione
quarter	quarto
half	mezza
three quarters	tre quarti

MONEY

Is there a bank/currency exchange office nearby?
C'è una banca/un ufficio di cambio qui vicino?

Can I cash this here?
Posso incassare questo?

I'd like to change sterling/dollars into euros
Vorrei cambiare sterline/dollari in euro

Can I use my credit card to withdraw cash?
Posso usare la mia carta di credito per prelevare contanti?

IN TROUBLE

Help!
Aiuto!

Stop, thief!
Al ladro!

Can you help me, please?
Può aiutarmi, per favore?

Call the fire brigade/police/an ambulance
Chiami i pompieri/la polizia/un'ambulanza

I have lost my passport/wallet/purse
Ho perso il passaporto/il portafoglio/il borsellino

Where is the police station?
Dov'è il commissariato?

I have been robbed
Sono stato/a derubato/a

I need to see a doctor/dentist
Ho bisogno di un medico/dentista

Where is the hospital?
Dov'è l'ospedale?

I am allergic to ...
Sono allergico/a a...

I have a heart condition
Ho disturbi cardiaci

GETTING AROUND

Where is the train/bus station?
Dov'è la stazione ferroviaria/degli autobus (dei pullman–*long distance*)?

Does this train/bus go to ...?
È questo il treno/l'autobus (il pullman—*long distance*) per ...?

Where are we?
Dove siamo?

Do I have to get off here?
Devo scendere qui?

When is the first/last bus to ...?
Quando c'è il primo/l'ultimo autobus per ...?

Can I have a single/return ticket to ... please?
Un biglietto di andata/andata e ritorno per ... per favore

I would like a standard/first-class ticket to ...
Un biglietto di seconda/prima classe per ...

Where is the timetable?
Dov'è l'orario?

Do you have a subway/bus map?
Ha una piantina della metropolitana/ degli autobus?

Where can I find a taxi?
Dove posso trovare un tassì?

Please take me to ...
Per favore, mi porti a ...

How much is the journey?
Quanto costerà il viaggio?

Please turn on the meter
Accenda il tassametro, per favore

I'd like to get out here, please
Vorrei scendere qui, per favore

Is this the way to ...?
È questa la strada per ...?

Excuse me, I think I am lost
Mi scusi, penso di essermi perduto/a

AROUND THE TOWN

on/to the right ....a destra
on/to the left .... a sinistra
around the corner............all'angolo
opposite .... di fronte a ...
at the bottom (of) ....in fondo (a)
straight on................ sempre dritto
near.................................vicino a
cross over .... attraversi
in front of............................. davanti
behind.................................... dietro
north .... nord
south...sud
east ....est
west ....ovest
free..gratis
donation .... donazione
open .... aperto
closed...................................... chiuso
cathedral..........................cattedrale
church ....chiesa
castle................................... castello
museum...................................museo
monument .... monumento
palace.....................................palazzo
gallery .... galleria
town...città
old town ....centro storico
town hall .... municipio

boulevard ....corso
square ....piazza
street.. via
avenue .... viale
island .... isola
river.. fiume
lake...lago
bridge.. ponte
no entry ....vietato l'accesso
push ....spingere
pull .... tirare
entrance............................. ingresso
exit .... uscita

TOURIST INFORMATION

Where is the tourist information office/tourist information desk, please?
Dov'è l'ufficio turistico/il banco informazioni turistiche, per favore?

Do you have a city map?
Avete una cartina della città?

Can you give me some information about ...?
Puo darmi delle informazioni su ...?

What sights/hotels/restaurants can you recommend?
Quali monumenti/alberghi/ ristoranti mi consiglia?

Can you point them out on the map?
Me li può indicare sulla cartina?

What is the admission price?
Quant'è il biglietto d'ingresso?

Is there a discount for senior citizens/students?
Ci sono riduzioni per anziani/ studenti?

Is there an English-speaking guide?
C'è una guida di lingue inglese?

Are there organized excursions?
Ci sono escursioni organizzate?

Do you have a brochure in English?
Avete un opuscolo in inglese?

Could you reserve tickets for me?
Mi può prenotare dei biglietti?

Can we make reservations here?
Possiamo prenotare qui?

RESTAURANTS

Waiter/waitress
Cameriere/cameriera

I'd like to reserve a table for ... people at ...
Vorrei prenotare un tavolo per ... persone a ...

A table for ..., please
Una tavola per ..., per favore

Can we sit there?
Possiamo sederci qui?

Is this table taken?
Questa tavola è occupata?

Are there tables outside?
Ci sono tavole all'aperto?

We would like to wait for a table
Aspettiamo che si liberi una tavola

Could we see the menu/wine list?
Possiamo vedere il menù/la lista dei vini?

Do you have a menu/wine list in English?
Avete un menù/una lista dei vini in inglese?

What do you recommend?
Cosa consiglia?

What is the house special?
Qual è la specialità della casa?

I can't eat wheat/sugar/salt/ pork/beef/dairy
Non posso mangiare grano/ zucchero/sale/maiale/manzo/latticini

I am a vegetarian
Sono vegetariano/a

I'd like ...
Vorrei ...

May I have an ashtray?
Può portare un portacenere?

I ordered ...
Ho ordinato ...

Could we have some salt and pepper?
Può portare del sale e del pepe?

The food is cold
Il cibo è freddo

The meat is overcooked/too rare
La carne è troppo cotta/non è abbastanza cotta

This is not what I ordered
Non ho ordinato questo

Can I have the bill, please?
Il conto, per favore?

Is service included?
Il servizio è compreso?

The bill is not right
Il conto è sbagliato
We didn't have this
Non abbiamo avuto questo

HOTELS

I have made a reservation for ... nights
Ho prenotato per ... notti

Do you have a room?
Avete camere libere?

How much per night?
Quanto costa una notte?

Double/single room
Camera doppia/singola

Twin room
Camera a due letti

With bath/shower
Con bagno/doccia

May I see the room?
Posso vedere la camera?

I'll take this room
Prendo questa camera

Could I have another room?
Vorrei cambiare camera

Is there a lift in the hotel?
C'è un ascensore nell'albergo?

Is the room air-conditioned/heated?
C'è aria condizionata/riscaldamento nella camera?

Is breakfast included in the price?
La colazione è compreso?

When is breakfast served?
A che ora è servita la colazione?

The room is too hot/too cold/dirty
La camera è troppo calda/ troppo fredda/sporca

I am leaving this morning
Parto stamattina

Can I pay my bill?
Posso pagare il conto?

TIMES/DAYS/MONTHS

Monday	lunedì
Tuesday	martedì
Wednesday	mercoledì
Thursday	giovedì
Friday	venerdì
Saturday	sabato
Sunday	domenica
day	giorno
week	settimana
today	oggi
yesterday	ieri
tomorrow	domani
January	gennaio
February	febbraio
March	marzo
April	aprile
May	maggio
June	giugno
July	luglio
August	agosto
September	settembre
October	ottobre
November	novembre
December	dicembre

COLOURS

black	nero
brown	marrone
pink	rosa
red	rosso
orange	arancia
yellow	giallo
green	verde
light blue	celeste
sky blue	azzuro
purple	viola
white	bianco
grey	grigio

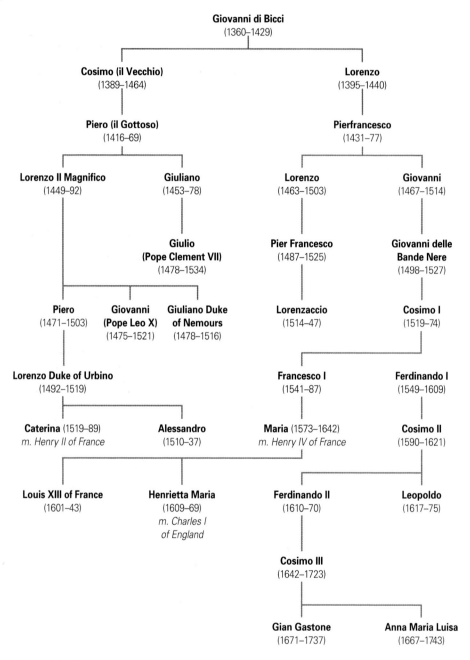

Giovanni di Bicci
(1360–1429)

Cosimo (il Vecchio)
(1389–1464)

Lorenzo
(1395–1440)

Piero (il Gottoso)
(1416–69)

Pierfrancesco
(1431–77)

Lorenzo II Magnifico
(1449–92)

Giuliano
(1453–78)

Lorenzo
(1463–1503)

Giovanni
(1467–1514)

**Giulio
(Pope Clement VII)**
(1478–1534)

Pier Francesco
(1487–1525)

**Giovanni delle
Bande Nere**
(1498–1527)

Piero
(1471–1503)

**Giovanni
(Pope Leo X)**
(1475–1521)

**Giuliano Duke
of Nemours**
(1478–1516)

Lorenzaccio
(1514–47)

Cosimo I
(1519–74)

Lorenzo Duke of Urbino
(1492–1519)

Francesco I
(1541–87)

Ferdinando I
(1549–1609)

Caterina (1519–89)
m. Henry II of France

Alessandro
(1510–37)

Maria (1573–1642)
m. Henry IV of France

Cosimo II
(1590–1621)

Louis XIII of France
(1601–43)

Henrietta Maria
(1609–69)
*m. Charles I
of England*

Ferdinando II
(1610–70)

Leopoldo
(1617–75)

Cosimo III
(1642–1723)

Gian Gastone
(1671–1737)

Anna Maria Luisa
(1667–1743)

Little could the Medici's 14th-century founding father have suspected the extent to which his family would dominate Florence and Tuscany, nor how his descendants would include popes and cardinals and marry into some of Europe's most prestigious noble and royal families. The direct Medici male line died out in the 18th century but Medici blood still flows in the royal and aristocratic veins of countless European families.

Aisle: the interior corridors of a church, running either side of the nave

Apse: the semicircular end of a church or chapel

Architrave: a moulded frame around a door or window

Atrium: an inner courtyard, open to the sky

Baldacchino/baldacchin: a canopy, usually over a throne or altar

Baroque: architectural style popular in the 17th century. It is characterized by elaborate decoration of convex and concave curves

Byzantine: architectural style developed after AD330, when Byzantium became capital of the Eastern Empire. It is characterized by Eastern influences and highly decorated style

Campanile: a bell tower, often separate from the main building

Capital: top of a column

Chancel: the eastern end of a church, where the high altar is found

Chiaroscuro: exaggerated light and shade effects in a painting

Classical: architectural style characterized by the use of elements from Ancient Greece or Rome, including finely proportioned, simple shapes, and which has its roots in the fifth century BC.

It has seen many revivals, including in the 16th century and in neoclassicism, which was popular between the late 18th and early 19th centuries

Cloister: a courtyard, often in a monastic building, surrounded by a covered passageway with an open arcade or colonnade on the interior side

Coffering: ceiling decoration made up from patterns of recessed squares or other shapes

Colonnade: a row of columns supporting a beam

Column: an upright, usually used as a load-bearing support, but can be

freestanding as a monument

Confessio: an underground area of a church, usually below the altar, which houses relics

Crossing: the area of a church where the transepts, nave and chancel intersect

Crypt: area below a church, usually for graves

Cupola: a domed roof

Etruscans: a race of people who inhabited Tuscany from around the 10th century BC. Their architecture was similar in style to that of the Greeks of the same period

Fresco: a painting made directly onto damp plaster so that the image becomes permanent

Frieze: a decorated band, often along the top of a wall

Gothic: architectural style popular between the late 12th century and the mid-16th century, recognizable by its pointed arches and ribbed vaulting

Greek cross: a church layout, whose ground plan resembles a cross with four equal arms (see also Latin cross)

Grotesque: style based on ancient Roman decoration found in underground ruins

Latin cross: a church layout, whose ground plan resembles a cross with three short arms and one longer one

Loggia: a room or gallery that is open on one or more sides

Mannerism: a style in art and architecture, popular between 1530 and 1600, that is characterized by distortion and exaggeration of perspective and the human body for dramatic effect

Nave: the long arm of a Latin cross church; the opposite end to the apse

Pediment: in classical architecture, a low gable and entablature forming a triangular shape. Usually on the outside of a building, but also above doorways and fireplaces

Peristyle: columns ranged around a building or courtyard

Portico: a roofed area, usually

the focus of a building's façade, supported by columns and topped with a pediment (see above)

Reliquary: an elaborate container holding part of a deceased holy person's body

Rococo: architectural and artistic style popular in the 18th century that is characterized by asymmetry and exaggerated curves

Romanesque: an architectural style popular in the 11th–12th centuries, combining classicism with influences from Byzantium and Islam

Sacristy: room in a church where the vestments and liturgical vessels are kept

Sepulchre: a tomb cut from rock, or built from stone or brick

Stucco/stuccowork: a slow-setting plaster, used to form intricate decoration

Transept: the short arms of a Latin cross church

Triptych: a picture or carving on three panels, often used as an altarpiece

Trompe l'oeil: illusionistic effect in painting, giving a striking impression of three-dimensional space

Tympanum: space between the lintel over a door and the arch above it. Also, the flat area inside a pediment (see above)

Vaulting: an arched ceiling or roof

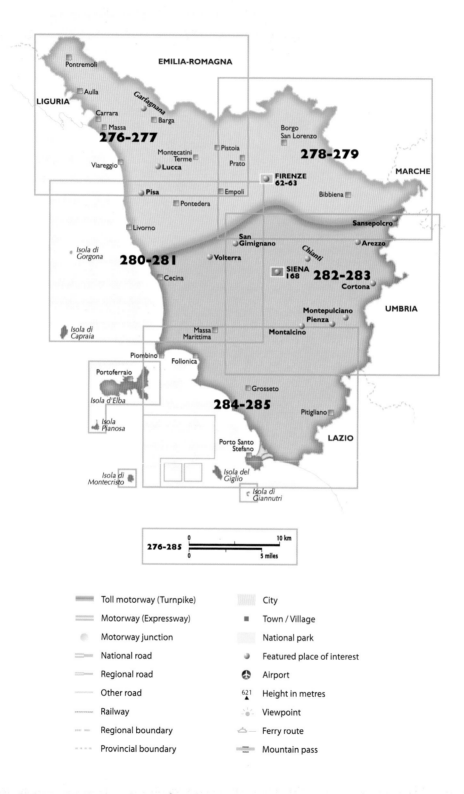

Pontremoli

EMILIA-ROMAGNA

Aulla

LIGURIA

Garfagnana

Carrara

Barga

Massa

276-277

Montecatini
Terme

Pistoia

Borgo
San Lorenzo

278-279

MARCHE

Viareggio

Lucca

Prato

Pisa

Empoli

FIRENZE
62-63

Bibbiena

Pontedera

Sansepolcro

Livorno

San
Gimignano

Arezzo

Isola di
Gorgona

280-281

Volterra

Chianti

Cecina

SIENA
168

282-283

Cortona

Montepulciano
Pienza

UMBRIA

Isola di
Capraia

Massa
Marittima

Montalcino

Piombino

Follonica

Portoferraio

Isola d'Elba

Grosseto

284-285

Pitigliano

Isola
Pianosa

LAZIO

Porto Santo
Stefano

Isola di
Montecristo

Isola del
Giglio

Isola di
Giannutri

	0		10 km
276-285			
	0		5 miles

▬▬	Toll motorway (Turnpike)	▨	City
═══	Motorway (Expressway)	■	Town / Village
●	Motorway junction	▨	National park
═▷	National road	●	Featured place of interest
═▷	Regional road	✈	Airport
──	Other road	621 ▲	Height in metres
┈┈	Railway	☀	Viewpoint
─ ─	Regional boundary	⌂─	Ferry route
┈┈┈	Provincial boundary	▭═	Mountain pass

MAPS

Map references for the sights refer to the atlas pages within this section or to the individual town plans within the regions. For example, Siena has the reference ✚ 282 G7, indicating the page on which the map is found (282) and the grid square in which Siena sits (G7).

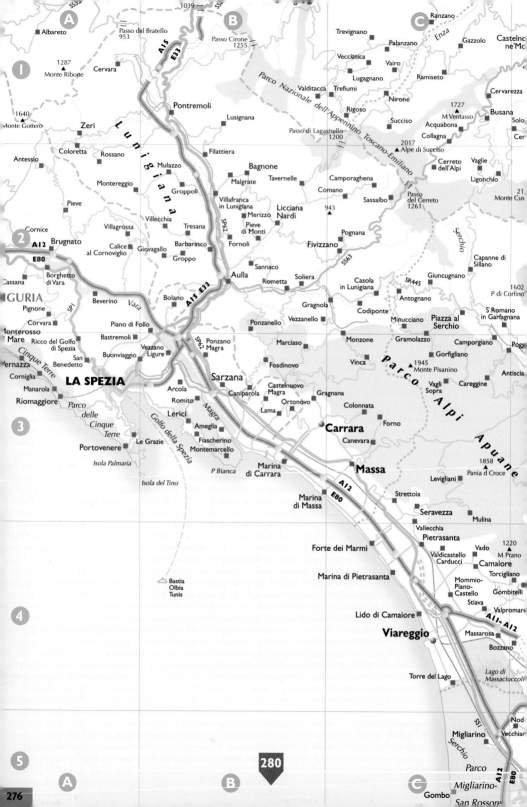

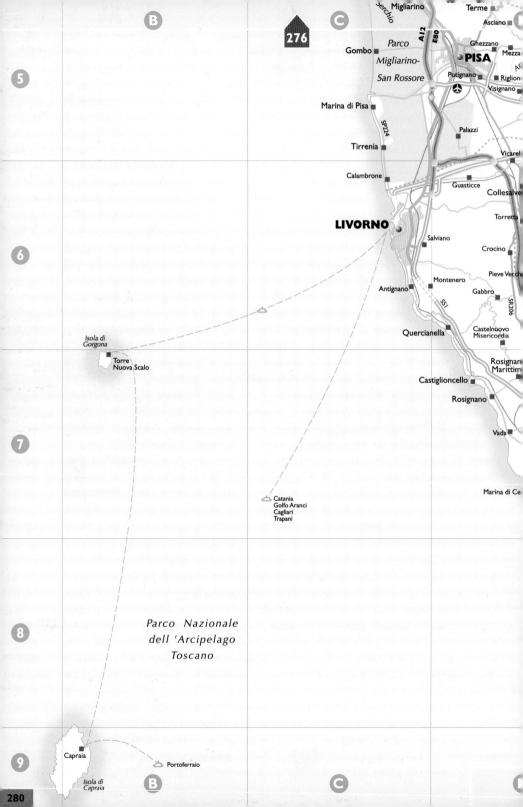

B

C

Migliarino

Terme

Asciano

Parco

Ghezzano

Mezza

Gombo

PISA

Migliarino-

Putignano

Riglion

San Rossore

Visignano

Marina di Pisa

Palazzi

Tirrenia

Vicarel

Calambrone

Guasticce

Collesalve

Torretta

LIVORNO

Salviano

Crocino

Pieve Vecc

Montenero

Gabbro

Antignano

SR206

Castelnuovo
Misericordia

Quercianella

Rosignan
Marittim

Castiglioncello

Rosignano

Isola di
Gorgona

Vada

Torre
Nuova Scalo

Marina di Ce

Catania
Golfo Aranci
Cagliari
Trapani

Parco Nazionale
dell'Arcipelago
Toscano

Capraia

B

C

Portoferraio

Isola di
Capraia

Maestrello 283 L8
Magione 283 L8
Magliano in
Toscano 285 G11
Magonfia 277 D1
Malgrate 276 B2
Malignano 282 G7
Malmantile 278 F5
Manarola 276 A3
Manciano 285 H11
Mantignano 278 G5
Marano s Panaro 277 F1
Marcena 279 K6
Marcialla 278 G6
Marciana 284 C10
Marciana Marina 284 C10
Marciano d Chiana 283 J7
Marciaso 276 B3
Marcignana 281 F5
Marina di Alberese 284 F11
Marina di Campo 284 C10
Marina di Carrara 276 B3
Marina di Castagneto
Donoratico 281 D8
Marina di Cecina 281 D7
Marina di Grosseto 284 F10
Marina di Massa 276 B3
Marina di
Pietrasanta 276 C4
Marina di Pisa 280 C5
Marlia 277 D4
Marliana 277 E4
Marradi 278 H3
Marsciano 283 L9
Marsiliana 285 H11
Massa 276 C3
Massa 277 D1
Massa Marittima 281 F9
Massarosa 276 C4
Meldola 279 K3
Meleto 278 H6
Mensa 279 L2
Mercatale 278 G5
Mercatale 278 H2
Mercatale 283 L7
Mercatello 283 L9
Mercatello sul
Metauro 279 L5
Mercato Saraceno 279 L3
Merizzo 276 B2
Mezzana 280 D5
Micciano 281 E7
Miemo 281 E7
Migliano 283 L9
Migliarino 276 C5
Minucciano 276 C2
Missiano 283 L9
Modigliana 279 J2
Moggiona 279 J4
Moiano 283 K9
Molazzana 277 D3
Molino d Piano 278 H4
Molino Nuovo 277 E4
Mommio-Piano-Castello 276 C4
Monghidoro 278 G2
Monsagrati 277 D4
Monsigliolo 283 K7
Monsummano
Terme 277 E4
Montagnano 283 J7
Montaione 281 F6
Montalcino 282 H8
Montale 277 F4
Montalla 283 K7
Montalto
di Castro 285 J12
Montaperti 282 H7
Montardone 277 E1
Monteacuto
d Alpi 277 F3
Monteacuto
Ragazza 278 G2
Montebonello 277 E1
Montecarelli 278 G3
Montecarlo 277 E4
Montecastelli 281 F7
Montecastelli 283 L7
Montecastello 281 E5
Monte Castello
di Vibio 283 M10
Montecatini Terme 277 E4
Montecatini
Val di Cecina 281 E7
Montecchio 281 E6
Montecchio 282 G7
Montecchio 283 K8
Montecontieri 282 H8
Montecopiolo 279 L4
Montecorone 277 F1
Montecreto 277 E2
Montefegatesi 277 D3
Montefiorino 277 E1
Montefiridolfi 278 G5
Montefollonico 283 J8
Montefoscoli 281 E6
Montefredente 278 G2
Montegabbione 283 L9
Montegelli 279 L3
Montegiove 283 L9
Montegiovi 279 K6
Montegiovi 285 H9
Montegonzi 282 H6
Monteguidi 281 F7
Monte Lattaia 282 G9
Monteleone d'Orvieto 283 K9
Montelifre 282 J8
Montelupo Fiorentino 281 F5
Montemarcello 276 B3
Montemassi 284 F9
Monte Melino 283 L8
Montemerano 285 H11
Montemignaio 278 J5
Montemurlo 278 F4
Montenero 280 D6
Montenero 282 H9
Monte Ombraro 277 F1
Montepaststore 277 F1
Montepescali 284 F9
Montepulciano 283 J8
Montepulciano Staz 283 K8
Monterappoli 281 F5
Monterchi 283 L6
Montereggio 276 A2
Monteriggioni 282 G7
Monteroni d'Arbia 282 H8
Monterosso al Mare 276 A3
Monterotondo
Marittimo 281 F8
Monte San Savino 283 J7
Montescudaio 281 E7
Montese 277 F2
Monte S Maria
Tiberina 283 L6
Monte Sperello 283 L8
Montespertoli 278 F5
Montevarchi 282 H6
Monteverdi Maritt 281 E8
Montiano 279 L3
Montiano 285 G11
Monticchiello 283 J8
Monticello Amiata 285 H9
Monticiano 282 G8
Montieri 281 F8
Montioni 284 E9
Montisi 282 J8
Montone 283 L7
Montopoli in
Val d'Arno 281 E5
Montorgiali 285 G10
Montorsaio 285 G9
Monzone 276 C2
Morcella 283 L9
Moronico 279 J2
Morra 283 L7
Motrone 277 D3
Mugnano 283 L8
Mulazzo 276 B2
Mulina 276 C3
Mura 281 F6
Murci 285 H10
Murlo 282 H8
Musignano 285 J12

Nave 277 D4
Nirone 276 C1
Nodica 276 D5
Novafeltria 279 L4
Nozzano-Castello 277 D4
Nusenna 282 H6

Olevole 283 K9
Oliveto 277 F1
Oliveto 283 J7
Olmi 277 F4
Olmo 283 J6
Onano 285 J10
Orbetello 285 G12
Orbetello Scalo 285 G12
Orciano Pisano 281 D6
Orciatico 281 E6
Orentano 277 E5
Ortimino 281 F5
Ortonovo 276 B3
Ospitaletto 277 F1
Ossaia 283 K7
Ost di Piavola 279 L3

Paciano 283 K9
Padonchia 283 K6
Paganico 285 G9
Palagano 277 E2
Palaia 281 E6
Palanzano 276 C1
Palazzi 280 D5
Palazzuolo sul Senio 278 H3
Pancole 285 G10
Panicale 283 L9
Panicarola 283 K8
Panzano 282 G6
Papiano 283 M9
Pari 282 G8
Parrano 283 L10
Partigliano 277 D4
Passignano sul
Trasimeno 283 L8
Pastina 281 D6
Pavullo nel Frignano 277 E2
Pazzere 277 E4
Peccioli 281 E6
Pelago 278 H5
Pennabilli 279 L4
Pereta 285 G11
Perticara 279 L4
Perugia 283 M8
Pescaglia 277 D4
Pescaia 283 J7
Pescia 277 E4
Pescia Fiorentina 285 H12
Pescia Romana 285 H12
Petrazzi 281 F6
Petricci 285 H10
Petrignano 283 K8
Pian di Sco 278 H5
Piana 283 K8
Piancaldoli 278 H2
Piancastagnaio 285 J10
Piandelagotti 277 D2
Pianella 282 H7
Pianetto 279 K3
Piano 283 J8
Piano degli Ontani 277 E3
Piano di Coreglia 277 D3
Piano di Follo 276 B2
Pianosa 284 C11
Pianosinatico 277 E3
Piansano 285 K11
Piastre 277 E3
Piazza 282 G6
Piazza al Serchio 276 C2
Piazzano 277 D4
Piazze 283 K9
Piegaro 283 K9

Name	No.	Ref	Name	No.	Ref	Name	No.	Ref	Name	No.	Ref
Pienza	282	J8	Ponzalla	278	H3	Ricco del Golfo			Sannaco	276	B2
Pierantonio	283	M7	Ponzanello	276	B2	di Spezia	276	A3	San Pellegrno		
Pietrafitta	282	G6	Ponzano	277	F1	Riglione	280	D5	in Alpe	277	D2
Pietrafitta	283	L9	Ponzano Magra	276	B3	Rigomagno	282	J7	San Quirico		
Pietraia	283	K8	Popiglio	277	E3	Rigoso	276	C1	d'Orcia	282	J8
Pietralunga	283	M6	Poppi	279	J5	Rimigliano	281	D9	San Rabino	284	G11
Pietramala	278	G2	Populonia	284	D9	Riolunato	277	E2	S Ansano	277	F5
Pietrapiana	278	H5	Porcari	277	E4	Riomaggiore	276	A3	Sansepolcro	279	L6
Pietrasanta	276	C4	Pornello	283	L9	Rio Marina	284	D10	Santa Luce	281	D6
Pietre	277	D1	Porretta Terme	277	F3	Rio nell' Elba	284	D10	Sant'Anna Pelago	277	D2
Pieve	276	A2	Portico di Romagna	279	J3	Riotorto	284	E9	Santa Sofia	279	K4
Pieve a Presciano	282	J6	Porto	283	K8	Ripalvella	283	L10	San Venanzo	283	L9
Pieve di Brancoli	277	D4	Porto Azzurro	284	D10	Riparbella	281	E7	San Vincenzo	281	D8
Pieve di Chio	283	K7	Porto Ercole	285	G12	Rispescia	285	G10	Saragiolo	285	J10
Pieve di Monti	276	B2	Portoferraio	284	C10	Rocca d'Orcia	282	J9	Sarsina	279	L4
Pieve di Panzano	282	G6	Porto Santo			Rocca San			Sarteano	283	K9
Pieve di Santa Luce	281	D6	Stefano	284	G12	Casciano	279	J3	Sarzana	276	B3
Pieve Fosciana	277	D3	Portovenere	276	A3	Roccalbegna	285	H10	Sassa	281	E7
Pievepelago	277	E2	Pozzo	283	J7	Roccastrada	282	G9	Sassalbo	276	C2
Pieve San			Pozzo Nuovo	283	K7	Roccatederighi	281	F9	Sasseta	278	G3
Giovanni	283	J6	Pozzuolo	283	K8	Rometta	276	B2	Sassetta	281	E8
Pieve Santo			Pracchia	277	F3	Romita	278	G6	Sassi	277	D3
Stefano	279	K5	Prata	281	F8	Romito	276	B3	Sassofortino	282	G9
Pieve Socana	279	J5	Pratantico	283	J6	Ronco	279	K2	Sassoleone	278	H2
Pieve Vecchia	280	D6	Prato	278	F4	Roncobilaccio	278	G3	Saturnia	285	H11
Pignone	276	A2	Prato di Strada	279	J5	Roncofreddo	279	L3	Savaiana	277	F3
Pila	283	L8	Prato Ranieri	284	E9	Rondelli	284	E9	Savignano s		
Pino	283	J8	Pratolino	278	G4	Rosia	282	G7	Panaro	277	F1
Piombino	284	D9	Predappio	279	K3	Rosignano	280	D7	Savignano sul		
Piosina	283	L6	Preggio	283	L7	Rosignano			Rubicone	279	M3
Pisa	280	D5	Premilcuore	279	J3	Marittimo	280	D7	S Benedetto		
Pisignano	279	L2	Presciano	282	H7	Rossano	276	A2	V d Sam	278	G2
Pistoia	277	F4	Prignano S Secchia	277	E1	Rufina	278	H4	S Brigida	278	H4
Pistrino	283	L6	Principina a Mare	284	F11	Ruota	277	D5	Scala	281	F5
Piteccio	277	F3	Procchio	284	C10	Ruscello	283	J6	Scandicci	278	G5
Piteglio	277	E3	Proceno	285	J10				Scansano	285	G11
Pitigliano	283	L6	Prunetta	277	E3	S Agata	278	G3	Scarlino	284	F9
Pitigliano	285	J11	Pte Cappuccini	279	L4	S Agata	279	L4	S Carlo	279	L3
Poggibonsi	282	G6	Pucciarelli	283	K8	S Agata	283	K7	S Carlo	281	D8
Poggi d Sasso	285	G9	Puglia	283	K6	Sala	279	L2	Scarperia	278	G3
Poggio	276	C3	Punta Ala	284	E10	Saline di Volterra	281	E7	S Caterina	283	K7
Poggio a Caiano	278	F4	Putignano	280	D5	Salivoli	284	D9	S Colomb	278	G5
Poggio Berni	279	M3				Saltino	278	H5	S Colombano	279	K3
Poggio Cavallo	285	G10	Quarata	283	J6	Salviano	280	C6	Scorgiano	282	G7
Poggio d'Acona	279	K5	Quarrata	277	F4	Sambuca	278	G6	S Croce sull' Arno	281	E5
Poggioferro	285	H10	Quartaia	281	F7	Sambuca Pistoiese	277	F3	S Dalmazio	281	F7
Pogi	282	J6	Quattro Strade	281	E5	San Benedetto	276	A3	S Damiano	279	L3
Pognana	276	C2	Querceto	281	E7	San Benedetto			S Donato	278	H5
Polveraia	285	G10	Quercianella	280	D6	in Alpe	279	J3	S Donato	282	G6
Pomarance	281	F7				San Casciano			S Donato	285	G11
Pomonte	284	C10	Radda in Chianti	282	H6	dei Bagni	283	K9	S Donato Vecchio	285	G11
Ponsacco	281	E5	Radicofani	285	J9	San Casciano			S Donnino	278	G4
Pontassieve	278	H5	Radicondoli	281	F7	in Val di Pesa	278	G5	Seano	277	F4
Ponte a Cappiano	277	E5	Raggiolo	279	J5	S Andrea	279	L2	Seggiano	285	H9
Ponte a Egola	281	E5	Ramiseto	276	C1	Sanfatucchio	283	K8	S Egidio	279	L2
Ponte a Moriano	277	D4	Ranchio	279	K3	S Angelo	279	L2	Selci	283	L6
Ponte Buggianese	277	E4	Ranzano	276	C1	S Angelo in Colle	282	H9	S Ellero	278	H5
Pontedera	281	E5	Rapolano Terme	282	J7	San Gimignano	281	F6	Selva	285	J10
Ponte di Masino	277	E5	Rassina	279	J5	San Giuliano Terme	277	D5	Semproniano	285	H10
Ponte Pattoli	283	M8	Ravi	284	F9	San Godenzo	278	J4	Seravezza	276	C3
Pontepetri	277	F3	Reggello	278	H5	San Marcello			Serramazzoni	277	E1
Ponticino	283	J6	Ribolla	284	F9	Pistoiese	277	E3	Serravalle	282	H8
Pontremoli	276	B1	Riccio	283	K8	San Miniato	281	E5	Serravalle Pist	277	E4

Place			Place			Place			Place		
Sesto Fiorentino	278	G4	Spergolaia	284	F11	Tole	277	F2	Vicchio	278	H4
Sestola	277	E2	S Piero a Ema	278	G5	Torcigliano	276	D4	Viciomaggio	283	J6
Settignano	278	G5	S Piero a Sieve	278	G4	Torre	282	H6	Vico d'Elsa	281	F6
Settimello	278	G4	S Piero in Bagno	279	K4	Torre del Lago	276	C4	Vico Pancellorum	277	E3
S Feliciano	283	L8	S Piero in Campo	284	C10	Torre Nuova Scalo	280	B7	Vicopisano	281	D5
S Filippo	282	G6	S Piero in Frassino	279	J5	Torrenieri	282	H8	Vidiciatico	277	F2
S Fiora	285	H10	S Pietro Belvedere	281	E6	Torretta	280	D6	Vignola	277	F1
S Firmina	283	K6	Spina	283	L9	Torriana	279	M3	Villa a Sesta	282	H7
S Giovanni	282	H7	S Polo in Chianti	278	H5	Torrita di Siena	283	J8	Villa Basilica	277	E4
S Giovanni			S Quirico	277	E4	Trassilico	277	D3	Villa d'Aiano	277	F2
alla Vena	281	D5	S Quirico	285	J11	Traversa	278	G3	Villa di Baggio	277	F3
S Giovanni			S Rocco	277	D3	Trecine	283	L8	Villafranca in		
d Contee	285	J10	S Rocco	277	F4	Trefiumi	276	C1	Lunigiana	276	B2
S Giovanni			S Rocco a Pilli	282	G7	Trentola	279	L2	Villagrossa	276	A2
d'Asso	282	H8	S Romano in			Treppio	278	F3	Villalta	279	L2
S Giovanni			Garfagnana	276	C2	Trequanda	282	J8	Villamagna	281	E6
Valdarno	278	H6	S Savino	283	K8	Tresana	276	B2	Villa Minozzo	277	D1
S Giuseppe	283	K9	S Savino	283	L8	Trestina	283	L7	Villanova	279	K2
S Giustino	279	L6	S Sisto	279	L5	Trevignano	276	C1	Villanova	279	L4
S Giustino			Staffoli	277	E5	Triana	285	H10	Villanova	281	F5
Valdarno	279	J6	Staggia	282	G7	Tuoro sul			Villa Ranuzzi	278	G2
S Giusto			Stia	279	J4	Trasimeno	283	K8	Villa Saletta	281	E6
Alle Monache	282	H7	Stiava	276	C4				Villastrada	283	K9
Siena	282	G7	Sticciano	285	G9	Uliveto Terme	281	D5	Villecchia	276	B2
Signa	278	F5	Sticciano Scalo	284	G9	Umbertide	283	L7	Villore	278	H4
S Ilario in Campo	284	C10	Stigliano	282	G8	Usigliano	281	D6	Vimignano	278	F2
Sillico	277	D3	Strada in Chianti	278	G5				Vinca	276	C3
Sinalunga	283	J8	Strettoia	276	C3	Vada	280	D7	Vinci	277	F5
S Leo	279	L4	Subbiano	279	K6	Vado	276	C4	Visignano	280	D5
S Lorenzo	285	H9	Succiso	276	C1	Vagli Sopra	276	C3	Vitigliano	278	G6
S Lorenzo a Merse	282	G8	Suvereto	281	E8	Vaglia	278	G4	Vitriola	277	E1
S Lorenzo a Pagnat	281	D5	Suvignano	282	H8	Vagliagli	282	G7	Vivo d'Orcia	285	J9
S Lucia	283	L6	S Varano	279	K2	Vaglie	276	C2	Vizzaneta	277	E3
S Macario in Piano	277	D4	S Vincenzo a Torri	278	F5	Vaiano	278	G4	Volterra	281	F7
S Marco	283	M8	S Vito in Monte	283	L9	Vairo	276	C1	Voltre	279	K3
S Maria Nova	279	L2	S Vittore	279	L3	Valdicastello					
S Mariano	283	L8	S Vivaldo	281	F6	Carducci	276	C4	Zeri	276	A1
S Martino	282	G6				Valditacca	276	B1			
S Martino al Vento	282	H6	Talamello	279	L4	Valdottavo	277	D4			
S Martino in Strada	279	K2	Talamone	285	G11	Valentano	285	J11			
S Martino in			Talciana	282	G6	Valiano	283	K8			
Tremoleto	279	J5	Talla	279	J5	Vallecchia	276	C3			
S Martino Sopr' Arno	279	J6	Tatti	284	F9	Vallecchio	281	F5			
S Martino sul Fiora	285	J11	Tavarnelle			Vallerona	285	H10			
S Mauro	279	M3	Val di Pesa	278	G6	Vallombrosa	278	H5			
S Miniato Basso	281	E5	Tavernelle	276	B2	Valpiana	284	F9			
S Nicolo di Celle	283	M9	Tavernelle	283	L9	Valpromaro	276	D4			
Soanne	279	L4	Tavola	278	F4	Varna	281	F6			
Soci	279	J5	Teodorano	279	K3	Vecchiano	276	D5			
Sodo	283	K7	Tereglio	277	D3	Vecciatica	276	C1			
Sogliano al			Terme di Firenze	278	G5	Veggio	278	G2			
Rubicone	279	L3	Terontola Staz	283	K8	Venturina	284	E9			
Soliera	276	B2	Terra del Sole	279	K2	Vergato	277	F2			
Sologno	276	D1	Terranuova			Verghereto	279	K4			
Sommocolonia	277	D3	Bracciolini	278	H6	Vernazza	276	A3			
Sorano	285	J11	Terriccola	281	E6	Vernio	278	G3			
Sorrivoli	279	L3	Tessennano	285	J12	Vescovado	282	H8			
Sottili	281	E5	Tirli	284	F10	Vetulonia	284	F10			
Sovana	285	J11	Tirrenia	280	C5	Vezza	279	J6			
Sovicille	282	G7	Toano	277	D1	Vezzanello	276	B2			
S Pancrazio	278	G5	Tobbiana	278	F4	Vezzano Ligure	276	B3			
Spedaletto	281	E6	Toiano	277	F5	Viareggio	276	C4			
S Pellegrino	278	H3	Toiano	281	E6	Vicarello	280	D5			

4

126 AA/S McBride;
130 AA/C Sawyer;
132 AA/T Harris;
133 AA/C Sawyer;
134 AA/T Harris;
135 AA/K Paterson;
136 AA/T Harris;
137 AA/C Sawyer;
138 AA/T Harris;
140 AA/C Sawyer;
141 AA/T Harris;
142l AA/T Harris;
142r AA/T Harris;
143 AA/T Harris;
144 AA/T Harris;
145 AA/K Paterson;
146 AA/T Harris;
147t AA/T Harris;
147b AA/T Harris;
148 AA/T Harris;
149 © CuboImages srl/Alamy;
150 AA/K Paterson;
152 AA/C Sawyer;
156 AA/C Sawyer;
158 Ingram;
161 AA/C Sawyer;
162 AA/K Paterson;
164 Hotel Locanda L'Elisa;
166 AA/C Sawyer;
170 AA/T Harris;
171 AA/T Harris;
172 AA/T Harris;
173 Luca Lozzi/Getty Images;
174 AA/S McBride;
175 AA/C Sawyer;
176 AA/T Harris;
177l AA/T Harris;
177r AA/T Harris;
178 AA/T Harris;
179 AA/T Harris;
180 AA/T Harris;
181 Photo Scala, Florence - courtesy of the Ministero Beni e Att. Culturali;
182 AA/T Harris;
183 AA/T Harris;
184 AA/S McBride;
186 AA/S McBride;
188 AA/T Harris;
190 AA/T Harris;
192 AA/C Sawyer;
194 AA/T Harris;
195 AA/S McBride;
196 AA/S McBride;
197 AA/C Sawyer;
198 AA/K Paterson;
199 AA/C Sawyer;
200 AA/K Paterson;

201 AA/T Harris;
202 AA/T Harris;
203 AA/C Sawyer;
204 AA/K Paterson;
205 AA/C Sawyer;
206 AA/T Harris;
207 AA/S McBride;
208 AA/K Paterson;
209 AA/K Paterson;
210 AA/S McBride;
211 © Christine Webb / Alamy;
212 AA/ K Paterson;
213 AA/R Ireland;
214 AA/K Paterson;
216 AA/S McBride;
217 AA/S McBride;
218 AA/R Ireland;
219 AA/T Harris;
220 AA/K Paterson;
222 AA/T Harris;
224 AA/T Harris;
226 AA/R Ireland;
228 AA/T Harris;
230 AA/T Harris;
234 AA/R Ireland;
238 AA/C Sawyer;
239 AA/M Jourdan;
241 AA/C Sawyer;
243 AA/M Jourdan;
244 AA/T Harris;
245t Digitalvision;
245b AA/T Harris;
246 AA/K Paterson;
247t AA/C Sawyer;
247b AA/T Harris;
248 AA/T Harris;
252 AA/S McBride;
253 AA/T Harris;
254 AA/T Harris;
255t AA/S McBride;
255b AA/M Jourdan;
256 Photodisc;
258 Photodisc;
259 Photodisc;
260l Photodisc;
260r AA/S McBride;
261 Simeone Huber/Getty Images;
262 AA/M Jourdan;
264 AA/T Harris;
265 AA/S McBride;
266 AA/T Harris;
275 AA/S McBride.

FLORENCE AND TUSCANY

ACKNOWLEDGMENTS

CREDITS

Managing editor
Marie-Claire Jefferies

Project editor
Laura Linder

Design
Drew Jones, pentacorbig, Nick Otway

Picture research
Liz Stacey

Image retouching and repro
Michael Moody

Main contributors
Rebecca Ford, Tim Jepson, Sally Roy, Nicky Swallow, James Taylor, The Content Works, Frances Wolverton

Updater
Tim Jepson

Indexer
Marie Lorimer

Production
Rachel Davis

Published by AA Publishing, a trading name of AA Media Limited, whose registered office is Fanum House, Basing View, Basingstoke, RG21 4EA. Registered number 06112600.
A CIP catalogue record for this book is available from the British Library.

ISBN 978-0-7495-6230-4

KeyGuide is a registered trademark in Australia and is used under license.
Colour separation by Keenes, Andover, UK
Printed and bound by Leo Paper Products, China

We believe the contents of this book are correct at the time of printing. However, some details, particularly prices, opening times and telephone numbers do change. We do not accept responsibility for any consequences arising from the use of this book.
This does not affect your statutory rights. We would be grateful if readers would advise us of any inaccuracies they may encounter, or any suggestions they might like to make to improve the book. There is a form provided at the back of the book for this purpose, or you can email us at Keyguides@theaa.com

A03807
Maps in this title produced from mapping © MAIRDUMONT / Falk Verlag 2009 and with reference to mapping © ISTITUTO GEOGRAFICO DE AGOSTINI S.p.A., NOVARA 2008
Transport map © Communicarta Ltd, UK
Weather chart statistics supplied by Weatherbase © Copyright 2004 Canty and Associates, LLC.

Find out more about AA Publishing and the wide range of travel publications and services the AA provides by visiting our website at **www.theAA.com/bookshop**

Thank you for buying this KeyGuide. Your comments and opinions are very important to us, so please help us to improve our travel guides by taking a few minutes to complete this questionnaire.

You do not need a stamp (unless posted outside the UK). If you do not want to cut this page from your guide, then photocopy it or write your answers on a plain sheet of paper.

Send to: **KeyGuide Editor, AA World Travel Guides**
FREEPOST SCE 4598, Basingstoke RG21 4GY

Find out more about AA Publishing and the wide range of travel publications the AA provides by visiting our website at www.theAA.com/bookshop

ABOUT THIS GUIDE

Which KeyGuide did you buy? ....

Where did you buy it? ....

When? ....month .... year

Why did you choose this AA KeyGuide?
☐ Price ☐ AA Publication
☐ Used this series before; title
☐ Cover ☐ Other (please state)

Please let us know how helpful the following features of the guide were to you by circling the appropriate category: very helpful (VH), helpful (H) or little help (LH)

Size	VH	H	LH
Layout	VH	H	LH
Photos	VH	H	LH
Excursions	VH	H	LH
Entertainment	VH	H	LH
Hotels	VH	H	LH
Maps	VH	H	LH
Practical info	VH	H	LH
Restaurants	VH	H	LH
Shopping	VH	H	LH
Walks	VH	H	LH
Sights	VH	H	LH
Transport info	VH	H	LH

What was your favourite sight, attraction or feature listed in the guide?

Page.................. Please give your reason ....
....

Which features in the guide could be changed or improved? Or are there any other comments you would like to make?

....

ABOUT YOU

Name (Mr/Mrs/Ms) ....

Address ....

....

....

Postcode.. Daytime tel nos...

Email...
Please only give us your mobile phone number/email if you wish to hear from us about other products and services from the AA and partners by text or mms.

Which age group are you in?
Under 25 ☐   25–34 ☐   35–44 ☐   45–54 ☐   55+ ☐

How many trips do you make a year?
Less than1 ☐   1 ☐   2 ☐   3 or more ☐

ABOUT YOUR TRIP

Are you an AA member?   Yes ☐ No ☐

When did you book? .... month .... year

When did you travel? .... month .... year

Reason for your trip?   Business ☐   Leisure ☐

How many nights did you stay? ....

How did you travel?   Individual ☐   Couple ☐   Family ☐   Group ☐

Did you buy any other travel guides for your trip? ....

If yes, which ones?..

Thank you for taking the time to complete this questionnaire. Please send it to us as soon as possible, and remember, you do not need a stamp (unless posted outside the UK).
AA Travel Insurance call 0800 072 4168 or visit www.theaa.com

Titles in the KeyGuide series:
Australia, Barcelona, Britain, Brittany, Canada, China, Costa Rica, Croatia, Florence and Tuscany, France, Germany, Ireland, Italy, London, Mallorca, Mexico, New York, New Zealand, Normandy, Paris, Portugal, Prague, Provence and the Côte d'Azur, Rome, Scotland, South Africa, Spain, Thailand, Venice, Vietnam, Western European Cities.
Published in July 2009: Berlin

The information we hold about you will be used to provide the products and services requested and for identification, account administration, analysis, and fraud/loss prevention purposes. More details about how that information is used is in our privacy statement, which you'll find under the heading "Personal Information" in our terms and conditions and on our website: www.theAA.com. Copies are also available from us by post, by contacting the Data Protection Manager at AA, Fanum House, Basing View, Basingstoke, Hampshire RG21 4EA.

We may want to contact you about other products and services provided by us, or our partners (by mail, telephone, email) but please tick the box if you DO NOT wish to hear about such products and services from us. ☐

AA Travel Insurance call 0800 072 4168 or visit www.theaa.com